PATHS TO JUSTICE SCOTLAND
What People in Scotland Do and Think About Going to Law

Paths to Justice Scotland

What People in Scotland Do and Think About Going to Law

PROFESSOR HAZEL GENN

Faculty of Laws
University College London
and

PROFESSOR ALAN PATERSON

Law School
Strathclyde University

With
The National Centre for Social Research

Funded by the Nuffield Foundation

·HART·
PUBLISHING

OXFORD—PORTLAND OREGON
2001

Hart Publishing
Oxford and Portland, Oregon

Published in North America (US and Canada) by
Hart Publishing
c/o International Specialized Book Services
5804 NE Hassalo Street
Portland, Oregon
97213-3644
USA

Distributed in the Netherlands, Belgium and Luxembourg by
Intersentia, Churchillaan 108
B2900 Schoten
Antwerpen
Belgium

Hart Publishing is a specialist legal publisher based in Oxford,
England. To order further copies of this book or to request a list
of other publications please write to:

Hart Publishing, Salter's Boatyard, Folly Bridge,
Abingdon Rd, Oxford OX1 4LB
Telephone: +44 (0)1865 245533 or Fax: +44 (0)1865 794882
e-mail: mail@hartpub.co.uk
WEBSITE: http://www.hartpub.co.uk

British Library Cataloguing in Publication Data
Data Available
ISBN 1 84113–040–0 (paperback)

Typeset by Hope Services (Abingdon) Ltd.
Printed in Great Britain on acid-free paper by
Creative Print & Design, Wales, Ebbw Vale

Contents

Foreword

The Nuffield Foundation has long been interested in promoting access to justice. In the heady days of the 1970s, this was equated with giving everyone equal access to legal help in dealing with all the legal processes which might affect their lives, not only in the ordinary courts but also before tribunals and other decision making bodies. It was assumed that everyone shared the lawyers' assumptions about what was and was not a legal problem and that going to law was ultimately the best way to solve such problems. In the 1990s we all began to realise that, viewed in that light, the potential demand for legal services was infinite but the resources to meet it were not. But we also began to wonder whether other people shared the lawyers' assumptions. How often did they encounter a problem in their everyday lives which lawyers would perceive as having a legal solution? What did they do about it? Did they do nothing, try to solve it themselves, go to others for advice and help, go to law? And how did they feel abut it all?

We therefore commissioned Professor Hazel Genn of University College London, together with the National Centre for Social Research, to conduct a large-scale study of these issues. A specialist advisory committee, which I chaired, helped to develop a concrete series of problems in everyday life to which there might be a legal solution, conceptualised for the purpose of the research as a "justiciable event". There was then a large screen to assess the incidence of such problems and an in depth study of those who had experienced them. The results were published as *Paths to Justice: What People Do and Think about going to Law* (Hart Publishing, 1999). This has given us some fascinating insights: principally that such events are very common but most types of problem rarely lead to legal proceedings. It has also had a real impact upon the Government and the Legal Services Commission as they consider how best to serve the needs of ordinary people for legal information, advice and help.

That study was limited to England and Wales. Scotland, as is well known, has a completely separate legal system and in many areas completely different laws. There has been no equivalent to the recent wholesale changes to civil procedure in England and Wales following Lord Woolf's Report. We soon began to think that there would be real benefits in carrying out essentially the same study in Scotland, properly adapted to meet the differences between the two legal systems. We could then learn more about the experiences of individuals within those two systems, which in turn might influence thinking about the development of community legal services, and the legal system in Scotland.

We therefore turned once again to Professor Genn and the National Centre for Social Research, but this time in partnership with Professor Alan Paterson of Strathclyde University, and assisted by a Scottish advisory Committee, chaired by Sheriff Principal Gordon Nicholson. We are particularly grateful to the advisory committee for all the help and advice they have given to this project. Once again, the results have been fascinating.

They would be fascinating in their own right, irrespective of any comparison with England and Wales. But the comparison is also fascinating. For me, three points stand out. The first is the lower reported incidence of justiciable events in Scotland. There is, as the authors say, no obvious reason for this. Is it that the Scots have a more stoical attitude to the vicissitudes of life than do the English – the "Ach tae hell with it" syndrome – and so put such matters out of their minds? Or is it the stronger socialist tradition, which looks to community solutions rather than to individual action? There is much food for thought and material for further research there.

The second, however, is the even lower perception of the legal system held by the Scots, and particularly those who have direct experience of it. As the authors report, "The survey suggests that whatever may be the position amongst the Scottish judiciary and legal profession, many people in Scotland feel no pride or ownership in 'their' justice system nor confidence in its ability to reach a fair result." This comes as something of a shock to a former member of the English Law Commission who has worked closely with colleagues in the Scottish Law Commission over many years. The authors suggest that the media and the parties' own advisers may be partly to blame.

But thirdly, as the authors also comment, the similarities between the findings of the two studies are much greater and more interesting than the differences. How people tackle particular types of problem differs more from problem to problem than from country to country. Differences in substantive law and procedures have little effect upon this. One might think, for example, that there would be considerable differences between the incidence of and reactions to problems with buying and selling a house, where the procedures are entirely different: but there are not.

This is a salutary lesson for all lawyers, north or south of the border. We are dealing here with the stuff of everyday life, and as the authors say, "the problems of everyday life are pretty similar in Scotland and in England. For such problems any developed legal system will attempt to provide answers, and although the route to those solutions may vary from jurisdiction to jurisdiction, the outcome may look surprisingly alike . . . Although the rules and procedures may appear distinctive to the lawyers, judges and academics who use and analyse them and to which they become attached . . . viewed pragmatically they lead to very similar outcomes."

They suggest that what is needed is clear guidance, information and education about obligations, rights, remedies and procedures, together with "accessible, affordable court procedures which will encourage settlement or provide for relatively painless adjudication". And so of course, say all of us: but experience south of the border of trying to achieve this has only served to emphasise how very difficult it is. For, as long as we regard the traditional adversarial process, in which the best lawyers and advocates often win, as the Rolls Royce of dispute resolution, the chances of our attaining this goal are slim indeed.

This book should be compulsory reading for all with an interest in achieving real access to justice north or south of the border. The Nuffield Foundation is proud to have sown the seed and grateful to everyone for bringing it to such magnificent fruition.

Dame Brenda Hale
Lord Justice of Appeal and Trustee of the Nuffield Foundation

Acknowledgements

This ambitious project could not have been accomplished without the contribution of a large number of people. First, the study benefited greatly from the wisdom of a distinguished Advisory Panel who generously gave their time to offer guidance on the design and analysis of the research. The Panel members were: Peter Anderson (Simpson & Warwick W.S.); Peter Beaton (Justice Department, Scottish Executive); Micheline Brannan (Justice Department, Scottish Executive); Michael Clancy (Law Society of Scotland); Alisdair McIntosh (Access to Justice, Diligence & European Co-ordination, Scottish Executive); Susan McPhee (Citizens Advice Scotland); Dr Claire Monaghan (Head of Civil Law Research Branch, Scottish Executive); Lindsay Montgomery (Chief Executive, Scottish Legal Aid Board); Sheriff Principal Gordon Nicholson QC; Sarah O'Neill (Scottish Consumer Council); Catherine Palmer (Civil Law Research Branch, Scottish Executive); Dr Sue Warner (Equality Unit).

Sharon Witherspoon (Deputy Director of the Nuffield Foundation) has provided critical insight and enthusiastic support from inception to completion of the project and we are very grateful for her contribution to the research.

At the National Centre Sarah Beinart, Emily Charkin, and Patten Smith all contributed to the design of the fieldwork and Steven Finch assisted with data analysis. The fieldwork for the project was expertly carried out by the National Centre's team of interviewers. The quality of the data available for analysis was a direct result of the care with which interviews were undertaken and the interest in the research shown by interviewers. We would also like to record our gratitude to Kit Ward and Hilary Legard who conducted lengthy and challenging qualitative interviews to supplement the screening and main survey interviews. The insights gained as a result of their skilful interviewing techniques have greatly enriched the study.

We would like to thank Andrew Horne for assisting Alan Paterson in Strathclyde in the early stages of the research, and James Shirley at UCL for helping Hazel Genn prepare the final manuscript for publication. We are grateful to Theresa O'Neill, assistant to Sharon Witherspoon, for her help in maintaining liaison between the

researchers, the Foundation, and the Advisory Panel, and to Lisa
Penfold at UCL for managing affairs relating to publication and the
launch of the findings.

Special thanks again to Richard Hart and the team at Hart
Publishing for their high standards of professionalism in producing this
volume and for their tolerant help when working under considerable
time pressure.

Finally we would both like to pay tribute to Helen Ghosh at UCL
whose utterly dependable and conscientious support throughout the
life of the project has been exceptional.

Hazel Genn
Alan Paterson
October 2001

List of Figures

List of Tables

List of Tables

1

Introduction

*"I'm all for justice, but I think the price of justice is probably too high
for most of us lesser mortals. I think it's basically too expensive"*
[Survey respondent who did not pursue an employment problem]

Only a legal surrogate for Rip van Winkle could have failed to notice
that the UK is experiencing an era of almost unprecedented interest in
the resolution of civil disputes and in the procedures and public funding available to assist in the process. The spate of consultation and
white papers touching on these topics[1] on both sides of the Border in
the last decade conveys an impression of policy turmoil that has been
surprising to those who see few votes in civil justice. But even seasoned
observers were intrigued by the initiation of two inquiries in Scotland
in the same week in November 2000. The first was the establishment of
the Scottish Executive's Working Party on Community Legal Services.[2]
The second, entitled "Scotland's Access to Justice" was labelled as "a
major inquiry into the Scottish Legal Aid system" and launched by the
Justice and Home Affairs Committee[3] of the Scottish Parliament on the
9th November 2000. It cannot thus be denied that "Access to Justice"
and "Community Legal Services" are firmly on the political agenda in
Scotland. Unfortunately, there the certainties end. There is no consensus as to the meaning of either phrase among policymakers or commentators. Indeed, apart from a "feelgood" factor, which makes it
difficult to dissent from the view that each of them is or would be "a
good thing", it might be argued that both phrases are so opaque that
they offer little concrete guidance for reformers.

---

[1] See the reports by the Rt Hon the Lord Woolf MR, *Access to Justice: Interim Report*,
Lord Chancellor's Department 1995; *Access to Justice: Final Report*, Lord Chancellor's
Department 1996; *Access to Justice Beyond the Year 2000*, A Consultation Paper,
Scottish Office Home Department, 1998; *Modernising Justice*, A Consultation Paper,
Lord Chancellor's Department, November 1998, HMSO; *Access to Justice Act* 1999.

[2] Although the working party was announced on the 10th October 2000 by the Justice
Minister (Jim Wallace) in a speech to celebrate 50 years of legal aid in Scotland, it was
not established until November.

[3] As it was then known. It is now the Justice 1 Committee.

Academic commentators have at least made a stab at it. Some twenty years ago Cappelletti and Garth in their seminal work on access to justice offered an idealist perspective,[4]

> "The words 'access to justice' are admittedly not easily defined, but they serve to focus on two basic purposes of the legal system—the system by which people may vindicate their rights and/or resolve their disputes under the auspices of the State. First, the system must be equally accessible to all, and second, it must lead to results that are individually and socially just".

A more pragmatic stance, however, would view the aim of the system as 'justice according to law' rather than 'justice' per se and note that in an era of finite resources, it is not just equal access, but how much effective access, that matters. For example, in 1950, 80% of the Scottish population was eligible for civil legal aid, judged on income grounds. It could thus be fairly argued that the purpose of legal aid was to enable those of low or moderate income, who had a reasonable case, to raise or defend an action without the handicap of inadequate resources or a fear of having to pay crippling expense should they lose.[5] Equality of access really meant equality for all users of the system. By 1985, however, the Scottish Office was arguing that this was a distortion and that the purpose of civil legal aid was, and had always been, merely to "permit those of insufficient means that same opportunity to pursue their rights as is available to those of moderate rather than abundant means".[6] In short, that equality of misery was all that legal aid sought to achieve. If someone of moderate means could not afford to litigate, neither should those from the lower income sector. This, almost perverse view of access to

---

[4] Cappelletti and Garth (eds), *Access to Justice: A World Survey*, Sijhoff and Noordhoff, Alphen aan den Rijn, 1978.

[5] "The object of the [legal aid] scheme is to provide assistance in a more effective form in the conduct of civil proceedings and legal advice for those of slender means and resources, so that no one will be financially unable to prosecute a just and reasonable claim or defend a legal right, and to allow counsel and solicitors to be remunerated for their services." *Legal Aid Bill 1948: Summary of the Proposed New Service*, Cmnd 7563, HMSO, London, November 1948.

[6] Scottish Home and Health Department Consultation Paper on Legal Aid, 1985 SLT(News) 113. The argument involves a subtle gloss on the English "hypothetical paying client" test as to the reasonableness of legal aid being awarded in a civil case. That test required the Legal Aid Board to consider whether a person of *sufficient* though not superabundant means would pursue the action. The key difference is the reference to "sufficient" in the English test. Despite this, the Scottish Legal Aid Board's guidelines on the reasonableness test today are punctuated with a series of references to the "privately funded litigant of moderate but not abundant means". The Scottish Legal Aid Handbook 5th edition, SLAB, April 2000 Ch.6. For a critique of the Scottish Office argument see A. Paterson, "The Purpose of Legal Aid" 1985 SLT(News) 232.

justice, stems from a modern fear that it would be unfair for a publicly funded litigant to be put in a stronger position than a privately paying litigant.[7] One task that faced both inquiries, therefore, was to establish in their own minds what the purpose of legal aid in Scotland should be at the start of the twenty-first century.[8]

THE UNMET NEED FOR LEGAL SERVICES

Any dismay that members of the inquiries who were new to the field may have felt that "access to justice" and the "purpose of legal aid" are issues about which there is substantial disagreement, can only have been compounded by the reality that concepts such as "the unmet need for legal services" or even the question as to what is a "legal problem" do not lend themselves to easy analysis either. In fact, the prevailing orthodoxy is probably that both of them are subjective in nature and are not open to objective verification. Thus unmet need is not a matter of estimating the incidence of legal problems in the community and noting how many are not taken to a lawyer. First, because it is now widely accepted that legal services will often be provided by

[7] Thus C. Stoddart and H.Neilson assert in *The Law and Practice of Legal Aid in Scotland* (4th edn) T & T Clark, 1994, para 9.19 "legal aid was never intended to place an assisted person in a more advantaged position than an ordinary fee-paying client, but only to equate their relative positions". The allegation that legally aided clients have an unfair advantage over those ineligible for legal aid is one that has frequently been used by the insurance lobby, which before the recent switch to Conditional Fee Agreements in England, was predominantly associated with the interests of defenders. It is certainly the case that one function of the reasonableness test has always been to prevent legal aid being granted for a case which no private client, however wealthy, would pursue if they were acting rationally. Cf. *McColl v. Strathclyde Regional Council* 1983 SLT 616. However, that need not be equated with the "equality of misery" approach. In fairness, it is unclear that the "equality of misery" is the current policy for the Scottish Executive. Thus, in a recent pronouncement, the Government Annual Expenditure report 2000, the purpose of legal aid is described as "To ensure access to justice for those people who could not otherwise afford it". Moreover in its evidence to the Justice Committee Inquiry the Executive states that "legal aid is intended to provide the means whereby individuals on low and modest incomes can be given access to the legal system". However, the practical impact of the SLAB guidelines on reasonableness (see note 5 above) seems still to reflect the "equality of misery" approach.

[8] Curiously, the cuts in financial eligibility in 1993 may have undermined the "equality of misery" approach by leaving the poorest in society able to litigate as easily as the richest but squeezing out those of modest means either through the threat of substantial contributions or through the lowness of the upper levels for income and capital in terms of eligibility. There is some evidence both from Netherlands and from the present study to suggest that those with the lowest income do in fact use solicitors to a greater extent than those of moderate means.

non-lawyers. Secondly, and more importantly, a statement that a particular problem is a legal one is not a statement of fact but an assertion that, of the available options for dealing with the problem, resorting to the law and legal services is the most appropriate.[9] Similarly, to assert that one has a need for legal services is not to make a statement of fact so much as to make a subjective value judgement. Necessarily, such judgements are open to challenge. No amount of fieldwork, therefore, could establish the "true" extent of the need for legal services in Scotland.

How then can policymakers and reformers resolve questions as to whether there are access to justice problems, unmet needs or deficiencies in the existing supply of legal services in Scotland? The prevailing solution among contemporary thinkers to these problems of definition and analysis is that identified by the Hughes Royal Commission on Legal Services in Scotland,[10] namely, stipulation. As the Hughes Commission recognised, the fact that tackling these problems requires the making of value or policy judgements, does not mean that the judgements cannot be defended on rational grounds.

We have already seen that there is an ongoing debate as to the current purpose of legal aid. Perhaps, therefore a reasonable starting point in determining what stipulations policymakers should make, would be the underlying philosophical justification for the state to provide legal services to its citizens. Over the years scholars have put forward a variety of arguments on this.[11] Foremost among them is Griffiths who concluded that the best argument for state funded legal services is:

> "not that they are a form of wealth, not that they are good for people, not that social change will result from distributing them, but rather that the just operation of the legal system demands a more equal distribution of the use of facilities collectively believed to be important to the realisation of legal entitlements and protections".[12]

This, of course, is close to the answer that in an adversarial jurisdiction such as Scotland, poverty legal services are necessary to provide "equal

---

[9] See P.Lewis, "Unmet Legal Needs" in P. Morris *et al., Social Needs and Legal Action,* London, Martin Robertson, 1973.

[10] Report of the Royal Commission on Legal Services in Scotland (1980) (Cmnd 7846, HMSO, Edinburgh).

[11] For a convenient summary of these see T.Goriely and A.Paterson, "Introduction: Resourcing Civil Justice" in Paterson and Goriely (eds) *Resourcing Civil Justice,* Oxford, Oxford University Press,1996. (pp.1–35).

[12] J.Griffiths, "The Distribution of Legal Services in the Netherlands" (1977) 4 *British Journal of Law and Society* 282–6.

access to justice". However, as we saw earlier, such an argument fails to address the question of limited resources. If "access to justice" is seen as an ideal, clients and legal service providers alike will always want more resources. The access argument provides administrators with little help in using a limited budget. Yet in a world of finite resources some form of rationing is inevitable.[13]

In truth, we could do a lot worse than to begin with the definitions and policy judgements that the Hughes Commission made in this field:

Unmet Need
2.9 Where a citizen finds a non-legal solution that satisfies him, we would not be justified in claiming that he is deprived of legal services. That would depend on his awareness of his legal rights. In assessing the need for legal services we must therefore think in terms of two stages—firstly enabling the client to identify and, if he judges it appropriate, to choose a legal solution; and, secondly, enabling the client to pursue a chosen legal solution.

2.10 Accordingly, when we speak of a need for legal services in our Report we are speaking of a need for services—facilities, advice, assistance, information or action—to enable a citizen with a problem to assert or protect his rights in law by identifying and, if he so chooses, pursuing a legal solution, that is a solution which involves a knowledge of rights and obligations or of legal procedures. When we speak of "unmet need" we are concerned about instances where a citizen is unaware that he has a legal right, or where he would prefer to assert or defend a right but fails to do so for want of legal services of adequate quality or supply.

Hughes, it will be seen, starts from the client's perception of need. It has the merit of avoiding paternalism and highlighting the citizen's needs for information and education with respect to legal services.[14] However, by not looking sufficiently at the interests of other stakeholders, and notably the Treasury, Hughes, like so many who came after them, failed to grapple adequately with the problem of finite resources.

---

[13] See Goriely and Paterson, *op.cit.* at p.31. Perhaps surprisingly, the European Human Rights Convention would be of relatively little value in this context. The flexibility in the interpretation of its provisions throughout the EU helps to explain the dramatic variations between EU jurisdictions in terms of expenditure per capita on legal aid.

[14] Cf. the Association of Scottish Legal Advice Networks (ASLAN) *Manifesto For a Community Legal Service*, "The law is the guardian of people's rights. If people are ignorant of their rights and there is no guide to help them through the maze then they are excluded from the benefits of Scotland's legal system. Although we work with thousands of people every year, we know that many more do not have the legal information, advice and representation to influence the major decisions which will impact on their lives such as stopping an eviction, negotiating debt and defending unfair dismissal." ASLAN Committee, June 2000.

This problem, as discussed earlier, cannot be resolved by empirical research however expertly conceived and executed. Nevertheless, given that some form of rationing and prioritisation seems inevitable, empirical research can play a vital role in helping to ensure that available funds are targeted to geographic areas and legal fields that rank most highly in terms of relative need[15] and that the spend is in the most cost-effective, quality assured fashion. Such research can range from surveys of the incidence of different problem types which raise legal issues, to needs assessments based on statistical proxies and from the impact of economic incentives on the behaviour of service providers to the assessment of the relative attainment of providers in terms of quality standards and outcomes. Despite its current importance, little empirical work on these lines has yet been conducted in Scotland.

THE BROADER CONTEXT

Hopefully, the Justice 1 Committee report and any initiatives that stem from it will not be restricted to the narrow confines of the legal aid system. However we define it, the effective pursuit of "access to justice" requires not only a strategic vision in relation to the provision of legal services, but also of court procedures or court-annexed procedures as well as the legal rights and entitlements of the citizen. The notion that the operation of the legal aid system and the incidence of legal aid expenditure is in some way separable from changes in the law or state recognised forms of dispute resolution, including court procedures, is surely untenable. Regrettably, policymakers have not always accepted the truth of this insight. Yet increases in legal aid expenditure are more often caused by changes in legal entitlements[16] or procedures or in the level of court fees, than by lawyers responding to economic incentives.[17] Alternatively, a reduction in the required separation periods in divorce cases in Scotland or a simplification in the associated procedures could prove a more cost effective way of pursuing "access to justice" than continuing to pump ever more public resources into the

[15] Once the criteria for "need" have been stipulated. One reason for the revival in interest in "legal needs" research (see below) is that a concern with value for money or prioritisation in legal aid spend entails looking at how and why people utilise the civil justice system and an understanding of the effectiveness of the services provided. See P. Pleasence et al., *Local Legal Need*, London, Legal Services Research Centre, 2001.

[16] E.g. the Children (Scotland) Act or the Human Rights Act 1998.

[17] See Goriely & Paterson *op.cit.* p.19.

litigation of family disputes—consistently the biggest area of civil legal aid expenditure in Scotland.

Despite this, one of the most remarkable aspects of the current era, is the extent to which the tidal wave of reform in relation to civil procedure that has swept over the litigation landscape in England and Wales for the last decade has passed Scotland by. There was no counterpart to the original Civil Justice Review[18] nor to its more radical successor under the aegis of Lord Woolf.[19] Although critical voices have been raised from time to time[20] suggesting that the defects of delay, excessive cost, uncertainty and incomprehensibility that Lord Woolf detected in England and Wales are not unknown in Scotland, there has been a fierce resistance by successive governments in Scotland to any systematic or strategic review of the civil justice system. Instead the preference has been for a series of small-scale, self-contained, ad-hoc reviews of different aspects of the Scottish system, spread over the decade, not all of which have been implemented.[21] This piecemeal approach has ensured that there has been no attempt to harmonise the jurisdiction or procedures of the Scottish Civil Courts.

If Scotland has been slower to embrace strategic reform in relation to civil procedure than its immediate neighbours, it is perhaps not surprising that ADR also appears to be generally less developed in Scotland, whether in relation to family, community or commercial

---

[18] Report of the Review Body on Civil Justice (1988), Cmnd. 394, HMSO, London.

[19] The Rt. Hon. The Lord Woolf, *Access to Justice: Interim Report,* LCD, 1995; *Access to Justice: Final Report,* LCD, 1996 and the Access to Justice Act 1999.

[20] E.g. Lord Gill, "The Case for a Civil Justice Review" (1995) 40 *J.L.S.S.*129; R. Wadia, "Judicial Case Management in Scotland" 1997 S.L.T. (News) 255; R. Mays, "Frying Pan, Fire, or Melting Pot?—reforming Scottish Civil justice in the 1990s" 1997 *J.R.* 91; H.Jones et al, *Small Claims in the Sheriff Court in Scotland* (Scottish Office Central Research Unit, 1991, Edinburgh). That said, research commissioned by Scottish Courts Administration on the Scottish courts in the 1990s did not reproduce the largely critical picture with respect to delay which emerged from the civil justice review. On the other hand only one looked at client satisfaction and none at value for money. See *Sheriff Courts Customer Survey,* Edinburgh, MVA Consultancy, 1992; S. Morris and D. Headrick, *Pilgrim's Progress? Defended Actions in the Sheriff's Ordinary Court,* (Scottish Office Central Research Unit, 1995, Edinburgh); E. Samuel and R. Bell, *Defended Ordinary Actions in the Sheriff Court: Implementing Ordinary Cause Rules 1993* (Scottish Office Central Research Unit, 1997, Edinburgh) and G. Cameron and R. Johnston, *Personal Injury Litigation in the Scottish Courts: A Descriptive Analysis* (Scottish Office Central Research Unit, 1995, Edinburgh).

[21] E.g. Lord Coulsfield, *Report of the Working Party on Commercial Causes,* Edinburgh, 1993; Lord Cullen, *Review of the Business of the Outer House of the Court of Session,* Edinburgh, 1995; The Sheriff Court Rules Council, "The New Ordinary Cause Rules" 1993 *J.L.S.S.*35; *A Consultation Paper on Proposed New Rules for Summary Cause and Small Claims in the Sheriff Court* (1998).

disputes.[22] Certainly, Scotland lags far behind England in relation to the availability of In-Court Adviser programmes and there are no court-based ADR initiatives as yet.

Curiously, such procedural or dispute processing reforms as have been introduced North of the Border have rarely been based on research evidence of litigants' perceptions of the system.[23] It follows that discussion about access to justice and the reform of court procedures proceeds largely in the absence of reliable quantitative data about the needs, interests and experiences of the community that the system is there to serve. There is as little information available about who litigates and why they litigate as there is about who chooses not to litigate and who feels that they are being denied access to the courts. With odd exceptions,[24] we have surprisingly scant knowledge of the kinds of cases that actually reach the civil courts or the dispute resolution activity that takes place in the shadow of the courts. Equally, we know remarkably little about what the civil justice system actually delivers and the extent to which the courts are regarded as valuable or irrelevant to those for whom they ostensibly exist. The result is that we lack a context for evaluating proposals for change. Here an equivalent to the English Civil Justice Council might be of assistance in highlighting the gaps in our knowledge. Unfortunately the Justice Minister has

[22] See e.g. B.Clark and R.Mays, *Alternative Dispute Resolution* (Scottish Office Central Research Unit, 1996, Edinburgh) and A. Paterson, T. Bates and M. Poustie, *The Legal System of Scotland* (4th edn) (W.Green, 1999) pp.13–26. Evidence of the relatively low rate of actual mediations even in Family law cases comes from S. Morris et al, *Family Business in the Scottish Sheriff Courts in 1992* (Scottish Office Central Research Unit, 1997, Edinburgh) and J. Lewis, *The Role of Mediation in Family Disputes in Scotland* (Scottish Office Central Research Unit, 1999, Edinburgh).

[23] At least the evaluation of the Edinburgh In-Court Adviser Project surveyed those who had used the Adviser's services as to their perceptions of the project and their experiences of the courts. E. Samuel, *Supporting Court Users: The Pilot In-Court Advice Project in Edinburgh Sheriff Court* (Scottish Office Central Research Unit, 1999, Edinburgh). The reform of the Commercial Cause procedure in the Court of Session was a partial exception to this generalisation. The Scottish Office Central Research Unit is also to be commended for commissioning "before and after" studies of the introduction of the New Ordinary Cause Rules in the Sheriff Court, but even here the principal focus was on the professionals', as opposed to the litigants', perceptions of the process. S.Morris and D. Headrick, *Pilgrim's Progress? Defended Actions in the Sheriff's Ordinary Court*, (Scottish Office Central Research Unit, 1995, Edinburgh); E.Samuel and R.Bell, *Defended Ordinary Actions in the Sheriff Court: Implementing Ordinary Cause Rules 1993* (Scottish Office Central Research Unit, 1997, Edinburgh).

[24] E.g. the Ordinary Cause in the Sheriff Court (including Family Business); Small Claims (Jones et al *op.cit.*) and Personal Injury cases (G.Cameron and R.Johnston, *Personal Injury Litigation in the Scottish Courts: A Descriptive Analysis* (Scottish Office Central Research Unit, 1995, Edinburgh).

refused to establish a Scottish Civil Justice Council, suggesting that interested stakeholders should settle for the unofficial Civil Justice Forum initiated by the Law Society of Scotland in 1998. Given that this body has no standing, no powers, and no resources its value as more than a talking shop is difficult to ascertain and already it appears to have lost much of its original momentum.[25]

COMMUNITY LEGAL SERVICES

While there is no shortage of commentators who regret that Scotland appears to be lagging behind England in relation to ADR and state sanctioned dispute resolution, there are far fewer out and out enthusiasts in Scotland for the dramatic legal aid reforms contained in the Access to Justice Act 1999. The cutbacks in civil legal aid, and in relation to personal injury litigation in particular, the exponential growth in the use of conditional fees, the detailed and bureaucratic Funding Code, the capped legal aid budget and the introduction of contracts have dismayed Northern observers. For most, the disinclination of the Scottish Office to embrace such radical proposals in its consultation paper, *Access to Justice Beyond the Year 2000*[26] or to issue its White Paper[27] following the consultation exercise, have been seen as positive developments. Only the introduction of a Legal Services Commission with a proactive, strategic remit in relation to the provision of poverty legal services, and the launching of the Community Legal Service have been seen as causes for envy.

Even this is too simple. The general enthusiasm among stakeholders in the Scottish justice system for community legal services does not extend to the model of it that pertains in England and Wales. The idea of contracting for advice and assistance work is viewed with considerable suspicion, there is more tension among the "not-for-profit" sector in Scotland on the issue of non-lawyers receiving legal aid funding than exists in England and the principled commitment of the CABx movement to a free, non-means tested information and advice service is also stronger than in England and Wales. The Scottish Executive's working group into community legal services were conscious from an early

---

[25] This is a disappointing contrast with the Criminal Justice Forum in Scotland which has both standing and funding from the Scottish Executive.

[26] SOHD, 1998.

[27] Equivalent to the English and Welsh, *Modernising Justice* (LCD,1998).

stage that the distinctive features of the justice system in Scotland would significantly impact on the character of any community legal services programme introduced north of the border.

The working description adopted by the Group suggested that the threefold purpose of a community legal service in Scotland should be:

- To ensure that there is a joined-up network across Scotland of providers of quality-assured information, advice, assistance and representation on issues involving people's legal rights and obligations and legal procedures;
- To set out a general policy framework to allow local assessment of the adequacy of provision;
- And to encourage more effective partnership between service providers and funders.[28]

Clearly, the achievement of such ambitious goals would be greatly facilitated by the availability of reliable quantitative data on a wide range of issues, including:

- the incidence of problems, particularly but not exclusively in the social welfare field, which raise or potentially raise a legal issue;
- the response of the public (broken down by socio-economic groupings) to those problems (whether, to whom and why they went for advice when confronted by the problem e.g. taking no action—"lumping it", talking to the other side, consulting friends or relatives, going to an advice agency or a solicitor);
- the range of agencies (including law firms) consulted by the public and the reasons for selecting them and the order in which they are selected (if more than one is consulted);
- the pattern of access revealed by (1) correlating agencies consulted with the problem type perceived by the client (2) the distance travelled by clients (3) the modes of transport used (4) whether the attempt to obtain advice from an agency was successful or not;
- the referral process between agencies, its efficacy and quality;
- the levels of help obtained and from whom (signposting, information, advice assistance and representation);[29]
- results achieved, and with what levels of help;

---

[28] Speech by Jim Wallace on the 10th October 2000 at a conference in Edinburgh to celebrate 50 years of legal aid.

[29] See R. Moorhead, *Pioneers in Practice*, London, LCD, 2000.

• the quality of service received by clients and their satisfaction with the services received from the different providers.

In short, implementing an effective community legal service in Scotland will require a detailed understanding of "advice-seeking behaviour" by Scottish clients or potential clients. Although there is a long tradition of studies in the "legal needs" field in the UK and elsewhere, and a steady stream of empirical research studies into various aspects of legal services in Scotland, taken collectively, surprisingly little of the information outlined above is available to the policymakers—either at all or in an up to date form.

THE USE OF LEGAL AND ADVICE SERVICES

Taking first the studies into the use of advice and legal services. An excellent history of these is contained in Pleasence's *Local Legal Needs Project*[30] based on work by Tamara Goriely. The first study was conducted in the USA in 1938,[31] but there were no serious successors until the late 1960s and early 1970s when there was a rash of similar studies in the USA, England and Wales, Australia, Canada and the Netherlands.[32] Almost all of them followed the methodology of the original survey, by setting out a list of 20 or so problem areas which the researchers regarded as legal because the law provided a solution or rules for solving them, and therefore a lawyer would help to solve them or ought to be used to do so. They then asked whether respondents had experienced any of the problems in the last few years and if so, whether they had consulted a lawyer. Perhaps unsurprisingly, the surveys all found many instances where the problems had been encountered but no lawyer used. In the heady days of the sixties when lawyers were more sure of themselves and researchers believed that lawyers could significantly help the poor, these surveys served the useful function of

---

[30] P. Pleasence et al., *Local Legal Need*, London, Legal Services Research Centre, 2001. See also H.Genn, *Paths to Justice*, Oxford, Hart Publishing, 1999, pp.5–9.

[31] See C. Clarke and E. Corstvet, "The Lawyer and the Public" 47 (1938) *Yale Law Journal* 1972.

[32] E.g. B. Abel-Smith, M.Zander and R.Brooke, *Legal Problems and the Citizen*, London, Heinemann, 1973; M. Cass and R. Sackville, *Legal Needs for the Poor*, Canberra, Australian Government Publishing Service, 1975; C. Messier, *Les Mains de la Loi* (In the Hands of the Law), Montreal, Commission des Services Juridiques, 1975; K.Schuyt, K.Groenendijk and B. Sloot, *De Weg naar Het Recht* (The Road to Justice), Deventer, Kluwer, 1976.

highlighting potential deficiencies in the legal aid system and barriers to access to the law. However, by the end of the 1970s the weakness of these surveys was coming under increasing attack.[33] Legal needs and legal problems had been seen as facts to be found rather than policy judgments. The researchers had imposed their values on the data both by focusing on the narrowly traditional problems typically taken to private practitioners and by assuming that recourse to lawyers was the best solution to the problems they had listed. The surveys had become studies of who used lawyers and why. Much less was known about those who had problems in less "traditional"[34] areas and what steps they took outside the formal legal system. Nevertheless, comparisons of the use of the Advice and Assistance scheme and CABx inquiries in relation to the social welfare law areas of housing, debt, employment and welfare benefit suggested that such problems were far more frequently brought to CABx than to lawyers.[35]

Attempts to measure legal need continued despite the criticisms, but the rebukes stung and researchers were more cautious about referring to need or assuming that people who encountered the problems on the questionnaire ought to use a lawyer. A good exemplar was Barbara Curran's monumental work for the American Bar Association and the American Bar Foundation.[36] It focused on "the circumstances under which the public seeks the advice or help of lawyers" and sought to "identify factors which appeared to influence decisions to consult or not consult lawyers".[37] The interest of this research is that it was the first to recognise that the other weakness of the prior legal needs studies was their concentration on the kinds of people who used lawyers

[33] See Lewis, *op. cit* and Griffiths, *op. cit*. For a summary of the critiques see, J. Johnsen, "Legal Needs Studies in a Market Context" in F.Regan, A.Paterson, T.Goriely and D.Fleming (eds), *The Transformation of Legal Aid*, Oxford, Oxford University Press, 1999.

[34] From the point of view of the typical high street lawyer. Abel-Smith et al. were to an extent honourable exceptions to this charge.

[35] This is still the case—see T. Goriely with A. Paterson, *Access to Legal Services: A European Comparison*, The Law Society RRPU and the Scottish Executive CRU, London, The Law Society, 2000 at p.46.

[36] B. Curran, *The Legal Needs of the Public*, American Bar Foundation, Chicago, 1977. Curran's interviewers were instructed not to mention that the research was about legal problems or lawyers but rather that it was about "general problem solving". However her list of fact situations were chosen because they implied legal need in that it would have been a reasonable and appropriate course of action to have consulted a lawyer in connection with the problem.

[37] Ibid., p.9

rather than on the problems which they took to lawyers. What Curran showed was that people's likelihood of using a lawyer was predominantly determined by the kind of problem they were confronting. Thus she discovered that for some problems the poor or black respondents were far more likely to use a lawyer than wealthier or white respondents. Finally, Curran also showed that in choosing whether to use a lawyer people were quite sophisticated, entering into a highly rational cost benefit analysis.

Seventeen years later, the ABA updated Curran's study, although this time they looked at more problem types and restricted themselves to low and moderate income households.[38] Surprisingly, gone was the caution of its predecessor about using the phrase "legal needs" or trying to avoid the appearance of making value judgements. They found relatively little difference between the two sets of households in terms of the incidence of "needs" or in the resort to lawyers. Indeed, the great majority of the situations faced by the households did not find their way into the formal justice system, and the most common course of action in dealing with a "legal need" was to try to handle the situation on their own.

In the last five years or so there has been a resurgence of interest in legal needs studies around the world. The primary reason is the increasingly open recognition by governments that expenditure on poverty legal services has to be rationed. For years, legal aid was a demand-led budget. Expenditure was re-active, the scope for forward-planning by the administrators was limited, and strategic thinking was restricted to reformers or to the salaried sector (if any). With the decline of the welfare state, policymakers have become more committed to the notion that scarce resources should be targeted to areas where they will make the most significant impact. Legal needs studies, they hope, will help them to prioritise areas for expenditure.

Australia is perhaps the clearest example of this. In the 1990s it was the first jurisdiction with a highly developed legal aid programme to move to a fixed annual budget. It therefore became imperative that the Commonwealth administrators came up with an acceptable formula based on relative need to allocate funding as between the States. They used two approaches; needs assessment based on proxies for demand (see below) and a survey of the "unmet needs" of the low-income population. Here, they catered for the "policy value" question

---

[38] American Bar Association, *Report of the Legal Needs of the Low-and Moderate-Income Public*, Chicago, 1994.

as the Hughes Commission had proposed, by separately surveying the "felt needs" of the respondents for legal aid and contrasting them with the "normative needs" stipulated by the experts (providers, administrators and community groups).[39]

At about the same time legal aid was reformed in New Zealand and each local district was charged with identifying the legal needs in their areas, monitoring the provision of legal aid and recommending improvements to the Board. This could have been the start of an early form of community legal services, but due to a shortage of resources, the reform achieved little. This prompted the Legal Services Board to commission a nationwide survey of legal needs.[40] Using the standard formula of a questionnaire with a list of common problems experienced in the last three years[41] the survey found about half of the respondents had had such a problem and the researchers deemed about half of them to be examples of an unmet need.[42] This survey endeavours to place its findings in a comparative context by juxtaposing them with the results from surveys in England, Australia, and the USA. However, the authors rightly recognise that this is ultimately a rather fruitless exercise. Indeed it has become a matter of international consensus[43] that comparisons between legal needs surveys not only between jurisdictions but within them, over time, are of limited utility, because of differences in wording, design, methodology, time frame, problem areas and sectors of the population covered not to mention cultural differences between countries and the justice systems. The New Zealand research highlighted another drawback in the dominant form of legal needs study, the lack of nuanced, qualitative data which brings the national picture down to the ground.[44] Certainly, the Legal Services Board found it less helpful than they had hoped.[45] Their

---

[39] John Walker Crime Trends Analysis and Rush Social Research, *Legal Aid Funding Model*, Canberra, Attorney-General's Department, 1999.

[40] G.Maxwell, C.Smith, P. Shepherd and A. Morris, *Meeting Legal Service Needs*, Wellington, Institute of Criminology, Victoria University of Wellington, 1999.

[41] The problems were chosen to cover areas likely to have been encountered by the lower income individuals (not groups) which the researchers considered were amenable to some form of legal solution.

[42] Half the respondents were seen as having remediable information or access problems. The researchers' assessments of unmet need were, of course, judgements of policy value.

[43] Apart from the New Zealand researchers, Tamara Goriely in Pleasence, *op.cit.*, Genn, *op.cit.* and ABA (1994) have all reached similar conclusions.

[44] One critic described the New Zealand survey as "access to justice from 10,000 feet up".

[45] See A. Opie and D. Smith, "Needs Assessments" in A. Sherr and A. Paterson (eds.) *Legal Aid in the New Millennium* Special Issue of 33(2) 2000 *University of British Columbia Law Review* at p.405.

response was to follow an approach to establishing the existence of legal needs, which had been pioneered by Johnsen in Scandinavia, namely, action research.[46] Pioneer projects were established in disadvantaged rural communities to provide legal education and information, but also to interview members of the local community with a view to providing a detailed account of the needs of that district.[47]

ESTIMATING LEGAL NEEDS

The recent history of legal needs research in New Zealand and Australia is instructive. It shows that policymakers want several kinds of information about legal needs. This holds true for the designers of the Community Legal Service programmes in the UK as well. The starting point is the desire to know how legal services are currently used—who goes to which providers and for what. At its most basic this can be done by looking at the statistics kept by providing organisations e.g. the legal aid boards[48] or Citizens Advice Bureaux. By aggregating this information it becomes possible to map the supply of legal services within a jurisdiction. This is harder than it sounds due to the lack of consensus among the different providers as to the definition to be given to "legal services" or "legal needs". Moreover the myriad of different agencies within a country and the need to look at patterns of access and advice-seeking behaviour entails that detailed mapping is best done at the local level. Indeed, it has been starting point for the work of the English Community Legal Service Partnerships.[49] Mapping the use of legal services, however, tells one little about the incidence of potential

[46] See J. Johnsen, "Studies of Legal Needs and Legal Aid in a Market Context" in F. Regan et al. (eds.) *The Transformation of Legal Aid*, Oxford University Press, 1999 at p. 205.

[47] Mitchell Research (1999) *Unmet Legal Need in the Taranaki Region* and A. Pitman (1999), *A Needs Analysis for Legal Services in the Tai Tokerau Legal Services District*.

[48] See e.g. the work done for the Scottish Legal Aid Board mapping the use of all forms of legal aid in Scotland on a geographic basis, A. Paterson and M. Turner-Kerr, "Research Report on the Distribution of Supply of Legal Aid in Scotland", Edinburgh, Scottish Legal Aid Board, 1993.

[49] The CLS Partnerships are locally based arrangements for joint working between the principal funders of legal services. Their functions include improving the co-ordination between funders and suppliers in the provision of legal services through: better mapping of the supply of legal and advice services; better assessment of the relative need for legal and advice services, and bridging the gap between the two, in part through the development of effective referral systems between suppliers of legal and advice services. See R. Moorhead, *Pioneers in Practice,* London, LCD, 2000.

"legal problems" or people who do not use legal services, for whatever reason.

To get this information requires either a legal needs study of the traditional approach set out above, taking care to avoid unintended value judgements about "legal problems" and "unmet legal need", or needs assessment through the use of statistical proxies. In Australia the Commonwealth opted for the latter strategy in devising their model for allocating funds between the States. They assumed that the States would continue to fund their traditional areas of criminal and family work, and that the budget should be distributed between the States on a per capita basis. The allocations were then weighted by statistical proxies for demand through the use of three need factors: demographic factors, socio-economic factors and cost-increasing factors.

England and Wales has been a test-bed for both approaches. Taking first needs assessment. As part of its work on targeting resources to the areas of greatest need, the English Legal Aid Board, now Legal Services Commission has been working for nearly eight years on proxies for needs assessment. Typically the Board produced an additive formula of relevant census or deprivation factors to proxy the need for advice and assistance in the social welfare law fields (debt, housing, employment, social security and health and community care). Thus the formula for proxying the need for housing advice in an area includes three components: levels of unfit households, overcrowded households and homelessness. Again the formula for proxying the need for debt advice includes two components: levels of unemployment and of undefended debt cases in the courts. Although intuitively attractive, the Board's formulae are questionable on statistical and other grounds. Certainly far from all the CLS pilot Partnerships chose to use the Board's formulae when conducting needs assessments, although the latter were deployed more widely than any of the alternatives.[50] Pascoe Pleasence of the Legal Services Research Centre, with the assistance of a range of other researchers, has recently completed a substantial re-examination of the Board's formulae in comparison with deprivation indices used in other spheres.[51] He concludes that, on balance, the Board's approach is to be preferred to other approaches. However, since there are no objectively established "true" needs for legal advice, it is difficult to see how

---

[50] Most commonly these were local authority deprivation indices or the proportion of Council Tax Benefit claimants in a given area. See Moorhead, *op.cit.*
[51] P. Pleasence et al., *Local Legal Need*, London, Legal Services Research Centre, 2001.

Pleasence is able to conclude that one formula is more adequate than another. Given that proxies for need are only (1) indicators of relative need between different geographic areas and (2) a rough starting point which the CLS partnerships are supposed to refine, drawing on their local knowledge, there is a strong case for pragmatically settling for simpler, possibly univariate formulae which will deliver much of the functionality of the more complex formulae espoused by the Commission.[52]

Armed with their supply maps and their proxy patterns of need, the CLS Partnerships are expected to seek to bridge the gap between the two. Gaps there will certainly be, as Pleasence's finding that over 70% of wards in England and Wales saw no delivery of legally aided advice level work of any description within them despite containing 60% of the population, seems to suggest. Similarly, Paterson and Montgomery showed that the substantial variations in the delivery of advice and assistance in the social welfare law field in different parts of rural Scotland[53] were as much due to the presence in some of the areas of "niche" specialist solicitors as to differences in demand proxies.[54] Here the need for a clearer understanding of "advice seeking behaviour" is vital. Not simply the who, why and why-not questions, but also the operation of referral networks. The low percentage of generalist advice agency clients that are referred on to solicitors in private practice on either side of the Border hints at a culture of "non-referral",[55] despite the desirability of a seamless local network of advisers. Miller's study of referrals to Scottish solicitors showed not only a low rate of referral but also an "attrition effect"—20% of referrals to solicitors never arrive—which suggests that it may be more important to concentrate on getting the client to the most appropriate agency, first time round. To achieve this will require a better understanding of why clients choose the agencies which they do,[56] how rational these choices are,[57]

[52] For a limited attempt at legal needs assessment (using univariate proxies), and its relationship to supply in Scotland, see A. Paterson and P. Montgomery, "Access to and Demand for Welfare Legal Services in Rural Scotland", Edinburgh, Scottish Legal Aid Board, 1996.

[53] See A. Paterson and M. Turner-Kerr, *Research Report on the Distribution of Supply of Legal Aid in Scotland*, Edinburgh, SLAB, 1993.

[54] See Paterson and Montgomery, *op. cit.*

[55] See, J. Steele and G. Bull, *Fast, friendly and expert?* London, Policy Studies Institute, 1996; C. Miller Research, *Referrals between Advice Agencies and Solicitors*, Edinburgh, CRU, 1999.

[56] See E. Kempson,(1989) *Legal Advice and Assistance*, Policy Studies Institute.

[57] Here there are the makings of an interesting debate between Kempson, *op. cit* and A. Lindley, (1997) "Access to Legal Advice", *Consumer Policy Review*, vol.7 no.4 July/August p.143. Kempson, building on research of Gillian Borrie, *Advice Agencies: What They Do*

and how far they are prepared to travel for different types of service.[58]

Another key component in "advice-seeking behaviour" is determining why so many people with problems which might potentially benefit from the provision of legal services, choose not to seek help from any provider. This has led some scholars to focus their energies on the early stages of disputes in order to theorise disputing behaviour, although this has been hampered by a lack of empirical data. One of the most influential theories on disputing behaviour[59] visualises access to justice as a path with barriers, which some travellers will surmount, while others fall by the wayside. The logical steps along the path involve the recognition of particular kinds of events as "injurious" (naming): the identification of the event as a grievance for which another is responsible (blaming); the confrontation of the wrongdoer with the complaint (claiming); and finally, if the response of the wrongdoer fails to provide satisfaction, the decision to pursue a remedy through the courts. According to this model, the litigants who find their way into the formal dispute resolution system are those who, following the occurrence of a potentially injurious event, attribute blame to another person or body, have the consciousness of a legal remedy, and are prepared to seek such a remedy rather than simply ignoring the event (lumping it) or attributing the event to bad luck or an act of God.

Although this model is a helpful starting point in identifying the psychological processes and structural barriers that affect choice, it is important not to underestimate the complex interaction of factors that influence decisions about how to deal with problems raising legal issues and the fact that the model may be more appropriate for certain types of legal problem than for others. Indeed one of the difficulties of theorising about disputing behaviour in the access to justice context has been the failure to recognise the *dissimilarity* of problems for which legal remedies exist and the responses to those problems. Not everyone involved in circumstances for which a legal remedy is available necessarily feels a

and Who Uses Them, London, NCC, 1982, argues that although patterns of access vary as a reflection of the different providers in separate localities, in most districts there is relatively little overlap between the work done by the agencies and the law firms. Her conclusion is therefore that the public are surprisingly sophisticated in their use of legal and advice agencies. Lindley begs to differ.

[58] See A. Millar and S. Morris, *Legal Services in Scotland: Consumer Survey* Edinburgh, CRU, 1992.

[59] W. Felstiner et al (1981) "The Emergence and Transformation of Disputes: Naming, Blaming, Claiming . . .", 15 *Law and Society Review* 631.

grievance. Not everyone blames another. Those who claim may not blame and those who blame may not claim. Not everyone is interested in the remedy that is provided by the law. Those who neither blame nor claim may not necessarily "lump it", but may seek a self-help remedy that is likely to secure a desired outcome.

Understanding advice-seeking behaviour, therefore, must lie at the heart of any attempt to develop a community legal service which takes seriously public perceptions of legal and advice services. It is also central to attempts to reform civil procedure or to foster ADR. The best way to study it is through a sophisticated legal needs survey. Certainly, that was the conclusion of the National Consumer Council of England and Wales at the time of the Woolf *Access to Justice Review*[60] when they sought to look at the use of legal and advice services to resolve civil disputes. They screened over 8,000 respondents by asking whether they had been involved in a serious dispute in the last three years in relation to a series of listed problems. Those who had, were asked about their experiences of the civil justice system. Thirteen per cent of the population had experienced one or more of the 13 listed problems and a very high percentage of them (nearly 80%) had sought outside help (usually from solicitors or CABx) about resolving the dispute. These results alone reveal the limitations of the research as an indicator of the adequacy of the existing justice system. The low incidence of the 13 everyday problems on the list clearly reflects the phrasing of the key question. Respondents appear to have interpreted "serious disputes" as akin to "legal disputes".[61] This in turn would explain why such a high proportion sought outside help. It would seem that the survey tells us more about respondents who perceived their problems as a legal disputes meriting the use of the formal justice system than those who had problems in their day-to-day lives which raised legal issues, possibly serious ones, but which were not seen as worth disputing or as being disputable. The survey is unable to cast light on how the latter group handled their problems. The Scottish Consumer Council carried out a parallel study using the same questionnaire, a year later. Interestingly, 18.5% reported having experienced a serious civil dispute in the last three years and twice as many had experienced faulty goods or unsatisfactory services as their English counterparts. Explaining these

---

[60] Rt. Hon. the Lord Woolf MR *Access to Justice: Interim Report*, Lord Chancellor's Department 1995; *Access to Justice: Final Report*, Lord Chancellor's Department 1996

[61] Perhaps because the question was preceded by a reference to the Woolf Inquiry, *op.cit.*

differences is not easy, but the answer may be partly linguistic. Thus Goriely has suggested that perhaps the canny Scots regarded a poor quality purchase as more "serious" than the English[62]—the latter being presumably more resigned to built in obsolescence, or perhaps that North of the Border the word "dispute" is taken to mean an "argument" without any quasi-legal connotations.[63] At any rate the Consumer Council surveys are a reminder as to the major impact which subtle differences of phraseology can make to research results.

Like the Consumer Council surveys, this book reports on "advice seeking behaviour" by the public in England and Scotland. Conceived in a context of increasing concern over access to justice and impending changes to the civil justice system, at least in England, the research has become, if anything more timely with the emergence of the community legal services initiatives on both sides of the Border. Like the Consumer Council surveys the research was conducted over slightly different timeframes in England and Scotland. The former study was awarded a grant by the Nuffield Foundation in the summer of 1996 and its results were published in 1999.[64] It sought to fill some of the existing information void and to provide a factual basis that would inform debate and policy choices. It presents the results of a national survey of households in England and Wales. The broad primary objective of the study was to establish the frequency with which members of the public were faced with problems which raised legal issues, ("justiciable problems"), to map the response of the public to those problems, whether and where they went for help, and the results. Although the study represented the most comprehensive attempt in England and Wales to estimate the volume of such problems from the "bottom-up", it built on the well-established tradition of legal needs surveys which has been set out above. It was recognised, however, that the distinctiveness of the civil justice system in Scotland, including its substantive law, court procedures,[65] court system,[66] legal aid provision [67]and the organisation of its

[62] It may be relevant that Scottish consumers are poorer and are more likely to live in rural areas than their English counterparts.

[63] See P. Pleasence et al, *Local Legal Need*, *op.cit*. para. 2.2.16.

[64] Genn, *op.cit*.

[65] In the absence of a civil justice review, judicial case management is much less developed in Scotland, even in relation to the small claims procedure.

[66] Again the lack of enthusiasm for a rationalisation of court jurisdictions in Scotland has left the Sheriff Court with a far wider substantive jurisdiction than the County Court. See Paterson, Bates and Poustie, *The Legal System of Scotland op.cit*. chapter 2.

[67] Scotland has no legal aid franchises or contracts. Most cases in Scotland begin on Advice and Assistance and only after sufficient evidence has been gathered can the case

legal profession[68] was such as to merit a separate survey. Not only would this yield important data about the use (and non-use) of legal and advice services in Scotland but it would allow a comparison between the jurisdictions which might cast light on the importance of cultural and structural differences in influencing advice seeking behaviour in the two countries.

THE PATHS TO JUSTICE SCOTLAND SURVEY

The focus of the study was on the behaviour of the public in Scotland[69] in dealing with non-trivial justiciable civil problems and disputes, as potential pursuers or potential defenders. The approach represented an attempt to map strategies from the bottom-up and was distinctive in that it was not limited to use of legal services to achieve court-based solutions for disputes and grievances. The study was designed to include the widest range of events (experienced by individuals as private persons) for which legal remedies are available under the civil justice system, subject only to a "triviality" threshold. Whether or not individuals were included or excluded from the study depends crucially on several key definitions used in the study as follows:

"Justiciable event": For the purposes of the study a justiciable event was defined as a matter experienced by a respondent which raised legal issues, whether or not it was recognised by the respondent as being "legal" and whether or not any action taken by the respondent to deal with the event involved the use of any part of the civil justice system. Fourteen broad categories and over sixty sub-categories of justiciable event were identified for inclusion in the study ranging across employment, divorce, family, money, health, injury, immigration, property, discrimination issues etc (see Chapter 2 for full list). The justiciable events included in the study related only to *civil* matters, so where a

progress to getting a full civil legal aid certificate. There is also a stiffer merits test for legal aid in civil cases in Scotland. As a result, the ratio of legally aided personal injury cases per 100,000 of the population in Scotland was less than one-third of the figure in England and Wales in 1997.

[68] There are far fewer (proportionally) advice agencies in Scotland who employ a salaried solicitor. On the other hand, there are proportionately more community law centres in Scotland.

[69] For logistical and cost reasons, the survey excluded Scotland North of the Caledonian Canal.

respondent had been the victim of a crime this was not normally included. However, there were situations where violence raised the possibility of civil actions and these cases were included.

"Non-trivial": In order to avoid the study being swamped with trivial matters it was necessary to impose a triviality threshold. Using imposed or self-selected severity thresholds involved difficulties. For example, imposed thresholds ignore respondents' perceptions of the importance of an event. If a respondent felt that the threshold was too low they might be irritated by having to answer further questions about a matter to which they attached little importance. If the threshold was set too high, a respondent might feel frustrated about not being permitted to talk about a matter that was important to them. On the other hand, self-selected severity inevitably involves differential interpretation of terms such as "serious" and "major", resulting in the loss of information about strategies adopted to deal with some relatively serious events and the possibility of being swamped by relatively trivial events. In the end a mixture of imposed and self-selected triviality criteria was adopted. This involved a two stage approach: first respondents were asked to report all justiciable events that they had experienced as defined by the study irrespective of the seriousness of the event; second, events that had been reported were excluded from further questioning if respondents said that they had taken no action whatsoever to deal with the problem because the problem had not been regarded as important enough to warrant any action. Thus exclusion from further investigation was based on respondents' subjective perceptions of triviality. Some events, however, were automatically deemed to be relevant for further investigation. These were, divorce, being threatened with or the subject of legal proceedings, or having considered or commenced legal proceedings against another person or organisation[70]. Finally, events were not included in the main survey if respondents said that they had taken no action to deal with the problem because they did not regard themselves as being in dispute since they believed that the other side was right, or that no one was to blame[71].

[70] The American Bar Association Comprehensive Legal Needs Study (1994) adopted a slightly different approach. Some matters were included automatically such as homelessness, discrimination, dismissal from work. For all other types of events the questions were framed in such a way that words such as "serious problem/dispute" or "major difficulties" were incorporated into the question.

[71] In both the England and Wales and the Scotland studies, this approach excluded undefended debt actions, a common "problem" faced by the public in both jurisdictions.

"Private individuals": The study was concerned with the response of *individuals* to justiciable events. Thus businesses, institutions, associations, etc were excluded from the study. This raised some difficulties when an individual was in business on his own account and it was decided that such individuals would be included if they reported a justiciable event occurring in their private capacity, but that any justiciable event occurring in relation to their work activities would be excluded. A self-employed plumber suing an electrician who carried out work on the plumber's house would therefore be included. If, however, the same plumber had been sued by a householder as a result of his own faulty workmanship, that event *would not* be included in the study.

Objectives

The survey was designed to provide information and offer analyses of the following:

- The *incidence* of justiciable problems within the population.
- The *responses* of the public to justiciable matters, including use of legal and other advice sources, alternative dispute resolution methods, self-help strategies (and what these entail—for example involving the police in civil disputes), and simply doing nothing.
- Perceived *barriers* to access to justice, including the types of issues that are being denied access to the courts, when access is desired; the factors perceived as representing the main barriers to access—such as cost, lack of information, lack of confidence.
- The *motivation* for taking action to resolve problems and for using courts or alternative forms of dispute resolution, or for avoiding legal processes.
- The *outcome* of different strategies for resolving justiciable disputes and the cost.
- The public's *experiences and perceptions* of legal proceedings, the courts, and the judiciary.

Central to the survey's objectives and subsequent analysis was a desire to convey the *dissimilarity* of the range of justiciable problems that might face members of the public at different times, and the way in which strategies for the resolution of justiciable problems are as much influenced by the characteristics of the problem as by the characteristics of the person experiencing the problem.

Method[72]

The research comprised four distinct stages:

(i)   Qualitative developmental work involving group discussions to assist in the design of the screening questionnaire.

(ii) A face-to-face screening survey of the general population of adults (over 18) conducted in their homes, designed to estimate the incidence of events for which legal remedies exist ("justiciable problems") in the five years since January 1992. This involved a random sample of 2,684 individuals ("the screening survey").

(iii) Follow-up face-to-face interviews with 472 adults in their homes who had been identified as having experienced a non-trivial justiciable problem during the previous five years ("the main survey");

(iv) In-depth face-to-face qualitative interviews with 29 respondents who had experienced a justiciable problem ("the qualitative interviews").

Qualitative Developmental Work

The screening survey replicated the survey instrument used in the England and Wales study, with necessary adjustments to take account of the distinctive features of the Scottish legal system. The English questionnaire was preceded by a lengthy developmental stage in order to ensure that the questions included on the screening questionnaire covered the widest possible range of potentially justiciable problems, not merely the more obvious events that many people would recognise as being potentially "legal" problems. Moreover, it was important that the wording of the questions was appropriate, containing comprehensive memory prompts in order to maximise recall and reporting. The developmental work in Scotland included a series of group discussions with members of the public, solicitors, and advice agency workers. The discussions took place during evenings and lasted for about two hours. All group discussions were tape-recorded and verbatim transcripts produced.

   Topics explored during group discussions with members of the public included: experiences of justiciable events and the terminology used by the public when referring to "justiciable problems"; the various strategies adopted to try and resolve justiciable problems; the range of

---

[72] A full technical report is provided in Appendix A.

advice sources used by the public in dealing with justiciable problems; experience of the accessibility of advice and assistance; motivations for taking action to try and reslove problems; experience of and attitudes to the legal profession, the courts, and the judiciary.

Group discussions with solicitors and advice agency workers included exploration of the range of justiciable events dealt with by them; the types of advice and assistance provided for different categories of justiciable problem; routes to advisers and perceived barriers to advice; and perceptions of clients' attitudes to taking legal or other action to resolve justiciable problems.

In addition to group discussions, pilot surveys of the screening questionnaire and the main questionnaire were carried out in order to obtain a rough estimate of the likely strike rate for the main survey, and to modify and refine questions in the light of experience.

The Screening Survey

A random sample of 2,684 individuals aged 18 or over was screened in order to determine whether or not they had experienced problems of various sorts during the previous five years ("the survey period"). Interviewers presented respondents with a series of show cards each of which showed a list of problems of a particular type and respondents were asked whether or not they had experienced one or more of the problems on each card since January 1992. There were fourteen broad categories of problems and over sixty problem sub-categories included on the screening survey. The full range of questions asked, together with the material on the show cards is reproduced in Appendix C. The results of the screening survey are discussed in Chapter 2.

Main Survey

Respondents who said that they had experienced problems of a particular type were then asked for each problem mentioned (up to a maximum of three) whether they had taken any of a list of actions which were also shown on a card. Those saying that they had not taken any of these actions were then asked to say why not, again choosing their reasons from a card. Respondents were deemed eligible for a main interview if they had experienced one or more problems from the problem show cards and had *either* taken one of the specified actions about it *or* indicated that the reason they had not taken any such action was not to do with the triviality of the problem. In addition, respondents were automatically deemed eligible for a main interview if they had been involved in divorce proceedings, had legal action taken against them, had been threatened with legal action over a disagreement, or had started, or considered starting, court proceedings. If respondents mentioned having experienced more than one problem during the survey period, they were asked about the second most recent problem in the main interview. The second most recent problem was chosen in order to increase the likelihood that sufficient time would have elapsed for a resolution to have been achieved.

The main survey questionnaire covered the experiences of those who sought to deal with their problems or disputes through the legal system, those who used alternative methods of dispute resolution, those who adopted self-help strategies, and those who did nothing at all to seek a resolution of their problem or dispute. The interview covered details of the justiciable problem and what was at stake; the strategy adopted by the respondent, if any, in trying to achieve a resolution of the problem; details of any advice and assistance obtained; use and experience of legal processes; objectives in taking action; outcomes achieved. The survey also dealt with experiences and perceptions of processes and services and perceptions of those who did not use legal processes. All respondents were also questioned about attitudes to the courts, judiciary, and lawyers[73]. The main survey interviews lasted on average around forty-five minutes.

Qualitative Study

Although the screening survey and main survey provided reliable estimates of the incidence of justiciable events and responses to those events, qualitative interviews were conducted to provide in-depth information about behaviour, decision-making and motivation, permitting a more detailed tracing of the *processes* through which disputes were handled. In particular, qualitative interviews were able to explore in detail: influences on decisions about how to deal with disputes and problems; motivations and objectives underlying choices about particular courses of action; experiences of using legal and other advisers; perceived barriers to advice; experience of being involved in legal proceedings. The qualitative interviews also provided important

---

[73] A copy of the main questionnaire is reproduced at Appendix C.

information to supplement attitudinal questions posed on the main survey about attitudes to the courts and legal services[74].

Respondents included in the qualitative follow-up stage of the research were recruited from those who had been interviewed in the main survey and were selected on the basis of a mix of problem types and responses to those problems. Qualitative interviews were therefore conducted with respondents who had taken no action to resolve their justiciable problem; those who had taken action to resolve their problem and who had done so without seeking any advice or assistance; respondents who had sought advice from an advice agency or non-legal adviser and then handled the problem themselves; respondents who had sought legal advice and resolved the problem without becoming involved in court proceedings; and respondents who had sought legal advice and resolved their problem following a court or tribunal hearing.

All interviews were tape-recorded and verbatim transcripts produced. The interviews lasted for about one hour on average.

STRUCTURE OF THE BOOK

Chapter Two uses the results of the screening survey to estimate the incidence of different kinds of justiciable problems as reported by respondents to the screening survey, together with brief information about whether respondents took any action to deal with the problem. The Chapter identifies the most common problems experienced by members of the public, demographic variations in the reporting of justiciable problems, and the frequency with which individuals experienced problems of a particular kind during the survey period. For each of the fourteen broad problem areas covered in the screening survey, estimates are provided of the number of problems occurring per 1,000 population and the total number of problems occurring within the population of Scotland. There is also information provided about the types of problems that tend to cluster together. The second section of Chapter Two provides a breakdown of the main survey sample, based on the selection of respondents experiencing a "non-trivial" justiciable problem during the previous five years, and the demographic characteristics of respondents experiencing problems of different types are described.

---

[74] The topic guide used in the qualitative interviews is reproduced at Appendix A.

Chapter Three begins with an overview of the public response to justiciable problems, analysing the characteristics of "lumpers", "self-helpers", and those who obtained assistance in the process of resolving their problem. In order to gain a better understanding of the public need for advice in dealing with justiciable problems the Chapter describes barriers and pathways to advice, the choice of advisers, expectations of advisers, the nature of advice received and satisfaction with that advice.

Chapter Four lays bare the various strategies adopted by respondents in dealing with justiciable problems of different types and looks in more detail at some of the issues discussed in Chapter Three in relation to particular problem types. In the final section of Chapter Four, the results of multivariate analysis are presented in order to gain a better understanding of the factors associated with the likelihood that advice would be obtained during the process of resolving disputes.

In Chapter Five the outcomes of attempts to resolve problems are analysed. The Chapter reports the proportion of all those experiencing a justiciable problem who succeeded in achieving a resolution of their problem, the proportion who abandoned their attempts to seek a resolution and the proportion who became involved in legal proceedings. Differences in outcome are analysed in relation to whether or not advice was obtained and the kind of advice obtained, as well as in relation to the type of problem experienced. In the second section of the chapter the cost of taking action to resolve problems is described, together with information about those respondents whose legal costs were covered by legal aid or other sources. The final section of the Chapter uses the results of multivariate analysis to explain the factors most strongly associated with different problem outcomes, for example whether any resolution was achieved by agreement, or whether there was a court hearing or whether no resolution was achieved at all.

Respondents' motivations for taking action and the fulfilment of objectives are the subject of Chapter Six. The Chapter summarises the reported motivation of respondents for taking action to resolve justiciable problems and describes differences in motivation depending on the type of problem being experienced. There is also a summary of the amount of money being pursed or defended and the types of non-money remedy desired by respondents. Differences between problem types in the extent to which respondents' objectives were achieved are described, as are perceptions of the fairness of the outcomes obtained. The final section of the Chapter discusses the results of multivariate analysis identifying factors associated with the achievement of objectives and perceptions of fairness of outcome.

In Chapter Seven the experiences of those involved in ADR and court processes are described, followed by a detailed analysis of responses to attitude questions about the legal system. These data are supplemented by analysis of qualitative interviews in which respondents were given the opportunity to expand on their views of the legal system. The material in the chapter provides useful contextual information that can contribute to understanding of the influences on the public when they make decisions about how to deal with justiciable problems.

The concluding Chapter highlights some of the main findings of the study and draws together the various threads running through the discussion in previous chapters. It considers the significance of the courts in the resolution of civil disputes and the policy strategies that might rationally flow from the understanding of the needs and preferences of the public gained from the study.

A technical report providing details of sampling, response rates, data collection methods and weighting procedures is provided at Appendix A. Appendix B describes in more detail the approach of the multivariate analyses reported in Chapter 4, 5, and 6 and presents the full results of the analyses. The screening questionnaire, main survey questionnaire, advance letter, and qualitative interview topic guide are reproduced at Appendix C.

2

The Landscape of Justiciable Problems

COLLECTING INFORMATION ABOUT JUSTICIABLE PROBLEMS

The purpose of this chapter is to estimate the incidence of justiciable problems as defined in the survey and to look very broadly at public responses to these problems. The estimates are based on the replies of a random sample of 2,684 adults who were asked during a screening survey to recall whether they had experienced any of a wide range of problems during the previous five years and if so when, and on how many occasions. The analysis in this chapter is a comprehensive attempt to assess the frequency with which the population of Scotland faces a wide range of justiciable problems. The analysis is comparable with that carried out in England and Wales and reference is made throughout the chapter to similarities and significant differences between the findings of the two studies.

The range of problems included in the survey and the wording used to describe those problems were developed on the basis of focus group meetings held in Edinburgh with advice agencies, members of the public, and solicitors, followed by piloting of questionnaires. The questionnaire largely repeated the questions used in the England and Wales study with important modifications to make the language appropriate to Scotland and, in a few places, with different or additional items to cover differences in the Scottish legal system and legal procedures. After testing the wording of the screening survey and making some modifications, the survey was conducted during spring 1998. In the final form of the questionnaire, interviewers presented respondents with a series of cards, each of which showed a list of problems of a particular type, and respondents were asked whether or not they had experienced one or more of the problems on each card since January 1992. The types of problems covered in the screening survey were:

- employment problems;
- problems relating to owning residential property;
- problems with renting out rooms or property (including crofting);
- problems to do with living in rented accommodation;
- problems with faulty goods or services;
- problems to do with money;
- problems to do with relationships and other family matters;
- problems connected with having children aged less than 18;
- injuries and health problems arising from accidents or poor working conditions requiring medical treatment;
- death of child or partner as a result of an accident;
- problems with discrimination in relation to sex/race/disability;
- problems with unfair treatment by the police;
- problems with immigration or nationality issues;
- problems with receiving negligent/wrong medical or dental treatment;
- defamation (reputation or good name publicly questioned).

The list of types of problems differed from that used in England and Wales in that it included questions about accidental death of child or partner and defamation.

Because it was important to encourage memory recall, on each of the show cards dealing with a particular category of problem, there was a series of memory prompts indicating the kinds of problems that might arise in the general category. So, for example, the show card dealing with problems to do with living in rented accommodation offered the following prompts:

- poor or unsafe living conditions;
- getting a deposit back from the landlord or council;
- renting out rooms to lodgers or sub-letting;
- getting other people in the accommodation to pay their share of the bills;
- getting the landlord or council to do repairs *(e.g. dampness)*;
- agreeing on rent, council tax or housing benefit payments or other terms of the lease, missive or tenancy agreement;
- getting the landlord to provide a written lease, missive or tenancy agreement;
- neighbours *(e.g. disputes about noise, boundaries, access etc)*;
- harassment by the landlord;
- being evicted, or threatened with eviction.

In addition to this range of justiciable "problems", respondents were also asked whether, apart from anything already reported, they had been involved in divorce proceedings, had had legal action taken against them, had been threatened with legal action over a disagreement or had started or considered starting court proceedings for any reason.

Respondents who said that they had experienced any of these problems were then asked for each problem mentioned (up to a maximum of three) whether they had taken any of a list of actions which were also shown on a card as follows:

- Talked/wrote to other side about problem
- Sought advice about trying to solve problem
- Threatened other side with legal action
- Went to court/tribunal/arbitration or started a court or tribunal case or an arbitration
- Went to mediation or conciliation
- Took problem to an ombudsman
- Took other action to try to solve the problem
- Did nothing.

Those saying that they had not taken any of the actions on the card were then asked to say why not, again choosing their reasons from a card as follows:

- Other side was already taking action
- Thought it would cost too much
- Thought it would take too much time
- Did not think anything could be done
- Did not think it was very important
- No dispute with anybody/thought the other person/side was right
- Was scared to do anything
- Thought it would damage relationship with other side
- Other reason.

Respondents were deemed eligible for a "main" interview if they had experienced one or more problems and had either taken one of the specified actions to deal with the problem, or had failed to take action for a reason *other than* the triviality of the problem or that there was no dispute. Respondents were also included in the main survey if they had been involved in divorce proceedings, had had legal action taken against them, had been threatened with legal action over a disagreement about something, or had started or considered starting legal proceedings.

THE MOST COMMON PROBLEMS AND THEIR INCIDENCE

In total, some 26% of all respondents who answered the screening survey reported having experienced one or more justiciable problems during the previous five years. The type of problems most frequently experienced were money problems (experienced by seven percent of the total sample); those relating to faulty goods and services (experienced by six percent of the total sample); those relating to living in rented accommodation (six percent); those relating to owning residential property (five percent); employment problems (five percent); those relating to relationships and family matters (four percent); injuries/ health problems resulting from accidents or poor working conditions (three percent of the sample) (Figure 2.1). The problems least frequently experienced by the sample were those relating to: immigration or nationality issues (0.2% of the sample), discrimination on grounds of race, sex or disability (0.5% of the sample), defamation (0.6% of the sample), and negligent or wrong medical or dental treatment (0.6% of the sample).

Comparing these results with those obtained in the England and Wales study, the most important point to note is the significantly *lower* overall incidence of justiciable problems reported in Scotland. While in Scotland about *one in four* respondents reported having experienced one or more justiciable problems during the survey reference period (26%), the figure in England and Wales was about *two in five* (40%). In the case of each problem type the level of incidence was *lower* than, or in a few cases equal to, that found in England and Wales. Not only was the overall incidence of problems different between the two jurisdictions, but so too was the pattern of incidence. This divergence is discussed in more detail at the end of this Chapter and in Chapter 8.

The most commonly reported types of problem in Scotland were money problems and faulty goods and services. These two types of problems were also the most frequently experienced by the population of England and Wales. While in Scotland tenancy problems were the *third* most commonly experienced problem, they were the *fifth* most common in England. While in Scotland accidental injury or work-related ill-health was the *seventh* most commonly mentioned problem, in England it was the *fourth* most common. In both Scotland and England involvement in divorce proceedings was the eighth most commonly mentioned justiciable problem or event experienced (see Figure 2.1). In addition to these differences in the results in Scotland and England and Wales in terms of the *incidence* of broad categories of problems, there were also some curious differences in the *types* of problems experienced. These differences are discussed later in the Chapter[1].

Having been asked about experiences of specific problem types, respondents were then asked some additional questions in order to ensure that all those who had been involved in, or considered starting, any kind of legal proceedings were included in the main survey. Respondents were asked whether "apart from anything you have already told me about in this interview—since January 1992, has any legal action been taken against you, for example have you been sent a solicitor's letter or had court proceedings started against you?" and some additional questions about taking legal action and being threatened with legal action (see questionnaire in Appendix C for full text of questions). These "catch-all" questions produced some additional positive cases. About one percent of the sample reported that they had been the subject of legal action (as compared with three percent in England), about one percent of the sample reported having been *threatened* with legal action where they disputed the demand being made, and about one percent of the sample reported that they had started or *considered* starting some kind of legal proceeding through court, mediation or ombudsman. In all of these situations the proportions responding positively were somewhat *lower* in Scotland than in England and Wales.

The results of the screening survey can also be compared with the results of the Scottish Consumer Council study of experiences of civil disputes in Scotland ("SCC study").[2] That study found that 18% of their random sample of the general population of Scotland had recent experience of at least one serious civil dispute relating to the thirteen problem areas asked about. Provided the sample was representative of the population as a whole, this would correspond to just under one million Scots. This figure is considerably lower than the 26% of respondents in the present study who had experienced a justiciable problem in the previous five years. However, the SCC study counted only those

---

[1] Although immigration and asylum-seeking in particular are now political issues in Scotland, this was not the case in when the fieldwork was conducted.

[2] *Civil Disputes in Scotland*, Scottish Consumer Council, 1997.

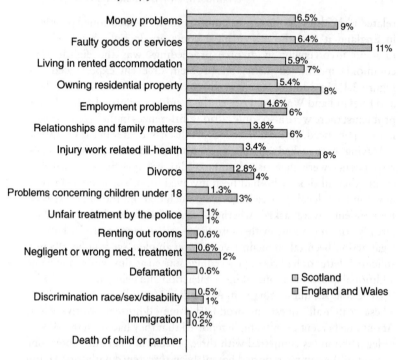

Figure 2.1 Incidence of problems of different types reported in screening survey in Scotland (Base=2,684) compared with England and Wales results.

members of the public who reported having experienced one of 13 types of "serious civil disputes" in the previous three years. Thus the range of matters about which respondents were asked was much narrower than in the present study which used 14 broad problem categories and about 65 different sub-categories of problem to prompt memory and to indicate the kinds of problems and events to be reported. The use of the criterion of "serious dispute" in the SCC study meant that those respondents who had experienced a problem, even one that was "difficult to solve", but avoided the matter from becoming a "serious dispute" by taking direct action, would probably not have been included in the SCC study although they would have been included in the present study. The differences between the overall incidence rate achieved in the two studies can also be partly accounted for by the longer reference period used in the present study (five years rather than the three-year reference period used in the SCC study). Finally, the SCC survey was not administered as a single omnibus study but as part of the System Three Scotland's Scottish Opinion Poll every month for a six-month period. This methodological difference from the present study may also have influenced the results attained.

There were also some divergences between the two studies in the estimated incidence of specific problem types, although this is partly a result of different definitions of problem categories in the two studies. The most common problems reported in the SCC study were faulty goods (17%) unsatisfactory services (15%), damage to a vehicle (11%) dispute with a local authority/agency (10%) problems with neighbours (9%), divorce (7%), injury (7%), problems at work (6%) and custody/ access to children (6%). The problem categories that are directly comparable with the present study, such as, injury and problems at work show that the SCC estimates are relatively similar. Other categories are more difficult to compare. For example, in the present study faulty goods and services were categorised together and had an incidence rate of 7%. In the SCC study faulty goods had an incidence of 17% and unsatisfactory services an incidence of 15%. Such marked differences defy easy explanation. Again the figure for the incidence of divorce in the SCC study is rather higher than in the present study (7% in the SCC study as compared with 3%). However, the figure for the incidence of divorce proceedings derived from the screening survey in the present study represents simply those respondents who had been involved in divorce proceedings during the previous five years, whereas the SCC study refers to people "involved in a serious dispute about divorce". It is therefore likely that the SCC figure includes matters that would have been categorised in the present study under "relationships and family matters".

DEMOGRAPHIC VARIATIONS

The only demographic information collected on the screening questionnaire was the age and sex of respondents[3]. Analysis of prevalence of justiciable disputes in relation to these factors indicated that there were no meaningful differences between men and women in the extent to which they reported having experienced these problems. This finding is reasonably consistent with the SCC study which found that while

[3] Full demographic information was collected during the main survey and is used throughout the analysis of main survey findings discussed in the following chapters.

18% of respondents reported having had a serious dispute, 20% were men and 17% were women, and is also consistent with the NCC study, which found few gender differences in the reporting of involvement in civil disputes. Moreover, within each problem type the proportion of men and women reporting having experienced the event was virtually identical (Table 2.1).

Table 2.1 Incidence of problems of different types by gender

Type of problem	Total	Gender Male	Female
	%	%	%
Money	7	8	5
Faulty goods or services	6	6	7
Living in rented accommodation	6	6	6
Owning residential property	5	5	5
Employment problems	5	5	4
Relationships and other family matters	4	4	4
Injuries / health problems	3	3	3
Divorce	3	2	3
Problems concerning children aged under 18	1	1	2
Unfair treatment by the police	1	2	*
Renting out rooms or property	1	1	1
Negligent or wrong medical treatment	1	1	1
Defamation	1	1	*
Discrimination race/sex/disability	1	1	*
Immigration or nationality issues	*	*	*
Any problem	26	26	26
Unweighted base	2684	1223	1433
Weighted base	2684	1214	1441

'*' denotes a non-zero quantity of less than half a per cent

There were, however, some differences in experience depending on age (Table 2.2). Younger people were more likely to have experienced problems than their older counterparts: a little over one third of those aged between 18 and 34 (between 34% and 38%) had experienced one or more problems, whereas about one in five of those aged between 55 and 64 had done so (20%) and fewer than one in ten of those aged 65 or over had done so (9%). The incidence of most problem types declined with increasing age. Some of these differences can be plausibly linked with age-related changes in life-style, notably those relating to problems with employment, living in rented accommodation, and having children under 18. However, the explanations of other age-related trends, such as those relating to faulty goods and services and money, are less obvious.

The findings in relation to age are consistent with those south of the Border, although the differences are somewhat more marked. For example, although a general decline in reporting of justiciable problems was found with increasing age, some 34% of those aged between 55 and 64 reported one or more justiciable problems during the survey reference period and 23% in the 65 plus age group reported one or more problems.

The SCC study confirmed the finding that younger persons were more likely to have experienced a dispute about custody and access (now known as residence and contact) with children but found that those over 55 were more likely to have had a dispute about unsatisfactory services and were twice as likely to have had a dispute with a government department or agency, as those under 55. Again, direct comparison with the present study is difficult, in part because of differences in problem categorisation.

Although the demographic and social classification data collected about screening respondents was rather limited, further analysis of the demographic characteristics of those reporting having experienced justiciable disputes in comparison with the general population is presented in the final section of this chapter.

An analysis was also undertaken of the incidence of justiciable problems by population density. From Table 2.3 it can be seen that only minor differences were observed in the incidence of justiciable problems in urban and rural areas. Thus while money problems were reported by eight percent of respondents to the screening survey living in urban areas the comparable figure for rural areas was five percent. As might be expected, problems arising from living in rented accommodation were reported by eight percent of those living in urban areas as compared with only four percent of those living in rural areas.

FREQUENCY OF JUSTICIABLE PROBLEMS

Many members of the public interviewed in the screening survey reported having experienced problems of a particular type on more than one

Table 2.2 Incidence of problems of different types by age [4]

Type of problem	Age						
	Total	18–24	25–34	35–44	45–54	55–64	65+
	%	%	%	%	%	%	%
Money	7	12	10	9	6	4	1
Faulty goods or services	6	6	9	10	8	4	2
Living in rented accommodation	6	18	10	4	4	3	2
Owning residential property	5	4	6	10	5	4	3
Employment	5	8	8	5	5	3	—
Relationships and family matters	4	3	8	7	3	1	1
Injury/work-related health problem needing treatment	3	4	4	5	3	3	2
Divorce proceedings	3	1	4	7	3	1	*
Children under 18	1	2	2	3	*	*	—
Unfair treatment by the police	1	2	3	1	1	—	—
Renting out rooms or property	1	1	1	1	1	1	*
Negligent medical/dental treatment	1	1	1	*	1	*	—
Defamation	1	1	1	*	*	1	*
Discrimination race/sex/disab	1	2	*	*	1	*	—
Immigration problem	*	*	*	—	*	—	—
Any problem	26	34	38	31	30	20	9
Unweighted base[5]:	2684	241	486	513	445	390	572
Weighted base[3]:	2684	258	497	512	442	379	558

occasion during the survey reference period. For most broad categories of problems the average number of problems experienced by individuals during the survey reference period was somewhere between 1.2 and 2.3

[4] Note that in all tables the symbol "*"denotes a non-zero quantity of less than half a per cent and the symbol "—" denotes zero.

[5] The number of unclear answers is not shown in these tables because it varied by type of problem.

Table 2.3 Incidence of problems of different types by population density

Type of problem	Population density		
	Total	"Urban"	"Rural"
	%	%	%
Money	7	8	5
Faulty goods or services	6	6	7
Living in rented accommodation	6	8	4
Owning residential property	5	5	6
Employment problems	5	5	4
Relationships and other family matters	4	4	3
Injuries / health problems	3	3	3
Divorce	3	3	2
Problems concerning children aged under 18	1	1	2
Unfair treatment by the police	1	1	1
Renting out rooms or property	1	1	1
Negligent or wrong medical treatment	1	1	1
Defamation	1	1	1
Discrimination race/sex/disability	1	1	1
Immigration or nationality issues	*	*	*
Any problem	26	28	23
Unweighted base	2684	1363	1262
Weighted base	2684	1377	1248

(Table 2.4). The average number of times people experienced a particular category of problem was notably higher for certain problem types. For example, the average number of problems experienced in the previous five years relating to renting property was 2.27, and for problems relating to owning residential property it was 1.53. In effect this means that individuals were more likely to experience problems of these types in clusters i.e. if they experienced the problem *at all* they were likely to experience it on more than one occasion (Table 2.4). From Table 2.4 it can also be seen that for many categories of problems, respondents in Scotland had suffered a *higher* average number of problems than those in England and Wales. Examples of this are problems arising from living in rented accommodation, discrimination, unfair treatment by the police or medical negligence, and owning residential property. Respondents in

Table 2.4 Mean number of problems: those with problems of a given sort.

Type of problem	Mean no. of problems	England and Wales	Weighted Base
Living in rented accommodation	2.27	1.78	146
Unfair treatment by the police, medical negligence, discrimination,	2.20	1.31	54
Owning residential property	1.53	1.43	137
Renting out rooms or property	1.51	1.46	16
Money	1.43	1.46	166
Faulty goods or services	1.41	1.38	171
Relationships and other family matters	1.41	1.38	85
Injuries/work related ill health	1.19	1.97	97
Employment problems	1.17	1.21	112
Children under 18	1.17	1.42	36

Scotland had experienced a lower average number of injuries and work-related ill health and problems relating to children.

INCIDENCE OF JUSTICIABLE PROBLEMS: NATIONAL ESTIMATES

Having calculated the proportion of the sample that experienced certain types of justiciable disputes, and the average number of times that each type of problem was experienced by individuals in the sample, it is possible to combine the information in order to show the proportion of all justiciable problems falling into any particular problem category, and to estimate rates per thousand population for each problem category. This information appears in Table 2.5. The most numerous problems experienced by the sample were those relating to:

• living in rented accommodation (123 problems per 1,000 people)
• faulty goods and services (90 problems per 1,000 people)
• money (88 problems per 1,000 people)
• owning residential accommodation (78 problems per 1,000 people).

It is also possible to estimate the total number of adults in Scotland affected by each type of problem over the survey reference period and the total number of problems of each type experienced over this

Table 2.5 Estimates of rates per thousand, numbers of adults in Scotland affected by problems of different types and of total number of problems of different types during previous five years.

Type of problem	Number of problems per 1,000 population over 18	England and Wales results per 1,000 population over 18	Estimate of number of adults with problem of this type	Total number of problems that are of this type
Living in rented accommodation	123	124	140939	491697
Faulty goods or services	90	153	165072	357712
Money	88	138	160245	352179
Owning residential property	78	119	132251	310979
Employment	49	73	108117	194412
Relationships and family matters	45	83	82053	177810
Discrimination, unfair treatment by the police, immigration, medical negligence	44	46	52128	176252
Accident or work-related health problem	43	90	93637	171253
Divorce proceedings	28	47	72400	111270
Problem with children under 18	16	43	34752	62490
Renting out rooms or property	9	16	15445	35844

period[6] (Table 2.5). By including the results for England and Wales it is possible to see that, in general, the pattern of rates per 1,000 population is similar in the two jurisdictions. However, the incidence per 1,000 adult population is higher in England and Wales for most categories of justiciable problems. This is particularly true for consumer problems (90 per 1,000 in Scotland compared with 153 per 1,000 in England and

---

[6] These estimates are affected by the way in which a "problem" is operationally defined. In making them, problems have been calculated as something linked to the individual. Thus two people involved in the same problem (whether on the same side or on different) sides would be counted twice.

Wales); money problems (88 per 1,000 in Scotland compared with 138 per 1,000 in England and Wales); accidental injury and problems with children under 18. Rates were much closer for problems such as living in rented accommodation (123 per 1,000 in Scotland as compared with 124 per 1,000 in England and Wales) and discrimination, negligence and unfair actions by the police (44 per 1,000 in Scotland compared with 46 per 1,000 in England and Wales).

PROBLEM CLUSTERS

In addition to looking at the incidence of problem types and the frequency with which individuals experienced problems of a certain type, an analysis was carried out in order to describe the *different* kinds of problems that survey respondents had experienced during the previous five years. Table 2.6 presents a cross-tabulation of the overlap between the incidence of different types of problems occurring during the survey reference period that had been defined as non-trivial[7]. From this table it can be seen that, for example, respondents reporting employment problems during the previous five years were also quite likely to have experienced money problems (29%), or problems to do with living in rented accommodation (27%). Respondents who were involved in divorce proceedings during the previous five years were very likely also to report family problems (50%), or money problems (20%). Victims of accidental injury or work-related ill-health were quite likely to mention that they had experienced money problems during the previous five years (27%) or employment problems (15%).

Respondents who reported having experienced money problems during the previous five years were likely also to have experienced problems with rented accommodation (27%), consumer problems (27%), or employment problems (20%).

These findings show clearly that respondents reporting having experienced a justiciable problem in the previous five years often experienced a problem more than once *and* more than one type of problem. While 14% of the population reported having experienced only one non-trivial justiciable problem during the previous five years, a further eight percent reported having experienced two or more prob-

---

[7] For technical reasons, justiciable problems that were regarded by respondents as too trivial to warrant taking any action were excluded from this analysis.

lems during the five year period. Looking more closely at those who had experienced more than one problem in the previous five years, five percent of the population reported having experienced two problems; two percent reported having experienced three problems; and in each case less than one percent reported having experienced four, five or six problems. No respondents reported having experienced more than six problems during the survey reference period.

Table 2.6 shows the ways in which problems of different types tend to cluster and an additional analysis was undertaken to identify the most common pairs of problems occurring together during the five years of the survey reference period.

An analysis of the relationship between pairs of problem types (Table 2.7) shows that those problem types most commonly experienced together were as follows (for ease of comparison the England and Wales correlation values are shown alongside in square brackets):

- divorce and family matters (0.45) [E & W: 0.53]
- family matters and children (0.33) [E & W: 0.26]
- divorce and children (0.22) [E & W: 0.20]
- money problems and family matters (0.20) [E & W: 0.09]
- money problems and living in rented accommodation (0.23) [E & W: 0.17]
- money problems and faulty goods or services (0.23) [E & W: 0.16]
- owning residential property and faulty goods or services (0.22) [E & W: 0.17]
- accident or injury and faulty goods or services (0.17) [E & W: 0.09]
- employment problems and money problems (0.20) [E & W: 0.19]
- employment problems and living in rented accommodation (0.18) [E & W: 0.9]
- police/immigration/negligence and living in rented accommodation (0.17) [E & W: 0.10]
- police/immigration/negligence and money (0.17) [E & W: 0.12]
- police/immigration/negligence and family matters (0.17) [E & W: 0.08].

All of the strongest correlations that were observed in the England and Wales data were also found in the Scotland data. However, in general, *stronger* correlations were observed between problem types in Scotland compared with England and Wales.

The results of the screening survey suggest therefore, that problems and misfortune have a tendency to come in clusters. This finding is consistent with other studies of legal problems and misfortune, and

Table 2.6 Percentage overlap between the incidence of eligible problems.

	Total	Q2 Employ- ment problem	Q3 Owning resid. Property	Q4 Renting out property	Q5 Living in rented accomm.	Q6 Faulty goods/ services
Unweighted base	2684	110	126	15	140	160
Weighted base	2684	113	126	15	148	161
	%	%	%	%	%	%
Q2 Employment	4	—	17	[12]	20	15
Q3 Owning residential property	5	19	—	[39]	6	23
Q4 Renting out property	1	2	5	—	2	1
Q5 Living in rented accomm.	6	27	7	[20]	—	16
Q6 Faulty goods or services	6	21	29	[14]	18	—
Q7 Money	6	29	20	[35]	31	28
Q8 Divorce	3	6	9	[13]	5	6
Q9 Family matters	3	11	14	[33]	14	11
Q10 Children	1	5	7	[20]	5	5
Q11 Accident or injury	3	10	11	[7]	7	14
Q13 Police etc.	2	7	6	[14]	11	6
Unweighted base	165	73	88	35	76	44
Weighted base	170	75	90	35	77	45
Q2 Employment	20	8	14	[16]	15	[18]
Q3 Owning residential property	15	15	19	[24]	18	[17]
Q4 Renting out property	3	3	5	[8]	1	[4]
Q5 Living in rented accomm.	27	9	23	[22]	14	[36]
Q6 Faulty goods or services	27	13	21	[22]	29	[23]
Q7 Money	—	20	31	[20]	27	[41]
Q8 Divorce	9	—	42	[36]	7	[13]
Q9 Family matters	16	50	—	[55]	10	[27]
Q10 Children	4	17	22	—	4	[6]
Q11 Accident or injury	12	7	8	[9]	—	[12]
Q13 Police etc.	11	8	14	[8]	7	—

[ ] Percentages based on fewer than 50 respondents are shown in brackets

Table 2.7 Correlations matrix for problem types.

	Q2 Employ- ment problem	Q3 Owning resid. property	Q4 Renting out property	Q5 Living in rented accomm.	Q6 Faulty goods/ services
Q3 Owning residential property	0.13				
Q4 Renting out property	0.03	0.13			
Q5 Living in rented accomm.	0.18	0.01	0.05		
Q6 Faulty goods or services	0.13	0.22	0.02	0.12	
Q7 Money	0.20	0.13	0.08	0.23	0.23
Q8 Divorce	0.03	0.08	0.05	0.03	0.04
Q9 Family matters	0.09	0.13	0.13	0.14	0.11
Q10 Children	0.06	0.10	0.12	0.09	0.08
Q11 Accident or injury	0.09	0.11	0.02	0.06	0.17
Q13 Police etc.	0.09	0.08	0.07	0.17	0.09

	Q7 Money	Q8 Divorce	Q9 Family matters	Q10 Children	Q11 Accident or injury
Q8 Divorce	0.09				
Q9 Family matters	0.20	0.45			
Q10 Children	0.07	0.22	0.33		
Q11 Accident or injury	0.14	0.04	0.06	0.04	
Q13 Police etc.	0.17	0.09	0.17	0.06	0.07

with studies of the experience of crime victims[8]. For example, aside from the obvious clustering of divorce with problems concerning the care of children, empirical studies of the consequences of divorce have demonstrated the disruption to families caused by the forced sale of the

---

[8] Surveys of criminal victimisation consistently reveal the clustering of incidents of victimisation. Certain individuals will be a victim of crime on more than one occasion during a survey reference period and such people may experience repeated instances of the same crime or instances of different crimes being committed against them. For a discussion of this phenomenon see Hazel Genn , "Multiple Victimisation", in M Maguire and J Pointing (eds) *Victims of Crime: A New Deal?* Open University Press, Milton Keynes, 1988.

48   *The Landscape of Justiciable Problems*

family home, and the frequent poverty and dependence on benefits that affects the lone parent shouldering childcare responsibilities after divorce. "[T]he burden of child-rearing after divorce falls mainly on [women's] shoulders and with lower wages for women combined with the opportunity costs of child-rearing, we have a growing population of economically vulnerable female-headed households."[9]

Similarly, empirical studies of the financial consequences of accidental injury and work-related ill health have shown that many victims suffer financial hardship and have problems with benefits in the immediate aftermath of an injury as a result of being unable to work[10]. In addition there may be longer-term employment consequences and financial hardship if the victim suffers a substantial degree of residual disability, even if compensation for the injury was obtained via the legal system. A study of the long term financial effects of personal injury conducted by the Law Commission showed that as well as losing earnings from work, accident victims often incur other costs (for example for medical treatment, rehabilitation etc) or suffer other losses and other household members may have to give up work altogether as result of the victim's accident, thereby causing a *further loss* in household income. The Law Commission study found that nine in ten victims of serious injury had received state benefits since the date of their accident. The report concluded that having to pay extra costs while living on a reduced income resulted in many accident victims experiencing financial problems, and many borrowed money or accumulated debts as a result of their accident.[11]

Certain types of situations can have a cascade effect. For example, threatened repossession of the family home can lead to marital strain and breakdown, mental health problems, leading to difficulties at work and problems in caring for children.

The financial vulnerability, emotional impact, and other consequences that can flow from many kinds of justiciable problem have implications for the type of advice and assistance that is needed when members of the public seek help to deal with problems.

[9] L J Weitzman and M Maclean (eds), *Economic Consequences of Divorce*, Oxford, Clarendon Press, 1992, p9.
[10] D Harris et al, *Compensation and Support for Illness and Injury*, Oxford, Clarendon Press, 1984.
[11] *Personal Injury Compensation: How Much is Enough?*, London, Law Commission, Report No 225, 1994.

TRIVIALITY THRESHOLD

In order to exclude from further analysis justiciable problems regarded by survey respondents as too trivial to bother about, all those who reported having experienced a problem during the survey reference period were asked whether they had taken any action to deal with the problem and if not, why they had failed to take action. Those respondents who reported lack of action in the screening survey because the problem was not regarded as important enough to warrant action were not included in the follow-up main survey [12].

However, the impact of applying the triviality criterion was relatively small for most problem types. As the discussion in the following section will show, rather few problems were reported in the survey that respondents had regarded as being too trivial to do anything about, although they may have failed to take action for other reasons. It may be, therefore, that the impact of the requirement that the problems or disputes be "difficult to solve", ensured that relatively few trivial problems were reported in the screening survey. So, for example, in the screening survey some six percent of the sample reported having been involved in a money problem. After removing those cases in which respondents said that the money problem was not important enough to take action, the estimate for non-trivial money problems remains at six percent of the total sample (Table 2.8). The same is true for most other problem types. In employment problems removing the trivial cases or those where it was thought that the other side was probably right makes a difference of one percent. This suggests that in most cases by choosing not to report events regarded as trivial, or simply by failing to remember them respondents had already filtered out most unimportant events. The result is that the population estimates for "non-trivial" justiciable events is almost identical to those for all justiciable events reported.

THE INCIDENCE OF DIFFERENT PROBLEMS AND WHETHER ANY
ACTION TAKEN

The following sections describe in more detail the nature of the problems reported by respondents during the screening survey. Relatively

[12] In addition, those respondents who said that they had not taken action because they were not in dispute or believed that the other side was right were not included in the main survey.

Table 2.8 Incidence of problems of different types since 1992: impact of applying the triviality criterion

Problem type	Estimate of the incidence in adult population before applying triviality criterion	Estimate of the incidence in adult population after applying triviality criterion
	%	%
Employment	5	4
Owning residential property	5	5
Renting out rooms or property	1	1
Living in rented accommodation	6	6
Faulty goods or services	6	6
Money	7	6
Relationships and other family matters	4	3
Problems concerning children aged under 18	1	1
Injuries / health problems	3	3
Discrimination, unfair treatment by the police, immigration, medical negligence	2	2
Unweighted base	2684	2684
Weighted base	2684	2684

brief information is also given about whether or not respondents reported during the screening survey having taken any action, no matter how limited, to try and resolve the problems that they had reported, since this information was used as the basis for inclusion in the main survey. Figure 2.2 below shows that although action was to taken to try and resolve most problems there was some variation between different types of problem. For example, where problems concerned children, action was almost always taken to seek some kind of resolution. On the other hand, no action was taken to seek a resolution for around one in three problems relating to unfair treatment by the police, discrimination, accidents, and work-related ill health. Full information about respondents' strategies for resolving disputes and their use of advisers,

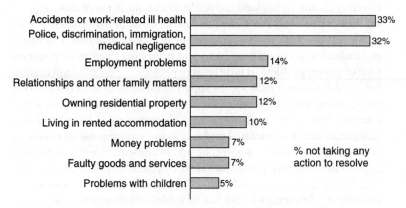

Figure 2.2 No action taken to resolve justiciable problem by problem type.

based on comprehensive information obtained in the main survey, is presented and discussed in Chapters 3 and 4.

Problems to do with money

The most common problem experienced by the general population sample was money problems. About seven percent of the total sample reported having experienced money problems that were difficult to solve during the previous five years. The screening questions relating to money were intended to distinguish between those people having difficulties meeting their outgoings, from specific problems that might give rise to a legal action either by the respondent or against the respondent. The most common kinds of money problems mentioned by respondents to the screening survey were problems over the refusal of benefits by DSS to which respondents felt they were entitled, incorrect or disputed tax demands, insurance companies unfairly rejecting claims, and getting someone to pay money that they owed. Less common problems reported were: incorrect advice about insurance, pensions etc, unfair refusal of credit, incorrect or disputed bills (Figure 2.3). Among those respondents who mentioned having experienced a money problem during the survey reference period, the average number of money problems experienced was 1.4.

The findings in Scotland differ significantly from those in England in relation to the reported incidence of insurance companies unfairly rejecting claims. In England and Wales about one in ten of those reporting money problems mentioned this as the cause of the problem (11%) and it was the sixth most common type of money problem. The figure in Scotland was one in five (20%) and it was the third most common type of money problem. It is difficult to provide an obvious explanation for the difference. There are no apparent differences between the two jurisdictions regarding insurance law, although there may be some common law contractual differences. Moreover, most large insurance companies are multinational and rely heavily on the use of choice of law and jurisdiction clauses in contract. In consequence it is difficult to explain the contrasting incidence rates by reference to law alone. They may be accounted for in differences in practices by the companies, or possibly by differences in the law of evidence between the two countries which leads insurance companies to resist cases more vigorously in Scotland on the ground that it would be harder for a disgruntled pursuer to prove loss or damage in court. It is, of course, also possible that there are more claims by Scottish insureds and that this makes the companies wary and more likely to reject claims. Door to door collection of premiums is expensive and more prevalent in Scotland than England, which might incline companies to seek to minimise payments on claims in Scotland. This is an area that would benefit from further investigation.

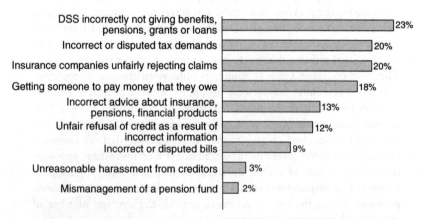

Figure 2.3 Breakdown of problems or disputes that were difficult to solve to do with money since January 1992—percentages of all respondents reporting money problems (Unweighted base = 171).

Respondents were very likely to have taken action to deal with money problems. In over nine out of ten money problems reported in the screening survey, respondents said that they had taken some action to try to resolve the problem. Most often this involved writing or talking to the other side. Advice was sought for less than one in three money problems experienced by the sample and in only a small proportion of money problems did the respondent go to court either to pursue or defend a claim (Figure 2.4).

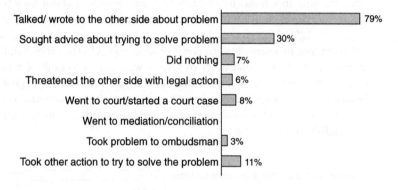

Figure 2.4 Action taken to resolve problems to do with money (Unweighted base problems = 226).

In the very small proportion of cases (less than one in ten) in which respondents had failed to take any action to resolve a money problem, the most common reasons given for the failure were that respondent thought that the problem was unimportant or that nothing could be done to resolve the problem.

Problems with receiving faulty goods or services

The second most common type of justiciable problem experienced by the general population sample involved faulty goods or services. Six per cent of the total sample had experienced one or more of these types of problems during the survey reference period. This is a five percent lower figure across the population than that found in England and Wales, where it was the most common type of problem mentioned by the survey sample. There are few variations between Scots law and

English law that would account for these differences[13]. The average number of problems experienced by those reporting consumer problems was 1.4 per person.

Brief information obtained on the screening survey about action taken to deal with consumer problems revealed that the vast majority of respondents took action to try and remedy consumer problems. Some steps had been taken to resolve the problem for about 93% of the consumer problems that had been experienced and reported in the survey. The most common action taken was to speak or write to the other side, but only in a minority of cases was advice sought about how to resolve the problem (31% of consumer problems). In just under one in five cases (18%) legal action was threatened, but in virtually no cases did consumer problems lead to court proceedings. On the other hand, in a handful of cases consumer problems were taken to ombudsmen (2%) or mediation (1%) (Figure 2.5). In comparison with the English findings, the Scots appeared to be more proactive about contacting the other side to try and resolve the problem and they were less likely than the English to do nothing.

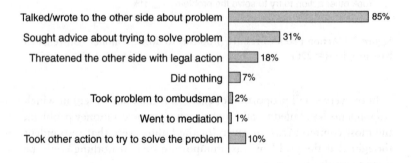

Figure 2.5 Action taken to try and resolve problems with receiving faulty goods or services (Unweighted base problems = 211).

---

[13] The situation is also complicated by the fact that the SCC survey found a nine percent *greater* instance of problems with faulty goods in Scotland than in England and an eight percent greater instance of problems with services, although as was pointed out in Chapter 1, there were important differences in the design and administration of the SCC survey as compared with the present study.

In only about seven percent of cases respondents said that they had taken no action whatsoever to try and resolve the problem and the most common reason given (seven out of thirteen respondents) was that the respondent did not think that the problem was very important. A detailed discussion of the most common approaches to dealing with consumer and other disputes, based on information obtained during the main survey, appears in Chapter 4.

Employment problems

About five percent of the Scottish population had experienced one or more problems relating to their employment. The most common types of employment problem suffered were: losing a job (33% of respondents who had experienced employment problems), experiencing changed terms or conditions of employment (20%), and other rights at work (20%). Harassment at work was also reported fairly frequently (18% of respondents who had experienced employment problems), as was unfair disciplinary procedures (13%) and unsatisfactory or unsafe working conditions (12%) (Figure 2.6).

Although employment law is the same throughout the UK, employment varies between the two jurisdictions in that a very high proportion of Scots work in small businesses. The proportion of the sample experiencing employment problems in Scotland was roughly consistent with that in England (six percent) and the frequency with which specific types of problems had been experienced was also broadly consistent although a higher percentage of English employment problems concerned losing a job (41%). On the other hand, a greater percentage of Scots respondents said that their problem concerned "other rights at work" (20% in Scotland compared with 12% in England). These findings are broadly consistent with the CAS survey carried out in 1996/7 which found that Scots had fewer dismissal problems than those in England, but a greater instance of problems concerning changes to terms and conditions of work.

Among those reporting having experienced employment problems, the average number of these problems experienced during the previous five years was 1.2.

Most respondents took some action to deal with their employment problems. By far the most common actions taken were talking or writing to the other side (55%) and seeking advice about the problem (51%). In a relatively substantial minority of cases (13%) the respondent had

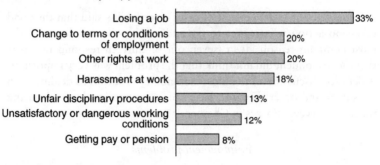

*Figure 2.*6 Breakdown of problems or disputes that were difficult to solve to do with employment since January 1992—percentages of all respondents reporting employment problems (Unweighted base = 120).

threatened legal action. The approach to dealing with employment problems is explored more fully in Chapter 4. This approach to dealing with employment problems is, again, broadly consistent with the approach in England and Wales.

In about fourteen percent of employment problems, respondents said that they had done nothing about the problem. This is a relatively *high* figure in comparison with other problem types and compared with sixteen percent in England who did nothing. The main reasons given by respondents for doing nothing about their employment problem were that they did not think that anything could be done (mentioned for about a two out of five problems), or that they thought that the other side was right (mentioned for about a quarter of employment problems). In a small number of cases respondents took no action because they were scared to do anything, or because they thought it would damage their relationship with the other side. The following extract from a qualitative interview provides a good illustration of these concerns, together with another fear, occasionally expressed in employment cases, about getting a reputation as a "troublemaker":

> "I didn't think there was anything I could do in law. I sought no legal advice whatsoever. I did think of speaking to someone at the Citizen's Advice Bureau, but I didn't in fact do that. ..I thought I was wasting my time. There didn't seem any point in venting my spleen . . . going through the story to Citizen's Advice and, y'know, speaking to my neighbour about it. I just felt it was a bruising time and I should find a new job as quickly as possible . . . I just felt there was nothing in law I could do about it: it was such a horrid

experience I just quickly wanted to get on with my life, rather than trying to have a protracted legal situation with an employer, and very often you'll find with employers' forms they'll ask you 'Have you been involved in any litigation?' Which, if you're filling in forms, you don't want to be telling lies about it."[Unfairly dismissed from work]

Problems with owning residential property

About five percent of the sample had experienced one or more problems to do with owning residential property. This is a lower figure than in England and Wales where eight percent of the population had experienced such problems. However, in Scotland there is a nine percent lesser instance of owner occupation than in England and a twelve percent lesser instance than in Wales which might well account for the lower rate of reporting such problems. The average number of problems experienced during the previous five years was 1.5 per person.

The most frequently experienced problems in this category were to do with neighbours (51% of respondents who had problems with residential property), communal repairs or maintenance (24%), and alterations to property or planning permission (20%) (Figure 2.7). There are some interesting similarities and differences here in comparison with the England and Wales findings. The first similarity to comment on is the consistency between the proportion of those experiencing problems about buying and selling property in the two countries. Seventeen percent of those with problems concerning ownership of real property in England said that they had experienced a problem relating to buying or selling property. The figure in Scotland was also seventeen percent, despite the fact that the law in the respective countries is vastly different. The Scottish system demands that a solicitor be involved in at least some of the transaction, while in England there is no requirement for a solicitor to deal with the transaction. DIY conveyancing is almost unknown in Scotland whereas in England it is more common and one might expect that this could lead to a higher incidence of problems. Another difference in conveyancing practice is that in England the initial offer and acceptance does not create a binding contract in sales of immovable property (thereby leading to the practice known as gazumping). This might lead one to expect that the English survey would have shown a significantly higher level of conveyancing problems, which was not the case. A possible counterbalancing difference in practice is that the English offer and acceptance system is slightly simpler than that in Scotland as a result of standard form offers and this might lead to *fewer* problems. The position in Scotland regarding missives is quite different—each is individually drawn up by the respective parties' solicitors, necessitating a close examination of each offer and acceptance received, which may increase the potential for problems occurring.

A *difference* between the English and Scots findings was in relation to communal repairs and maintenance. Although one in four of those experiencing problems with ownership of residential property in Scotland mentioned problems to do with communal repairs or maintenance, only a little over one in ten mentioned this south of the Border (12%). An explanation for this could lie in the difference in the law of tenement between the two countries. In Scotland there are more tenements than in England and the tenement stock may be older and of poorer quality in Scotland.

A final similarity is in the incidence of neighbour problems. In both Scotland and England this was the most common type of problem reported in relation to ownership of residential property. In Scotland some 51% of those experiencing a problem concerning ownership of property said that the problem was to do with neighbours, and in England and Wales the figure was 57%. In both countries difficulties with neighbours is a common and intractable problem, as will be seen from the discussion in Chapter 5.

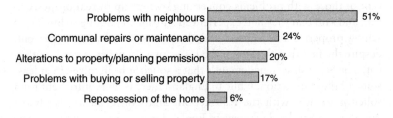

Figure 2.7 Problems or disputes that were difficult to solve to do with owning residential property since January 1992—percentages of all respondents reporting residential property problems (Unweighted base = 144).

Respondents reported that they had taken action to try and resolve residential property problems in the overwhelming majority of cases (88% of problems experienced). The main actions taken by respondents were to talk or write to the other side about the problem (62% of problems) and to seek advice about solving it (43% of problems). In about 11% of problems the action taken was to threaten the other side with legal action. About four percent of problems resulted in legal proceedings, about four percent went to mediation/conciliation, and a similar proportion took their case to an ombudsman. This approach to dealing with problems concerning residential property was broadly consistent with that taken in England and Wales. A notable difference, however, was in the proportion of respondents who reported that they had sought advice about their problem. In England and Wales a significantly *higher* proportion of respondents experiencing this type of problem sought advice about trying to resolve the problem (56% of English respondents obtained advice as compared with 43% in Scotland).

In Scotland, respondents had taken no action to try and resolve their problems to do with owning property in about 12% of cases, which is a relatively low rate of inaction in comparison with some other problem types. The main reasons mentioned for doing nothing were: feeling that the problem was not very important and thinking that nothing could be done. This level of inaction is entirely consistent with that found in England and Wales.

Problems to do with living in rented accommodation

About six percent of the total sample had experienced problems relating to living in rented accommodation. The main problems with living in rented accommodation were with getting the landlord to do repairs (44% of respondents who had problems in this category) and problems with neighbours (38%). Other problems mentioned with some frequency were poor or unsafe living conditions (17% of respondents who had problems in this category), getting a deposit back from the landlord (16%), harassment by the landlord (11%) and being evicted or being threatened with eviction (11%).

There are some interesting points of comparison with the English data in relation to these figures. Demographically, the Scots have higher levels of living in rented accommodation than the English or the Welsh (41% as compared with 33% and 29% respectively) and the Scots have a lower instance of private rented occupancy than in England, and a slightly lower instance than in Wales[14]. Similar levels of

---

[14] *Population Trends*: Office of National Statistics 1998.

leasing from housing associations are found in all of the jurisdictions with only a one percent higher instance of such leasing in England than in the other jurisdictions. However, the Scots have a higher instance of rental from local authorities than the English—as much as about twelve percent higher. Despite these differences, the reported incidence of problems relating to living in rented accommodation was similar in the two jurisdictions, with six percent of respondents in Scotland reporting having experienced such problems as compared with seven percent of respondents in England and Wales. In both jurisdictions the most common problem experienced was getting the landlord to do repairs to the property (44% in Scotland and 48% in England and Wales). The pattern of problems was broadly consistent between the two jurisdictions with two or three notable exceptions. First, problems with neighbours were mentioned more frequently than in England and Wales. Almost two in five people who had problems relating to rented accommodation in Scotland reported problems with neighbours (38%) as compared with only one in four in England and Wales (25%).

A second notable difference was in the frequency of problems about getting the landlord to provide a written lease or tenancy agreement. In Scotland this accounted for twelve percent of people who reported problems with renting and was the fifth most common problem mentioned, whereas in England and Wales it accounted for only three percent of people who reported problems to do with renting and was one of the least common problems. The discrepancy in the figures is likely to relate to private tenancies where there is a prevalence of licence agreements (a lesser form of tenancy) in Scotland.

Finally, there was a greater incidence reported in Scotland of harassment by landlords, which may well be consistent with the greater level of problems reported relating to written leases. In Scotland, harassment by the landlord was the joint sixth most common problem reported in relation to renting property and was reported by eleven percent of people who experienced problems in this category. In England and Wales it was the *least* common problem reported and was mentioned by only three percent of those experiencing problems in renting property. These two last points of difference create a picture of a smaller privately rented sector in Scotland, but one in which more landlords misbehave. In England and Wales harassment of tenants by landlords is a criminal offence and this may have an effect on landlords' behaviour. The differences in the results of England and Scotland in these respects may be a reflection of a greater tendency and greater freedom among Scots landlords to treat tenants badly. The following provides a graphic example of the problems:

"I was given a month contract, no deposit and there was only half rent for the first month, so since I was a student it was ideal. Once I had signed the lease for the month he moved all his things back in to the house so he was living there as well. It didn't seem to be a problem at the time. It was during my summer so I was working part-time and I didn't really have much money so I was stuck there until the October. I didn't even know he'd be living there initially..I would have left but I wasn't able to do that financially because I didn't have the money for a deposit . . . by the July I didn't have a contract, or lease. I would ask and he would say 'Oh well it doesn't matter'. It was going along like that and the whole thing just became more and more awkward.. He was a bully, basically. A very bullying person. Towards the end there was nonsense about whether I was ruining cushion covers in the living room and he was demanding all this money . . . He would talk about having all this knowledge of the legal profession and what he would do if I didn't pay this money up, and he was looking for deposits for electricity. And I don't know if it was a bluff or not, but he said if I didn't pay this money he would take legal action in a small court and that would result in me not being able to work for any local authority for so many years. I didn't know

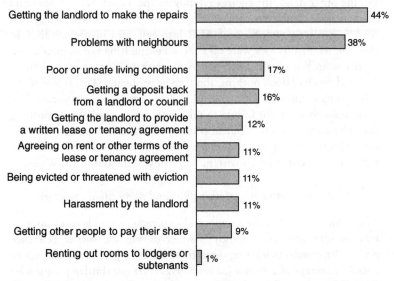

Figure 2.8 Problems or disputes that were difficult to solve to do with living in rented accommodation since January 1992—percentages of respondents reporting such problems (Unweighted base problems =149)

what the position was with that. I didn't know can he do that? Part of me suspected that he couldn't because technically he didn't have a lease that I had signed to be staying there. So I don't know."

In nine out of ten problems relating to renting accommodation respondents had taken some action to try to resolve the problem. Respondents had spoken or written to the other side in about two thirds of cases (69%) and had sought advice for over half of all problems to do with renting property (51%). In two percent of cases there had been a mediation and in the same proportion of cases the problem had been taken to an ombudsman. In a high proportion of cases (21%) legal proceedings had been threatened and in about four percent of cases there had been court proceedings.

Respondents in Scotland appeared to be more likely than those in England and Wales to take advice about a problem relating to renting (51% in Scotland as compared with 37% in England) and also more likely to threaten legal proceedings (21% in Scotland as compared with five percent in England and Wales). These figures suggest that the Scots are quite vigorous in their approach to resolving disputes concerning rented accommodation by comparison with those south of the border. On the other hand, the figures relating to the use of ADR in Scotland to deal with problems over renting, while still very low, suggest a *slightly* greater penetration of ADR into this area of dispute than in England where *no* cases were taken to an ombudsman or to mediation.

In one in ten of all problems to do with renting property (10%) respondents had done nothing about their problems. This figure is relatively low compared with some of the other problem categories. The main reasons given for failure to take action was a belief that nothing could be done, that the problem was not sufficiently important to warrant action, or that the respondent thought that the other side was right. These figures are consistent with those in England and Wales.

Problems to do with relationships and other family matters

About four percent of the sample had experienced problems to do with relationships and other family matters during the survey reference period. Respondents who reported these kinds of problems had experienced an average of 1.4 since January 1992. Over one third of people who experienced problems in this category reported problems getting or paying maintenance or child support payments (38%), another third reported problems concerned the division of money or property in connection with a divorce or separation (34%), and a notably significant proportion (30%) reported violent or abusive relationships with a partner, ex-partner or other family member. A further one quarter (28%) reported problems after the death of a family member or partner (Figure 2.9).

Comparing these results with those in England and Wales we find a somewhat higher level of reporting of violent or abusive relationships in Scotland than in England and Wales (30% of those who experienced problems to do with relationships in Scotland as compared with 22% in England and Wales). There are several potential explanations for the observed difference. First, the findings might simply suggest that the Scots are more violent or abusive than their English counterparts. A second explanation might be that the Scots *perceive* domestic violence as more of a problem than the English or are more willing to report such occurrences in survey interviews. A heightened level of awareness of domestic violence and remedies may have occurred as a result of the highly successful "Zero Tolerance" campaign adopted by the Scottish Office in the 1990's which was broader and more sustained than its counterpart south of the border. The third explanation may be that the Scots are more likely to take action over domestic violence and abuse than the English, again as a result of this awareness-raising strategy. This important topic is worthy of further investigation. An example of the problems experienced as a result of domestic violence was provided in a qualitative interview as follows:

> "I had to leave the house because I was scared. There was a lot of tension, fights. He never actually hit me, but the pushing and shoving ..he'd push me to the floor and he'd sit on me and hold me. I ended up walking out of there covered in bruises. He threatened to break into the house and kill me. This is why I left. Prior to me leaving there was a big argument on the Thursday night and it went on until about three or four in the morning. The following morning the police arrive and explained that somebody had called them and they were quite worried. They said 'You dinnae have to put up with this; there's so many options that you have—you can get out.' The police were absolutely wonderful. I went to the Women's Aid—the refuge."

Another difference between the Scots and English results in relation to family and relationship problems concerns the incidence of problems following the death of a family member. This accounted for more than one in four of respondents who experienced problems in this category in Scotland (28%) as compared with only fourteen percent in England and Wales. This finding is rather curious since in Scotland the rules for intestate succession are fairly settled and normally pose few problems, although obviously winding up an estate causes more difficulties if there has been no will. Since testate succession does not generally create a problem and the law in the two jurisdictions is relatively similar, the difference in the incidence is somewhat surprising. Figures from Scotland[15] indicate that some 75% of Scots dying in 1998 had made a will, so unusually high levels of intestacy cannot explain the difference. Evidence from questionnaires and qualitative interviews suggests that the problems may in fact be disputes over dispositions made in wills raising the question of whether the Scots are more prone than the English to challenge wills. Examples of problems relating to wills, as explained in qualitative interviews, are as follows:

"My father passed away. I hadn't been in contact with my father for years and years, and we were informed that he'd died and there wasn't a Will. It turned out that because of Scottish law if he doesn't fill in his Will, all his stuff goes directly to his children, and I presume he did that deliberately, didn't bother writing out a Will. So it was a case of us getting in contact wi' the solicitors to claim through his estate to split it three ways.. It was kind of touchy because my father's sister decided that she deserved it more than we did. She was trying to make things a wee bit more awkward, but I think she probably knew, deep down inside, that she didn't have a leg to stand on because of the way the law is."

"When my mother died it came to light that she had made a will without anybody knowing, behind my stepfather's back. He knew that she'd made a will, but she then went and made a different will and that came as a big surprise to him as it went not in his favour. Rather than the house and things going to him automatically, she fenced off half of it to make sure that half of her estate would come directly to her children. My father was to be able to stay in the house, but she wanted to guarantee that when he died, what was hers was going to pass to her children because she knew that we didn't get on with him particularly well. None of us knew about that. She didn't tell any of us about that when she was alive so this came to light the day that she died and the dispute really arose because my stepfather was very upset by that. The wording of the will was ambiguous about how much she had left to him and how much she had left to us and that's where the dispute mainly arose from. It split the family because of her will. The impact's still really going on."

Advice had been sought about problems to do with relationships and family matters in over half of all cases (51%) and in slightly lower proportion of cases the respondent had talked or written to the other side (44%). In 17% of problems about relationship and family matters

---

[15] Extracted from figures maintained at Edinburgh Sheriff Court for 1998.

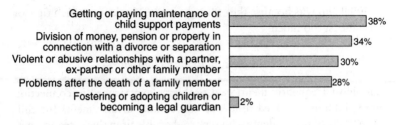

Figure 2.9 Problems with relationships and other family matters since January 1992—percentages of respondents reporting such problems (Unweighted base = 120).

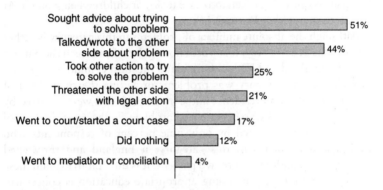

Figure 2.10 Actions taken about problems with relationships and family matters; all such problems since January 1992 (Unweighted base problems = 120).

court proceedings were commenced, which is a relatively high proportion by comparison with other problem types.

About 12% of respondents experiencing family or relationship problems did not take any action to deal with the problem and this figure is relatively low when compared with other problem types, although not the lowest. The most common reasons for not taking action in order to try and resolve a problem relating to relationships and family matters were that the respondent did not consider that the matter was a dispute or did not think that anything could be done about the problem. In one or two cases respondents said that they were scared to do anything or thought that it would damage the relationship with the other side. In no case did respondents say that their failure to take action to resolve the problem was because they thought it would take too much time or would cost too much.

Problems to do with children

The most frequently mentioned problems experienced in connection with children, involved residence and contact arrangements for children (56% of respondents who reported problems in this category) getting children to a desired school or obtaining the kind of education that they needed (31%), and children being unfairly excluded or suspended from school (28%). A small minority of respondents reported a problem concerned involvement with the Children's Panel about a child being at risk or being taken into care (6%), or children being on the At Risk Register (11%) (Figure 2.11).

Although the absolute number of problems in this category is rather small in the Scots survey, it is worth noting the difference in the pattern found in England and Wales . In England the most commonly reported problem in this category was problems in getting the rights kind of schooling (55%) and residence and contact problems were reported by 35% of respondents who experienced problems in the category. School exclusions were reported by only nine percent of respondents who experienced problems in this category in England and threatened abduction of children a mere two percent. It is difficult to explain these differences. As far as obtaining appropriate education is concerned, there are no substantive law or procedural differences between the two jurisdictions that might explain the much higher proportion of the English sample who experienced problems of these types. There are no indications of the prevalence of special needs education as between the two jurisdictions that might explain the difference. A partial explanation for the difference might be that in Scotland (and particularly in rural areas) there is less choice of State schooling available to parents and therefore disputes about admission to a preferred school are less likely to arise.

Another significant difference is in the proportions experiencing school exclusions. Over one in four of those reporting problems to do with children in Scotland mentioned this as a problem (28%) as compared with only nine percent in the England and Wales study. Finally, the Scots study revealed a significantly high proportion of cases in this category relating to residence and contact problems than in the English study (56% as compared with 35% in England and Wales).

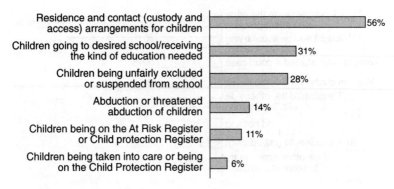

Residence and contact (custody and access) arrangements for children — 56%

Children going to desired school/receiving the kind of education needed — 31%

Children being unfairly excluded or suspended from school — 28%

Abduction or threatened abduction of children — 14%

Children being on the At Risk Register or Child protection Register — 11%

Children being taken into care or being on the Child Protection Register — 6%

Figure 2.11 Problems or disputes that were difficult to solve to do with children under 18 since January 1992—percentages of respondents reporting such problems (Unweighted base =36).

There was a very high level of action taken in relation to these kinds of problems. In 95% of the problems reported, respondents said that they took some action to try and resolve the problem. The most common actions taken were talking or writing to the other side or seeking advice about the problem (Figure 2.12). Respondents also threatened or began legal proceedings in a high proportion of cases relating to problems with children. Over one in four respondents started a court or tribunal case and just under one in five respondents said that they had threatened the other side with legal action.

Another notable difference from the English findings was the proportion of problems in this category that was reported to have been taken to mediation. In Scotland nearly *one in four* problems relating to children under 18 was said to have been taken to mediation or conciliation. The equivalent proportion in England and Wales was only eight percent. This finding is a little puzzling since, as will be seen in Chapters 3 and 7, very few respondents to the main survey said that they had used mediation services or been advised to do so. A possible explanation for this inconsistency is that at the screening stage, where the questioning about action taken to resolve disputes was not detailed, respondents were confusing pre-separation marriage guidance counselling with post separation dispute mediation services.

In only five percent of cases did respondents say that they had done nothing to try and resolve the problem concerning children under 18. This is a very low figure by comparison with other problem types and

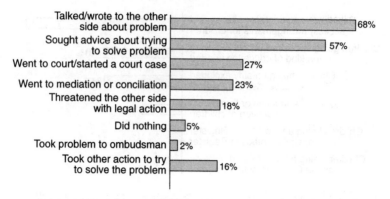

Figure 2.12 Actions taken about problems with children; all such problems since January 1992 (Unweighted base problems=44)

indicates the importance attached to resolving problems of this nature when they occurred. It is consistent with that found in England and Wales.

Injuries and health problems

Some three per cent of respondents had suffered an injury or health problem resulting from an accident or from poor working conditions in the survey reference period. Respondents took action to obtain a remedy for fewer problems of this type than they did for any other problem type. In *one third* of cases of accidental injury or work-related ill health, respondents did nothing. In the sixty seven per cent of problems where respondents took action, the main approach was talking or writing to the other side (36%) or seeking advice about the problem (34%). Although a relatively high proportion threatened legal proceedings (16%) only five percent said that they actually *started* court proceedings.

The failure of one in three respondents experiencing an accidental injury or work related illness requiring medical treatment to take any action is explored in more detail in Chapter 4 (the finding is consistent with that in England). At the screening stage the reason most often given by injury victims for failure to take action was because respondents felt that they were not in dispute or that the other side was right—in other words that they did not believe that anyone else was to

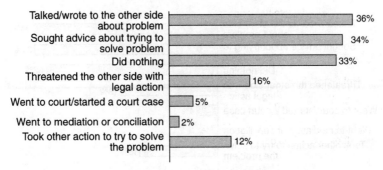

Figure 2.13 Actions taken about injuries or work-related ill health; all such problems since January 1992 (Unweighted base problems=112)

blame for the injury or ill-health. Other common reasons for not taking action were that respondents thought that nothing could be done, or that it was not important enough to take action.

Problems with discrimination, unfair treatment by the police, immigration, nationality or medical negligence

These heterogeneous problems were presented to respondents together on the same show card and were treated as a single group of problems for the purposes of asking the follow-up questions about actions undertaken and reasons for doing nothing. For this reason they are discussed together here.

A relatively small proportion of the sample had experienced problems of these sorts. One percent of the sample as a whole had suffered unfair treatment by the police. About 0.6% had suffered some form of medical negligence during the survey reference period and about 0.6% said that they had suffered defamation during the reference period. About 0.5% of the sample as a whole had experienced one or more instances of discrimination on the grounds of race, sex or disability and about 0.2% had experienced an immigration problem.

Looking at the group as a whole, there was a relatively low level of action taken to resolve this group of problems. Respondents said that they had taken some action to resolve the problem in about two thirds (65%) of cases. The most common action taken was talking or writing to the other side (34% of problems), or seeking advice (34%).

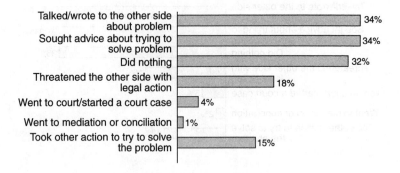

Figure 2.14 Actions taken about discrimination, unfair treatment by the police, immigration/nationality or medical negligence (Unweighted base problems=71).

Respondents did nothing about one third of these problems, which is a relatively high proportion. The chief reasons given for failure to take action were that it was believed that nothing could be done about the problem or that taking action might damage a relationship with the other side.

SECTION 2. THE "MAIN SAMPLE" OF NON-TRIVIAL JUSTICIABLE PROBLEMS

Respondents were deemed eligible for a main interview if they had experienced one or more problems from the problem show cards and had either taken one of the specified actions about it or indicated that they had not taken any such action for reasons other than that the problem was too trivial. Respondents were also deemed eligible if they had been involved in divorce proceedings, had had legal action taken against them, had been threatened with legal action over a disagreement about something, or had started or considered starting court proceedings. Overall 621 of the 2684 individuals screened were eligible for the main survey (23%). A breakdown of the main survey respondents according to the type of non-trivial problem for which they were selected is presented in Table 2.9. The comparison shows that the pattern of problem types about which respondents were successfully

Table 2.9 Breakdown of main survey sample by problem type.

Problem category reported in screening questionnaire	% of problems reported in screening survey	% of problems in main survey	Unweighted Number of cases in main survey
Employment	7	8	47
Owning residential property	11	12	56
Renting out property	1	2	6
Living in rented accommodation	18	14	62
Faulty goods and services	13	20	77
Money	13	17	83
Divorce proceedings	4	3	19
Family matters	7	5	24
Children under 18	2	3	15
Accidental injury/work-related ill health	6	6	42
Discrimination/ police ill treatment/immigration/ clinical negligence	6	3	15
Subject to legal action	3	2	7
Threatened with legal action	3	1	5
Started or considered legal proceedings	5	2	12
Weighted base	1845	472	—
Unweighted base	1801	472	472

interviewed in the main survey broadly reflects the pattern reported in the screening survey.

REDEFINING PROBLEM TYPES

The analysis of data obtained during the screening survey has been presented in a way that is consistent with the structure of the screening questionnaire. However, as will be evident, many of the problems experienced by respondents that were collected together under broad categories of problem type in the screening questionnaire do not logically fit well together for analytical purposes. In order to reveal differences in approach and outcome for respondents experiencing different types of justiciable problem, the subcategories of problems were regrouped into nine categories that were more meaningful and which would offer sufficient cases in each subgroup for comparisons to be undertaken.

These nine problem types are as follows:

Problems with neighbours	including those owning and those renting property.
Divorce and separation	including divorce proceedings, problems with ex-partners, problems about residence and contact, problems about payment of maintenance, violent or abusive relationships with a partner or ex-partner.
Employment problems	
Consumer problems	including goods and services
Accidental injury and work-related ill health	excluding medical negligence
Problems over money	including money owed, insurance companies rejecting claims, incorrect bills, unfair tax demands, incorrect advice about insurance, pensions, etc., mismanagement of pension fund, unfair refusal of credit, harassment from creditors.
Problems with owning residential property	alterations to property, planning permission, buying or selling property, communal repairs or maintenance, repossession of the home, squatters
Problems with landlords	poor/unsafe living conditions, getting deposit back, getting landlord to do repairs, agreeing terms of lease, harassment by landlord, eviction or threats of eviction
Tribunal matters	including DSS benefits and education problems.

Since the number of cases reported in the screening survey relating to renting out property, the police, immigration, discrimination and medical negligence was very small, these cases have tended to be excluded from full analyses which specifically compare problem types.

COMPARISON OF MAIN SURVEY SAMPLE WITH ENGLISH SAMPLE AND
GENERAL POPULATION OF SCOTLAND

Aside from age and gender differences in the reporting of justiciable
problems discussed earlier, it was not possible to collect comprehensive
demographic data about respondents at the screening stage. This
information was collected, however, for all respondents selected for
the main survey and it is therefore possible to make some broad comparisons between the characteristics of the sample of respondents
reporting non-trivial justiciable problems during the previous five years
with the characteristics of the general population. This information is
presented as a rough guide to the ways in which the sample is similar
to, and differs from, the England and Wales main survey sample and
the population of Scotland at large.

Comparison with England and Wales Survey

The available information for comparison (Table 2.10) shows that the
age profile of the Scots main survey was similar to that in England and
Wales. The only point of difference was a somewhat larger proportion
of the Scots sample aged between 18 and 24. This also accounts for the
higher proportion of the Scots sample being in full time education (ten as
compared with three percent in England and Wales). The gender split
showing a higher proportion of females in the main survey is identical
with that in England and Wales, and as far as economic activity is concerned, the main survey sample in Scotland was marginally less likely to
be in full or part-time employment and more likely to be unemployed.

As far as educational qualifications are concerned there are some
striking differences between the Scots main sample and the English
main sample. While the proportions with no qualifications at all in the
two countries are similar, the proportion of respondents in the Scots
main sample with degree level qualifications is significantly *higher* than
in the English sample (41% in Scotland as compared with 29% in
England and Wales) and the proportion of respondents with only SCE
ordinary/O level/CSE or equivalent qualifications is significantly *lower*
than in the England and Wales sample (seven percent in Scotland as
compared with 32% in England and Wales). The Scots main survey
sample therefore appears to be more highly educated overall than the
English sample.

Comparison of Main Survey Sample with General Population of Scotland

Table 2.10 also shows that the main survey was somewhat younger than the general population of Scotland with a higher proportion of the main sample being under 34 than in the general population and a lower proportion being over the age of 55. This reflects the fact that older respondents to the screening survey were much less likely than other age groups to report having experienced justiciable problems. The gender split, however, in the main survey is roughly the same as that in the general population. The main survey sample comprised a greater proportion of economically inactive respondents than in the general population.

The social class and educational profile of the main survey sample was compared with the 1991 census data. Overall the social class pro-

Table 2.10 Comparison of characteristics of main survey sample of respondents experiencing justiciable disputes with England and Wales main survey sample and the general population of Scotland.

	% Scotland main survey sample	% England and Wales main survey sample	% Scotland General Population
Age			
18–24	16	11	11
25–34	29	29	19
35–44	26	26	19
45–54	14	16	17
55–64	8	7	13
65 or older	5	8	20
Sex			
Male	45	44	48
Female	55	56	52
Economic Activity			
In employment	56	61	69
Unemployed	6	4	8
Economically inactive	38	34	23

file of the main sample seems to be very similar to the general population as compared with the Census data, although respondents in
skilled manual occupations are somewhat underrepresented as are
those in unskilled occupations.

As far as educational qualifications are concerned, it is not possible to
provide a complete comparison, but the Table shows that the main survey sample comprised a significantly higher proportion of respondents
with degree level qualifications than would be expected from Census
data. This finding indicates either that less well-educated members of

Table 2.11 Comparison between Scotland main survey sample, England and
Wales main survey sample, and the general population of Scotland (%).

	Scotland Main Sample	England & Wales Main sample	Census 1991[16]
Social class[17]			
I (Professional)	5	5	4
II (Intermediate)	25	30	25
III (Skilled Non-Manual)	19	25	22
III (Skilled Manual)	14	18	21
IV (Semi-skilled)	16	15	17
V (Unskilled)	4	7	8
Educational qualifications[18]			
No qualifications	17	20	N/A
Degree etc.			
(Degree / Higher degree (or degree level qualification) Teach)	41	29	14
SCE Higher etc.			
(SCE Higher, ONC/OND, SCOYBEC/TEC or SCOTVEC)	20	20	N/A
Other	23	32	N/A
(SCE Ordinary etc)			

[16] Based on the 1% household Sample of Anonymised Records (SAR).

[17] Social class is based on respondent's own job (or last job if not in employment),
excluding those in the Armed Forces and any that have never worked.

[18] This definition applies to the main survey sample only.

the public experience fewer justiciable problems, or more probably, that there was systematic underreporting of justiciable problems by the less well-educated sector of Scottish society. This is the likely explanation for the under-representation of skilled and unskilled manual workers in the main survey sample as compared with the 1991 Census data.

CHARACTERISTICS OF RESPONDENTS EXPERIENCING PROBLEMS OF
DIFFERENT TYPES[19]

Consumer problems

Those respondents reporting consumer problems who were interviewed in the main survey were predominantly in the 25 to 54 age groups with slightly more women than men being interviewed about these problems (58% of those interviewed about consumer problems were women and 43% were men). Most were in full or part time work (65%) and there was a sizeable minority in full time education (11%). A very small minority of those interviewed about consumer problems was unemployed (2% although about 8% of the sample as a whole were unemployed). The income distribution of those complaining of consumer problems was rather different from the sample as a whole. Whereas about one third of the sample as a whole had incomes of below £10,000, only about six percent of those interviewed about consumer problems had incomes of that level. At the other end of the spectrum, about one in three of those reporting consumer problems had incomes in excess of £32,000 as compared with about one in five in the sample as a whole.

Although the main sample had a very high proportion of people with degree level qualifications, those with consumer problems were more likely than the sample as a whole to have obtained higher educational qualifications and somewhat less likely to have no qualifications. Thus over half of those interviewed about consumer problems (53%) had a degree level qualification as compared with 41% of the sample as a whole. Only about twelve percent of those reporting consumer problems had no qualifications (as compared with 17% in the sample).

[19] This analysis has been carried out for those categories of problems for which the largest number of unweighted cases was available in the main sample. Those categories *not* included were: disputes over ownership of residential property, disputes concerning benefits, education tribunals, unfair treatment by the police, immigration, and clinical negligence.

Respondents with consumer problems were also more likely than the sample as a whole to be owner occupiers (79% as compared with 53% in the sample as a whole).

About half of the complaints were against shops, mail order companies, travel agents and holiday companies (53%); about one in five complaints were against tradesmen such as plumbers and electricians (22%); and a smaller minority was complaints about professional services (11%). The remainder was spread across a wide range of persons and organisations. Although these figures are broadly consistent with England and Wales, the proportion of complaints about professional services was higher in Scotland than in England and Wales (11% of consumer problems as opposed to five percent in England and Wales).

Employment Problems

The age distribution of respondents interviewed about employment problems in the main survey was slightly different from that of the main survey as a whole, with those experiencing these problems being concentrated in two particular age groups. Almost half of all those interviewed about employment problems were between 25 and 34 (46% as compared with 29% in the sample as a whole) and a further quarter were aged between 45 and 54 (23% as compared with 14% in the sample as a whole). More women than men were interviewed about employment problems (57% were female as compared with 43% who were males) and this mirrors exactly the difference in the gender balance in the sample as a whole. This finding differs from those in England and Wales where more men than women were interviewed about employment problems, although there were also more women than men in the English main survey sample. Among those reporting employment problems a high proportion were in full time work than in the sample as a whole and a slightly lower proportion than in the sample as a whole were in part-time work. A higher proportion than in the sample as a whole were waiting to take up work (8% as compared with two percent in the sample) or were unemployed (8% as compared with 6% in the sample as a whole).

The income distribution of those complaining of employment problems was fairly similar to that in the sample as a whole, although a higher proportion of respondents experiencing employment problems fell within the highest income bracket (14% of those with employment problems as compared with ten percent in the sample). These findings are somewhat different from those in England where few respondents with incomes of below £10,000 reported employment problems.

The educational profile of those interviewed about employment problems was similar to that of the sample as a whole, as were levels of property ownership and rental.

The overwhelming majority of employment problems were with the respondent's employer (79% of employment problems), although 13% of cases concerned a work colleague.

Divorce proceedings and separation problems

This category includes cases relating to divorce proceedings and also other problems in relationships between partners, for example spousal violence and disputes over contact with children. Among those included in this category some 30% were included because they had been involved in divorce proceedings during the previous five years; 36% were included having reported a dispute with their ex-partner in relation to family matters such as child maintenance, division of property or violence; and 28% were in dispute with their ex-partner in relation to children under the age of 18. Some six percent were in dispute with the Child Support Agency. As compared with England and Wales, a higher proportion in the Scots sample involved children and a lower proportion related to divorce proceedings.

Those respondents reporting divorce and separation problems who were interviewed in the main survey were predominantly aged between 25 and 44 (82%). More women than men in the sample had reported a divorce and separation problem (60% of those reporting these problems were women and 40% were men). About half of those interviewed about divorce and separation problems were in full-time work (51%) and another 13% were in part-time work. About 17% were looking after the home and or family, which is somewhat higher than the average for the sample as a whole (11%).

The household income distribution of respondents interviewed about divorce and separation problems was similar to that of the sample as a whole although a slightly higher proportion was on a *low* income. About 40% of those interviewed about divorce and separation problems had household incomes of less than £10,000 as compared with 32% in the sample as a whole. This pattern is identical with that in England and Wales.

As far as education is concerned, respondents interviewed about divorce and separation problems were somewhat less likely than the sample as a whole to have a degree level qualification, and somewhat more likely to be educated only to the level of O level/CSE than the sample as a whole. The proportion with no qualifications was roughly the same as for the whole sample.

Respondents experiencing divorce or separation were more likely than the sample as a whole to be living rent free, including in a relative or friend's home, although in other respects their home occupation was similar to the sample as a whole.

Problems with neighbours

Neighbour disputes represented the most common problem experienced by those reporting problems to do with owning property and was also the second most common problem experienced by those reporting problems relating to living in rented accommodation (second only to the difficulty of getting landlords to carry out repairs to the premises). In the main survey about six in ten of those interviewed about problems with neighbours were living in property that they owned and the other four in ten were living in rented accommodation, which is similar to the pattern of occupation in the sample as a whole. Among those living in rented accommodation, respondents complaining of problems with neighbours were more likely than the sample as a whole to be living in property rented from the local authority (68% of those with neighbour problems compared with 54% of the sample). They were slightly less likely to be renting from a housing association (5% as compared with 10% in the sample) or from a private landlord (26% as compared with 32% in the sample).

The age distribution of those experiencing problems with neighbours was rather different from the sample as a whole, with a higher proportion of those with neighbour problems being in the 55+ age bracket (27% of those with neighbour problems were in this age group as compared with only 13% of the sample as a whole). There were also fewer respondents in the 25–44 age bracket complaining of neighbour problems as compared with the sample as a whole. Connected with the age distribution is the fact that women were over-represented among those complaining of neighbour problems (69% of those with neighbour problems compared with 55% in the sample as a whole). A difficulty with neighbours is clearly something that disproportionately afflicts older women.

There were no significant differences in economic activity between those complaining of neighbour problems and the sample as a whole, nor were there any significant differences in income, unlike England and Wales where those experiencing problems with neighbours were more likely to have lower household incomes.

The educational profile of those interviewed about neighbour problems was somewhat different from that of the sample as a whole. A significantly higher proportion of respondents complaining of neighbour problems had no educational qualifications (30% as compared with 17% in the sample) and significantly fewer had qualifications at A level or SCE Higher level (6% compared with 20% in the sample). These findings, which are consistent with those in England and Wales, are probably related to the relatively high number of older women reporting neighbour problems.

Money problems

Among those interviewed in the main survey about money problems excluding disputes relating to DSS benefits, the most common problems related to a dispute with an insurance company (27%), the local authority (21%) a bank, building society or mortgage company (11%), the Inland Revenue (10%), a utility (6%), or some other company (18%).

Although the age distribution of respondents interviewed about money problems largely reflected the age distribution of the sample as a whole, a greater proportion of young people aged 18–24 reported money problems (27% as compared with 16% in the sample). Rather more men than women reported money problems, representing a significantly higher proportion than in the sample as a whole (58% as compared with 43% male respondents in the sample). The economic activity of those reporting money problems was also not significantly different from the sample as a whole, except in respect of respondents classified as long term sick and disabled who represented 18% of those with money problems but only nine percent of the sample as a whole.

The income distribution of those complaining of problems to do with money did differ somewhat from that of the sample as a whole. All brackets were roughly similar except that there were more respondents with incomes below £10,000 (43% as compared with 32% in the sample as a whole).

As far as education was concerned, those reporting problems to do with money were slightly less likely than the sample as a whole to have degree level qualifications.

Although about 44% of those reporting money problems owned their home or were buying it with a mortgage, a slightly higher proportion of this group than the sample as a whole were living in rented accommodation, although more likely than the sample average to be renting it from the local authority (63% as compared with 54% in the sample).

Accidental injury and work-related ill health

Those respondents interviewed about injury and work-related ill health requiring medical treatment had most often suffered an accident or illness at work (44%) or a road accident (15%). About twelve percent were in dispute with the council as a result of falls in the street or other public places and one quarter said that their accident took place elsewhere.

Among those interviewed about accidents and ill-health there was a higher proportion of respondents over 65 than in the sample as a whole (13% as compared with 5% in the sample), and more women than men were interviewed about accidents (58% as compared with 42% of men). The relatively high proportion of elderly respondents in this category is consistent with the findings in England and Wales, although south of the border equal proportions of men and women were interviewed about accidental injury and work-related ill-health.

Most of those interviewed about accidents and work-related ill-health had a household income of between £10,000 and £20,000 (45% of all those suffering accidents).

About half of those interviewed about injury and ill-health were in full time employment. Unsurprisingly, a relatively high proportion of respondents suffering from these problems were long-term sick or disabled (13% as compared with 9% in the sample), or retired (12% as compared with 5% in the sample) and fewer were looking after the home (3% as compared with 11% in the sample as a whole).

Problems with landlords

Difficulties with landlords was the most common type of justiciable problem reported by respondents to the screening survey who said that they had experienced a problem relating to living in rented accommodation.

Those reporting problems with landlords were more likely to be in the age range 18–24 than the sample as a whole (51% as compared with 16% in the sample as a whole), and were more likely to be in full time education (25% of those with landlord problems as compared with 10% of the sample as a whole), or unemployed (14% as compared with 8% in the sample). Those who had experienced landlord problems were more likely than the sample as a whole to have low incomes (60% on incomes of less than £10,000 as compared with 32% of the sample as a whole).

Among those reporting problems with landlords 46% were renting from the local authority (as compared with 54% in the sample) and 48% were renting from a private landlord (as compared with 32% in the sample), thus confirming that respondents had proportionately greater problems with private landlords than with the local authority landlords.

CONCLUSION

The screening survey has revealed a relatively high incidence of justiciable problems within the general population. Over a five year period about 26% of the general population experienced one or more problems or events for which a legal remedy is available. For most problem types, the mean number of problems experienced by respondents was between 1.2 and around 1.5, although certain types of problems seem to occur with considerable frequency, such as problems to do with living in rented accommodation (2.3). The problems that have the highest rate of occurrence in the population are living in rented accommodation (123 problems per 1,000 adult population, those relating to faulty goods and services (about 90 problems per 1,000 adults over a five year period), money problems (about 88 problems per 1,000 adults over a five year period) and problems to do with home ownership (about 78 problems per 1,000 adults over a five year period). As we have seen, this pattern of problem incidence is very similar to that in England and Wales although in England and Wales consumer problems and money problems headed the list. The chief difference between the two jurisdictions, however, is in the incidence levels.

In Scotland respondents to the screening survey reported *fewer* experiences of each problem type during the survey reference period. Even in areas where the substantive law, the court procedures and the legal aid system were much the same in the two jurisdictions at the time of the surveys (e.g. divorce or personal injury) the Scottish incidence was significantly lower. Why should this be so? It seems somewhat difficult to account for such a large across-the-board difference. There are two possible explanations. The first is that there is actually a lower incidence of justiciable problems in Scotland. Given the breadth of the concept of justiciable problem there is no obvious reason why this should be the case[20]. The second, and more plausible explanation, is that there was a reporting difference in the Scottish survey caused by one, or a combination of factors influencing the perceptions of respondents to the screening survey.

In most cases the screening survey questions referred to "problems or disputes that were difficult to solve". It is possible that a greater sense of fatalism or powerlessness among segments of the Scottish population led to a systematic underreporting of problems. This could occur because problems and disputes were seen as incapable of resolution, or not worth the effort, or that trying to resolve a problem would not make any difference to their situation (a tendency once memorably described by the first Scottish Lay Observer, Joan MacIntosh as the "Ach tae hell with it" syndrome). In relation to this possible explanation for underreporting it may be relevant to note that those who did report justiciable problems in the screening survey were significantly more educated and younger as compared with the general population than those who reported nothing. It is reasonable to assume that low levels of education and advanced age might be associated with a greater sense of powerlessness or fatalism. Although the relationship between the reporting of justiciable disputes and age and education was noted in England and Wales, it was more pronounced in Scotland. The issue of powerlessness is discussed again at the beginning of the Chapter 3.

Underreporting might also have occurred because the Scottish population, with its strong socialist traditions, is more community-orientated than the English, and thus less likely to perceive disputes as being individual matters rather than collective problems. For example, if the great majority of local authority housing in an area suffers from

---

[20] The SCC study found an incidence rate of 18% while the NCC study in England and Wales found an incidence rate of 13% (see discussion in Chapter above).

dampness this may be seen as a feature of the community rather than as an individual problem.

Finally, a less plausible explanation in the light of the behaviour and views expressed by our Scottish respondents, is that the population of Scotland is more hardy, self-reliant and self assured than that in England and Wales, and is thus less likely than the English to perceive problems and disputes as being "difficult to resolve"[21].

Respondents who reported having experienced a justiciable problem in the previous five years often experienced a problem more than once *and* more than one type of problem. While 14% of the population reported having experienced only one non-trivial justiciable problem during the previous five years, a further eight percent reported having experienced two or more problems during the five year period. Pairs of problems that commonly tend to cluster together are: divorce and family matters; family matters and children; divorce and children; money problems and family matters; money problems and living in rented accommodation, money problems and faulty goods or services; employment problems and money problems.

For most problem types respondents reported that they had taken some action to try and resolve the reported problem, most commonly talking or writing to the other side and seeking advice. When action had not been taken this was most often because of a belief that nothing could be done about the problem or because the problem was regarded as unimportant. This behaviour varied by problem type and is explored in detail in Chapters 3 and 4.

The findings of the screening survey demonstrate that the general public of Scotland experiences a high volume of events for which the legal system could be mobilised. The workload of the civil justice system is the result of the cumulative choices of members of the public about whether to resort to legal proceedings in order to resolve such justiciable problems. An analysis of the behaviour of respondents reporting justiciable problems in relation to these issues, the influences on their choices, and their motivations for taking action or failing to take action are explored in the remainder of this book.

---

[21] To the extent that the stereotype of the "thrawn Scot" actually exists, it may be a contributing factor to perceptual differences that influencing reporting in the Scottish screening survey.

3

Strategies for Resolving
Justiciable Problems

This chapter describes the way the public in Scotland approaches the resolution of justiciable problems and disputes. The data used in the analysis was obtained during full interviews with respondents identified during the screening survey as having been involved in a non-trivial justiciable problem during the survey period. When respondents had reported experiencing more than one problem during the previous five years, they were asked during the main interview only about the *second* most recent problem.

The chapter deals with broad patterns of behaviour in the whole sample: whether respondents took any action to try and resolve their problem; whether they handled problems themselves; whether they obtained advice about how to resolve the problem and where they went to get that advice. Attention is paid to barriers and pathways to advice in order to gain a better understanding of the circumstances under which members of the public seek advice when faced with a justiciable problem. The chapter also provides information about what members of the public were looking for from advisers, what help they received and how useful that help was found to be. Since the approach taken to problem resolution varied substantially depending on the type of problem being faced, a more detailed discussion of advice-seeking in relation to particular types of problem is provided in the next chapter[1].

OVERVIEW

The first step in dealing with a justiciable problem for the overwhelming majority of members of the public interviewed in the survey was to

---

[1] Where the size of the subgroup permits this type of analysis. For the purpose of this and later analyses, problems were re-classified into narrower more consistent groupings than the broad categories used in the screening questionnaire (see discussion at end of Chapter 2).

try to resolve the problem directly themselves by contacting the other person or organisation involved in the problem or dispute. Over three-quarters (78%) of those who had experienced a non-trivial justiciable problems reported that they had made some contact directly with the other side in order to try to resolve the problem, whether or not they went on to obtain advice. This figure is significantly higher than the comparable figure in England and Wales where about two in three respondents said that their first step was to make contact with the other side to try and reach a resolution of the problem. Only when direct action failed to produce a result did many people go on to obtain advice about resolving the problem. A little under three-quarters of those who obtained advice had first made contact with the other side, but the remaining one in four of those receiving advice apparently went directly to advisers without first making contact with the other party to try and resolve the problem and a small minority did nothing at all.

Overall about three percent of respondents did nothing ("the lumpers"), about one- third (32%) tried to resolve the problem without help ("the self-helpers") and about two thirds (65%) tried to resolve the problem with advice or help from an outside adviser ("the advised") (Figure 3.1). These figures are virtually identical with the results in England and Wales (5% lumpers; 35% self-helpers and 60% advised).

Among all respondents interviewed about a recent justiciable problem, a little over nine out of ten (93%) had received advice in the past from a wide range of advice sources to help resolve other matters, and about two out of three (68%) respondents interviewed said that they had taken legal advice at least once some time in the past, regardless of how the problem about which they were being interviewed had been dealt with (this figure is identical to that reported in the England and Wales study). This shows that a high proportion of respondents reporting having experienced non-trivial justiciable disputes during the previous five years had previously sought advice, regardless of how they had handled the matter about which they were being interviewed.

"THE LUMPERS": NO ADVICE, NO CONTACT, NO ACTION

In common with the England and Wales survey, among members of the public in Scotland who had experienced non-trivial justiciable problems, only a very small proportion failed to take any kind of action to

No action taken to resolve problem 3%

Handled alone 32%

Obtained advice about resolving problem 65%

Figure 3.1 Broad Strategy for dealing with justiciable problems (Base = whole sample 472 weighted).

deal with their justiciable problems (one in thirty), despite the fact that the problems had been important enough to remember and to report during the screening survey.

This small group of "lumpers" is interesting and has some distinctive characteristics. First, those members of the public who took no action at all to try and resolve their problem were most likely to have experienced problems relating to clinical negligence, benefits, consumer problems, employment problems and personal injuries. Although the number of cases is rather small, the indication is that respondents in Scotland were *less* likely to lump money problems other than those concerning benefits than respondents in England and Wales, but more likely to lump problems to do with benefits. Scottish respondents were also less likely than those in England and Wales to lump problems about accidental injury. Respondents in Scotland who had taken no action to resolve their problem were less likely to have obtained outside advice about any problem in the past than respondents who had taken some action to resolve their recent problem. A little under half of those failed to take action to resolve their problem had an annual income of less than £10,000 (44% compared with 32% of self-helpers and 30% of those taking action with advice). A difference worth noting is that in contrast with the results in England and Wales, in Scotland there were *no* significant differences in educational attainment between respondents who took some action to resolve their problem and those who did not. There were also no significant gender differences between those who took action to resolve their problem and those who took no action at all.

The main reasons given by respondents for failing to take any action to resolve their problem were that there was nothing that could be done about the problem (about half of those who did nothing), or that the problem was over and done with (about one in four cases). Those who said that there was nothing that could be done about the problem were, of course, making this judgement without the benefit of any advice.

The decision not to take action to resolve the problem was generally reached after considering possible courses of action and rejecting those possibilities. For example, considering the cost of taking action, the possible stress and inconvenience, and concern about causing difficulties in existing relationships—or even making matters worse rather than better. In fact, the line between "lumpers" and those self-helpers who took some perfunctory and ineffective steps to resolve their problem is fine. In qualitative interviews "lumpers" were questioned closely about their reasons for failing to take action to resolve their problem. The explanations given convey negative perceptions of the cost and trouble that flow from involvement with lawyers and legal actions, as well as the same kind of powerlessness that was expressed by lumpers in England and Wales. The problems dealt with during the survey had been defined by the respondents themselves as non-trivial and therefore something that they cared about. In this context the failure to take action was generally not "accidental", but the result of deliberate choice or a sense of helplessness.

Other respondents who failed to take any action offered similar expressions of powerlessness, fear of becoming involved in acrimony, and concern about the cost of taking formal action. For example:

"I thought about it but I didn't want to ruffle any feathers . . . [and] everything with the legal system takes ages. There's nothing ever very forthcoming with it . . . . you go into the legal situation, you get bogged down by a whole lot of different things, and I just never even thought about it, to tell you the truth. It would need to be something where I was really desperate before I would take that avenue . . . The expense; the time; . . . I would never consider it unless it was really really desperate . . . I wouldn't have wanted to ruffle any feather by going to court, they could have been awkward. So there's just no way I would make things worse than what they already were..I knew that he had to be in the education system for so many years, and I was just wanting the best for him, so there's no way that I would want to make enemies with the education department." [Special needs requirement for child refused by local education authority]

Some of the difficulties expressed by those who failed to take action to resolve their problem were similar to explanations given by respondents who had tried to handle the problem themselves, but who would have liked advice and assistance in dealing with the problem.

THE SELF-HELPERS: PROBLEMS HANDLED WITHOUT ANY ADVICE

Just under one-third of respondents (31%) tried to resolve their problem by handling the matter themselves, and without obtaining any advice. (This figure is almost identical to that found in England and Wales (35%). The types of problems that respondents were most likely to have attempted to resolve without obtaining advice were consumer problems, money problems, and problems to do with benefits or schooling for children. Respondents were least likely to handle matters on their own when they were dealing with problems to do with divorce or separation or when claiming compensation for an injury. Although the majority of self-helpers reported that they had obtained advice in the past about a problem (81%), a higher proportion of self-helpers than those who obtained advice about their problem claimed *never* to have received outside advice in the past to deal with any matter (19% compared with one percent of the advised). These figures are identical to those found in England and Wales, although a slightly lower proportion of lumpers (17%) reported never having obtained advice about a problem than in England and Wales (29%).

About one-quarter of problems and disputes in Scotland concerned the respondent seeking a money remedy, either the payment of compensation or the reduction of an amount being claimed from the respondent. Among disputes concerning a money remedy, a self-help strategy was more likely to be adopted when the amount in dispute was £500 or less, than when it was for a larger sum. In cases involving disputed sums of over £3,000, virtually no one chose to try and resolve the problem without advice. For disputed sums of less than £500 about half of the respondents said that they had tried to resolve the problem without advice, whereas for sums of between £1000 and £3000 only about 17% tried to resolve the problem without obtaining advice.

Self-helpers can be distinguished from those who took no action at all to resolve their problem, those who took some direct action to resolve the problem and then sought advice about how to continue, and also from those who went directly for advice without ever trying to resolve the problem directly themselves. However, the label "self-helper" includes widely differing approaches to dealing with problems. Some self-helpers were able to solve their problem relatively easily by approaching the other side directly and requesting some action to remedy the problem. Consumer difficulties provide examples of this kind of successful direct approach to problem resolution:

> "I'd bought a second-hand freezer and when I got home the door was a wee bit skew whiff and wouldnae work. So I phoned a couple of times so someone could come and repair it but nobody ever appeared. But I was calling all the shots because I hadnae paid for the freezer. So I didnae pay for all of it. We agreed a price across the phone. I think it ended up sixty quid aff it. I think it was probably about two hundred quid and I think I gave him a hundred and forty."

There were also cases when respondents showed considerable determination and creativity in seeking redress for their consumer problem. For example:

> "We wrote back saying it wasn't as advertised and could we have a refund please and that was thoroughly ignored. I then wrote to the newspaper which unfortunately had changed its address. Then I wrote to the supplier and that was ignored. Then another letter went to the supplier and then we saw it advertised in the Exchange and Mart and the Express so we wrote to them saying that one of their advertisers had not responded to a fair request for a refund. The letter to the supplier threatened exposure to the press. Within a few days after that the supplier did actually send a refund. No apology. Basically a cheque in the post, end of story. I must admit I've had quite a lot of dealings with suppliers getting money back. I think I've picked up a lot of tips from problems pages in newspapers."

> "[We bought a kitchen and] two or three years later we noticed the doors, the vinyl was peeling away at the corners. We went back to [the store where we bought the units] and they sent somebody out, and the first thing the chap said was that we had built it too close to the cooker . . . and since the kitchen hadn't been fitted by themselves they would look at it but he didn't know how the thing would come out. We persevered. Phoned them regularly for two or three months and nothing seemed to be happening and it was a few months later before someone eventually came and eventually . . . legal action was threatened. We said that if we didn't get satisfaction . . . we set down a timescale, we would certainly be taking legal advice. I continued to press for it and eventually we did actually get new doors. It was settled without any need for court action . . . We felt we were in the right . . . It took between six months and a year."

However, as will be discussed in Chapter 5, a minority of these self-helpers were successful in achieving a resolution of their problem.

Analysis of the outcome of problems at the time of the interview shows that fewer than half of those who tried to resolve their problem by handling the matter entirely alone succeeded in achieving a resolution by agreement. Whether or not a self-help strategy will be successful depends on the nature of the problem, the confidence, competence, and persistence of the complainant, and the intransigence of the other party involved in the problem.

The experiences recounted by respondents in dealing with their justiciable problems, suggests that although it is possible to distinguish between those who take no action to try and resolve their problem and those who take some action but fail, the differences at the margin are fairly minor. Self-helpers cover a broad spectrum, ranging from those who make perhaps one rather ineffectual attempt to achieve a resolution and then give up, to those who take positive and sustained action only to be thwarted in the end, to those who take a relatively simple step and are rewarded with a remedy, and finally to those who battle on until they achieve a satisfactory outcome.

Although the "lumpers" are an interesting atypical group, in seeking to understand how the public responds to justiciable problems and why they respond in the way they do, an important question is less why a small minority of people do not even try to resolve the problem, but why the numerically much larger group of defeated self-helpers fails to obtain advice or assistance in trying to achieve a satisfactory resolution of the problem. Information shedding light on this question was obtained from survey responses and from qualitative interviews with self-helpers.

BARRIERS TO ADVICE

Respondents interviewed on the main survey about the action that they took to resolve their problem were asked whether they had actually attempted but failed to make contact with a chosen adviser. About six percent of all those interviewed said that they had unsuccessfully tried to contact one of the advice organisations—the most common being the CAB (32%), a social worker or social services department (22%), a consumer advice centre or Trading Standards Officer (14%), the police (11%), MP or local councillor (6%), or an advice agency (5%). Aside from failed attempts to contact the CAB, the sources of advice that respondents in Scotland had unsuccessfully tried to contact were somewhat different from the pattern in England and Wales where trades unions, welfare rights officers and professional bodies were more likely to be mentioned.

There was also evidence that a substantial minority of respondents (about one in four) experiencing justiciable problems had considered seeking advice, but in the event failed to take any steps to do so. The most common sources of advice *considered* but not contacted by respondents were CABx (mentioned by 38% of those who considered approaching an advice source and 10% of the sample as a whole) and solicitors (mentioned by about 30% of those considering contacting an advice source and five percent of the sample as a whole). The most common reasons for not making contact, even though consideration had been given to the possibility, was a belief that the adviser could not or would not help with the problem (27%). Other common reasons for not trying to make contact with an advice source were that nothing could be done about the problem (8%), thought it would be better to wait to see what happened before contacting an adviser (8%) or that it was too much hassle or bother to make contact (6%). In some cases advisers were not contacted because the other side responded to demands before contact was made.

Accounts of behaviour given during qualitative interviews provided vivid insights into some of the anticipated and real barriers to advice-seeking among those who considered trying to get help with their problem, but in the end failed to do so. Factors that emerged from interviews as being important influences on decisions about what action to take were: fear of legal costs and a perception of the withering away of legal aid; inaccessibility of good quality advice about legal rights; previous negative experiences of legal advisers or legal processes; a sense of powerlessness about certain types of problem; and in some cases a sense of alienation from the legal system. In these respects the responses were consistent with those found in England and Wales. The frequent references to legal aid "withering away" are interesting in that they seem to reflect developments in England and Wales reported in the UK media, rather than any significant changes to Scottish Legal Aid. The impact of UK-wide media reporting on the development of perceptions of the Scottish legal system is discussed at length in Chapter 7.

General negativity about legal processes

During qualitative interviews, many respondents expressed strongly negative feelings about involvement in legal processes. This negativity is a mixture of concern about the cost of legal advice, a sense that unwitting lay people are tricked and trapped during court hearings, and perceptions of the trauma that seems to be inevitable in the lengthy workings of the legal system. These negative feelings were expressed both by those who had attempted to pursue a remedy or resolution of their problem and by those who made little effort to secure a remedy. For example:

"I think I would consider myself to be fairly average and for me I think the cost and probably the intimidating purgatory you would go through trying to pursue your case—even though no matter how squeaky clean it was, there's always a doubt in the back of your mind that you could lose it for whatever reason—a technicality. Something comes up out of the blue which you haven't thought of. I think it would be a very worrying time and there could be nights in the run-up to the case you could probably lose quite a lot of sleep. And that could have a knock-on effect to your family. So it could be all-round quite a harrowing time."

"It's a shame that it wasn't possible to do what I think in law would be right, but it just wasn't possible. If it weren't that everybody that I've ever read about in the papers ends up suffering for what they've done, I would have said I should have gone to court and said I'd been constructively dismissed, but I've never read of case where that's happened, where the victim has ended up anything but still a victim"

"Sometimes I wonder why something should take so long. I'd watch cases on television and I say 'My goodness, it would be terrible to be wrongfully accused of something and wait fifteen months before the court case comes up.' You know, that is pretty frightening. I think the other problem is that if somebody's been under a lot of stress, and they're up against a system or an organisation which has battened down the hatches, it's very difficult for one person really to fight the organisation."

"[It's possible to get justice] if you're prepared to take the time and money. It certainly takes time. There's nae question about taking time, because there's the legal system. Dosnae matter whether it's criminal or civil or anything, it takes forever, or it appears to take forever. You speak to anybody that's had any problems. It seems to drag on and drag on. You might take things to court if they went really belly up. I suppose that's your last resort. There's surely better ways to resolve situations than taking things to court."

Accessibility of Advice Agencies

As far as obtaining advice was concerned, interviews suggest that while some people were unsure about where to go for advice, most respondents were aware of the existence of the Citizens Advice Bureaux. Indeed, about half of all respondents to the main survey (49%) said that they had actually obtained advice from a CAB at some time in the past[2].

Despite this general knowledge about the existence of CABx and other local advice centres, if they existed, it was also clear that the public often experienced problems in finding out about opening times, managing to get through on the telephone, and being forced to take time off work in order to visit a CAB because they were only open during working hours. All of these matters created barriers to advice-seeking, even among those who were relatively knowledgeable about sources of advice and might have used advisers in the past. There was also some evidence of a lack of confidence in the quality of advice provided by CABx.

Practical problems in obtaining advice from CABx and other advice agencies provided a regular explanation for the failure to obtain advice when self-help strategies had failed to achieve a resolution to the problem[3]. Although there were some concerns about the quality of advice offered at CABx, rather more common complaints related to the limited opening hours of CABx, waiting times for an appointment, and difficulty in making telephone contact to arrange an appointment. Some of those who had been quite determined about trying to resolve their problem were, in the end, defeated by lack of availability of free or low cost advice:

"I mean the Citizen's Advice Bureau in Glasgow is in the middle of town to start off with and I've been there once, and you had to wait and wait and wait and wait and wait and wait and there's an assumption that everybody's gonna wait, they're that desperate, they're gonna wait, but people get fed up and they go away, but it's in the middle of town, you know, if you've got

---

[2] Since interviewers accepted the name of the advice agency given by respondents, it is possible that other advice agencies have been included in the category "CAB" if respondents used that as a generic term for advice agency.

[3] Proportionately there are rather more CABx and their outreach offices in England and Wales than in Scotland. Thus the ration of CABx to the population is 1:74,000 in England and Wales and 1:86,000 in Scotland. Again the greater rurality of Scotland entails that those wanting to consult a CAB in rural Scotland may have to travel greater distances than their counterparts south of the border.

somebody that stays in the outskirts and it's not even the bus for going into town, it's to go away to Citizen's Advice. There should be many more Citizen's Advice Bureaux."

"I have been to the CAB, but not for anything major, just for queries with employers and things like that, just checking laws. I do think they're a worthwhile service, but they're no' enough staff in it. You can sit on the phone for all day trying to get through. Especially here, it's a really small office we've got and it's only open for six hours a day or so."

"Whenever I've been to the [CAB] there's been nothing. They're always that busy. You know they say make appointments for six month's time. Sometimes you can't even get them on the phone. The phone just rings out constantly."

"There's the Citizens Advice Bureau and places like that people can go to initially to find out, but I had a problem finding one. I was phoning around here there and everywhere before I finally got somebody and it was the Consumer people in Grampian that I finally got. So I had a wee bit of difficulty trying to find help. I think they should advertise a bit more. The Citizens Advice Bureau, when they were in their infancy, their advertising was good. I don't think people had a problem then trying to find them. But I was surprised when I got the phone book out and I started phoning around and I was getting all sorts of vague remarks—'Oh no, that's not here'. The nearest is in Aberdeen and I couldn't get them. I just couldn't get them. They had a Bureau number and I could never get anybody and then finally got through and they said that it wasn't manned—only certain hours and things like that. In fact I finally gave up and I got on to the Council Consumer Affairs."

"I was just at a loss. I was going through the phone book thinking, 'Well, maybe this could help me, maybe that could help me, maybe the next thing'. Because I'd gone through a whole lot of different places, you know, a lot of different charities to see if they could help . . . I just wanted somebody that would help me. I knew there had to be something. I wasnae too sure what, and I just went through the phone book and explained to them—I went on to the NSPCC first and they put me . . . into another few directions . . . They couldn't actually help me as such, but I just ploughed my way through till I actually got somebody that could help."

The common experience and expectation that obtaining advice from a CAB is extremely difficult presents a policy challenge to the architects of the Scottish community legal service. Knowledge of the existence of CABx is widespread, as is a general belief that useful guidance and assistance might be obtained from CABx. However, the evidence of the survey indicates a substantial unmet need for such advice and assistance. Prospective clients are discouraged as a result of limited opening times, unanswered telephones, full offices, and queues. These findings are consistent with the findings in the England and Wales study and with previous studies. For example, an analysis of reasons for lack of representation at tribunals conducted over ten years ago produced identical evidence about the problems of congestion in CABx[4].

Quality of free advice

Although not an overwhelming concern, there were some respondents who were mistrustful of the sort of advice that might be offered by a CAB and some whose experience led them to feel that CABx could not provide good quality advice.

"I thought of Citizen's Advice, but it has been so run down. They shut most of the shops, the advice centres in Glasgow. And when you go up there, I think they may be well-intentioned do-gooders, but they don't give you really great advice. They'll give you overall pointers, but I don't see them being that effective. I see them being another arm of Government. They're far too middle class to represent the lower classes. I went to see them when I was fighting for a grant and they gave me some advice, but it was advice more or less to keep my head under the parapet, don't make waves."

"There's the obvious ones [advice agencies] like the Citizens' Advice Bureaux and things like that, but I've not actually met anyone in those organisations that knows any more than I do. I've been to the CAB years ago with housing questions, and I found that the people who staffed it weren't actually up to date with the information I needed. They weren't actually telling me anything that I didn't already know. I needed someone to actually help me access the person I needed to talk to, to get my claim processed quickly, because I wasn't fit to work and I was gonna' lose the place that I was living in, and the people that I went to see at the CAB couldn't actually help me. They didn't know any short cuts. They were well-meaning, but undereducated in the day to day running of just the way the system works, which is very complicated."

"I'm nae worldly-wise in how the law works and I wouldnae have kent what my actual rights would have been. That would have been my biggest problem. And if you're unsure of your rights and if you phone some of these guys

---

[4] H Genn and Y Genn, *The Effectiveness of Representation at Tribunals*, Lord Chancellor's Department, 1989, pp. 223–224.

up, they can just talk you round the block and make you look a right numpty, which is nae the ideal situation. My first stop would probably be the Citizens Advice. But they're nae always the most informative either. The last time I went they werenae in my situation, probably because they weren't just schooled up in that particular area. They passed me on to some other guy to take it up, but I didnae."

Dissatisfaction with advice may also relate to a feeling that the advice was not what was wanted at the time, rather than that the advice was of poor quality. There is a problem stemming from a clash between the ethos of empowerment, which underpins the approach of the CABx, and the desire of many members of the public to be saved from their problem (see discussion later in this chapter relating to respondents' expectations of advisers). This was true in England and Wales where respondents complained of needing positive assistance with their problem rather than merely being told, for example, to go away and write a letter. To the extent that our speculation that there is a greater sense of powerlessness pervading some sections of the Scottish population is true, then this problem will be exacerbated in Scotland.

There were, however, respondents whose experience of the CAB was good. They did not seem to complain of particular difficulty in obtaining advice and found the advice received, and sometimes a referral, helpful. For example:

"Most people know that the CAB exists and they may be covering a wide range of things, but they're a first port of call and if they have the appropriate leaflets et cetera, perhaps with another contact number after that, I think that's probably the best way of working. But to have a single point of call that most people can find out about and can easily access, I think is quite important . . . I think they're quite well clued up at a basic level. They're not lawyers, but I think in terms of consumer law they're probably more clued up than the majority of lawyers."

General aversion to solicitors

Although the cost of legal advice (discussed below) was a very important factor in deterring some respondents from consulting solicitors about the possibilities of pursuing their claim or defending their position, there was also clear evidence of a strong strand of general "lawyer aversion" expressed during qualitative interviews. The nature of the aversion derived not simply from costs fears, although these were considerable, but sometimes from previous experience and a sense of class and power differences. One or two respondents provided very clear and evocative explanations of their reluctance to go to solicitors:

> "When you go in and visit a solicitor they are normally sitting on a high chair behind a massive desk, like the king at his throne, and you're immediately psychologically at a loss there, because they're towering over you and imposing themselves, imposing their will upon you, even though they're working for you. It would be better to have a more informal approach, rather than the very strict formal, sitting either side of a desk type approach. Where you could go along and have a chat with a solicitor."

> "I went to Money Matters. I felt more comfortable going there than I would be going up a Victorian staircase to a lawyer's office. When people are working in an open plan office and there are people buzzing about, you're less intimidated than being sat in a leather upholstered armchair in front of a mahogany desk with a roll top and ink-wells or whatever. Now that's intimidating for a start, just theatrically. And lawyers' offices tend to be either super modern or super Victorian; you know the smell of beeswax. And that separates you and you think what's this going to cost you. That's the first thing that comes into your mind. And I'm separated away from what is usual to me. This is the use of power, or the perception of power. You see someone that's got the trappings of success, wealth, security and it's the superiority as well. This professional veil that people hide behind, even the pin striped suit. I know it's there for the detachment of professionalism, but I'd rather sit down opposite someone dressed like myself."

Cost of obtaining legal advice

Respondents to survey interviews and qualitative interviews expressed a pervasive feeling that obtaining legal advice was hugely expensive and that for many kinds of problems obtaining such advice was simply not an option. Respondents who said that they had considered consulting a solicitor, but in the end had not done so, mainly gave concern about cost as the reason for not making contact. The following extracts from qualitative interviews provide graphic illustrations of concern about costs and the influence of media reports on the development of those perceptions.

> "Fundamentally you always come back to the cost of doing it. If it was only a case of two or three hundred pounds to put yourself through a court situation, even with all the purgatory that goes with it, most people would be probably prepared to do that—let's say even five hundred pounds. But more

often than not, some of these very long, protracted legal cases run for months and months, and the legal fee's tens and tens of thousands of pounds. Now, no one bringing up a family, paying a mortgage, could do that. You just simply couldn't do—couldn't contemplate it, unless they have a very big sum of money deposited somewhere. So I think for most of us, the civil side of law is probably out the question."

A respondent who failed to take action to pursue an employment problem, and who subsequently lost her job, explained clearly the dilemma about taking legal advice, particularly when the individual is contemplating action against a powerful institutional defender with potentially considerable resources:

"I could not have afforded a solicitor. At the time I was earning about £14,000 and I certainly wouldn't have qualified for legal aid and my husband couldn't have paid for a solicitor. Cost certainly did come into it. If cost hadn't come into it I might have pursued the case. The cost to me and the cost of trying to keep up with someone like the [institutional employer] who have got so much more money, clout with the legal department into the bargain . . . I couldn't afford to begin to pay the sort of thing that could have developed . . . you've got to think about what might happen when you start. There had been a case in the paper about a year before and it had gone into thousands and thousands and thousands of pounds—so there was just no way I could do anything like that."

A respondent whose husband was suffering from a long-term incurable sickness had struggled to receive the benefits to which she thought she was entitled as sole carer. She had corresponded with the local authority, written to the newspapers and her MP but failed to achieve her objective. She considered the possibility of pursuing the case through court but decided against it, largely on the grounds of cost:

"There was no way I would have got legal aid for that. If I'd got plenty of money I would have gone ahead with it . . . Money was the main reason [for not going ahead]. It could have cost thousands for the court case. I didn't feel as if I could have represented him—I would definitely have had to have a solicitor to do that. I don't think I would have been educated enough to cope. Answering questions and that would have been nae problem, but I don't think I would have been able to put his case over properly. I think they're so learned, some of that lot in the courts."

"It's just what you hear on television—if it goes to queen's counsel, they are people who charge quite phenomenal fees because they've got to take it on again from a solicitor. You're then beginning to think of quite an extraordinary amount of money. But I've no hard factual information at all: I just have this notion at the back of my mind that we're talking quite a lot of money."

Legal Aid and the "middle income trap"

Concern about legal costs was often inextricably linked with complaints about the perceived lack of availability of legal aid for those with modest incomes. Several respondents in qualitative interviews made reference to the plight of "those in the middle"—people who were neither wealthy enough to contemplate taking legal advice with equanimity, nor poor enough to qualify for legal aid. Representatives from this group felt themselves to be particularly disadvantaged in the search for justice. For example:

"The courts are very important for the people who need them. It's important to know that it's there behind you, in case you have a problem, that there's some remedy, because I'm sure it would be soul-destroying if you felt there was something legally wrong in your life that you couldn't get sorted out. I'm sure costs put people off. I'm sure there's a lot of people out there with grievances that could be dealt with through the courts, whether it's against a big company or whether it's a divorce or family law or whatever. And it'll be the fees. It'll be the lack of support from the legal aid system. It's the in-between—it's the people that are not well enough off to pay it themselves, and the people who are not poor enough to actually get the legal aid. It's the ones actually in between. And that batch of people in between seems to be getting bigger, because the legal aid system seems to be getting tougher to get."

"When I had a problem with my husband's ex-wife I went straight to a CAB and a legal aid solicitor because I had no income. It's easy if you have no money. You go to a CAB and get help. But on a decent salary, forget it. It is impossible for people in the middle of society, which can't be what anybody ever intended."

"I would have to pay if I went to a solicitor. I don't have the luxury of knowing well, 'I'll just send a solicitor's letter here, there and everywhere.' I would have to think about that, I would have to pay for it. I think there really is a problem here. There's an unfairness to that. If you don't work, if you're on income support you can afford this system, and if you've got any money at all, you can't afford this system. There's an iniquity there, and some people say the poorest people can't afford the law. It's not the poorest, it's the people just above the poorest people!"

"If you're unemployed it's no problem to walk up to a lawyer. In fact they do it all the time because it's not costing them. But if you're a guy that's earning £200 a week, for me to go to a lawyer—I'm caught out in a Catch-22."

In at least one case, however, the problem was expressed rather differently. From the view of a person caught in the middle-income trap, Legal Aid appeared to be *too* freely available for legal advice in minor disputes:

"To be honest I think Legal Aid is too open. I think it makes it too easy for people at the bottom end and the top end to abuse the system. If people were in the situation I was, where it was going to cost them every penny to pursue it, then they wouldn't pursue it. All these petty suing for wee bumps on cars would be thought of a lot more seriously if they knew that they might be hit for a couple of thousand pounds bill at the end of it. I think Legal Aid is too liberal from that point of view."

These quotes highlight the question raised in Chapter 1 about whether the thrust of legal aid policy should be to ensure that the poor with legal aid do not get an unfair advantage over middle income groups, or whether it should be to address the problem of how middle income groups can access civil justice.

Despite the concerns expressed about the cost of legal advice by those who *did not* go to a solicitor to seek assistance in resolving their problem, anxiety about cost clearly did not afflict everyone. As will be seen below, many respondents went directly to solicitors for legal advice about their problem, either because the matter was so serious that they were prepared to risk the cost, or because they knew, or were told by friends and relatives, that they would be entitled to receive legal aid. These experiences are discussed in the next section.

THE ADVISED: OBTAINING ADVICE ABOUT RESOLVING PROBLEMS

Just under two in every three people who had experienced a non-trivial justiciable problem obtained some kind of outside advice about how to resolve their problem. Although most people sought advice only after having tried first to resolve the problem by direct contact with the other side, a minority obtained advice directly and without any prior contact with their opponent.

Those experiencing justiciable problems used an extremely wide range of advice sources for their first port of call (Figure 3.2). The single most common first point of contact was a solicitor, with three in ten of those obtaining advice going first to solicitors (29%, representing 19% of all those experiencing a non-trivial justiciable problem). The next most common first point of contact was a Citizens Advice Bureau with just under one in five(17%) of those obtaining advice going first to the CAB (11% of all those with a justiciable problem). Apart from these two major advice sources, the most common places to which respondents turned for advice were the police (9% of advice seekers) a trade union or staff association (6%) and a department in the local council (5%). This pattern of first advice sources is almost identical to that found in England and Wales, as are the proportions of advice seekers going to the different sources.

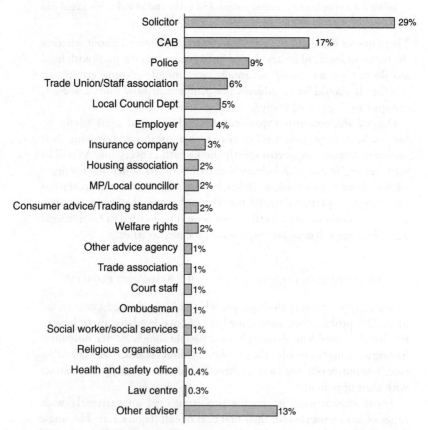

Figure 3.2 First source of advice (Base = all those obtaining advice 304 weighted).

Over half of all those respondents who obtained advice went to only one advice source (57%), and a little over one third (38%) took advice from two or three sources. Only a tiny proportion of people went to more than three different advisers (5%). These figures are comparable with England and Wales, although a higher proportion of respondents in Scotland did not go beyond their first adviser (57% as compared with 49% in England and Wales).

The list of second advisers is almost as varied as the first, and again the most common second adviser was a solicitor in private practice, followed by a local council department.

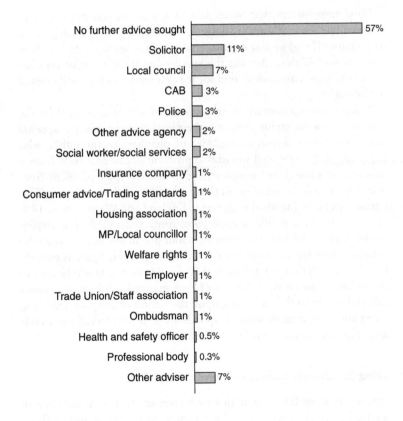

Figure 3.3 Second source of advice (Base = all those obtaining advice 304 weighted).

In cases when more than one adviser was contacted, the most common, but by no means the only pattern, was for people to go first to a CAB and then to contact a solicitor for further advice. Of those respondents whose first contact was with a CAB about one in three took no further advice (33%) while another third (33%) took advice from a solicitor (these figures are identical to the English results)[5]. About eight percent of those who went first to the CAB went on to take advice from the local council, about six percent went on to a welfare rights officer, about four percent went to the consumer advice centre or trading standards office, a similar proportion went to another advice agency, and about four percent went on to obtain advice from their MP or local councillor.

Most respondents who went first to a solicitor did not go on to obtain advice from a second adviser. About eight in ten of those going to solicitors (79%) sought no further advice (as compared with 67% in England and Wales). Among the small minority who went on elsewhere the most common second source of advice was the local council or the police.

Taking into account *all* of the sources of advice contacted by the respondents while trying to resolve their justiciable problem, it appears that a little over one-quarter (29%) of members of the public who experienced a non-trivial justiciable problem obtained advice from a solicitor *at some point* about trying to resolve their problem (representing almost one-half of all those who obtained any advice). This figure is virtually identical with that in England and Wales. About 14% of members of the public *at some point* contacted a CAB about trying to resolve the problem, representing about one in five of all those who sought advice (22%) about their problem. Again this figure is entirely consistent with that in England and Wales. However, as will be seen in the following sections, the choice of both first and subsequent advisers differed significantly depending upon the nature of the problem being faced and the extent to which respondents were able to call on friends and relatives who could offer professional advice.

Using friends and relatives with professional skills

About one in ten (11%) of all those who obtained advice turned first to a friend or relative who was also a professional adviser and in about

[5] On the face of it this seems to be inconsistent with the results of research by Carol Miller, op. cit 1999.

half of these cases the friend or relative was a solicitor, representing some 17% of those whose first adviser was a solicitor. In contrast with the English data, respondents did not use friends and relatives among the police, or local councils and none of the respondents in Scotland who went first to the CAB said that their contact had been a friend or relative.

> "I think if they didn't have their own lawyer most people would probably ask friends—you know, depending on what age they were, I think they'd probably ask friends; family; get a recommendation. In Scotland particularly I think there's a lot of personal recommendations. I think for law firms there's a kind of—'Oh, well, he seemed quite good with such and such', or 'He did this for me', or whatever. And round the area here you've got quite a lot of the lawyers, particular ones that specialise in the criminal cases, and undoubtedly word gets round who they are. 'Oh, see so-and-so, because he got me off six months'! There's no doubt that goes on quite a bit."

Choice of adviser: People type and problem type

An analysis of choice of adviser in relation to demographic characteristics reveals some interesting differences in relation to first adviser. For example, there was a significant difference in the use of solicitors as first advisers depending on income. Respondents with incomes of below £10,000 were significantly less likely to seek initial advice from a solicitor than those in other income brackets. Similarly, they were significantly more likely to seek advice in the first instance from a CAB (Figure 3.3)[6]. These results are different from those in England and Wales where it was found that there was little difference between income bands in their choice of first adviser. However, when we look at *all advice* obtained about trying to resolve the problem, and not just in relation to first advisers, the picture changes. In analysing all sources of advice obtained to try and resolve the problem, Figure 3.5 shows that there is a suggestion of a rough U-shaped distribution and a significant difference between use of solicitors between those with household incomes of £10,000 or less and those with household incomes of between £32,000 and £41,000. Those on the lowest incomes who obtained any advice about resolving their problem were as likely to obtain advice from a solicitor at some point as those on the highest incomes. This fact is important in that it suggests that the effect of existing legal aid provision is to make it possible for individuals on the

[6] See SCC study, p 17, op cit.

lowest incomes to have access to legal advice with at least the same frequency as those on higher incomes (see discussion of results of multivariate analysis in Chapter 4 for further discussion).

A notable feature of advice-seeking behaviour in relation to income is that although the heaviest use of the CAB as first advice source was made by those on the lowest incomes, only the highest earners in the main sample failed to make any appreciable use of CAB as a first source of advice (Figure 3.4). These results are again broadly similar to the English data, although in all income brackets *over* £10,000 the use made of the CAB as a first adviser was *lower* in Scotland than in England. Looking at all sources of advice, we find that among the lowest earners, over one in three consulted a CAB at some point about their problem (37% of those obtaining advice with incomes below £10,000). Among those with incomes of between £10,000–£19,999 about 17% of those obtaining advice used the CAB; among those with incomes of between £20,000–£31,999 a similar proportion (16%) used the CAB, and the proportion falls slightly to 14% for those on incomes of between £32,000–£40,999. However, among respondents with incomes of £41,000 or more, only seven percent of those obtaining advice went to the CAB. These figures indicate the fact that there is a demand for free advice about justiciable matters among most income groups and that such advice is currently being made available and being used across a wide income spectrum, although as compared with the results in England it seems that less heavy use is made of the CAB by those with household incomes above £10,000. It also shows that for the poorest income groups, the first step in seeking advice is most frequently to visit a CAB.

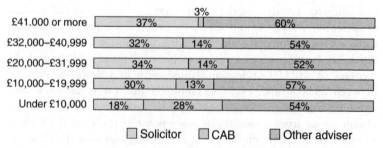

Figure 3.4 First adviser in relation to respondents' income (Base = all who obtained advice 304 weighted).

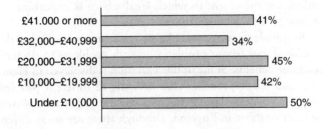

Figure 3.5 Advice obtained from a solicitor at any point while resolving problem in relation to respondents' income (Base = all those who obtained advice 304 weighted)

Education did not appear to be significantly associated with either choice of first adviser or whether advice was obtained from a solicitor at any point about the problem, nor, as will be discussed later, did it appear to be related to whether or not advice would be obtained *at all* about the problem.

The propensity to obtain advice from a solicitor or other adviser, however, did vary substantially between different problem types as is illustrated in Figure 3.6. Those *least* likely to seek advice were respondents facing consumer problems, benefit problems and other tribunal matters, and money problems. Although this is broadly consistent with the findings in England and Wales, Figure 3 shows that in general advice seeking was somewhat higher in Scotland for most problem types and that there were notable differences between the Scots and English results in one or two areas. For example, victims of accidental injury and those with landlord problems in Scotland were *more* likely to seek advice than their English counterparts,

As well as variation between problem types in the propensity to obtain advice at all, there were also immediately evident differences in the *type* of advisers to whom people turned when faced with certain problems. For example, solicitors and other legal advisers were the most frequent first contact point for those with problems relating to divorce and other family matters, underlining the perceived importance of these problems to those who experience them and the current significance of legal advice in seeking to resolve such matters. Solicitors were also the most frequent first point of contact for respondents who suffered accidental injury or work-related health problems, again indicating the extent to which legal advice is important in seeking a remedy for these misfortunes.

Respondents were most likely to go first to a CAB when dealing with landlord and tenant problems or with problems to do with employment or benefits. Some of this variation is displayed in Figures 3.7 and 3.8, and the approaches characteristic of different problem types is explored in detail later in the next chapter. The patterns are again very similar to those in England, although there are some differences. For example, in Scotland solicitors were less frequently consulted about employment problems, owning property or tribunal matters, and more likely than in England to be consulted about landlord and tenant problems.

Delay before obtaining advice

All respondents were asked about how long after the problem started they contacted their first adviser. This had to be slightly modified for some problem types, such as divorce. There was some variation in the length of time taken by respondents to obtain advice after the problem started, although the majority of respondents appeared to have acted quite promptly. About one-third of those who took advice did so as

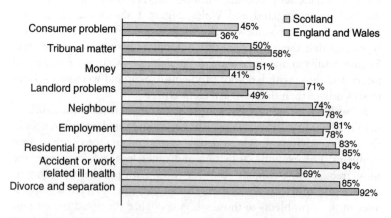

Figure 3.6 Percentage obtaining advice by problem type in Scotland (Base = All respondents 472 weighted) and in England and Wales (Base = All respondents 1134 weighted).

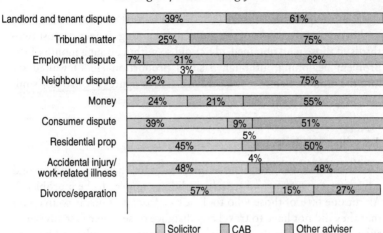

Figure 3.7 First adviser by problem type (Base = all who obtained advice 304 weighted).

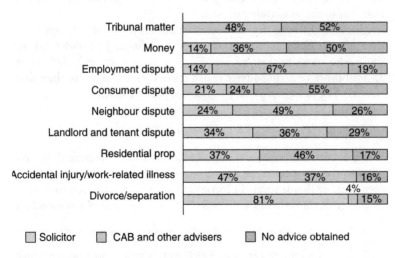

Figure 3.8 Advice from solicitors and other advisers at any time to resolve problem by type of problem (Base = 472 weighted cases).

soon as the problem started (32%), and a further 18% took advice within one or two weeks of the problem beginning. In fact, almost two-thirds of those who obtained advice did so within about a month of the problem beginning, although a small proportion (13%) waited six months or more before seeking advice. These figures are broadly similar to the English approach to speed of advice-seeking.

Travelling to advisers

Most respondents (about three-quarters) met their first and second advisers face to face, and travelling did not appear to be a problem[7]. About one fifth of those who took advice from an outside source said that they did not have to travel any distance to see their first adviser (a slightly lower figure than in England). Among those who did have to travel, most had a journey of *less* than five miles, although a small minority travelled considerable distances (about one percent of those who obtained advice had to travel more than 50 miles). This suggests that for most respondents using advisers at the time of the survey, geographical accessibility of advisers was not a problem. This was confirmed in qualitative interviews in which complaints about accessibility of free legal advice related to opening times and waiting times of advice agencies, and complaints about inaccessibility of legal advice related to cost, not to the availability of outlets[8].

All but a tiny minority of those respondents using advisers spoke to their adviser either in person or on the telephone. Just under half of those who spoke to their adviser did so once or twice only and about 17% of those receiving advice spoke more than ten times to their first adviser. The pattern was very similar for second advisers.

Pathways to advice

When asked what made the respondent think of contacting their first adviser, the most frequent answers were that it was the respondent's own idea, or that it seemed obvious (55%); that it had been suggested by a friend/relative/work colleague (17%); or because the respondent

---

[7] It should be noted here, however, that the population in the most remote areas of Scotland was not covered in the screening survey.

[8] This is consistent with a study published by the Scottish Office Central Research Unit in 1994 (Anne Millar and Sue Morris, *Legal Services in Scotland: Consumer Survey 1992*, Legal Studies Research Findings No. 1, The Scottish Office, 1994).

had had experience of a similar situation (7%). Respondents' accounts of how they found their adviser varied depending on the type of adviser. Where CABx were concerned, respondents mostly seemed to know where they were located although there was difficulty in establishing opening times and getting appointments. In the case of solicitors, respondents asked among friends and work colleagues, walked into the nearest office to where they lived or worked, or used the Yellow Pages[9]. The following are typical examples of the path to advice:

"I would look up the Yellow Pages. I think most people would. A lot of peoples' first contact with a solicitor is maybe when they're buying a house, or whatever, you know, and you hear it from somebody else, 'Well, she was quite good, or he was quite good or whatever'. I'd probably look up Yellow Pages and see what was handy."

"I think lawyers are quite freely accessible at the end of the day, unless they're trying to reduce legal aid, which is an entirely different thing. They're available through Yellow Pages. There's a list of lawyers in there. When I was trying to get different lawyers' opinions, it wasn't a problem phoning up several companies and going, 'Can I speak to a lawyer, please, I want to clarify something,' They were quite free and easy with their information as well, I didn't feel like it was time is money sort of thing, you know? So I don't think there's a problem with that."

Reference was also made to free interviews with solicitors and the availability of no-win, no-fee arrangements, which appeared to be quite well understood among respondents to the main survey in Scotland.

"I've seen it in the Yellow Pages. Nowadays you actually will find lawyer ads with your first interview free. I've seen the ads on the TV—'Have you had an accident? Are you suffering because of this? Call us.' You know—no win no fee type of thing. I found [the free interview] excellent because it was a very informal thing. The fact that you can get in there and talk to someone. It's a bit like the chap on the radio except you've got it all to yourself, and your question gets answered."

---

[9] This accords very much with previous studies in Scotland which established that 15–32% of respondents had a family lawyer or had used one before, 29–47% were recommended a solicitor by a friend or relative or simply happened to know a solicitor and 4–30% found their lawyer from the Yellow pages or from passing their office by chance. See Hughes Commission on Legal Services in Scotland Vol II Table 30 p.63 (1980), Scottish Consumer Council Study (1995) and System Three Survey for the Scottish Law Society (1998).

Another useful pathway to advice was by using friends and relatives whose job was the provision of advice. As discussed earlier in the chapter, a substantial minority of professional first advisers was actually friends or relatives of the respondent. Interviews illustrated how those experiencing a problem might call up a friend or relative who was a solicitor or other adviser and pick their brains about how to deal with the matter. In some cases this resulted in the friend actually taking some action, such as writing a letter on the respondent's behalf without charge, or taking on the case with an understanding that only a minimal charge might be made

It is important to realise that many of those who obtained advice did so from only one source and sometimes that source was not particularly helpful in suggesting a route for resolution of the problem. Thus within the category of "the advised", as among "self-helpers", there are groups with very different experiences who had access to advice of varying intensity and sophistication.

What is wanted from advisers

Respondents who sought help from advisers were principally looking for advice about how to solve their problem (about three out of four (73%) of those who sought advice said that this was what they wanted) and, to a lesser extent, advice about their legal rights (46%). About one in three of those who obtained advice said that they wanted advice about court procedures for dealing with the problem (34%) and almost one in four (23%) wanted advice about their financial position. A small minority was looking for someone who could represent them in a court or tribunal hearing (9%). This pattern was repeated for second advisers as well. It therefore seems that although solving the problem is a priority, in seeking advice many people are looking specifically for information about their legal rights. As the discussion in Chapter 4 demonstrates, the requirement for information of a specifically legal nature varied substantially between different problem categories.

Advice received

In over eight out of ten cases where advice was obtained (83%), the first adviser thought that something could be done about the problem. However, the effect of being told by a first adviser that nothing could be done about the problem, unsurprisingly, had a substantial impact on subsequent behaviour. Of those who were told that nothing could be done about their problem, a little under half (43%) did *not* obtain any further advice (see Figure 5.1 Chapter 5). Among those who did go on to obtain further advice, the majority went to solicitors, CABx, the local council and the police.

First advisers gave advice about procedures, for example how to deal with summonses or court procedures (51%), about legal rights (45%), and about the financial position of the respondent (21%). In a little under one-third of cases, however, first advisers did not offer advice about any of these matters

The type of advice received from the most common first sources varied depending on who was providing the advice. So, for example, the most common advice given by the CAB was to contact the other side involved in the problem (90%), or to obtain help from another organisation (27%). In only a minority of cases did the CAB suggest threatening the other side with legal action (11%) or taking legal proceedings (13%). Advice to go to mediation or an ombudsman occurred very rarely (2% and 3% of those taking advice from the CAB respectively).

The police as first advisers most often told people to seek advice from elsewhere (64%), or to go to court (50%). They also suggested contacting the other side involved in the problem in about one-third of cases (38%). The most common advice given by local councils was to contact the other side (79%), to threaten legal proceedings (29%) or to seek advice from elsewhere (26%). Unsurprisingly, the most common advice given by solicitors was to contact the other side (41%), to threaten the other side with legal proceedings (42%) or to go to court (26%). Solicitors recommended trying mediation in about 3% of cases.

The very low rate at which either CABx or solicitors advised clients to consider mediation or other alternatives to traditional methods of dispute resolution was consistent with the picture in England. This demonstrates the rather minimal impact that ADR has had to date on the thinking of advisers and, therefore, on the strategies adopted by the public for dealing with disputes.

Referrals

Those who sought advice first from a CAB were referred on to a variety of second advisers. In a little under half the cases where CABx made a referral this was to a solicitor (46%). Almost one in five cases of referrals were to a consumer advice centre (18%), and in about 10% of cases where a CAB made a referral this was to the local council. Legal advisers were less likely than CABx to refer clients on, but when they did, it was most often to a department of the local council.

First advisers other than the CAB or solicitors were also quite likely to refer respondents on to other organisations. Most commonly other advisers suggested contacting a solicitor (20%), the local council (8%), a law centre (8%) or the police (6%). These patterns are broadly similar to those found in England and Wales, although there was a slight tendency for respondents to be referred more frequently to local council departments than in England and Wales[10].

Assistance

Those respondents who had contacted an adviser were asked what kind of assistance they had received. For example, whether the adviser had contacted the other side involved in the problem on the respondent's behalf, whether the adviser had negotiated with the other side on the respondent's behalf, whether the adviser had made contact or helped to make contact with another organisation, or whether the adviser had accompanied the respondent to any kind of court or tribunal proceeding. In a little under half of the cases (44%), first advisers gave no assistance of this kind. The most common type of assistance provided by first advisers was to contact the other side on the respondent's behalf (40% of cases), to negotiate on the respondents behalf (20% of cases), to contact another person or organisation who might be able to provide help (12% of cases) or to help the respondent make contact with another person or organisation (8%). In about four percent of cases the first adviser accompanied the respondent to a court or tribunal. This pattern is virtually identical with that found in England and Wales.

Comparing the type of help offered by solicitors, CABx and all other types of advisers, it appears that CABx were *less likely* than solicitors or all other advisers together to provide these kinds of direct assistance (74% of those going first to a CAB received no help of this kind compared with 47% of those going to other advisers and 19% of those going to legal advisers). This finding is consistent with the CAB philosophy of empowerment. Legal advisers were much more likely than

---

[10] For a fuller, but consistent, analysis of referrals from advice agencies to solicitors see C. Miller, *Referrals between Advice Agencies and Solicitors*, The Scottish Office Central Research unit, 1999 at p. 28.

other types of advisers to contact the other side involved in the problem or negotiate with the other side. They were also much more likely to accompany respondents to a court or tribunal. When CABx gave assistance of this kind it was most frequently to help the respondent make contact with another person or organisation that might be able to assist in resolving the problem. Non-CAB non-legal advisers (for example local authorities, the police, local councillors) were also more likely than CABx to make contact with the other side on the respondent's behalf (this occurred in 40% of cases), to negotiate with the other side (16%) or to contact another person or organisation on the respondent's behalf (14%). Again these figures are virtually identical to those found in the England and Wales study.

These findings indicating the kind of help that is currently available to members of the public with justiciable problems from the advice sector and from private legal practice has a direct bearing on policy discussions concerning the future scope of the community legal service in Scotland.

Helpfulness of advisers

Levels of satisfaction with first advisers were very similar among those who used CABx, solicitors, and trades unions or staff associations. Among first advisers, the greatest satisfaction expressed was with advice from trades unions or staff associations, with 60% of respondents who used them saying that they had been very helpful. Of those who sought advice first from solicitors, just under half (48%) said that they had found the advice very helpful. CABx were rated as very helpful by 41% of those who had obtained initial advice from there and the police were rated as very helpful by 43% of those went there first for advice. These figures are very similar to those in England and Wales, although satisfaction with solicitors was somewhat higher in England and Wales with 56% rating their solicitor as very helpful.

When asked whether they would recommend first advisers to others in a similar situation, respondents were generally quite positive. There were however some differences depending on the type of adviser. Among those whose first adviser was a solicitor or other legal adviser some 13% said that they would probably or definitely *not* recommend others to seek advice from that source. Among those whose first adviser was a CAB about 17% said that they would probably or definitely *not* recommend the CAB as a source of advice and a similar proportion

(18%) of those using other non-legal advisers said that they would probably or definitely *not* recommend their advice source to others.

The degree of satisfaction with advisers expressed by respondents appears to increase with the level of help offered by the adviser. When advisers contacted the other side on the respondent's behalf, this was felt to be helpful or very helpful in 80% of cases. When advisers negotiated on the respondent's behalf 85% thought this was helpful or very helpful (most saying very helpful) and similar levels of satisfaction were expressed when advisers contacted another person or organisation on the respondent's behalf. When advisers helped respondents to contact another organisation by making an appointment or giving a list of people to approach some 98% of respondents found this to be helpful or very helpful (mostly very helpful). These figures are indistinguishable from those in England and Wales.

Expectations of advisers

Information gathered during in-depth interviews fills in some of the detail on expectations of advisers and also goes some way to explain why many of those who received advice nonetheless failed to achieve a resolution of their problem. Although over six in ten respondents sought and obtained advice from at least one source in order to try and resolve their problem, it is also clear that over half of those who obtained advice (58%) nonetheless failed to achieve a satisfactory resolution of their problem.

Obtaining advice does not in itself ensure any kind of success in dispute resolution either through legal or other procedures. A complicated mix of factors influences the outcome of different kinds of problems and disputes and this is explored in Chapter 4. However, in-depth interviews with respondents raised issues about the mismatch between public need for advice and assistance and what was sometimes on offer, in particular the perceived inadequacy of mere "advice". Several respondents explained the futility of being told to write letters or make telephone calls when they felt that they lacked the necessary confidence, vocabulary, and basic knowledge about rights and remedies. What people need when they go for advice will depend on the type of problem that they are experiencing and, importantly, their own personal competencies (e.g. confidence, verbal skills, literacy) as well as their emotional state. Many respondents who were relatively well-educated and knowledgeable felt a need for information about how to enforce their rights—where to go, who to write to and what exactly their rights were in certain situations. For those respondents the rovision of information met their perceived needs. For many others, however, the provision of information and guidance about how to take a problem forward did not meet perceived needs. What was wanted was someone to take over and deal with the problem—to make difficult phone calls or to write difficult letters. Moreover, some respondents were so emotionally drained by the worry about the problem that even if they would normally feel competent and confident, at that particular time and in those particular circumstances they were not able to manage dealing with the problem. They did not want to be *empowered*, they wanted to be saved. When respondents commonly talk about abandoning or giving up because of "the hassle" involved in trying to deal with a problem, this simple colloquialism actually obscures what is in many cases an important form of paralysis. For example:

> "I was looking for somebody to take me by the hands and lead me . . . I was totally exasperated. I didnae know what I was doing: I had never been in this situation before and nobody was forthcoming with any kind of help. You know, I found out eventually that I could have claimed for a lot of different things and nobody had ever told me about these things . . . it took a long long time to get these things for him. So . . . basically I was left with this wee disabled boy and nobody was gonna' help me."

The striking messages that emerges from interviews with members of the public about the need for advice and active assistance in dealing with justiciable problems has important implications for policy on the provision of advice and assistance.

CONCLUSION

The survey provides ample evidence that when faced with a justiciable problem the overwhelming majority of members of the public in Scotland tried to resolve the problem directly by contacting the other person or organisation involved. Those who went on to obtain advice generally did so only after having tried a direct approach.

A very small minority of "lumpers" took no action whatsoever to resolve their problem and members of this group were less likely to have obtained outside advice about any problem in the past than respondents who had taken some action to resolve their recent problem. This suggests that in Scotland there may be a persistent tendency to "lump" problems, stemming from a sense of fatalism or powerlessness and this was to some extent borne out by qualitative interviews in which respondents referred the cost and trouble that flow from involvement with legal action and a perception that little could be done to solve problems and disputes.

About one in three respondents adopted a self-help strategy. Self-helpers who attempted to resolve their problem without taking outside advice were often required to show determination and creativity in order to secure a satisfactory resolution. Self-help strategies ranged from brief attempts to achieve a resolution to sustained campaigns. Many were defeated in their attempts and gave up without ever seeking any assistance in their efforts. The experiences of self-helpers provide a wealth of information about barriers to obtaining advice such as inaccessibility of good quality advice about legal rights; fear of legal costs and some negative experiences or beliefs about legal advisers and the legal system. Practical problems in obtaining advice from CABx and other advice agencies provided a regular explanation for failure to obtain advice when self-help strategies had failed, as did fear of the cost of seeking legal advice from solicitors.

Nearly two in three respondents who had experienced a non-trivial justiciable problem obtained advice about resolving their problem and the majority did so having first tried to resolve the problem by themselves. A very wide range of advisers was used but by far the most common were solicitors in private practice and CABx. Over half of all those respondents who obtained advice went to only one advice source and most of the remainder went to two or three sources. These figures are comparable with England and Wales, although a higher proportion of respondents in Scotland did not go beyond their first adviser (57% as compared with 49% in England and Wales). Taking into account all sources of advice contacted by respondents while trying to resolve their justiciable problems, it appears that a little over one-quarter of members of the public obtained advice from a solicitor at some point about trying to resolve their problem (representing almost one-half of all those who obtained any advice). An analysis of use of solicitors by income showed that those on the lowest incomes were as likely to obtain advice from a solicitor at some point as those on the highest incomes. The analysis suggests a U shaped curve in which middle-income respondents used solicitors *less* than either those on lower incomes or those who were better off. This is important since it suggests that the effect of existing legal aid provision in Scotland is to make it possible for those in the lowest incomes to have access to legal advice with at least the same frequency as those on higher incomes.

The propensity to obtain advice and the choice of advisers varied significantly depending on the type of problem being faced. Issues relating to divorce and family matters, accidental injury, ownership of residential property, and landlord and tenant disputes were the *most* likely to be taken to solicitors, while matters relating to benefits, money, and employment disputes were the *least* likely to be taken to solicitors. These findings to some extent differ from those in England and Wales where respondents were more likely than those in Scotland to consult solicitors about problems relating to employment and ownership of residential property, and less likely to consult solicitors about landlord and tenant problems.

The results presented in this Chapter also indicate a widespread feeling of ignorance about legal rights that exists across most social groups. Different levels of personal confidence and resources will affect what can be done with information and advice, but the need for easily accessible free or low cost advice is profound. There is a demand for free advice among most income groups and such advice is currently being made available and being used across a wide income spectrum. This fact is important for policy decisions about the shape and scope of any new Scottish community legal service. The current level of demand for free advice appears to exceed the resources available. The accounts of difficulties in accessing free advice from CABx and other advice agencies contrasts sharply with the ease with which advice can be obtained from solicitors if members of the public in Scotland can afford to pay for such advice and are willing to do so.

Respondents reported few difficulties in knowing where to find advisers or in travelling to meet them. Most said that they either did not have to travel at all or had a journey of less than five miles although in fairness, it should be remembered that the survey excluded the most remote areas of Scotland. However, it suggests that despite recent concerns among the legal profession as to the continued viability of legal advice and assistance and civil legal aid work, for most of the population there is still a good network to act as the basis for a Scottish community legal service.

Finally, interviews with respondents revealed the mismatch between the public need for free advice and assistance and what was sometimes on offer, in particular the perceived inadequacy of information and advice when what was needed was more positive assistance. CABx were less likely than solicitors or all other advisers to provide direct assistance such as contacting the other side or negotiating on the respondent's behalf. They were also extremely unlikely to recommend threatening the other side with legal action or taking legal proceedings. Given the behaviour and intransigence of some opponents described by respondents in this chapter, it is unsurprising that by the time members of the public seek help they feel a need for active assistance and sometimes for credible threats to be made. These matters are again relevant to the provision of advice and assistance under any future Scottish community legal service.

4

The Response to Problems of Different Types

As the last Chapter made clear, the way that members of the public approached the resolution of problems and disputes varied substantially according to the type of problem being faced. In this Chapter, therefore, the discussion focuses on a more detailed description of how respondents dealt with problems of different types, highlighting variations in approach and the features distinctive to citizens against whom some action is being taken (potential defenders)[1]. An important factor in the approach to problem resolution was the extent to which different groups sought and obtained advice about their problem, and the chapter therefore concludes with a discussion of the results of a multivariate analysis which identifies the factors associated with obtaining advice about justiciable problems. In this chapter we present relatively detailed analyses of the following problems types:

- consumer problems
- money problems (excluding benefits)
- divorce/separation problems
- neighbour problems
- problems with landlords
- employment problems
- accidental injury or work related ill health.

The discussion is limited to these specific groups because the number of respondents in the other problem type subgroups is too small for analysis. Even within the above subgroups, the number of cases available for analysis is too small for a detailed discussion. However, broad trends have been presented and attention has been drawn to instances where the results are consistent with those in England and Wales. In relation

---

[1] For the purpose of this and later analyses problems were re-classified into narrower more consistent groupings than the broad categories used in the screening questionnaire (see the discussion at the end of Chapter 2).

to each problem type there is a brief discussion of respondents' propensity to obtain advice, the purpose of advice seeking, advice received, and satisfaction with advice. In addition, some brief information is given at the end of the first section of the chapter about the approach to resolution of problems relating to benefits, schooling, disputes concerning residential property, and when the respondent was having action taken *against them* by another.

CONSUMER PROBLEMS (FAULTY GOODS AND SERVICES)

About half of the complaints within this broad problem category were against shops, mail order companies, travel agents and holiday companies (53%); about one in five complaints was against tradesmen such as plumbers and electricians (22%); and a smaller minority was complaints about professional services (11%). The remainder was spread across a wide range of persons and organisations. Although these figures are broadly consistent with England and Wales, a higher proportion of complaints in Scotland was about professional services (11% of consumer problems as opposed to five percent in England and Wales).

As with most categories of problem, the overwhelming majority of those who experienced a consumer problem took some action to deal with it. Only three percent of those with consumer problems said that they had taken no steps to resolve the problem.

Consumer problems were the most likely of all problem types to be handled directly by respondents without obtaining any outside advice[2]. Just over half of all those interviewed about consumer problems said that they had dealt with the problem themselves (52%). This figure can be compared with 49% of those who experienced money problems, 14% of those with employment problems and 11% of those who had experienced divorce or separation problems

The most common strategy adopted for consumer problems by self-helpers was for the respondent to contact the other side to seek to resolve the problem directly (94%) and a sizeable minority (18%) said that they had threatened the other side with legal action. As will be seen in the next chapter, these self-help strategies had a relatively high rate of success when members of the public were dealing with consumer problems.

---

[2] See SCC study, *Civil Disputes in Scotland*, 1997, (op. cit.), p.14.

Nearly half (45%) of those with problems relating to consumer goods or services obtained outside advice about solving the problem. This was one of the *lowest* rates of advice-seeking of all problem types. For example, 81% of those with employment problems obtained advice about resolving their problem, 85% of those with divorce or separation problems obtained advice, 84% of those suffering an accidental injury or work-illness obtained advice, and 74% of those experiencing problems with neighbours obtained advice about trying to resolve the problem.

Most of those with consumer problems who took advice went to one source only (84%), and the remainder went to two or three advisers. Among those who sought advice about their consumer problem, the first point of contact was most often a solicitor (40%), which is rather different from the situation in England and Wales where the most common first source of advice for consumer problems was a CAB (30%) and only about one in five went first to a solicitor. In fact, less than one in ten (9%) of respondents in Scotland facing consumer problems said that they went *first* to a CAB for advice. About nine percent went to consumer advice or trading standards departments, a similar proportion said that they first took advice from an insurance company and about seven percent took advice from court staff about their problem.

Of all those who took advice about a consumer problem, a little under one-half obtained legal advice at some point about their problem and about twelve percent contacted a CAB about the problem[3]. Some seven percent of those obtaining advice about a consumer problem said that they went directly to obtain advice from court staff. These results indicate a significantly *greater* propensity to obtain legal advice about consumer problems in Scotland than in England and Wales where only eighteen percent of those experiencing consumer problems obtained advice about resolving the problem.

Most respondents with consumer problems said that the idea of making contact with their first source of advice was their own (57%) and almost one in five said that they had done the same on a previous similar occasion, which is a significantly higher proportion than in England and Wales. Suggestions from friends and relatives were acted upon in around 16% of cases, which is rather lower than the English results.

[3] These figures are slightly higher for solicitors and slightly lower for CABx than those found in the SCC study. It may be partly attributable to the high proportion of service complaints in the present study and the high level of education among those reporting problems relating to goods and services.

Among people with consumer problems who took advice about dealing with the problem, more than nine in ten had already either been in contact with the other side or tried unsuccessfully to contact them before obtaining advice, demonstrating that that the overwhelming majority of people with consumer problems attempt to resolve the problem directly before obtaining advice about how to proceed and only seek advice once their own efforts to obtain redress have failed. Advice was generally obtained fairly soon after the problem started with a little under half of those obtaining advice doing so within one to two weeks of the start of the problem.

Consumer problems: Advice needs

What members of the public experiencing consumer problems were looking for from advisers, initially at least, was advice about how to solve the problem (about seven out of ten mentioned this) and to a lesser extent, advice about their legal rights (47% of respondents with consumer problems saying that this was what they wanted). About one in three wanted advice about dealing with court procedures, and about five per cent wanted someone to represent them in a court hearing.

Consumer problems: Advice received

Most people obtaining advice about a consumer problem were told that something could be done about the problem (86%) and the most common advice given was to contact the other side to try and resolve the problem (46%) or to obtain help from another organisation (22%). About 15% were told to threaten the other side with legal action and a small minority was advised to begin court proceedings (7%). In no cases were respondents advised to take their case to an ombudsman or to mediation or conciliation, demonstrating the lack of impact that these alternatives to traditional methods of dispute resolution have had on the advisers' thinking.

Consumer problems: Satisfaction with advice

Members of the public experiencing consumer problems expressed a relatively high degree of satisfaction with the advice received from their first point of contact. About half thought the advice had been very helpful and a further 29% thought the advice was fairly helpful. The remainder thought that the advice was not very helpful (10%) or not helpful at all (12%)

DIVORCE AND SEPARATION PROBLEMS

This category includes both cases relating to divorce proceedings and also other problems in relationships between partners, for example disputes over the division of property and child maintenance, disputes over contact with children and spousal violence. Among those included in this category, some 30% were included because they had been involved in divorce proceedings during the previous five years; 36% were included having reported a dispute with their ex-partner in relation to family matters such as child maintenance, division of property or violence; and 28% were in dispute with their ex-partner in relation to children under the age of 18. Some six percent were in dispute with the Child Support Agency. As compared with England and Wales, a higher proportion in the Scots sample involved children and a lower proportion related to divorce proceedings.

Although the vast majority of those respondents experiencing divorce or separation problems took some action to resolve their problem, in common with other problem types a very small minority reported that they had done nothing to try and resolve the problems (4%). Although the difference is small, it is interesting to note that in England and Wales virtually no respondents reported having "lumped" a divorce or separation problem.

In common with the English results only a small proportion of Scottish respondents experiencing divorce or separation problems said that they had tried to deal with the matter themselves without taking advice at any point (11% which is similar to the figure in England of seven per cent). This figure can be compared with 52% of those experiencing consumer problems and 49% of those with money problems.

Most of this small group of self-helpers had some contact with their partner to seek to resolve the problem. When there was no contact in this group it was generally because there had been no attempt to contact the partner. The strategy adopted among self-helpers was generally simply to contact their partner or ex-partner directly to seek to resolve the dispute.

About 85% of those who had been divorced or who had problems to do with partners obtained advice about dealing with the matter. This is the highest rate of advice-seeking among all problem types, although only slightly higher than for accidental injury (84%) and problems to do with owning property (83%), and somewhat lower than the figure for divorce and separation problems in England and Wales (92%). The figure can be compared with 45% for consumer problems, 51% for money problems, and 74% for neighbour problems.

About half took advice from only one outside source (52%) although about 45% consulted two or three outside sources.

The pattern of advice-seeking among divorcees and those with relationship problems was rather different from other problem types. A much more limited range of advice sources was used and there was a much greater concentration on legal advice. The first point of contact was most often a solicitor, with about three in five respondents going *directly* to obtain legal advice from a solicitor (59%). The next most common first contact was with the police (17%), which is a rather different result from the situation in England and Wales where the police were the first advice contact in divorce and separation problems in only six percent of cases. This is a reflection of the number of cases involving violent and abusive relationships reported above in Chapter 2. CABx were the first destination for 15 percent of those with divorce and separation problems, which is somewhat lower than in England and Wales where about one in four went first for advice to a CAB.

Looking at all of those members of the public who experienced divorce and separation problems, just over eight out of ten obtained advice at some time from a solicitor in private practice (81%). About 17% were in contact with the police at some time in connection with the divorce or separation problem, and about 13% contacted a CAB at some time about the problem. This group had the highest rate of contact with legal advisers of all problem types and can be compared with 14% in employment cases, 14% for money problems, 34% in landlord problems, 25% in neighbour problems, 47% in accidental injury cases, and 21% for consumer problems. These figures are roughly similar to those in England and Wales, although in several categories of cases use of lawyers was somewhat higher in Scotland (landlord, money, consumer problems) and somewhat lower than in England for employment cases.

Most of those obtaining advice about divorce and separation problems had contacted their partner to try and resolve the problem before obtaining advice (82%), leaving a significant minority (18%) who apparently had made *no attempt* to resolve the problem before turning to outside advisers. Among those who had not contacted their partner about the problem most had made no attempt at contact.

Although about half of those obtaining advice about divorce and separation problems did so within one month of the problem emerging, the other half of these respondents often took quite a long time before obtaining advice. About one in four waited for more than six months before obtaining advice.

Advice wanted

In seeking initial advice there was a heavy emphasis on wanting advice about ways to solve the problem (63% said that they wanted this, among other things, from their first adviser), about legal rights (59%) about procedures (42% mentioned this), and advice about their financial position (39%). About 17% were looking specifically for someone to represent them in court proceedings. Although problem solving was mentioned by almost two-thirds of those with problems relating to divorce and separation, the high demand for advice about legal rights and procedures underlines the significance of legal advice in the resolution of matters concerning divorce and separation referred to in the previous chapter. The fact that such a high proportion of those involved in divorce and separation matters obtained legal advice is a reflection of a number of factors: the seriousness with which such matters are regarded by the parties involved; the current availability of public funding of legal advice for disputes related to the breakdown of relationships and arrangements over children and property for those with limited resources; and the willingness of others to bear the cost of obtaining legal advice.

Although the use of traditional court-based solutions to these problems and disputes is fundamental, there was a suggestion in the screening survey of a greater use of mediation in family cases in Scotland than was found in England and Wales. While respondents to the main survey appeared to have little experience of mediation, as reported in the previous chapter, data from the screening survey suggest that in Scotland nearly *one in four* problems relating to children under 18 were said to have been taken to mediation or conciliation. The equivalent proportion in England and Wales was only eight percent. However, in the light of the main survey responses these figures are not entirely convincing. It is possible that at the screening survey stage some respondents were making reference to attendance at marriage guidance counselling rather than mediation to settle disputes *following* the decision to divorce.

Divorce and separation: Advice obtained

A very high proportion of those seeking advice about divorce and separation problems were told by their first adviser that something could be done about the problem (85%). The most common course of action recommended by first advisers was to contact the other side (suggested by first advisers to 52% of those receiving advice), seek advice or help from elsewhere (30%), or go to court (26%). This is a slightly different approach to that found in England where the most common advice given by first advisers was to go to court (45% of those receiving advice) or to threaten the other side with legal action (suggested to 38% of those receiving advice).

In only a small minority of cases (7%) did a first adviser suggest that the respondent go to mediation or conciliation to try and seek a resolution of their divorce or separation problem. This is consistent with the position in England and Wales but tends to run counter to the suggestion in the screening survey of high use of mediation. It is also consistent with the findings of Chapter 5, which show only a tiny proportion of respondents who used mediation to resolve disputes relating to divorce and separation.

Divorce and separation: Satisfaction with advice

The level of satisfaction expressed with first advisers among respondents experiencing divorce and separation problems was slightly below average in comparison with other problem types. About one third (34%) said that they found the advice very helpful, and a similar proportion found it fairly helpful (37%). This is a somewhat lower level of satisfaction than expressed about first advisers who assisted with consumer problems or problems to do with owning property.

PROBLEMS WITH NEIGHBOURS

This category includes both owners of residential property and those living in rented accommodation who reported having experienced a problem with a neighbour during the survey period. In common with the findings in England and Wales, neighbour disputes represented the most prevalent difficulty experienced by those reporting problems to do with owning property. Although traditional stereotypes might suggest that neighbour disputes disproportionately afflict those living in rented accommodation, this was the second most common problem experienced by those living in rented accommodation (second only to the difficulty of getting landlords to carry out repairs to the premises) and was again consistent with results in England and Wales.

None of the survey respondents reporting neighbour problems said that they had "lumped" the problem, indicating that members of the public are not prepared to endure these problems without at least taking some kind of action, despite the fact that in reality neighbour problems are among the most difficult to resolve (see Chapter 5).

A little over one in four of those who experienced a problem with a neighbour tried to handle the problem without advice, and this is a relatively low figure by comparison with other problem types. Almost all of those who adopted this strategy tried to resolve the problem simply by contacting their neighbour directly and none reported having threatened their neighbour with legal action.

Neighbour problems: Obtaining Advice

About three-quarters of those experiencing problems with neighbours obtained advice about solving the problem (74%) which is a relatively high rate of advice-seeking and compares with 45% for consumer problems, 51% for money problems, 81% for employment problems, 84% for personal injury, and 85% for divorce and separation problems. This rate of advice-seeking demonstrates the seriousness with which neighbour problems are treated by members of the public and also the difficulty of achieving a resolution simply by adopting a self-help strategy.

A little under half of those with neighbour problems took advice from only one outside source (47%), but a similar proportion (44%) consulted two or three outside sources (38%). About eight percent took advice from four or more sources and this figure is rather higher than for many other problem types where no respondents reported consulting more than three advisers. In common with the English results, the Scottish findings indicate a substantial demand for advice among those with neighbour problems and highlight the extent to which the public will explore all avenues in order to achieve some sort of resolution.

The sources of initial advice used by those with neighbour problems were also somewhat different from other problem types. The most common first point of contact was the police with about *one in three* of those obtaining advice going there first (33%). The second most common source of advice was the local council, with one-quarter of advice-seekers going there first (these figures are similar to England but reversed with one third there going first to the council and one-quarter going first to the police). Solicitors were also quite frequently used as a first source of advice (22% of advice-seekers' initial contact). The CAB was very rarely the first choice for those with neighbour problems (only 3% going first to a CAB).

The local council was the most common second source of advice for neighbour problems , which suggests that first advisers were frequently referring people on to the council. After the local council the most common second sources of advice were the police, and housing associations.

Taking all of those experiencing neighbour problems as a whole, 37% contacted the police at some time about the problem, 33% contacted their local council, 33% contacted solicitors, and 3% contacted the CAB about trying to resolve the problem with their neighbour. This latter figure is much lower than that in England and Wales where some 25% of those with neighbour problems at some time contacted a CAB about the problem.

The vast majority of people with neighbour problems attempted to resolve the problem directly before obtaining advice about how to proceed. Among respondents who obtained advice, around eight in ten had either been in contact with the other side or tried unsuccessfully to contact them before obtaining advice.

Although about half of those who obtained advice about neighbour problems did so quite rapidly after the problem started, a substantial proportion of those with neighbour problems waited quite a long time before obtaining advice. Approaching one in five (17%) waited six months or more before taking advice.

Neighbour problems: Advice wanted

What people involved in neighbour problems were looking for overwhelmingly was advice on how to solve the problem (83% of those with neighbour problems were looking for this kind of advice). Only one in three mentioned wanting advice about their legal rights (a somewhat lower proportion than in some other problem types) and only a small proportion mentioned wanting advice about court procedures (13%), again a lower figure than in other problem types.

Advice obtained

Although the majority of those experiencing neighbour problems were told by their first adviser that something could be done about the problem, the proportion was the lowest percentage of all problem types (72%). For example, the figure can be compared with 85% of those suffering accidental injury or work-related ill health who were told that something could be done about their problem, and with consumer problems when 86% were told by their first adviser that something could be done to resolve the problem. The most common advice given by first advisers to those with neighbour problems was to contact the other side to try and resolve the problem (20%), seek help from another person (20%), threaten the other side with legal proceedings (13%), or take the case to court (6%). Second advisers were more likely to recommend threatening the other side with legal proceedings (28%) and less likely to suggest making contact with the other side to try and resolve the problem (16%). In no case did a first or second adviser suggest that the respondent try mediation to resolve the problem with their neighbour. This finding is again completely consistent with the situation found in England and Wales.

Neighbour problems: Satisfaction with advice

On the whole members of the public experiencing problems with neighbours expressed a somewhat lower level of satisfaction with their first advisers than other respondents, with about two-thirds saying that they thought the advice very helpful or helpful. This slightly higher level of dissatisfaction may be a reflection of the intractability of neighbour problems and the limited extent to which the law is able to offer a remedy to those locked into disputes with their neighbours. Neighbour problems have some characteristics in common with employment problems and divorce and separation problems in that the protagonists are often caught in an unhappy relationship from which it is difficult to escape and for which the possibilities of reaching a satisfactory resolution are slim.

MONEY PROBLEMS

This category *excludes* respondents who were involved in disputes over social security benefits, but covers matters to do with disputed bills, disputed tax demands, problems with pensions, or loans. Among those interviewed in the main survey about money problems (excluding disputes relating to DSS benefits) the most common problems related to a dispute with an insurance company (27%), the local authority (21%), a bank, building society or mortgage company (11%), the Inland Revenue (10%), a utility (6%), or some other company (18%). In contrast with the English findings, none of those respondents interviewed about a money problem said that they had "lumped" the problem. All had either taken steps alone to resolve the problem or had sought advice. By contrast, in the English study about ten percent of those with money problems took no advice about resolving their dispute and made no attempt to contact the other side, which was a relatively high proportion in comparison with other problem types. The approach to money problems thus appears to be somewhat different in Scotland.

Those experiencing money problems were divided equally between those who attempted to deal with the problem alone and those who sought advice from one or more sources. Some 49% of those with money problems took action to resolve the problem without obtaining any advice about how to resolve the problem, which is one of the highest proportions of self-helpers among all problem types (for example 12% in divorce and separation cases, 13% in injury cases, 14% in employment disputes, and 27% in neighbour disputes). The most common strategy adopted was simply to contact the other side involved in the problem, although in about 14% of cases the respondent threatened the other side with legal action.

Money problems: Obtaining advice

Half of those with money problems obtained outside advice about dealing with the problem (41%). This figure is relatively low and can be compared with 45% obtaining advice for consumer problems, 80% for employment problems, 74% for neighbour problems, 85% for divorce and separation problems, and 84% for personal injury. Just under three in five of those with money problems took advice from just one outside source (57%), with the remainder consulting two or three advisers.

The most common first point of contact for those with money problems was a solicitor (26% going there first). The next most common source of advice was a CAB (22%). This is again different from the picture in England and Wales where the CAB was more popular as the first point for advice for money problems.

Taking all of those with money problems as a whole about 28% obtained advice at some time from a CAB about dealing with the problem and about 29% obtained advice from a solicitor. This spread of advice is rather different from England and Wales where a rather lower proportion of those with money problems obtained advice from solicitors (12%), although interestingly almost one in five of first advisers on money problems in Scotland were friends or relatives of the respondent (18%).

Although a large proportion of respondents with money problems said that the idea of making contact with their first source of advice was their own (48%), around 15% said that the suggestion had come from a friend or relative, and around one in five said that their first adviser was a personal contact, friend or relative. About seven percent said that they had specifically wanted "legal" help.

Around three in five respondents with money problems said that they had made contact with the other side before obtaining outside advice (59%), a lower proportion than in England and Wales. Most people who obtained advice about money problems did so quite quickly. About two in five obtained advice as soon as the problem started (41%) and another quarter said that they obtained advice within four weeks. However, about one-fifth waited more than six months before obtaining advice.

Money problems: Advice wanted

The vast majority of those with money problems were unsurprisingly seeking advice from their first adviser about how to solve the problem (85% of respondents with money problems mentioned this). However, the next most common advice wanted was about court procedures (44%), demonstrating the perceived emphasis on legal aspects of money problems. About one-third said that they wanted advice about their legal position (31%) and about five percent were looking for someone to represent them in court proceedings. A little over one-third said that they wanted to be advised about their financial position (37%).

Money problems: Advice obtained

In quite a high proportion of cases the first adviser thought that some-thing could be done about the money problem (82%). This figure was about average and compared well with 72% for neighbour problems, which had the lowest level of positive advice. The most common advice given by first advisers was to contact the other the side to try and resolve the problem (48%) or to seek help from another person or organisation (21%). In about one in ten cases (9%) respondents were advised to threaten the other side with legal proceedings and in five per-cent of cases respondents were advised to go court. In eight percent of cases respondents were advised to take the case to an ombudsman, but in no case were respondents advised to try mediation.

Money problems: Satisfaction with advice

On the whole those with money problems were fairly satisfied with the advice received from their first contact. Three quarters of respondents thought that the advice received had been very or fairly helpful, although nearly one in five thought that the advice had been not at all helpful (18%). This represents a fairly high degree of dissatisfaction as compared with other problem types.

PROBLEMS WITH LANDLORDS

Difficulties with landlords was the most common type of justiciable problem reported by respondents to the screening survey who said that they had experienced a problem relating to living in rented accom-modation. The main problems with living in rented accommodation were getting the landlord to do repairs and problems with neighbours. About two percent of the surveyed population reported having had one or more problems relating to getting landlords to do repairs during the previous five years. These respondents were fairly evenly split between local authority housing (45%) and privately rented property (48%). About seven percent of those with problems with landlords were rent-ing from housing associations. Other relatively frequent problems to do with renting property were poor or unsafe living conditions, getting a deposit back from the landlord, harassment by the landlord and being evicted or being threatened with eviction.

All respondents interviewed in the main survey who had experienced problems with landlords had tried to do something about the problem either alone or following advice from an outside advice source.

Just under one in three respondents with landlord problems had tried to resolve the problem without obtaining any advice (30%) and the overwhelming majority of self-helpers did nothing much else other than make contact with the other side to try and achieve some sort of resolution to the problem. They do not appear to have threatened legal action or done anything else. As will be seen in the next chapter, these self-help strategies had a rather low rate of success.

Landlord Problems: Obtaining Advice

About 70% of those interviewed who had experienced problems with landlords sought advice about the problem. This compares with 73% for neighbour problems, 45% for consumer problems, 81% for employment problems, and 85% for divorce and separation problems. Almost two out of every three of those with landlord problems who sought advice went to two or three advisers (63%).

The first point of contact for those experiencing problems with their landlord was most often the CAB (40%). About ten percent went first to the local council and *none* went first to see a solicitor. Where a second adviser was contacted this was most often a solicitor (37% of second advisers), a CAB (12%), or the local council (12%).

Among those experiencing problems with landlords as a whole, 52% were in contact with a CAB at some time about their problem and 45% contacted a solicitor for help in solving the problem. The rate at which solicitors were consulted about landlord problems was significantly greater than in the England and Wales study.

In nine out of ten cases where advice was sought about problems with landlords the respondent had been in contact with the landlord about the problem before obtaining advice (90%) and advice was generally obtained quite quickly after the problem started.

Landlord Problems: Advice Wanted

Respondents dealing with landlord problems were initially generally looking for advice about how to solve the problem (90% of those obtaining advice), advice about court procedures (48% mentioning this), and advice about legal rights (45% mentioning this). About 12%

wanted advice about their financial position, but none wanted the first adviser to represent them in court proceedings.

Landlord Problems: Advice obtained

A very high proportion of those obtaining advice about problems with their landlord was told that something could be done about the problem (83%). This figure can be compared with the lower figure for example in neighbour disputes (72%). The most common advice received from first advisers was to contact the other side to try and resolve the problem (65%), or to seek advice or help from another person (35%). In almost one-quarter of cases, first advisers suggested that respondents threaten court proceedings and in six percent of cases advisers suggested taking the case to an ombudsman. In no cases did first advisers suggest trying mediation. Second advisers were most likely to suggest contacting the other side (69%), threaten the other side with legal proceedings (32%), take the problem to an ombudsman (20%) or, interestingly, attempt to resolve the problem via mediation (15%).

Landlord Problems: Satisfaction with Advice

Respondents who were interviewed about their approach to resolving problems with landlords expressed only moderate satisfaction with the advice received from their first point of contact. A little over one in three (37%) said that the advice had been very helpful, and a further 27% said that the advice was fairly helpful. However, over one in three respondents said that the advice received from their first adviser was not very or not at all helpful (37%).

EMPLOYMENT PROBLEMS

The number of cases involving employment problems is rather small for separate analysis and the summary information following should therefore be treated as indicative. However, attention has been drawn to findings that are consistent with those in England and Wales and in which it is therefore possible to have greater confidence.

About six percent of respondents interviewed about employment problems said that they had simply "lumped" the problem, making no attempt to resolve the problem directly with their employer nor obtaining advice. This figure is similar to that in England and Wales.

About 14% of respondents who had experienced problems to do with employment said that they had attempted to reach a resolution of the problem without obtaining any outside advice. This figure is relatively low by comparison, for example, with those experiencing consumer disputes, but is consistent with the English results.

About eight out of ten respondents with problems relating to employment obtained advice about solving the problem (81%). This figure, consistent with England, is relatively high and can be compared with 45% for consumer problems, 51% for money problems, 84% for accidents and work-illness, 74% for neighbour problems, and 85% for divorce and separation problems.

About two thirds of respondents experiencing problems at work (69%) took advice from only one outside source and about one in four (28%) consulted two or three outside sources. Only a small minority took advice from four or more sources (3%).

The first point of contact for those with employment problems was most often the CAB (31%), or a Trade Union or staff association (28%). Solicitors were the first source of advice in only a small proportion of cases concerning employment problems (7%). Employers were also used as an initial source of advice (14%).

Although a large proportion of respondents said that the idea of making contact with their first adviser was their own (57%), just under one-fifth said that the suggestion had come from a friend or relative (18%), and about 14% said that they had used the same source of advice on a previous similar occasion.

Looking at the sample of those experiencing employment problems as a whole, and at all sources of advice, fewer than one in five of those experiencing employment problems obtained legal advice at some point about the problem (17%), a figure which is significantly *lower* than in England and Wales where the proportion was one in three. The figure can also be compared with 95% of those in divorce and separation cases obtaining legal advice, 45% of those with landlord problems, 29 of those with money problems, 33% of those with neighbour problems, 56% of those suffering accidental injury, and 46% of those with consumer problems. On the other hand about one in three of those with employment problems in Scotland (34%) at some time consulted a CAB about trying to resolve their employment problem.

In most cases advice was obtained fairly rapidly after the problem started. Over half (57%) obtained advice within one or two weeks of the problem starting.

Employment problems: Advice wanted

In common with most other problem types and the English results, people were initially seeking advice about how to solve the problem (69%) and advice about their legal rights (55%). About one third mentioned that they wanted advice about court procedures (33%) and a substantial minority mentioned that they wanted someone to represent them at a court or tribunal hearing (14%). These figures are almost exactly the same as those in England and Wales. Most people obtaining advice about an employment problem were told that something could be done about the problem (78%) and this figure is higher than that in England (69%).

Employment problems: Advice obtained

Most of those obtaining advice about employment problems were told that something could be done about the problem (78%) although advisers' confidence was somewhat lower in employment problems than for other problem types. For example, in consumer cases 87% were told something could be done and the figure for injury cases and divorce and separation cases was 85%. The only problem type with a lower proportion of advisers feeling something could be done was neighbour disputes where only 72% of first advisers though that something could be done to resolve the problem. As one respondent explained:

> "I was out of work for two years. I now work on a much lower salary. But I took the advice of the [union] man which was 'Don't even try it.' There wasn't anyone else to discuss it with. I was a union member. Why pay a solicitor if you're already paying union dues?" [Constructive dismissal]

First advisers visited by those with employment problems were most likely to suggest that the respondent contact the other side to seek a resolution of the problem (37%) or to seek help or advice from another source (19%). In 14% of cases first advisers suggested taking the case to a court or tribunal, and in eight percent of cases the first adviser suggested threatening the other side with legal action. In about three percent of employment cases, however, first advisers suggested taking the case to a mediator to try and resolve the problem.

Employment problems: Satisfaction with advice

In common with English findings, Scots respondents who had experienced employment problems expressed a rather *low degree of satisfaction* with the advice received from their first point of contact. About one in three respondents obtaining advice about employment problems thought that the advice received from their first adviser was either not very helpful (17%) or not at all helpful (14%). Only 31% found the advice very helpful which is the lowest proportion of all problem types.

ACCIDENTAL INJURY AND WORK-RELATED ILL-HEALTH

About three percent of the surveyed population reported having had one or more injury or health problem in the last five years that resulted from an accident, or from poor working conditions and which necessitated a visit to a doctor or hospital. Those respondents interviewed about injury and work-related ill health requiring medical treatment had most often suffered an accident or illness at work (44%) or a road accident (15%). About twelve percent were in dispute with the council as a result of falls in the street or other public places and one-quarter said that their accident took place elsewhere.

In contrast with the English findings only three percent of those who experienced an accidental injury or work related illness requiring medical treatment took no action to gain redress (as compared with 15% in England and Wales).

Rather few victims of accidental injury or work-related ill-health tried to take action to obtain redress on their own. About 13% of all those interviewed about injury said that they had tried to handle the matter on their own. In general this amounted to little more than making contact with the other side. They do not appear to have threatened legal action or done anything else. The relatively modest success of this strategy is discussed in Chapter 5.

140   *The Response to Problems of Different Types*

Accidental Injury: Obtaining Advice

Over eight in ten (84%) respondents suffering accidents or work related health problems obtained advice about the problem. This is a relatively high rate of advice seeking by comparison with other problems and higher than the figure in England and Wales which was just under seven in ten (69%).

The first point of contact for respondents who suffered injury or work-related illness was most often a solicitor, with about half of those seeking advice going directly to a solicitor (48% as compared with 32% in the English survey). The next most common initial contacts were with trades unions (30% of first advisers), and the police (11%). Unlike other problem types, CABx were only used as an initial source of advice by a small minority of accident victims (4% of first advisers).

Although a large proportion of respondents said that the idea of making contact with their first source of advice was their own (52%), around one-quarter said that the suggestion had come from a friend or relative (26%), and about 13% said that they were following their employer's procedure.

Among all victims of accidental injury and work-related illness in the sample, over half (56%) contacted a solicitor at some time to obtain advice about the problem.

In nearly two out of three cases (62%) where advice was obtained about compensation for injury or illness, the respondent had *not* been in contact with the other side before seeking advice, nor had they generally tried to make contact with the other side. This suggests that respondents are aware that if they are going to seek any kind of remedy against the person responsible for the injury or illness, success will depend on more than direct negotiations or other self-help remedies.

Advice was generally obtained very rapidly after the accident or illness. About two in five of those who obtained advice said that they did so immediately (40%). An additional one-quarter (24%) obtained advice within two weeks.

Accidental injury: Advice wanted

What respondents were looking for from advisers, at least initially, was advice about legal rights (74% of respondents mentioning this), advice about court procedures (54%), and advice about how to solve the problem (56%). Around one in three accident victims wanted their first adviser to represent them in court. This demonstrates a rather stronger emphasis on legal redress than in the English sample.

Accidental Injury: Advice obtained

A very high proportion of those obtaining advice about an accident or work-related illness was told that something could be done about the problem (85%). This figure can be compared with the somewhat lower figures of 72% for neighbour problems and 78% for employment problems, although the results in Scotland suggest that for most problem categories, first advisers were optimistic about the chances of achieving some kind of resolution to problems or form of redress. The most common advice given by first advisers was to to contact the other side to try and resolve the problem (32%) to threaten the other side with legal action (29%), or to seek advice or help from another person (17%). In no case did a first adviser suggested going to mediation.

Accidental Injury: Satisfaction with advice

Respondents with injury and health problems expressed an about average degree of satisfaction with the advice received from their first point of contact. A little under half(46%) said that the advice had been very helpful and a further fifth (21%) said that the advice was fairly helpful. A very high proportion of those experiencing accidental injuries said that they would definitely recommend their first adviser to others (78% compared with 55% of first advisers for employment problems, 48% of consumer problem first advisers and 47% of those advising on neighbour problems).

OTHER PROBLEMS

There were several other types of problems that respondents reported during the screening survey and about which they were interviewed in the main survey. However, because of the relative rarity of these types of problems the number of cases about which information is available is small, making full analysis unreliable. The following information is presented as indicative, however, of the approaches taken by those experiencing these rather less common problems. In general unweighted numbers have been given rather than percentages.

Problems with owning residential property

Some 24 respondents to the main survey were interviewed about problems to do with owning residential property (other than neighbour problems). Of this number all took some action to deal with the problem, and a high proportion (20 out of 24) obtained advice about how to resolve the problem. Only four respondents attempted to resolve the problem without obtaining advice. Those who went to advisers most often went first to a solicitor (9 of the 24), although three went first to an ombudsman. Only one of the 24 respondents went first to a CAB for advice about the problem affecting their property.

Tribunal issues

Some 22 respondents to the main survey were interviewed about problems to do with receiving benefits or problems over schooling, both of which are dealt with in special tribunals. Of this number only two failed to take any action to try and deal with the problem. About half obtained advice about trying to resolve the problem (27 out of 39) and none of these obtained advice from a solicitor.

Those having action taken against them

In only a small proportion of cases (one in ten) did respondents report that action was being taken against them, rather than them taking action against another. Those who were having action taken against them were concentrated among divorce and separation problems (12%), money problems, and landlord and tenant problems. Among respondents who said that they were having action taken against them about two percent said that they had done nothing to try and resolve the problem. About four in ten (41%) said that they tried to resolve the problem without advice and the remaining 57% sought advice about the problem. As compared with respondents who were potential pursuers as a whole, there was no significant difference in the propensity to take action or to seek advice about the problem. However, those having action taken against them were more likely to have sought advice from a CAB than those taking action, although the rates at which advice was sought from lawyers was roughly similar. This is in contrast to the results in England and Wales where although potential defenders were less likely to seek advice overall, those who did obtain advice were more likely go to lawyers than other advisers.

SECTION 2: EXPLAINING ADVICE-SEEKING

In order to try and understand more fully the factors associated with the likelihood that respondents would seek advice about trying to resolve a justiciable dispute a multiple regression analysis was conducted. Using this type of analysis it is possible to identify factors that are significantly associated with the likelihood that advice will be obtained when members of the public are faced with different types of justiciable problems, and to estimate whether certain groups are more or less likely than average to seek advice[4].

The purpose of the analysis was to try and isolate factors associated with *any* kind of advice-seeking and no distinction was made at this point between different types of adviser. The factors included in the analysis of whether or not advice would be obtained, on the basis of the results of earlier cross classification of variables were: the type of problem being experienced by the respondent and the type of remedy being sought, and whether the respondent was taking action or having action taken against them; the respondent's age, sex, social class, education, employment status, and income; and finally an indicator of the extent to which respondents reported having suffered negative effects from dealing with their problems, and an indicator of respondents' attitude to the legal system.

Although an identical procedure was adopted in the analysis of the England and Wales data, the limitations of the sample size in Scotland has meant that the analysis is rather less robust and the results, therefore, rather more tentative. In particular, results that differ substantially from those found in England and Wales might easily reflect the smaller sample size rather than a real difference in significant factors.

Taking all of the various factors included in the analysis into account, the results of the multiple regression analysis indicated that the factors found to be significantly associated with the likelihood that advice would be obtained to resolve the problem were:

- type of justiciable problem experienced
- respondent's household income
- respondent's employment status.

[4] The full results of the regression analysis are presented in Appendix B.

Of these three factors found to be significantly associated with whether or not advice would be obtained about the problem, the factors showing by far the strongest correlation were *problem type, followed by respondent's employment status.*

Type of justiciable problem

Employment problems, neighbour problems, divorce/separation, accident or injury problems and problems to do with owning residential property were all associated with an *increased* likelihood that respondents experiencing those problems would obtain advice about resolving the problem. On the other hand, money problems, and consumer problems were associated with *decreased* odds of obtaining advice.

Income

Respondents with relatively low household income of between £8,000 and £14,999 were more likely to seek advice compared with those who have lower incomes or higher incomes.

Employment status

Respondents who were self-employed or managers were more likely to seek advice compared with other employment groups.

COMPARISON WITH ENGLAND AND WALES MULTIVARIATE ANALYSIS

In the England and Wales study, the type of justiciable problem experienced by respondents was also the factor most strongly associated with advice seeking and the same problem types were positively associated with advice seeking. Income was also a significant factor associated with advice-seeking in England and Wales, although the pattern of the results was strikingly *different* from that in Scotland. In England and Wales respondents who had *higher* incomes (£15,000 or more) were *more* likely to seek advice, whereas the corresponding group in Scotland was *less* likely to seek advice. Employment status, which was the second most strongly correlated factor in Scotland, was not found to be significant in England and Wales. Factors that were found to be significant in England and Wales but not Scotland were age, amount of money sought, attitude to the legal system, educational qualifications and sex. However, in drawing conclusions from the results of the multivariate analysis in Scotland, it must be stressed that it is to be expected that fewer factors will be found to be significant, since the sample size for analysis was relatively small.[5]

THE INTERACTION OF FACTORS ASSOCIATED WITH ADVICE SEEKING

The analysis thus far has identified a number of factors that are associated with the likelihood that advice will be obtained in order to try and resolve a justiciable problem. It is not clear, however, how these various factors interact. To address this question a further analysis was undertaken[6] in order to identify the characteristics of subgroups of respondents which differ in terms of their propensity to seek advice about their justiciable problem. The analysis produced four different (mutually exclusive and exhaustive) groups for which the percentage of cases obtaining advice about a justiciable problem varied from 47% to 85%. The characteristics of these groups are discussed below.

Low propensity to obtain outside advice

The analysis suggests that the group of respondents in the sample *least* likely of all to obtain advice about dealing with a justiciable dispute had the following characteristics:

• Problems concerning goods and services, money problems, and benefits or education problems.

Within this particular group about 47% obtained advice and the group comprised over one-third (39%) of the main survey sample.

Average propensity to obtain outside advice

Two groups with middling rates of advice seeking comprise respondents experiencing landlord and tenant problems, neighbour problems and miscellaneous other problems. These groups were subdivided according to gender with the male group being much more likely than the female group to seek advice (76% compared with 60%).

---

[5] This categorisation was chosen because, as will be seen in Chapter 6, the amounts of money at issue were generally quite low, with a high proportion under £500.

[6] The CHAID (Chi-squared Automatic Interaction Detector) module within SPSS. The full results of the CHAID analysis are given in Appendix.

High propensity to obtain advice

The group with the highest rate of advice seeking comprised respondents experiencing divorce or separation problems, employment problems, accident or injury problems and problems to do with owning property. The rate at which advice was sought among this group was 85% and the group comprised just over one-quarter of the main survey sample (28%).

This analysis identified fewer groups than that for the England and Wales study (four instead of twelve). Common features of the CHAID groups on both studies were that respondents who had money or consumer problems were classified in groups with relatively low rates of advice seeking while respondents with employment, neighbour, owning property or accident or injury problems were classified in groups with relatively high rates of advice seeking.

CONCLUSION

This chapter has built on the discussion in Chapter 3 presenting a wealth of data about how members of the public in Scotland, faced with particular kinds of justiciable disputes, sought to deal with those problems. As discussed in the previous chapter, it appears that the overwhelming majority of respondents who perceived and defined a problem as being more than trivial took steps to do something about it. Among the few who did absolutely nothing, the failure to take action was not the result of inadvertence, but generally seemed to flow from a weighing of options.

Among those who took steps to resolve the problem most tried first to deal with the matter themselves and only resorted to advice when their efforts proved fruitless. The exceptions to this rule were some divorce and separation problems, some neighbour problems and some accidental injuries, when respondents went directly to seek advice, rather than attempting to deal directly with their opponent as a result of fear of the consequences, a total breakdown of communication or a sense that a direct approach would be futile.

It is also clear that whether members of the public obtain advice, where they go for advice, and whether they are prepared to pay for that advice is greatly influenced by the nature of the problem. The results of the multivariate analysis confirm that problem type tends to swamp other considerations, although they also suggest that some personal factors, such as income and employment status, are also important.

The problems about which advice was most likely to be sought were employment problems, neighbour problems, divorce and separation problems, accidental injury, and problems to do with owning residential property. What most of these problems have in common is the likely importance of the matters to the parties and the relative intractability of the issues that might be involved. For example, in employment problems, neighbour problems and divorce and separation problems the parties have been in a relationship. Where neighbour problems and divorce and separation problems are concerned, the parties may still be locked into a continuing relationship. These are problems that cannot be solved by a simple transfer of money. In employment cases an employee may be struggling to hold on to a job, or may be hoping to improve or preserve the conditions under which he or she is working. The increased propensity to obtain advice for these problems is a reflection of the complexity of the issues and the difficulty of achieving a resolution by means of self-help strategies.

Those problems about which advice was less likely to be obtained were consumer problems and money problems which reflects the fact that the issues involved might have been relatively uncomplicated and had less serious implications. As a result respondents may feel less inclined to go to the trouble and potential expense of obtaining advice.

It seems clear that very few members of the public would remain supine in the face of *any* justiciable problem. Decisions about whether to take action, what action to take, and when to give up, are influenced by respondents' own capacities and resources, and by the character of the opposition in the context of the severity of the problem.

Table 4.1 below suggests the combination of factors that seem to influence the extent to which members of the public faced with a justiciable problem will be able to resolve that problem alone and whether they are likely to need help. The level of need for advice and assistance will depend on the capacity and resources of the party facing the problem, the importance of the problem to that party, and the intransigence of the opponent. Thus those members of the public with low levels of competence in terms of education, income, confidence, verbal skill, literacy skill, and emotional fortitude are likely to need some help in resolving justiciable problems no matter what the importance of the problem and no matter how intransigent or accommodating the opposition, although this need will increase as problem severity and opponent intransigence increases.

A high level of need for advice might also be experienced by members of the public with medium to high levels of the necessary competencies, when faced with a problem of great importance or severity to themselves and an opponent who is intransigent. Examples here might be some divorce and separation problems, repossession of homes when people fall on hard times, accidental injury, and serious problems with neighbours.

A relatively low need for assistance, but a need nonetheless, might exist among those with medium to high levels of confidence, but who lack the specific knowledge about rights and procedures to mount a credible attack on an opponent or to present a convincing defence.

Table 4.1 Need for advice, assistance and/or representation.

Capacity/ Resources of Party	Importance of Problem to party	Intransigence of Opponent	Level of Need
LOW	MEDIUM/HIGH	LOW/MEDIUM/ HIGH	**MEDIUM/ HIGH**
MEDIUM/HIGH	MEDIUM/HIGH	HIGH	**HIGH**
MEDIUM/HIGH	LOW	HIGH	**MEDIUM**
MEDIUM/HIGH	LOW/MEDIUM/ HIGH	LOW	**LOW**

The question of whether or not people are willing to pay for advice involves another set of considerations that have to be overlaid on the suggested matrix. Does the problem involve some kind of immediate threat? Examples might be contact and residence cases, violent spouses, money being demanded, and employment problems. These are matters about which there might be a tangible threat of harm leading to an imperative for action. In these cases individuals might be prepared, if they must, to pay whatever it costs to avert the threat of harm or mitigate the damage.

Those situations can be distinguished from cases concerning recompense for harm already suffered, such as consumer problems, wrangles with insurance companies and accidental injury. In such cases what is being sought is a possible financial gain set against an uncertain outcome and the decision as to whether or not it is worth investing money in that doubtful outcome may lead to hesitation.

These issues are relevant to the debate surrounding the different levels of help that may be made available through the Scottish community legal services programme. Whether or not these varying levels of need will be addressed is a matter of prioritisation by policymakers and this is discussed further in Chapter 8.

5

Outcomes

The previous chapter looked in detail at the different approaches taken by respondents to the resolution of problems of different types. This chapter focuses more directly on the outcomes that were achieved by those trying to resolve their problem, and considers these outcomes in relation to the strategy adopted. The chief outcome with which the chapter is concerned is whether any resolution to the problem was achieved. In this context "resolution" is taken as meaning either that an agreement was reached to end or settle the problem (with or without the commencement of legal proceedings) ("agreement"), or that the matter ended with a court, tribunal or ombudsman's decision or order ("adjudication"). No judgement is made about whether agreements were good or bad or whether respondents were happy with the terms. The term "resolution" also includes cases where the respondent lost their case in court. "Unresolved" cases are those where action was taken to seek a resolution of the case but no agreement was ever reached to settle the matter and no court, tribunal or ombudsman's decision or order was ever obtained. These are, in effect, cases in which attempts to obtain a resolution were tried and then abandoned.

The first section of the chapter describes what happened when respondents handled the problem entirely alone; when they handled the problem with help from advisers, and when they turned to the legal system to achieve a resolution. The second section of the chapter presents information about the extent to which agreements and court decisions led to genuine resolution of problems and about some of the financial costs incurred by respondents in the process of trying to resolve their justiciable problems. The final section uses the results of multivariate analysis to try and explain the way in which certain characteristics of respondents and certain problem types are associated with different outcomes to justiciable problems

There is a wide range of possible outcomes to justiciable problems and the paths to those outcomes can be labyrinthine. Figure 5.1 displays the primary pathways that were followed by various groups of respondents interviewed in the main survey in order to try and achieve a resolution to their justiciable problem. Reconstructing behaviour from respondents' accounts of what happened is difficult because sometimes there is a lack of fine detail about deviations from primary routes, and because sometimes survey respondents give logically incompatible answers. This was not unexpected and reflects the confusion that many ordinary people feel in relation to legal and other dispute resolution processes that they do not fully understand and that are not adequately explained.

As Figure 5.1 shows, it is possible to resolve a dispute by handling it in a number of different ways: respondents could deal with the problem completely alone; they could obtain some advice and then continue alone; or they could obtain advice and then move toward a resolution with the aid of an adviser or representative. Even if legal proceedings had been started by the respondent, or against the respondent, a resolution could have been reached without a legal decision, or the case might have been abandoned. Thus the primary outcomes of agreement, adjudication or abandonment can be reached by a number of routes.

The Lumpers: No action, no resolution

Among all those interviewed in the main survey that had experienced a non-trivial justiciable problem, some three percent of respondents took no action to try and resolve the matter. This means that they did not contact the other side in the dispute or any other party or organisation, effectively eschewing the possibility of any resolution or remedy, despite the fact that these respondents all regarded their problem as non-trivial[1]. This figure is consistent with that in England and Wales (five percent).

---

[1] See discussion in Chapter 3 for details of characteristics of this group.

Resolved by agreement

According to respondents' accounts of their actions and the outcomes achieved, it seems that justiciable problems were eventually resolved *by agreement* in one-third of all cases (32%), and that in about one percent of all cases agreement was reached after the commencement of legal proceedings (see Figure 5.1). These results are also consistent with the English results in which 35% were resolved by agreements, with three percent following the commencement of legal proceedings.

Figure 5.1 also reveals that the proportions of the sample succeeding in reaching a resolution of their problem by means of agreement are very similar, whether or not advice had been taken. About 14% of the sample as a whole managed to resolve their problem by agreement without obtaining advice, while about 17% of the whole sample achieved a resolution of their problem after obtaining advice, but without becoming involved in any formal legal proceedings. These figures are *identical* to those found in the English study.

As the figure demonstrates, the general pattern of outcomes for justiciable problems in Scotland is consistent with that found in England and Wales. Indeed, in several cases the percentages are identical. Given the differences between the two jurisdictions in procedures and structures noted in Chapter 1, this consistency of outcome is notable and raises interesting questions.

Unresolved Cases: No agreement or adjudication

Over *half* of all respondents to the main questionnaire had not managed to achieve any kind of agreement to resolve their problem by the time of the interview (57%), nor had the problem been the subject of a court decision. In about three percent of these cases no action had been taken to resolve the dispute and four percent were unresolved after legal action had been commenced.

However, despite the absence of an agreement or decision to bring the problem to an end, about one third (38%) of these respondents said that at the time of the interview the problem was no longer ongoing— that the problem had in some sense resolved itself. The most common way in which the problem had resolved itself was by the respondent simply ceasing to pursue the complaint (32% of cases where respondents said problem had ended).

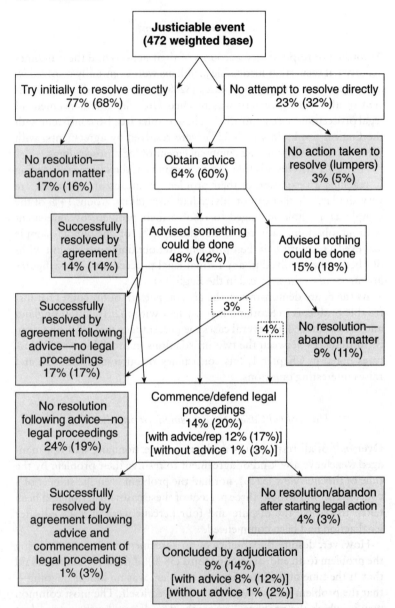

Figure 5.1 Paths and outcomes following justiciable event (All percentages given are of total sample 472—shaded boxes are final outcomes and English results given in brackets).

"We had a front door fitted which was faulty from the word go . . . so we phoned the firm up and eventually someone after about six or eight calls answered the phone and swore down the line and we didn't get any help at all with a lot of swearing. Then eventually he did come and brought someone to see the door and it was to be replaced. It never was replaced and after more phone calls we decided to go to the Consumer's Advice. I think I went to Citizen's Advice first and asked and they sent me to Trading Standards and they did go to a lot of bother, but found that [the firm] had gone down the tubes..but the bit that niggled me was that he was working from home and as far as we're concerned he's still making a living. The Trading Standards said they couldnae do anything else, they'd gone into liquidation."

In just under one in five of these cases, it was reported that the other side in the dispute had promised to do something that would bring the problem to an end (19%). In a small minority of cases the "resolution" of the problem was achieved by the respondent or the other side taking fairly drastic action. Among those respondents who said that the problem had ended, despite the absence of an agreement, in just over one in ten cases this was achieved by the respondent moving to a new house or area (13%). About 9% of respondents said that the problem ended when the respondent moved to another job. Some respondents who had been the subject of a complaint said that the problem had ended by the other side withdrawing or stopping pursuit of the respondent (4% of those saying that the problem had ended) or by the other side moving to a new house (4%).

In almost two-thirds of the cases in which there had been no agreement or adjudication the problem was still ongoing (62%) and in most of these cases respondents had no intention of taking any action to try and resolve the problem in the future. The most common reasons for not intending to take any further action were either that the respondent was waiting to see what might happen next (31%), or that the respondent felt there was nothing else that they could do to resolve the problem (30%). Other common reasons for giving up were that it would cost too much to do anything else (4%), that the respondent was fed up with the problem or had had enough of trying to sort it out (4%), or that it was not worth the hassle to continue (4%). The following examples of the reasoning behind decisions to give up after some attempts had been made to achieve a resolution or remedy are drawn from qualitative interviews:

"My doctor advised me to try. I was turned down. I got a letter back saying my appeal had been turned down, but I could go to a tribunal about it, by which point I'd been a year in the process and I couldn't be bothered any more. I'm now signed off permanently by the doctor. I don't work at all. It makes me very depressed and it's one of the reasons that I don't tend to follow through to the very end with things. I'm having to go over what's wrong with me, having to be examined by strange doctors gets me quite depressed." [Respondent trying to obtain disability benefit]

"Because I work in the health service—the floor above us, was the legal floor where they're currently handling all the cases that are coming in, that's why I probably wasn't too assertive. I didn't want to cause ripples, because I work in the system . . . . I have to work in this hospital—don't want to cause bad feeling." [Medical negligence]

"You hear reports in the news about these poor people that have got involved in court cases. Okay, they're phenomenal amounts of money you're talking about and big huge cases to be reported on the television, but seeing all their cases lost and they've got to pay thousands and thousands of pounds' worth of costs. So, it puts you off a little bit, even if it's a small thing you're thinking about—It is definitely the money you're thinking about."

An interesting concern offered by one or two respondents was the fear of a legal case being reported in the newspapers:

"One of the reasons I didn't want to [take it further] was I didn't want to make a big issue of it for [my son]. He would have been really angry at me if this had come in the papers." [Problem over schooling for sick son]

"If anything gets big enough to be noticed, and if I were against the Region it certainly would have got big enough to be noticed, at least locally, there would have been nasty things happening, newspapers, I don't need that." [Employment problem]

A clear factor influencing decisions whether to continue attempting to achieve some sort of resolution was a fairly generalised negative attitude towards various aspects of the legal system. Most of the people in the sample had made some attempt to resolve the problem themselves. Many had sought some advice about how they might achieve a resolution, but, as was noted in Chapter 3 and as will be seen further in Chapter 7, deep-rooted apprehension about becoming involved in legal proceedings prevented many people from pursuing their cases beyond a certain point. Apprehension about the legal system stems from what was occasionally described as a "cultural" aversion to involvement with lawyers, fears of the delay and trauma involved in legal processes and the overwhelming concern about legal expenses. The following examples drawn from qualitative interviews provide graphic illustrations of the concerns expressed and the direct link between law-aversion and their failure to press on with what they saw as justified causes:

"I don't think the legal system is very user-friendly. I feel that it's got an aura about it that normal human beings don't tend to get involved with it and if you do get involved with it, well poor you. It's a bit daunting. I feel that it's terribly complicated for normal Joe Bloggs that have no legal experience to be involved in and even someone like me that's got a little bit of knowledge from my work—it's still fairly daunting when its actually you that's involved. It's lack of control. Lack of knowledge and not being able to control it. I would have to go to someone to deal with it for me."

"I think it's long and tedious and drawn out. I think the whole of the legal system is actually. All Bills are passed and put in such a way that only certain people can understand them and unless you know, you've got hours to sit and study them. I think things could be a whole lot simpler, and I think they overcharge everybody. I really think the whole court system is vastly overpriced, and I think there must be a simpler way of doing it."

"You are going into this unknown world. You're going in there, and you don't know what you've to tell them and you don't what they're gonna charge you, and you don't know what they're gonna expect of you."

"An awful lot of people don't go to try and get justice because they are afraid of the cost, and in my case it's the psychological cost that is more frightening than the financial."

"You don't stand a chance. I think you really need to know what they're talking about and people with my kind of education, you've got no clue. Everything just seems so complicated. It just amazes me. It's the way they speak. They're so matter-of-fact and they expect you to know what they're talking about. They seem very intimidating as well. They really do. It just seems so much in another world to what I live in."

"I wouldnae even consider going to a lawyer unless I was absolutely desperate."

"I've not been brought up that you go to a solicitor to help solve your problems, I think it's a cultural thing . . . I suppose if it was something really important, and something immediate, something you knew you wanted do about it, or something that was against the law, you, you would maybe do that then."

LEGAL PROCEEDINGS AND ADJUDICATION[2]

In only about 9% of all cases of non-trivial justiciable problems was the matter concluded on the basis of a court, tribunal or ombudsman's adjudication, although the proportion of the sample involved in legal proceedings was rather higher at about 14%. This suggests that court and other legal proceedings play a very minor role in the resolution of justiciable problems afflicting ordinary members of the public as private individuals. Theories about the shadow cast by the law, however, would suggest that courts have a wide indirect impact on disputes resolved outwith the courts, and this is discussed further in Chapter 8.

As Figure 5.2 shows, involvement in legal proceedings was most common in cases concerning divorce and separation (45%), landlord problems (23%), accidental injury (19%) and owning residential property (17%). Involvement in legal proceedings was least common in neighbour disputes (6%) and consumer disputes (where there were no cases). Although this pattern is roughly consistent with that found in England and Wales there are some differences where involvement in legal proceedings in Scotland is either higher or lower than in England. For example, in England and Wales some 62% of divorce and separation problems led to legal proceedings, 37% of those experiencing problems with residential property were involved in legal proceedings, and 21% of those with employment problems were involved in legal proceedings. On the other hand only 11% of those in England dealing with landlord and tenant problems were involved in legal proceedings.

Moreover, as far as private individuals are concerned, it appears that their exposure to legal proceedings is more likely to be as a defender than as a pursuer. Those respondents who were having action taken *against* them were more likely to be involved in court proceedings than those respondents who had initiated action (see further below). Among those respondents who reported that they were having action taken against them, a little under one in three (29%) reported that they had been involved in legal proceedings in the course of resolving their problem.

[2] Respondents provided information about involvement in legal proceedings themselves. As in England and Wales, there was some evidence of confusion on the part of respondents about whether or not they had been involved in legal proceedings and, if so, what kinds of proceedings those were and what court or tribunal was dealing with the matter. Although this lack of understanding raises minor difficulties for the interpretation of the findings, it helpfully demonstrates the extent to which members of the public can be heavily involved in legal proceedings and yet have little understanding of those processes or terminology.

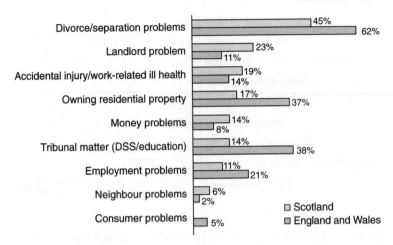

Figure 5.2 Involvement in formal legal proceedings by problem type (Weighted base = 472) compared with England and Wales.

Among respondents who were initiating action to try and resolve the justiciable problem, on the other hand, only 12% reported having been involved in legal proceedings. The experiences of defenders and pursuers diverge even further when looking at the distribution of court hearings. The proportion of respondents who reported that a hearing had taken place in connection with their case was about nine percent over the sample as a whole. Among respondents having action taken against them, however, about one in five (21%) said that their case had been decided on the basis of a decision by a court, tribunal or ombudsman as compared with only eight percent of those respondents who initiated action.

In a handful of cases (five) respondents said that their case had come before an ombudsman. These cases concerned disputes over money, landlords and residential property.

According to respondents their cases went to a variety of courts or tribunals, most commonly the Sheriff Court ordinary procedure, followed by the Sheriff Court summary cause procedure, and tribunals. A very small minority of those involved in court proceedings said that their case had been dealt with in the Court of Session (Figure 5.2). These figures have to be treated with some caution as a result of the confusion in minds of some respondents about the nature of the proceedings in which they had been involved.

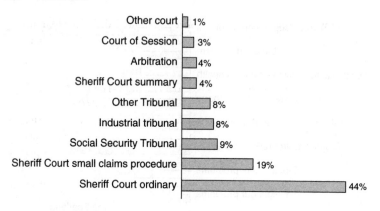

Figure 5.3 Respondents' reports of type of court/ tribunal dealing with problem. Base = all those involved in court proceedings 66 weighted).

"DEFENDERS": THOSE HAVING ACTION TAKEN AGAINST THEM

In only a small proportion of cases (one in ten) did respondents report that action was being taken against them, rather than them taking action against another. Those who were having action taken against them were concentrated among divorce and separation problems (12%), money problems, landlord and tenant problems. It is difficult to carry out a detailed analysis of the experience of those who said that their justiciable problem involved having action taken against them, since the unweighted number in the sample was rather small (about 42 respondents). A simple analysis suggests, however, that their experience was somewhat different from those respondents who were themselves the complainant or initiator of action.

A higher proportion of those who were having action taken against them reported that the problem had reached some sort of resolution (60% as compared with 41% among those who were initiating action). About 40% of all those who had action taken against them said that the problem had not been resolved by agreement or adjudication at the time of the interview (as compared with over half of those cases in which the respondent was initiating action (59%)). It is also notable that in those cases in which the respondent was the subject of action, the outcome of the case was more likely to be a court or tribunal decision than among those who were taking action (21% as compared with 8% of others).

In order to assess the influence of advice on the outcome of justiciable problems advice was initially divided into three categories: "lawyer advice", which was overwhelmingly advice from a solicitor in private practice with the odd case involving advice from a law centre; "other advice" which covered advice from a CAB and all other sources of advice from advice agencies and other sources identified in Chapter 3; and "no advice", where respondents reported that they had not obtained any advice from any source[3].

A simple breakdown of the outcome of justiciable problems in relation to these advice categories reveals some significant differences in outcome. As Figure 5.4 shows, respondents who obtained advice from a lawyer were *more* likely than others to have their case resolved on the basis of a court or tribunal adjudication. Those who received lawyer advice achieved a somewhat *lower* rate of agreement than those who received advice from other advisers, and the rate of non-resolution was similar between those advised by lawyers and those advised by other advisers. Among self-helpers who took action, the rates of agreement were slightly higher overall than among those who took advice (44% of self-helpers achieving an agreement compared with 24% of those who received lawyer advice and 35% of those who obtained other advice). These results differ somewhat from those in England and Wales where the type of advice received was related to the outcome of justiciable problems. It is arguable, of course, that those respondents who obtain advice from a solicitor are those experiencing the most intractable problems or those where a remedy cannot be obtained without assistance from a lawyer (for example compensation for accidental injury or divorce). The issues are, however, complicated and the role of advice is considered in more detail below in the analysis of outcome between problems of different types, and again in the final section in the explanation of outcome based on multivariate analysis.

---

[3] In the multivariate analysis in the final section of this chapter these definitions were further refined to distinguish between "other advisers" who provided positive assistance or representation and those who simply offered information and advice.

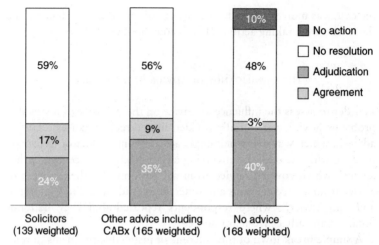

Figure 5.4 Outcome in relation to advice (Base whole sample 472 weighted)

OUTCOMES ACHIEVED FOR DIFFERENT PROBLEM TYPES

Just as there were substantial differences in the approaches taken to resolving disputes depending on the type of problem, so there appear to be substantial differences in the types of outcome achieved. From Figure 5.5 it can be seen clearly that although the average rate of resolution was 57%, there was considerable variation in the extent to which respondents experiencing different problems achieved any kind of resolution. Neighbour problems, landlord problems, and employment problems had very low resolution rates as compared with divorce and separation problems and consumer problems. These issues are explored more fully in the final section of the chapter.

Outcome of consumer problems

Almost all of those involved in consumer disputes took some action to try and resolve the problem. Only about three percent of respondents experiencing non-trivial consumer problems reported that they had taken no action to try and resolve the problem and respondents reporting consumer problems were the most successful in achieving some sort of agreement to resolve the problem. Among all consumer cases

DSS/school tribunal	23%	9%	59%	9%
Landlord	23%	9%	68%	4%
Money excluding benefits	46%	5%	48%	
Injury/work-related illness	31%	6%	59%	3%
Consumer	51%		46%	3%
Employment	19%	8%	67%	5%
Divorce/separation	37%	35%	47%	4%
Neighbour	26%	4%	69%	

☐ Agreement   ☐ Adjudication/court order   ☐ No resolution   ☐ No action

Figure 5.5 Final outcome of different problem types

included in the main survey, an agreement was reached to resolve the problem in over half the cases (51%). This can be compared with an overall agreement rate for example in employment cases of 19%, accidental injury 31%, divorce/separation, 13% and neighbour disputes 26%. These figures closely correspond with those in England and Wales.

Courts and ombudsmen seemed to play virtually no role at all in the in the resolution of consumer disputes. Among all consumer cases, none of those interviewed in the main survey had ended in any kind of court hearing, nor had proceedings been started.

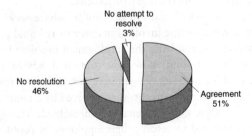

Figure 5.6 Outcome of consumer problems (Base = all consumer problems 96 weighted).

Looking at outcomes of consumer problems in relation to advice-seeking, it appears that those who did *not* obtain advice about solving their consumer problem were, on the whole, quite successful in achieving an agreement. About 53% of those who took action without advice succeeded in reaching some sort of agreement with the other side, which compared favourably with those who obtained advice about their consumer problem, of whom 50% succeeded in reaching an agreement with the other side. This finding may simply reflect the fact that advice was largely obtained once it was clear that a direct self-help approach had failed.

Those who were advised and those who handled their consumer cases alone also had similar rates of non-resolution (50% and 47% respectively). One could argue in relation to this finding that if cases taken to advisers are the most intractable cases, it is not surprising that they have a modest resolution rate. This finding also reflects the argument in Chapter 3 that the outcome of disputes depends on many factors including the person experiencing the problem, the nature of the problem and the characteristics and inclinations of the opponent.

Outcome of employment problems

Among all employment cases, about 5% of respondents took no action to resolve their problem, about 19% resolved the problem by means of an agreement with their employer and about 8% ended with a court or tribunal decision. In over two-thirds of employment problems (68%), no agreement was reached and no formal resolution to the problem was achieved. Of the handful of cases employment cases that went to a hearing, 90% were heard in industrial tribunals and ten percent were heard in the Sheriff Court ordinary procedure.

Comparing outcomes of cases in relation to advice-seeking, we find that all of those who became involved in court or tribunal proceedings, obtained advice about resolving the employment problem from an outside advice source. Among those who obtained advice about their employment problem, about one quarter succeeded in resolving the problem by agreement, ten percent were resolved by a court or tribunal decision, and two thirds (66%) remained unresolved. Among the small number who attempted to resolve their employment problem without obtaining advice, none succeeded in achieving a resolution of the problem. Whether or not advice was obtained about resolving employment problems, in over two-thirds of all employment cases agreement or legal decision achieved no resolution to the problem. This is one of the highest rates of non-resolution of all problem types and although the pattern of outcomes is comparable with England and Wales, the rate of non-resolution is considerably *higher* in Scotland (52% of employment not resolved in the England and Wales study).

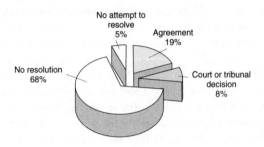

Figure 5.7 Outcome of employment problems (Weighted base = 37).

An example of the reasoning behind the decision to give up the attempt to seek a resolution to an employment problem was given by one respondent who, having received advice but having failed to secure a satisfactory response from the employer abandoned her potential suit:

> "I would have become very bitter and very nasty and I think I did a much better decision to get out. . . Because it's such a fight to get through anything like that . . . I think you need to be a Joan of Arc type to go ahead, and I'm not one. I'm much more interested in looking after my family . . . and it just wasn't worth it, I wasn't living life. I think that if you've got that sort of situation, unless it was spotted by somebody outside the two people involved, and immediately settled properly, with no hassle, no court, I can't see any point in anybody ever trying to do it, because if I'd won, what would I have? A place to work where I was hated. There is no win, is there?"

Outcome of divorce and separation problems

In a small minority of divorce and separation problems the respondent reported that no action had been taken to resolve the problem (four percent). Over one-third of all divorce and separation problems ended with a court decision or court order (36%). This is a much higher rate than for any other category of problem and is consistent with the findings in England and Wales. In only about thirteen percent of cases, however, had the problem been resolved by means of agreement, and this is somewhat lower than the proportion in England and Wales (21%). In three cases (six percent of the total) respondents reported that their divorce or separation problem had been dealt with by mediation and in all three cases an agreement was reached. The very small proportion of divorce and separation cases in the main survey reporting involvement with mediation is consistent with the findings of the English survey and at odds with the suggestion in the Scottish screening survey that mediation was more prevalent. As discussed in Chapter 2, the likely explanation for the relatively high reports of involvement with mediation at the screening stage is that respondents were referring to marriage guidance to try and avoid breakdown, rather than mediation to resolve outstanding disputes following the decision to divorce. At the time of the interviews there had been no agreement to resolve the problem in almost half of the cases (47%) and this figure is much higher than the non-resolution rate reported in the England and Wales study (22%).

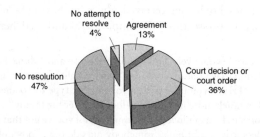

Figure 5.8 Outcome of divorce and separation problems (Weighted base = 47).

Outcome of neighbour problems

All of those respondents who had experienced a problem with a neighbour had taken some kind of action to try and resolve the problem, but as Figure 5.9 shows, neighbour disputes had a very low resolution rate. In just over a quarter of cases (27%) some kind of agreement was reached to resolve the dispute, and in a small minority of cases the neighbour dispute ended in a court hearing (4%), usually the Sheriff Court ordinary procedure. In about seven out of ten neighbour disputes no agreement was reached to resolve the dispute (69%), although in about half of these cases respondents said that the problem eventually resolved itself—in several cases by the respondent moving house. The non-resolution rate among neighbour cases was one of the highest of all problem types and these findings are again consistent with those in England and Wales.

Most respondents experiencing a problem with a neighbour had obtained advice about trying to resolve the problem (74%) and about one third of these sought advice from a lawyer.

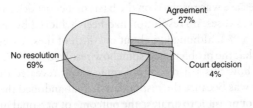

Figure 5.9 Outcome of neighbour problems (Weighted base = 49).

Outcome of money problems

No respondents who had experienced money problems (excluding benefits issues) had failed to take action to try and resolve the problem. A little under half (46%) of all of money problems ended with some agreement being reached between the parties And in a similar percentage of money cases (48%) there had been no resolution of the problem, although a minority of these said that the problem had somehow resolved itself (15%).

Outcome of accidental injury and work-related ill health cases

In about three percent of cases where respondents had suffered accidental injury or work-related ill health that required medical treatment, no action was taken to seek any compensation or other remedy. This was a much *smaller* proportion of "lumpers" than that found in England and Wales where some thirteen percent of those suffering injury or work-related ill-health had taken no action to obtain a remedy. Among those accident and ill-health victims who took some action to obtain redress in Scotland, only a small proportion tried to handle the problem themselves without first taking some advice (about 13%) and this figure is consistent with that in England and Wales. As far as the outcome of injury and occupational ill-health cases is concerned only about one in three (31%) led to an agreement between the parties to settle the claim. In a small number of cases (about six percent of claims) the case was resolved on the basis of a court decision. In almost six out of ten cases, no resolution had been achieved by the time of the interview (59%), although in about one-fifth of these cases the respondent said that the problem had somehow resolved itself. Further investigation of how this self-resolution came about revealed that in almost all cases it was because the respondent had abandoned the claim.

It was not possible to analyse the outcome of personal injury cases in relation to advice since the number of cases available for analysis is small and few respondents took any action to resolve the problem without obtaining advice. Accident victims appear either to do nothing, or to take action with the benefit of advice, usually from a lawyer adviser (see previous discussion in Chapter 3).

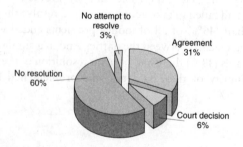

Figure 5.10 Outcome of accidental injury and work related ill-health (Weighted base = 31 weighted).

Outcome of landlord problems

In all problems relating to landlords, respondents took some action to try and resolve the difficulty. In no cases did respondents say that they had taken no advice or any other kind of action to deal with the problem. As compared with other categories of problem, difficulties with landlords appeared to be rather difficult to resolve. Over two in three of all landlord cases (68%) remained unresolved at the time of the interview. About one quarter of cases had been resolved on the basis of an agreement (23%) and about nine percent ended following a court decision. These figures are directly comparable with those found in England and Wales, although a very small proportion there (four percent) had taken no action to try and resolve the problem.

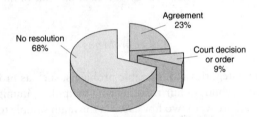

Figure 5.11 Outcome of problems with landlords (Weighted base = 43 weighted).

Outcome of benefit problems

Of the sixteen respondents interviewed in the main survey about problems to do with receiving benefits only two said that they had taken no action to deal with the problem. In a relatively high proportion of cases, by comparison with other problem types, problems to do with receiving benefits were resolved on the basis of an adjudication, although this is not surprising since benefits matters can only be heard in tribunals and any action taken by a respondent to challenge a decision about a benefit will automatically lead to a tribunal hearing. Of the 16 (unweighted) respondents interviewed in the main survey about problems relating to benefit, two reported that their cases had been decided at a tribunal hearing. Five respondents reported that the problem had been resolved by reaching an agreement with the other side, but in half of the cases (eight out of 16) respondents said that there had been no resolution of the problem.

About half of those respondents interviewed about benefit problems had obtained advice about their problem (eight out of 16).

Outcome of clinical negligence problems

Of the eight respondents interviewed about clinical negligence, seven reported that they had taken action to try and obtain a remedy. Of the seven respondents who said that they had taken some action, five had actually obtained advice. Of those respondents who took action to seek a remedy for an incident of clinical negligence, in one case the respondent reported that the matter had been resolved by agreement, and in the six remaining cases the matter was unresolved at the time of the interview.

Other problems

In the other categories of justiciable problems, such as problems over schooling of a child, unfair treatment by the police, immigration and defamation, there were two few cases in the main sample to undertake any reliable analysis.

DISPUTE RESOLUTION?

In the vast majority of cases where an agreement had been reached between the parties or a where a court or tribunal decision had been given, this effectively ended the dispute between the respondent and their opponent. In nine out of ten cases the respondent said that the agreement or decision had completely or partly ended the dispute between the two sides, although in seven percent of these cases the respondent said that the dispute had only been partly ended. Comparing agreements and court decisions it is clear that agreements appear to bring disputes to an end more completely than do court decisions. Among cases where the respondent reported that the matter had been resolved by agreement, 91% of those respondents said that the agreement had completely ended the dispute and seven percent said that it had partly ended the dispute. Only two percent of those who had reached an agreement with the other side said that the agreement had failed to end the dispute.

By contrast, those respondents whose cases had been resolved on the basis of a court, ombudsman, or tribunal adjudication were considerably *more* likely to say that the decision had *not* brought the dispute to an end. Almost one in three of respondents whose case ended with a court or tribunal hearing said that the decision had *not* ended the problem. A further seven percent said that the decision had only partly ended the dispute. In over half of those cases where agreements or court decisions had not wholly ended the dispute, the problem was reported to be still on going. These findings, together with evidence about abandoned cases suggest that in a high level of cases no resolution to problems is achieved and that simply taking advice does not necessarily lead to an agreement to resolve the problem. This reflects some of the problems with the kind of advice available to respondents, discussed in Chapter 3.

SECTION 2. THE FINANCIAL COST OF PURSUING
A RESOLUTION TO JUSTICIABLE DISPUTES

Legal Expenses

Among those cases where lawyer advice had been obtained or a decision given by a court, tribunal or ombudsman, 24% of respondents said that they had incurred no legal expenses; 13% said that their legal expenses had been paid by their opponent; and the remaining 64% said that their opponent did not pay their legal expenses, suggesting that the majority of people involved in legal proceedings were responsible for their own expenses or were in receipt of legal aid[4].

---

[4] It has to be borne in mind, however, that previous research seeking to ascertain information about legal expenses has shown that respondents are notoriously vague about expenses and responsibility for dealing with them. See Law Commission study on personal injury claims and Oxford survey of personal injury litigation op cit. See also John Baldwin, *Monitoring the Rise of the Small Claims Limit: Litigants' Experiences of Different Forms of Adjudication*, London, Lord Chancellor's Department, Research Series No 1/97, 1997. Baldwin comments, "Most of the people who were interviewed were surprisingly vague about how much they had actually expended on the litigation..an attempt to estimate the scale of expenses incurred in pursuing an action in the county courts had to be abandoned as it would have been too crude and inaccurate to be worthwhile." P 30.

Quite a high proportion of those respondents who had incurred legal expenses reported that they had been offered legal aid. About 43% of respondents who had incurred legal expenses said that they had been offered legal aid although of these, a relatively large figure of ten percent said that they had *refused* the offer of legal aid. The proportion of people being offered legal aid appears to be significantly higher than that found in England and Wales where about 27% of those who incurred legal expenses said that they had been offered legal aid[5].

The greatest use of legal aid in Scotland, as reported by respondents to the main survey, was among those experiencing problems with their landlord where two in three of those incurring legal expenses was offered legal aid (67%); divorce and separation problems, where over half of those incurring legal expenses were offered legal aid (56%), and those who had suffered an accidental injury or work-related illness when 36% were offered legal aid. Those experiencing other kinds of justiciable problem who incurred legal expenses were less likely to have received legal aid. For example, one in three of those with employment problems incurring legal expenses obtained legal aid; and about one in three of those with money problems said that they had been offered legal aid. Although the pattern of receipt of legal aid is roughly consistent with that in England and Wales, the position in Scotland suggests that higher proportions of those with landlord problems and injury problems were in receipt of legal aid than their counterparts south of the border[6].

About one percent of respondents with legal expenses had been supported by legal expenses insurance, and in less than one percent of cases where expenses had been incurred a trade union or staff association provided financial backing. About one percent of those incurring legal expenses said that they had been offered a speculative fee arrangement offered by a solicitor. Finally, about five percent of respondents who incurred legal expenses said that they had been offered free legal advice, generally by a solicitor or friend or relative.

Not all respondents who incurred legal expenses were, according to their reports, involved in formal legal proceedings. Among those who said that proceedings had been issued or a hearing held, about 42% said that they had been offered legal aid, but none said that they had

---

[5] Since there was no distinction made in the questionnaire between legal aid and legal advice and assistance it is not possible to ascertain to which respondents were referring.

[6] This is hard to reconcile with the fact that legal aid in personal injury cases per 100,000 population is one third lower in Scotland than in England and Wales.

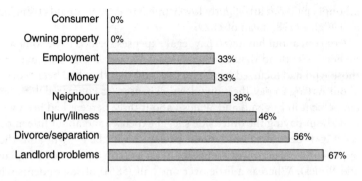

Figure 5.12 Proportion of respondents incurring legal expenses who were offered legal aid, within problem type (weighted base = 124 those incurring legal expenses).

had legal expenses insurance or been backed by a trade union or employer. This leaves over half (58%) of those involved in formal legal proceedings apparently responsible personally for their own legal expenses. In England and Wales the figure was somewhat higher at 68%.

Of all those respondents who incurred some legal expenses, whether or not legal proceedings were commenced, just over one in three said that they had paid some of those expenses personally (37%) and a further six percent said that they expected to have to pay some money in legal expenses. Among those who had paid some legal expenses themselves, the median amount paid was £150 (mean £597, range £7–£4993). One-quarter of all those who paid some legal expenses themselves said that they paid less than £75 (26%). Half of all those who had to pay legal expenses paid less than £150. Three-quarters of those who paid their own legal expenses said that they paid less than £800. If these figures are correct, then the fears expressed by respondents in Chapter 3, and those vividly expressed in Chapter 6 may be somewhat exaggerated, although for many people in difficult circumstances even £50 is an unaffordable amount of money to obtain redress. Moreover, among the group of respondents who reported that they had paid some legal expenses, about one-fifth said that they had *not* expected to have to pay anything in legal expenses, a figure which is identical to that found in England and Wales. In general, the figures on legal expenses are similar to those in England and Wales although the amounts paid out are slightly lower (median expenses paid in England and Wales £198, mean of £829).

Concern about having to pay legal expenses seemed to be somewhat higher in Scotland than in England and Wales. About one quarter of those who had incurred legal expenses said that they had been worried about having to pay their own legal expenses (as compared with only ten percent in England and Wales); about three percent had been worried about paying the other side's legal expenses and about fifteen percent had been worried about paying both their own and their opponent's expenses (as compared with only five percent in England and Wales). Whereas a little over one half (58%) of respondents who had incurred legal expenses said that they *had not been worried* at any stage about having to pay legal expenses, the comparable figure was 84% England and Wales. Moreover, even about ten percent of those who in fact incurred no legal expenses said that they had been worried at some time about having to pay legal expenses. The picture emerging is clearly of considerable concern about legal expenses which reflects the discussion in Chapter 3 about barriers to seeking legal advice and the discussion that follows in Chapter 7 about perceptions of the legal system.

Other costs

About 60% of *all* respondents to the main questionnaire reported that they had incurred costs in sorting out the problem. These costs were most often telephone calls (52%), travelling costs (22%) and, less often, loss of earnings (8%). In about one-half of cases these costs did not exceed £10 and in a further one-fifth of cases the costs did not exceed £50. In about two percent of cases, however, the cost of sorting out the problem was said to have been more than £10,000. About 17% of respondents said that they had to take time off work or used annual leave to sort out the problem.

SECTION 3. EXPLAINING OUTCOME

In order to identify whether there were any factors that were significantly associated with the outcome of cases, a multiple regression analysis, similar to that undertaken for advice-seeking, was carried

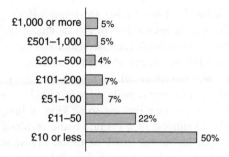

Figure 5.13 Cost of resolving dispute excluding legal expenses (Base = all those with costs 254 weighted).

out. The analysis of outcome distinguished between cases in which a resolution had been reached either through agreement or court decision or order, tribunal or ombudsman's adjudication (resolved), and those cases where there had been no agreement or adjudication or court order (not resolved).

The purpose of this analysis is to try and estimate the distinct contribution to different outcomes made by particular factors and to say whether respondents with specific characteristics might be more or less likely than the average respondent to achieve a resolution of their justiciable problem. The factors included in the analysis of outcome were demographic factors such as age, sex, education, income, class, employment status, as well as other factors hypothesised as likely to have an influence on outcome; for example the type of problem experienced, the type of remedy sought by the respondent; and whether the respondent was initiating the action or was the subject of action. The analysis also includes a variable concerning whether any advice was obtained and the nature of that advice. For the purposes of this analysis the definitions of advice used in the first section of the Chapter were further refined as follows: "legal advice" involving advice from a solicitor (and very occasionally a law centre); "other advice where action taken" which involved the adviser taking positive steps to assist in the resolution of the problem by contacting the other side, negotiating with the other side, contacting another person to try and resolve the problem, accompanying the respondent to a court or tribunal, or representing the respondent at a court or tribunal; "other advice where no action taken" which involved the adviser in simply offering information or advice or advising the respondent to go elsewhere; and "no advice".

The results of the multiple regression analysis indicate that *only one factor* was found to be associated with the outcome of justiciable problems and that was the nature of the remedy sought. Respondents who were *not* seeking a money remedy were *less* likely to resolve their dispute than those who were seeking some kind of lump sum payment. Moreover, the likelihood of a dispute being resolved is higher when larger lump sum payments (£501 or more) are at stake than lower amounts. In contrast, when the remedy sought was a weekly payment, respondents were less likely to achieve a resolution of the dispute, although their likelihood of achieving a resolution was still greater than when no money was at stake.[7]

This factor was also found to be significant in the England and Wales study where seeking larger lump sum payments was also strongly associated with increased likelihood of resolution. However, the other associations observed in Scotland were not seen for England and Wales. Several other factors were found to be associated with resolving disputes in England and Wales but not in Scotland: age, income, type of problem, employment status, educational qualification, type of advice sought, social class, whether the respondent was a defender and whether negative effects were reported. The considerably lower number of associations reported in Scotland relative to England and Wales may partly be explained by the smaller sample size in Scotland.[8]

INTERACTION OF FACTORS ASSOCIATED WITH OUTCOME

The analysis in this section so far has identified several factors that appear to be associated with the likelihood that a resolution of the justiciable problem would be achieved. It is not evident, however, how these various factors interact. To address this question an analysis similar to that carried out for advice-seeking was undertaken[9] and the results make it possible to identify a number of subgroups of respondents with

[7] Although employment status was significantly correlated with outcome, the correlation is fairly weak and the results for different categories were all on the borderline of significance.

[8] The results for those with degree level qualifications were on the borderline of significance.

[9] The CHAID (Chi-squared Automatic Interaction Detector) module within SPSS. The full results of the CHAID analysis are given in Appendix B.

similar characteristics and with varying propensity to achieve a resolution of their justiciable problem. The analysis produced six different (mutually exclusive and exhaustive) groups for which the percentage of cases achieving a resolution of the problem varied from 6% to 69%. The characteristics of these groups are discussed below.

Low propensity for cases to be resolved

The analysis suggests that the group of respondents least likely of all to achieve a resolution of their problem had the following characteristics:

- Problems to do with employment, neighbours, accidental injury, landlord and tenant, owning property, benefits/education
- No money amount was sought
- Respondent had relatively low educational attainment.

The rate at which this group achieved a resolution of their problem was about six per hundred and the group comprised about eleven percent of all respondents interviewed in the main survey.

The group with the next lowest propensity to achieve a resolution of their problem had similar characteristics in that they had experienced problems relating to employment, landlords, benefits or education problems, were not seeking money from the dispute but who had relatively high educational attainment.

High propensity for cases to be resolved

The group with the highest rate of achieving a resolution of their problem had the following characteristics:

- Respondents who were seeking a money remedy
- Respondents who used only non-legal sources of advice.

This group had a resolution rate of 69% and comprised about eleven percent of the main survey sample.

The other group with an above average rate of resolution (57%) consisted of respondents with a variety of problems (divorce/separation, consumer, neighbours, accident or injury or owning property) who had relatively high educational attainment and were not seeking a money remedy.

These findings have some common features with those for the CHAID analysis in the England and Wales study. In both studies the group with the lowest rate for resolving disputes included respondents in neighbour or landlord and tenant disputes who had low educational attainment.

CONCLUSION

The discussion in this chapter has focused on the outcome of justiciable problems. The chief outcome with which the chapter has been concerned is whether or not the justiciable problems experienced by members of the public had been resolved. "Resolution" has been defined as an agreement to end or settle the problem (with or without the commencement of legal proceedings) ("agreement"), or the conclusion of the matter by means of a court, tribunal or ombudsman's decision or order ("adjudication"). No judgement has been made about the quality of agreements or respondents' satisfaction with the terms of agreements. "Resolution" also includes both cases where the respondent won their case in court and where they lost their case in court. "Unresolved" cases are those that were in effect abandoned after action was taken, but in the absence of any settlement or adjudication.

The analysis has shown that over half of all members of the public in Scotland who experienced non-trivial justiciable problems failed to achieve any resolution to those problems, whether or not they had sought advice. However, this figure obscures two important facts. First, that the vast majority of those who sought advice had already tried to resolve their problem alone. This means that cases in which advice was sought are almost by definition the more serious or more intractable. Second, it obscures differences in the degree of assistance obtained from advisers.

A proportion of those who received advice were told that it was not worth pursuing the case and most respondents who received this advice took it. In this way the availability of good quality advice can filter weak cases out of the system and save individuals the time, expense and heartache that they might otherwise have spent in pursuing a fruitless cause. On the other hand, the relatively low level of advice to abandon cases that was actually given by advisers suggests that those taking the step of seeking advice had persevered with some justification. In those circumstances the very high failure rate is notable.

An important fact emerging clearly from the analysis in this chapter is the very limited use made by the public of formal legal proceedings to resolve justiciable problems. In almost nine out of ten problems no legal proceedings were commenced, no ombudsman was contacted and no ADR process was used. This is despite the fact that about two in three members of the public took some advice about trying to resolve their problem, and that of those, about half received advice from a solicitor at some point about their problem[10]. Involvement in legal proceedings was most common in cases concerning divorce and separation, landlord and tenant problems, accidental injury, and ownership of residential property. Involvement in legal proceedings was least common in consumer disputes and neighbour disputes. Although this pattern is roughly consistent with that found in England and Wales, involvement in legal proceedings was higher in Scotland for landlord and tenant problems and lower than in England for divorce and separation problems, employment problems, and disputes over residential property.

Only a very small proportion of cases ended on the basis of a court order or tribunal adjudication, and those members of the sample whose problem was resolved by adjudication were disproportionately members of the public who were being *pursued* via legal proceedings rather than those who were *initiating* action. In the case of defenders, problems were far more likely to be concluded on the basis of a court decision or order than in the case of pursuers, and far less likely to remain unresolved. This demonstrates the reluctance voluntarily to become involved in legal proceedings that was so graphically described by respondents in Chapter 3.

According to respondents' reports, the majority of people involved in legal proceedings and who incurred legal expenses were responsible for their own expenses or were in receipt of legal aid. A little over two in five respondents incurring legal expenses had been offered legal aid, although about ten percent of these had refused the offer. The proportion of people offered Legal Aid in Scotland was significantly *higher* than the proportion in England and Wales and this was before the reduction in the coverage of civil legal aid in England and Wales following the Access to Justice Act 1999. By far the greatest use of legal aid was among those experiencing landlord and tenant problems (where two thirds of those incurring legal expenses were offered legal

---

[10] See discussion in Chapter 3.

aid), divorce and separation problems, (where over half of those incurring legal expenses received legal aid), and those suffering accidental injury (among whom over one in three was offered legal aid)[11]. Legal expenses insurance was used by a handful of respondents who incurred legal expenses, as were speculative fee arrangements. A rather larger handful of those who incurred legal expenses had received free legal advice from a solicitor, friend or relative.

On the whole the amounts of money reported to have been paid out by respondents by way of legal expenses were relatively modest, although the information provided by respondents about their expenses might be unreliable. Concern about having to pay legal expenses seemed to be somewhat higher in Scotland than in England and Wales, and the picture that emerged reflects the discussion in Chapter 3 about barriers to seeking legal advice and the discussion that follows in Chapter 7 about perceptions of the legal system.

The results of multivariate analysis again confirm that problem type is important in the outcome of justiciable problems, although the type of remedy desired also helps to explain different outcomes. Some problems appear to have a generally low rate of resolution, for example employment problems, neighbour problems and problems with landlords. These types of problems combined with low educational achievement showed the lowest propensity to be resolved. Problems such as divorce and separation, consumer problems, accidental injury or problems relating to ownership of residential property had a higher propensity to be resolved where the respondent had a relatively high level of educational attainment.

In general, problems were more likely to reach some kind of resolution when a money remedy was being sought by or from the respondent, than when the remedy required was some change in behaviour. Using the law to change behaviour can be tortuous, expensive, and potentially damaging, but the use of alternative dispute resolution processes such as mediation among the sample of respondents dealing with justiciable problems was negligible. This fact is notable when considered in relation to the finding that agreements appear to bring disputes to an end more completely than do court decisions.

---

[11] This finding is frankly puzzling in the light of the available statistics on legal aid in Scotland.

6

Fulfilling Objectives?

This chapter focuses on respondents' reported motivations for taking action to try and resolve their justiciable problems, and the extent to which those objectives. The discussion also describes some of the effects of trying to achieve those objectives and the extent to which the outcomes achieved were regarded as fair. In the second section of the chapter the results of multivariate analysis are used to explain further the factors that are associated with the achievement of objectives and perceptions of the fairness of outcomes.

Identifying objectives

The approach taken to the identification of objectives in the survey was quite deliberate. Anticipating a complex and subtle mix of objectives and the possibility that objectives might develop and change over time, an elaborate series of questions was posed to respondents. Rather than suggesting a range of possible objectives or motivations to respondents, as has been the practice in other recent surveys[1], completely open questions were asked about objectives. This was done to avoid influencing responses by offering alternatives that might appear to be more socially acceptable motivations for taking action than simply the desire to obtain financial compensation.

First, respondents were asked about their initial main objective (*"Thinking back to when you first decided to do something about [the problem] what was the* main *thing you wanted to achieve?"*). This was

---

[1] For example the NCC survey in 1995, and the SCC survey in 1997. The approach adopted in these surveys was to ask, "What do/did you most want the law to help you to achieve?" Respondents were then asked to choose, from eight different outcomes, the one that was most important to them. The outcomes were: "Financial compensation; Prevent it happening again to me; Prevent it happening to someone else in future; An apology; Judgment about who is to blame; Clearing my name; An explanation; Public exposure of the culprit."

followed by supplementary questions designed to elicit additional objectives (*"At that stage, were there any other things that you hoped to achieve?"*); this question was repeated until all of the respondent's objectives had been identified. In addition to the questions about initial objectives, further questions were asked in order to capture any changes that might have occurred in respondents' objectives during the course of trying to resolve their problem (*"You've now told me about what you wanted to achieve initially. During the course of trying to sort out [the problem] did you change your mind at any time about what you wanted to achieve?"*). For each initial and subsequent objective recorded, respondents were asked to say whether they had achieved their objective completely, partly, or not at all. As will be seen in later discussion, the time taken in probing objectives and trying to capture changes in objectives yielded rather less than had been anticipated since respondents generally had only one driving motivation and that was very specifically calibrated to the nature of the problem.

Initial primary objectives

In response to the open question asked about main objectives, the single most common objective offered by respondents for taking action to resolve their problem was money or property related. About half of all respondents said that their main aim in taking action was money or property related (50% of all main aims), which is unsurprising given the balance of problem types in the sample. Examples of the kinds of money or property related aims mentioned by respondents to the survey were as follows:

• To get my rent paid for me
• To receive (increased) benefit payments
• Reduction of tax demand
• Compensation
• To get my money back/refund
• Want more time to make payments
• Reduction of bill.

The next most common motivation was to obtain some kind of change in behaviour on the part of the other person involved in the problem. About twelve percent of respondents said that this was their main objective and examples of the types of change wanted were:

- noise reduction
- to keep the other side away from the respondent of their family
- to prevent further annoyance or "hassle" from the other party.

About seven percent of respondents said that their main motivation in taking action was to achieve an objective in relation to their employment. For example:

- Change to job conditions
- Reinstatement in job.

About four percent of respondents said that their main objective was to obtain a separation or divorce, or to deal with property following divorce or separation, or to deal with matters relating to children as a result of a divorce or separation (about eight percent of respondents taking action).

About two percent of respondents wanted to prove their own innocence or to prove that the other side was in the wrong, or to enforce their rights. In just about one percent of cases, respondents said that that they wanted to prevent the same thing from happening to others, and a similar proportion of respondents said that their primary objective in taking action was to achieve an apology.

In a substantial number of cases the main objective given was either so broad or so specific to the particular problem being experienced, that it was difficult to code the responses into a common category. Occasionally this was because people simply said that they wanted "justice", but in other cases their objective was a very specific description of how they wanted their problem to be resolved. The pattern of responses to questions about main objectives in taking action is very similar to that in England and Wales, as can be seen from Figure 6.1.

Rather few respondents were able to specify more than one objective in taking action, which shows a high degree of single-mindedness and rather defeated the subtlety of questioning. In all, two-thirds of the sample said that they only had one objective in taking action. When respondents did mention a second objective, this tended to follow the pattern of first objectives, in that respondents predominantly mentioned money or property-related objectives, objectives relating to divorce or separation, and job-related objectives. Respondents occasionally mentioned as a second objective the desire to obtain an apology or to prevent the same thing from happening to others in a similar situation, but these were a very small minority.

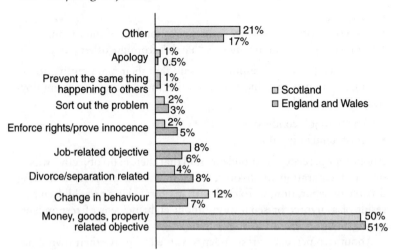

Figure 6.1 Main objectives in taking action (Base all who took action = 445 weighted) compared with England and Wales.

The type of objective desired by respondents naturally varied substantially by problem type. Although many respondents gave objectives that were so specific that they could not be properly categorised, varying patterns of motivation emerge between different problem types that reflect the nature of the problem and the range of possible remedies.

Consumer problems

A little under three quarters of those with consumer problems said that their main objective was money or property related (e.g. to get my money back or a refund, compensation, to get the property or goods repaired or maintained, to have the goods replaced); about three percent said that they wanted to sort out the problem; and two percent said that they wanted an apology. None of those with consumer problems said that their main objective in taking action was to prevent the same thing from happening to someone else, although in four percent of consumer cases the respondent said that their main objective was to achieve a change in behaviour on the part of the other person involved in the problem.

Money problems

Among those interviewed about money problems about 91% said that their main objective was money or property related (e.g. to get my money back, reduction of bill or demand) and about four percent said that they wanted to enforce their rights or prove their innocence. No respondents said that they wanted any apology or to prevent the same thing from happening to anyone else.

Employment problems

Over two-thirds of those experiencing employment problems mentioned a specific objective related to their job (68%) (e.g. reinstatement, change in conditions). About 18% mentioned money-related objectives such as getting money back or receiving payments that they were owed; six percent said that they wanted to prove their innocence. About nine percent of those experiencing employment problems said that they were primarily seeking a change in behaviour by their employer. None of the respondents interviewed about an employment problem said that their main motivation in taking action was to secure an apology or prevent the same thing from happening to others. This finding is slightly different from that in England and Wales where a relatively high proportion of those with employment problems were seeking an apology.

Divorce and separation

The most commonly cited primary objective of those experiencing divorce and separation problems was to obtain a divorce or separation (21%) or to obtain a fair split of assets or property after separation or divorce (14%). A large proportion offered family-related objectives to do with children (40%). About eleven percent said that they wanted to get the other side to pay child support; and about two percent said that they wanted to keep the other side away from them or their house. A further eight percent said that they just wanted no further trouble or hassle from the other side in the dispute. None of those involved in divorce or separation problems said that a primary objective was to receive an apology or to prevent the same thing from happening to others.

Neighbour problems

The most common objective among those experiencing problems with neighbours was to achieve a change in the behaviour of the other side (79%), for example noise reduction, to keep the other side away from the respondent's home, or to bring an end to hassle and aggravation. About four percent said that their objective was related to money or property, about two percent just wanted to sort out the problem and a further two percent said that they wanted to prove that the other side was wrong or to prove their own innocence. No respondents involved in neighbour disputes said that their primary objective was to receive an apology or to prevent the same thing from happening to others.

Accidental injury

Compensation was the most common motive for taking action among those suffering injury or work-related ill-health (36%); although about one-third mentioned a motive that was job-related (32%), and seven percent said that they wanted to enforce their rights. Not a single respondent experiencing accidental injury said that their primary motive in taking action was to receive an apology from the other side, despite the fact that this is often cited as a motivation for litigating. About eleven percent, however, said that their main objective in taking action was to prevent the same thing from happening to someone else. This may reflect the high number of work accidents and work-related illnesses in the sample.

Problems with landlords

Those experiencing problems with landlords offered an interesting range of motives for taking action. The most common objective was to get the property repaired or maintained (57%). The next most common objective mentioned by eight percent of respondents with landlord problems was in relation to the payment of rent. Another seven percent of respondents experiencing problems with landlords said that their main objective in taking action was to obtain an apology. This was the highest proportion of cases in which an apology was mentioned as the primary motive for taking action to deal with a problem. About four percent said that they wanted a reduction of a bill or demand by the landlord and two percent said that they wanted to keep the other side away from them or their family. These motives certainly support the picture of landlord misbehaviour commented on in Chapter 2.

CHANGING OBJECTIVES?

In order to gauge the extent to which respondents' objectives might have developed or changed over time, all were asked whether during the course of trying to sort out their problem, they had changed their mind at any time about what they wanted to achieve. Only about one in ten respondents said that there had been any change in what they had been wanting to achieve (10%), but even when this occurred there was little change between broad categories of objectives. So a respondent who had mentioned a money or property related objective as their initial primary objective would be most likely, if they reported having changed their mind about what they wanted, to mention another money related objective as their new objective.

MONEY CLAIMED AND OWED

A little under one in three respondents was seeking to obtain some money from the other person or organisation involved in their problem (29%); about eight percent of respondents wanted the other person or organisation to *reduce* the amount of money they were demanding from the respondent; the remaining 63% of respondents were seeking some other kind of outcome to their problem. This means that nearly two in three people were seeking a remedy *other* than direct payment of money. Among those respondents who were trying to get a reduction in the amount of money being demanded by their opponent about two-thirds (54%) were hoping to get a bill reduced, and about two-fifths (44%) were trying to get a reduction in regular payments that they were making or being asked to make.

Most of those who were trying to obtain money from their opponent in the dispute were hoping for a lump sum (71%) and most of the remainder wanted regular payments (although 5% wanted both). The amount of money being sought (or the amount by which the respondent wanted a bill reduced) was in the majority of cases relatively modest. Almost three quarters of respondents wanted no more than

£1000 (72% and most of those wanted no more than £500); about one-fifth of respondents wanted between £1000 and £5000 (21%); about six percent wanted between £5000 and £15000; and the remaining two percent were seeking over £15,000.

The handful of cases where the amount of money at stake exceeded £15,000 comprised injury and money problems excluding benefits.

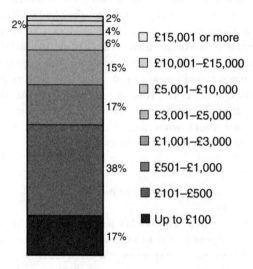

Figure 6.2 Amount of claim where respondent seeking lump sum (Base = 117 weighted all those seeking lump sum).

HOW EXPECTATIONS WERE FORMED

According to respondents, in two-thirds of the cases in which a sum of money was being claimed (69%), the sum being claimed was the respondent's *own* calculation of the amount he or she was entitled to. In other cases, respondents said that the figure had been suggested by a friend or work colleague (eight percent) or by another organisation (3%) or by a solicitor (6%). In five percent of cases respondents said that they had arrived at their assessment of the value of the claim on the basis of previous experience. Although in England and Wales about three percent of respondents said explicitly that they had based their assumption about the value of the claim on media reports of similar cases, no Scottish respondents mentioned this. Expectations of the amount likely to be recovered were thus rarely based on advice and this has implications for the extent to which respondents might feel that they had achieved their objectives.

AMOUNTS RECOVERED

Of those who succeeded in receiving money from the other side, the overwhelming majority received a lump sum rather than regular payments. The median amount recovered as a lump sum was £268 (mean £1,343) with a range of £3–£13,000. Although a little over one-half of respondents thought that the amount received was about the same as they had been expecting, about one-third received *much* or a *bit* less than they had hoped for. Interestingly, only about 13% of respondents said that they had received a little or much *more* than they had hoped for, and this figure is substantially lower than that in England and Wales (where one-quarter said that they received a little or much more than they had hoped for). Since most respondents said that they had not been advised about the amount of money that they should be claiming, but had worked it out largely for themselves, the high proportion of respondents obtaining the amount they expected might be taken as a sign of success. Indeed it seems that the majority who succeeded in obtaining a money settlement or court award achieved what they were hoping for or a bit more. However, about one in three were disappointed in the amount obtained, a higher figure than in England and Wales where about one in five recovered less than they were expecting.

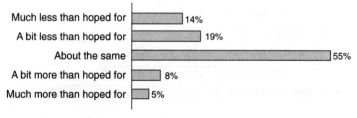

Much less than hoped for — 14%
A bit less than hoped for — 19%
About the same — 55%
A bit more than hoped for — 8%
Much more than hoped for — 5%

Figure 6.3 "Was this more, less or about the same amount of money as you had hoped for?" (Base = 59 weighted)

AMOUNTS PAID OUT

About two percent of respondents said that they had had to pay some of their opponent's legal expenses and some nine percent paid money by way of settlement to their opponent (about one-third paying lump sums and the other two-thirds making regular payments). The median lump sum paid by respondents to their opponent was £373 (mean £486, range £120–£1,100). Among those respondents who agreed to make regular payments to their opponent, the median payment was £35 (mean £198 and range £5–£625).

Respondents who had to pay money by way of a settlement were those involved in divorce and separation problems (36% of those paying money to the other side), respondents experiencing money problems (27% of those paying money to the other side), and those having problems with landlords (36%).

Although the number paying out money to their opponents was rather small, the analysis shows that expectations in relation to money paid out were rather different from those concerning money recovered. Only about one in five of those respondents who had to make a payment said that the amount they paid was about the same as expected. On the other hand, over *two thirds* (68%) said that they had had to pay a *little more* or *much more* than they had been expecting. About one in ten said that they had paid less than they had expected. These figures suggest that levels of disappointment about the amount of money to be paid out were higher in Scotland than in England and Wales where about half of those who paid out money said that the amount was what they had expected and only one-third said that they had to pay a little or much more than they were expecting.

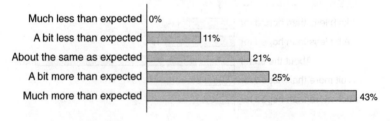

Figure 6.4 "Was this more, less or about the same amount of money as you had expected to pay?" (Base = 12 weighted).

OTHER AGREEMENTS—NO PAYMENT OF MONEY

In about 17% of all cases in the sample, respondents made agreements involving terms other than the direct payment of money to or by the respondent. Of the cases where a non-money agreement had been reached, the agreement nonetheless most often involved an agreement that related to money or to property. About 50% of agreements that did not directly involve the payment of money were money-related and about two-thirds of those agreements were to do with the repair, replacement, or maintenance of goods or property.

About a third of agreements that did not involve the payment of money concerned changes in the respondent's behaviour or in the behaviour of the other side. For example, keeping noise down, keeping away from the respondent or the respondent keeping away from the other side, or changes in working conditions.

IMPACT OF SORTING OUT PROBLEMS

All respondents who took any action were asked whether there had been any impact on their work or personal life as a result of trying to resolve their problem. Of the 61% of respondents who were in paid work during the course of sorting out the dispute, about one third reported that there had been a negative impact on their working life. The most common negative effects on working life were that the respondent had had to take time off work as a result of stress (27% of those reporting negative effects on work) or that relationships with colleagues had suffered (40%). About one-quarter of respondents reporting negative effects on work said that they had had to move to another job or leave their place of work, and about 17% said that their chances of promotion had been badly affected.

Such effects tended to be experienced *most often* by respondents whose problem involved employment disputes, and divorce or separation problems, although it was also mentioned by those with money problems and those suffering accidental injury. This suggests that respondents were probably referring as much to the impact of the problem itself as to the impact of trying to sort out the problem. Respondents who were *least likely* to report negative effects on their work were those who had been involved in consumer disputes and disputes with landlords.

All respondents who took action to resolve their problem, whether working or not, were asked whether they had experienced a range of both positive and negative feelings or situations listed on a show card (see below Table 6.1). Three out of four respondents (77%) reported having experienced one or more of the feelings or situations listed (exactly the same proportion as in England and Wales).

On the negative side almost three-quarters of those reporting some impact said that they had found the experience of trying to sort out the problem stressful. About four in ten said that they had had difficulty sleeping as a result of trying to sort out the problem (39% of cases)[2] and a slightly lower percentage said that their health had suffered (30%). About 15% of those reporting some impact said that their relationships with family and friends had suffered. About one in ten (11%) said that they had had to move to another house or flat as a result of trying to sort out the problem, and about five percent said that they had had to move to another area.

Those respondents reporting stressful effects tended to be concentrated among money, landlord, divorce and separation and employment problems, although consumer problems also appear to involve stress in resolving the problem. Those who had difficulty sleeping were most likely to be experiencing neighbour problems, divorce and separation, and landlord problems.

On the positive side, about one quarter of respondents reported that the experience had given them a sense of empowerment (26%) and about one third said that they were pleased to have been able to enforce their rights (32%). About four percent said that they were glad to have been able to clear their name. Those most likely to have experienced a positive feeling of empowerment as a result of resolving their problem were those involved in consumer problems and divorce and separation issues.

As Table 6.1 shows, these results bear a striking resemblance to those found in England and Wales. Although there is a suggestion of slightly higher levels of experienced stress in Scotland, the pattern between the two jurisdictions is virtually identical. This finding, bearing in mind the difference in cultures, the differences in the law and differences in procedures for dealing with disputes is notable. The results certainly indicate that in Scotland perceived unpleasantness and uncertainty of legal proceedings swamp other more positive aspects of enforcing or defending rights.

---

[2] The figures add up to more than 100% because respondents were able to refer to as many items as they had experienced.

Table 6.1 Negative and positive effects of sorting out problem (Base = all who took action 452 weighted)

Effects of sorting out the problem	% respondents taking action	% respondents experiencing effects	% respondents taking action England and Wales
None of these effects	23%		23%
Negative effects:			
I have found the experience of trying to sort out the problem stressful	56%	63%	49%
I have had difficulty sleeping	30%	28%	22%
My health has suffered	23%	29%	22%
My relationships with family and friends have suffered	11%	20%	15%
I have had to move to another house/flat	9%	11%	9%
I have had to move to another area	4%		
Positive effects:			
The experience has made me feel that I have some control over my situation	20%	26%	24%
I am glad to have enforced my rights	25%	32%	24%
I am glad to have cleared my name	3%	4%	5%
Life is more peaceful now that I have sorted it out	*	*	*
Other effect on life	6%	8%	9%

* Less than 1 percent (small type)

IMPACT AND OUTCOME

When comparing self-helpers with those who received advice about their problem it appears that those who received advice were *more* likely to report negative impacts than those who handled their problems alone. For example, 63% of those who received advice said that they found dealing with the problem stressful as compared with only 42% of self-helpers. This is likely, however, to be a reflection of the seriousness of the matter and possibly the degree of difficulty experienced in achieving a resolution.

There were, however, significant differences in impact depending on the means by which the problem was resolved. Those respondents who resolved their problem by agreement were the least *likely* to say that they had found the experience of sorting out the problem stressful (44%) and the most likely to say that the experience had made them feel in control of the situation (29%) or that they were glad to be enforcing their rights (33%). Respondents whose problem had led to a court or tribunal adjudication were the most likely to say that the experience of resolving the problem had been stressful (69%), that they had had difficulty sleeping (41%) and that their health had suffered (33%). Respondents who had failed to resolve their problem but who had taken some action to do so were also more likely than those who had reached an agreement to say that they had found the whole business stressful (62%), that they had had trouble sleeping (33%) or that their health had suffered (27%) (Figure 6.5)

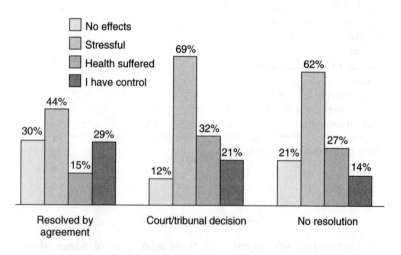

Figure 6.5 Impact of sorting out problem in relation to outcome (Base = all those who took action 452 weighted).

TIME TAKEN TO RESOLVE THE PROBLEM

Respondents were asked whether or not the time taken to resolve the problem had met with their expectations. In only about one-fifth of cases did the time taken meet expectations and in about six out of ten cases respondents said that the problem had take a *bit longer or much longer* than they had expected. In under one-fifth of cases did respondents report that the problem had taken *less* time than had been expected to sort out.

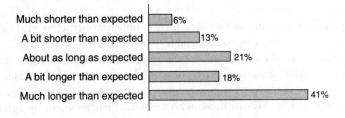

Figure 6.6 "Did solving this problem taken a shorter time than expected, about as long as expected, or a longer time than you expected?" (Base = resolved problems 266 weighted).

The respondents who were most likely to feel that the problem had taken much longer than expected to resolve were those who had experienced problems with a landlord (63% saying it had taken much longer), a money problem (59%), those who had dealt with consumer problems (49%), and those involved in divorce and separation (48%). Very few respondents in experiencing any type of problem said that the problem had taken much less time than expected to resolve. These findings differ a little from those in England and Wales where a somewhat lower proportion of respondents said that the problem had taken "much" longer than expected (33% in England and Wales) and where a slightly higher proportion thought that the problem had taken a much shorter time than expected (12%).

ACHIEVING OBJECTIVES?

For each objective that had been identified, respondents were asked whether they had achieved their main objective completely or partly. Among all respondents interviewed about their objectives in taking action, only a little over one-third said that their main objectives had been achieved completely (38%); about 15% thought that the aim had been partly achieved; and one-third (38%) thought that the aim had not been achieved. A further nine percent said that it was too early to say whether or not they would achieve their objective. The results for the achievement of secondary aims were very similar. Some respondents who did not resolve their problem nonetheless said that they had partially achieved their objectives.

Looking at the extent to which respondents felt that they had achieved their objectives in relation to the outcome of the case, it appears that there was a significant difference depending on the type of outcome. While 70% of those who resolved their problem by agreement said that they had completely or party achieved their main objective, only 43% of those whose problem was dealt with in a court or tribunal said that they had achieved their main objective either completely or partly.

The main objective that was most likely to be achieved was when the objective related to divorce or separation problems. Over two-thirds of those respondents who gave this as their main objective (69%) said that they had completely achieved their objective. This figure is almost twenty percent higher than the figure in England and Wales, although the number of cases in this category in Scotland was quite small. The next type of objective most likely to be completely achieved was changing behaviour. Just over half (52%) of those respondents who gave this as their primary motivation for taking action reported that they had completely achieved their objective. This finding is notable since in England and Wales, main objectives relating to changing behaviour were the *least likely* to be achieved. Only about one in five respondents in England and Wales who had wanted to change the other side's behaviour said that they had completely achieved their main objective.

Only about one third of those respondents whose main aim was money, property or goods related said that they had completely achieved their objective. This finding is more in line with the England and Wales figure where about 40% of those motivated by money or property objectives said that they had completely achieved their main objective. The objectives least likely to be achieved were a job-related aim where only 15% of respondents trying to secure a job-related objective said that they had completely achieved their objective. This figure is virtually identical to that in England and Wales (15%). The numbers for preventing the problem from happening to others and receiving an apology are too small to analyse.

The achievement of objectives varied substantially between problem types. Those respondents most likely to have completely or partly achieved their objectives were those dealing with divorce and separation problems, and accident victims (for whom compensation was the primary objective of taking action to resolve the justiciable problem). Those *least* likely to have achieved their objectives were tenants seeking remedies from landlords, those seeking to resolve a problem at work, and those dealing with money problems. It is interesting that in England and Wales neighbour problems appeared to be somewhat more intractable than in Scotland, divorce and separation problems appeared to be more difficult to resolve and landlord problems were equally difficult to resolve. In both jurisdictions, employment problems have very low levels of satisfactory resolution although the picture looks somewhat worse in Scotland (Figure 6.7).

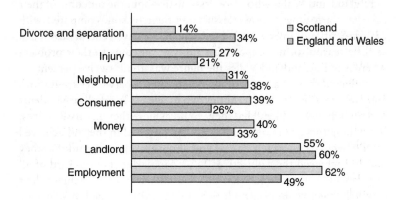

Figure 6.7 Proportion within each problem type *failing* to achieve their main objective (Base = all who took action 452) compared with England and Wales.

EXPECTATIONS OF FULFILLING OBJECTIVES

Although it is rather difficult to ask people after the event what their expectations had been when beginning to deal with a problem, respondents were all asked how likely they had thought it would be that they would achieve what they wanted when they first took action. On the whole, respondents claimed to have been fairly optimistic about the possibility of achieving their objectives when they had first taken action. About eight in ten respondents said that they had thought it very likely or fairly likely that they would achieve their objective (81%). Of the twenty percent one-quarter who reported that they had been less optimistic at the time they took action to deal with the problem, the main reasons for pessimism were: the past behaviour of the other side (34%); feeling of powerlessness (25%); general pessimism (22%); expectations of how the other side would respond (8%); lack of knowledge about this sort of problem (8%); that their own legal position seemed weak (4%); conflict of views with other side (4%); communication difficulties (1%). This pattern is very similar to that found in England and Wales. Notable differences, however, are expressions of powerlessness and general pessimism, which were more common in Scotland than in England and Wales. This issue was discussed in Chapters 1 and 3. So, for example, about eleven percent of respondents in England and Wales who were pessimistic about the outcome of their case gave a feeling of powerlessness as their reason, compared with 25% in Scotland. In Scotland about one in five gave general pessimism as their reason for not expecting a positive outcome to their problem whereas in England and Wales the figure was about twelve percent.

In general there was something of a mismatch between expectations and outcomes. For example, about two in five (43%) of all respondents had thought it very likely that they would achieve their main objectives, but among this group only half said that they had in the end achieved their objective completely (52%) and about one-quarter said that they had *not* achieved their objective (24%). Similarly, about a third of all respondents had imagined that they were fairly likely to achieve their original objective, but only a little over a third succeeded in achieving their objective completely (37%) and a relatively high proportion said that they had not achieved their objective at all (39%). Again these figures are remarkably similar to those found in England and Wales—both as to the expectations of respondents about the likely outcome of their case and as to the actual level of achievement of objectives. This mismatch between expectations and outcomes suggests that there is considerable scope for a programme of improved education on legal rights.

Those respondents who claimed to have been pessimistic all along about the likelihood of achieving their objectives were either proved correct, or had adjusted their reported expectation to coincide with outcome. Only about four percent of respondents reported that they had thought it not at all likely that they would achieve their objective. Nearly two in three of this group said that they had, indeed, failed to achieve their objective (63%). These findings are also consistent with those in England and Wales.

OUTCOME AND ACHIEVEMENT OF OBJECTIVES

Whether or not people reported that they had achieved their objectives differed depending on the nature of the outcome. Among those who had resolved their problem by agreement about seven in ten maintained that they had completely achieved their main objective in taking action and a further 18% said that they had partly achieved their objective. Only about one in ten (11%) of those respondents who had resolved their problem on the basis of an agreement said that they had *not* achieved their main objective.

Among those whose problem was resolved on the basis of a court or ombudsman's decision, a little over two in five said that they had achieved their main objective (43%), but a similar proportion (45%) said that they had *not* achieved their main objective. These findings differ from those in England and Wales in that achievement of objectives appeared to be lower when court or tribunal decisions were involved. For example, about 55% of respondents in England and Wales whose case was resolved on the basis of a court or tribunal decision said that they had achieved their main objective and fewer than one in three (30%) said that they had not.

FAIRNESS OF OUTCOME

All respondents whose problems were resolved by agreement or adjudication were asked whether, taking everything into consideration, they believed that the decision or agreement that brought the problem

to an end was fair. The responses to this question showed a striking difference between the views of those whose case had ended with a court
or tribunal decision and those who achieved settlement. The findings
are also significantly different from those in England and Wales.
Among those respondents whose dispute was resolved by an adjudicated decision only 48% said that the decision was fair (71% in England
and Wales). Of those respondents who had reached agreements to
resolve their disputes some 80% said that they thought the agreement
reached was fair (compared with 78% in England and Wales). The
chief difference, therefore, is in relation to the views of those whose
cases led to adjudication.

Fairness of agreements

Among those assessing the fairness of agreements there were some significant differences in perception based both on characteristics of
respondents and type of problem. For example, respondents involved
in problems with landlords, divorce and separation problems and
employment problems were significantly more likely to say that they
thought the agreement reached was *unfair* (60% of landlord agreements, 57% of agreements about employment problems, and 50% of
agreements about divorce and separation). On the other hand, respondents who reached agreements concerning neighbours all thought that
the agreement was *fair,* and respondents who reached agreements concerning accidental injury were also very likely to think that the agreement had been fair (only 10% saying not fair).

There was no difference in perception between men and women in
relation to the fairness of agreements, nor was there any significant
difference in perception between different age groups. There was,
however, a difference in perception depending on respondent's household income. The lowest earning respondents were the most likely of
all income groups to feel that agreements had been *unfair* (34% of
those with household incomes of under £10,000 and 24% of those
within incomes of between £10,000 and £20,000. There was some
evidence of dissatisfaction at the top end of the income scale as well
(which would be consistent with England and Wales), but the number
of cases in this category is very small for reliable conclusions to be
drawn. In England and Wales dissatisfaction with agreements was
much more prevalent at the top end of the income scale than at the
bottom end.

There was little difference overall in perceptions of the fairness of agreements between those taking action and those who had been the subject of action. Among those who were the subject of action (potential defenders) about one quarter (25%) thought that the agreement reached to resolve the dispute was unfair as compared with about 20% of those taking action.

Respondents who said that they thought their agreement was unfair were asked in what ways the agreement was unfair. The most common complaint was that the amount of money received as part of the agreement was not enough, or that the agreement was unfair because the other side had not honoured a previous agreement. A small proportion also felt the agreement was unfair because the problem had not been their fault.

All those who said that they felt the agreement was unfair were asked why they had agreed to settle the case if they did not feel it was fair. The most common reason given for submitting to what was seen as an unfair agreement was to avoid more bother, trouble, and inconvenience—in effect to get the problem over with (58%)[3]. This figure is much higher than that found in England and Wales where only a minority of respondents (14%) gave this as a reason. Another difference from England and Wales was the high proportion of respondents in Scotland who said that they had accepted an unfair agreement because of a general sense of powerlessness (23% as compared with 6% in England and Wales). Another common reason was to avoid any further disputes with the other side involved in the problem (22% of those who thought the agreement was unfair).

Fairness of court or tribunal decisions

Fewer than half of those whose problems ended in some kind of adjudication (mostly court decisions) said that they felt the decision was fair (45%), and as with agreements, there were some differences between groups of respondents in perceptions of the fairness of adjudicated decisions. Court and tribunal decisions principally affected those respondents involved in divorce and separation disputes (46% of all court/tribunal decisions), landlord disputes (11%) and disputes about ownership of residential property (11%). It is possible that

---

[3] These findings are consistent with other investigations of litigants' reasons for agreeing to settlements perceived to be unfair. See Harris et al (1984) op cit; Law Commission Report (1994) op. cit.

the nature of these disputes influences the broad views on fairness of outcome observed among those receiving court decisions. Unlike the findings in England and Wales, there was a clear difference in perception depending on whether the respondent had been taking action or was the subject of court action. Among those who had been taking action a little over half (52%) said that they thought the decision was fair, as compared with only a third (33%) of those who were having action taken against them. Unsurprisingly there was a significant difference in perception depending upon whether or not the respondent had won at his or her hearing (Figure 6.8) and this difference was more striking in Scotland than in England and Wales (although the numbers in Scotland are rather small). Among respondents who said that they had won at the hearing, although most thought that the decision was fair, as many as one in five (21%) were actually prepared to say that they thought the decision was unfair. This may be a reflection of a sense that winners had not been awarded sufficient compensation or that they received the wrong remedy. It also reinforces the impression that respondents who had been involved in legal proceedings were left with a rather negative view of the legal system.

Unsurprisingly in light of the previous finding, among those who lost at their hearing, the overwhelming majority thought that the decision had been *unfair*. Only *one in ten* of losers were prepared to say that the decision was fair as compared with one in three losers in England and Wales. This indicates a substantially more negative view of hearings in Scotland.

> "I really felt as if everything was taken out of your hands. The judge never asked 'How do you feel about this?' Everything was addressed to the lawyers; nothing was addressed to myself. To be honest, I don't know what it was about the judge but I didn't like him . . . I felt he was really quite biased. Things that my husband was bringing up were just unbelievable."

The perception of unfairness on the part of losers in court and tribunal hearings presents a problem for the courts and judiciary. Within the judicial system the most challenging objective is to make losing acceptable to those who bring their cases to court. Although it is to be expected that losers will feel bruised by their failure to obtain the desired outcome, it must be possible for claimants to leave the courts with a perception of having had a fair hearing, irrespective of the eventual outcome[4]. The problem of perceptions of the Scottish legal system is explored in detail in the next Chapter.

---

[4] See literature on perceptions of court procedure: Lind and Tyler; others.

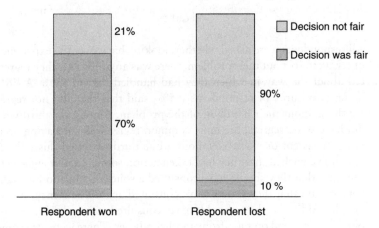

Figure 6.8 Perceptions of fairness of adjudication among those who won and lost. (Base = 44 decisions given).

Among respondents who received a court, tribunal or ombudsman's decision the most common reason for thinking that the decision was unfair was the respondent's belief that they should have won at the hearing (23% of those saying that the decision was unfair). For example:

"I felt total and utter disbelief. I mean, I came out and I couldn't believe it, to be honest, I was just so . . . gobsmacked, that nothing at all was going in my favour."

"I'd been left with this scar on my face which is there for life..I didn't want revenge, but some sort of satisfaction that something had been done. Basically she got away with this; she got no criminal charges brought against her; she had no compensation to pay; she got away with it, and that just wasn't fair. There could at least have been some sort of sign—in compensation towards me. But I got nothing. Nothing at all." [Refusal of criminal injuries compensation]

Other reasons given were that it is unfair to expect a person in the respondent's position to have to pay out money, or that the problem was not the respondent's fault. In addition there was a relatively long list of very specific reasons given as to why decisions had been unfair that related directly to the circumstances of the problem or the practical effect of the decision.

All respondents were asked whether, looking back over the experience of trying to sort out their problem, there was anything that they regretted about the way in which they had handled the situation. A little under two-thirds of respondents (65%) said that they did not regret anything about their handling of the problem. Among the third who did have some regrets, the most common regret was not having been more persistent or assertive (about a one third regretted this); about one in five wished that they had taken action sooner; about eight percent said that they should have consulted a solicitor and another eight percent said that they should have consulted an advice agency. A few people said that they should have consulted an ombudsman, or obtained a second opinion from another adviser. There were also some respondents who regretted seeking advice from solicitors or advice agencies.

There were some differences between problem types in the proportion of respondents admitting that they regretted the way they had handled their problem. The problem types with the highest proportion of respondents saying that they had regrets were employment disputes, problems with landlords, money problems and problems about ownership of property. Respondents expressing the fewest regrets were those who had suffered accidental injury and those dealing with divorce and separation problems. The pattern here is rather different from that in England and Wales where many regrets were expressed about the handling of divorce and separation problems. Indeed, the evidence of the Scottish survey suggests more generally that divorce and separation problems appear to be somewhat less adversarial and legalistic in Scotland than in England and Wales.

The most common regrets among those experiencing employment problems were not having been sufficiently assertive or persistent, and not having consulted a solicitor. Among those with landlord problems, the most common regrets were not having been more persistent or assertive and wishing that they had taken action to deal with the problem more quickly. Those respondents who were most likely to say that they wished they had gone to a solicitor were those experiencing consumer problems, those experiencing employment problems, and those with divorce and separation problems.

SECTION 2. EXPLAINING FULFILMENT OF OBJECTIVES AND
PERCEPTIONS OF FAIRNESS

In order to explore in a little more depth the factors that appear to be associated with the fulfilment of respondents' main objective in trying to resolve the problem and their perceptions of the fairness of the outcomes that they achieved, two further multiple regression analyses were conducted, similar to those carried out for advice-seeking and outcome of problem. Following the previous procedures, a number of factors likely to be associated with the achievement of objectives and perceptions of fairness of outcome were included in the analyses. These included: type of problem being experienced by the respondent and the type of remedy being sought, and whether the respondent was taking action or having action taken against them; whether the respondent had obtained advice; the respondent's age, sex, social class, education, employment status, and income; and finally an indicator of the extent to which respondents reported having suffered negative effects from dealing with their problems.

Achievement of main objectives

Unlike the results in England and Wales where *all* of the factors included in the analysis were significantly correlated with the achievement of respondents' main objectives, the Scottish analysis found *no* factors to be associated with respondents' perceptions of achievement of main objectives. This is a notable difference, which may be a function of the smaller sample size available for analysis in Scotland, or it may reflect a genuine difference in perceptions.

EXPLAINING PERCEPTIONS OF FAIRNESS

A final multivariate analysis was carried out to explore the factors associated with respondents' perceptions of the fairness of the outcome that they achieved. During the main survey respondents whose problem was concluded on the basis of an agreed settlement were asked whether or not they thought that the agreement reached was fair. Those respondents whose cases ended on the basis of a court order or court, tribunal or ombudsman's decision were asked whether they thought that the decision had been fair.

The factors included in the analysis were: the type of problem being experienced by the respondent and the type of remedy being sought, and whether the respondent was taking action or having action taken against them; whether or not the respondent had obtained advice from a solicitor or law centre; the respondent's age, sex, social class, education, employment status, and income; indicators of the extent to which respondents reported having suffered negative effects from dealing with their problems; and finally, attitude to the legal system (confident of a fair hearing if went to court).

The results of the analysis indicate that the variables that are significant for identifying factors associated with respondents' perceptions of the fairness of the outcomes to their disputes were:

- Problem type
- Type of remedy sought
- Whether any negative effects were experienced while sorting out problem.
- Attitude to law (whether confident of a fair hearing).

However, those factors most strongly correlated with perception of fairness were: the type of problem experienced by the respondents, an indicator of the respondent's attitude to the legal system (i.e. whether they believed that they would receive a fair hearing if they went to court), and the remedy being sought.

Type of problem

Problems to do with employment, divorce, landlord and tenant disputes and problems with owning property were associated with *decreased* odds of the respondent perceiving the outcome of the problem to be fair. In contrast, neighbour problems and consumer problems were associated with an increased likelihood that respondents would perceive the outcome as fair. This pattern is very similar to that found in England and Wales.

Remedy sought

Where respondents were seeking a money remedy with a value in excess of £500, respondents were least likely to perceive the outcome of their dispute as fair, presumably because the outcome fell significantly short of expectations.

Negative effects of resolving problem

The odds of perceiving the outcome as fair for those who experienced any negative effects while sorting out their problem were 50% *lower* than average.

Attitude to legal system

If respondents said that they were confident of a fair hearing if they had to go to court, or they had neither positive nor negative expectations, then the odds of thinking that the outcome of the problem was fair were *higher* than average. On the other hand, if respondents were not confident of a fair hearing, then the odds of them perceiving the outcome as fair were 67% *lower* than average.

These findings are consistent with those for the England and Wales study. However, that study also identified five other significant factors that were not found to be associated with perceptions of fairness of outcome in Scotland. These were: income, employment status, sex, whether the respondent was taking action or having action taken against them, and whether legal advice had been sought. The absence of any such association in Scotland may be in part due to the lower sample size.

CONCLUSION

The examination of respondents' objectives in taking action to deal with their justiciable problems has revealed some relatively simple truths. First, that the primary concern for most people is simply to solve the problem. How that is achieved depends on the nature of the problem. In some cases respondents wanted to prevent something dreadful from occurring. In other cases they just wanted to clear up a muddle. In other cases they simply wanted to get a piece of expensive equipment fixed, to obtain a refund for faulty goods, or to obtain compensation for harm suffered. There were also situations in which respondents passionately wanted to change the behaviour of someone who was making their life miserable. Most respondents had a clear sense of what would constitute a right, or fair, or proper outcome to the problem, and achieving that outcome would amount to obtaining justice.

The single most common objective for taking action to resolve justiciable problems was money or property related. Only a tiny proportion was interested in apologies or preventing the problem from happening to others. Very few respondents were able to specify more than one objective. Objectives varied depending on problem type in rather predictable ways, with money-related objectives being the most important in consumer, money and personal injury problems. Those experiencing divorce and relationship problems were often motivated by the need to make arrangements about children and property, while those experiencing neighbour problems predictably wanted to achieve a change in the behaviour of the person with whom they were in conflict. The pattern of objectives for taking action found in Scotland was virtually identical with that found in England and Wales.

Only a little over one-third of all respondents said that they had achieved their main objective completely and the same proportion said that they had not achieved their main objective. The achievement of objectives varied substantially between problem types. Those grappling with divorce and separation problems or accidental injury were the *most* likely to feel that they had achieved their objectives, while those *least* likely to have achieved their objectives were tenants seeking remedies from landlords and those with work or money problems.

Perceptions of fairness of outcome differed significantly between those whose problems had ended on the basis of an agreement and those whose disputes had gone to court. Where an agreement had been reached to resolve the problem, the vast majority of respondents (80%) said that the agreement was fair (the most common complaint about unfairness of agreements being that the amount of money received had been too low). On the other hand fewer than half of those whose cases ended with an adjudicated decision said that the decision was fair. This figure is significantly *lower* than in England and Wales where almost three-quarters of those going to court or tribunal said that the decision was fair. Moreover, perceptions of fairness were more strongly influenced than in England and Wales by the outcome of the hearing. Almost all of those who lost their hearing in Scotland said that the decision was unfair (90% in Scotland as compared with 67% in England and Wales) and even one-fifth of those in Scotland who *won* their hearing said that the decision was unfair. This slightly perverse outcome reinforces the impression that members of the public in Scotland involved in legal proceedings are left with a rather negative view of the legal system.

In the absence of education or advice about rights and obligations, information absorbed via the media plays an important part in forming beliefs about legal rights and understandings of entitlement as a consumer, as a spouse, as a parent, as a victim. Such informal sources of information influence expectations of how easy or difficult it might be to secure the desired outcome and advisers have an important role to play in making expectations realistic and outcomes more acceptable. These findings raise questions about the extent to which those expectations are well-informed and realistic.

The process of attempting to achieve a resolution of justiciable problems appears to take quite a toll on members of the public, and the negative effects of being involved in dealing with a problem are greatest for those who fail to achieve a resolution and those who find themselves involved in court or tribunal proceedings. According to respondents, problems to do with employment, divorce and separation, money, landlords and neighbours all have a substantial impact on health. On the other hand, only a minority of respondents was prepared to say that they regretted the way that they had dealt with their problem. The reported impact of sorting out problems was very similar to that reported in England and Wales. One difference, however, is in relation to divorce and separation problems where there seems to be some evidence that dealing with such problems is somewhat *less* adversarial and legalistic in Scotland than in England and Wales.

The results of the multivariate analyses suggest that problem type and remedy sought were strongly correlated with perceptions of fairness of the outcomes to disputes. Whether respondents were confident that they would receive a fair hearing if they went to court was also strongly correlated with perceptions of fairness of the outcome of cases, and this is relevant to the findings discussed in the next chapter about perceptions of the judicial system and levels of confidence in it.

Experiences and Perceptions of the Legal System

This chapter examines experiences of legal proceedings and attitudes to the legal system. In the first part of the chapter the experiences of respondents who were involved in court or alternative dispute resolution processes are described. Only a small minority of respondents experiencing justiciable disputes had been involved in legal proceedings at all (about 14%, see Chapter 4) and an even smaller proportion actually attended a court or tribunal hearing or a mediation session. Nonetheless, the experiences of these respondents are valuable for providing insights into the way in which the public experiences and responds to legal proceedings. The chapter begins with a description of the experiences of the handful of respondents who were involved in mediations and then goes on to describe the experiences of those involved in court and tribunal proceedings. The second section of the chapter looks more broadly at respondents' attitudes towards the courts, judiciary, and legal profession, including those respondents who had taken action to resolve their problem and those who had done nothing. These attitudes to the legal system provide useful contextual information that contributes to our understanding of the influences on the public when they make decisions about what to do in the face of a justiciable problem.

EXPERIENCES OF MEDIATION

Of all respondents to the main questionnaire only seven stated that they had had any involvement with a mediation or conciliation organisation. One other respondent said that a mediation or conciliation session was planned for the future. This represents about one percent of all respondents to the main survey and is roughly consistent with the picture in England and Wales where only 20 respondents had any involvement with mediation, representing two percent of the main survey sample. The small number of people using mediation as a means of resolving their disputes in Scotland is consistent with the findings in Chapters 3 and 4 that advisers rarely suggested trying mediation, although it conflicts with the results of the screening survey which suggested a much higher level of involvement in mediation for divorce and family disputes. As argued in Chapters 2 and 3, the inconsistency here is probably explained by the fact that respondents to the screening survey were conflating marriage guidance services used during partnership crises with mediation services geared to the resolution of disputes once the decision to separate has been taken.

However, with the benefit of hindsight, at least one respondent who had been involved in lengthy and acrimonious court proceedings following her divorce felt that mediation might have helped reduce the scope for post-divorce conflict. She had been offered mediation and her husband had agreed to attend, but she had refused the opportunity at the time:

> "Although I turned [family mediation] down at the time, I think it was silly because I think it would have helped, prior to allowing the divorce to go through. It actually gets the families with a mediator to talk. I think you can actually go through your lawyer to get one that does with the courts. I'm not exactly sure now. But I really think something like that where the kids are concerned should happen prior to the divorce being allowed to go through—make sure everything's sorted out, everybody's happy. Because at the time you're that stressed and you want it over and done with as quick as possible. And then you find it doesn't finish there—once you've got your bit of paper, you're not really finished there but it still carries on . . . He did go for the mediation, but he only went for mediation in the hope that we were going to get back together. And at that time I was scared to have anything to do with him, any contact. But I now think it would have been a lot easier on the kids and myself. I think it would have aired so much bitterness and so much resentment prior to the divorce."

Of the seven respondents who had been involved in a mediation or conciliation, one had used ACAS in the course of dealing with an employment problem, which is a statutory conciliation service rather than a voluntary ADR process. Other organisations used included the National Family Mediation Service (two respondents) and the SFLA (three respondents). One respondent did not know the name of the organisation used.

Those respondents who had contact with mediation organisations were divided between those experiencing employment problems and those dealing with problems to do with children following divorce or separation.

Most of the respondents had attended more than one session and two respondents had attended four or more sessions.

In most cases some kind of agreement was reached at the end of the mediation or conciliation (five out of seven), but in two cases where there had been some kind of agreement, respondents said that the case had gone on to be the subject of a court or tribunal decision. In the two cases where no agreement had been reached at the final mediation or conciliation session, both remained unresolved at the time of the main survey interview.

Advice and Representation

Of those respondents who had some involvement with mediation or conciliation services all had received some kind of advice about their problem. Three of the seven had received legal advice, and the others received advice from a trade union, a welfare rights officer and another advice agency.

All respondents were asked whether or not they had been accompanied at their mediation or conciliation and whether there had been anyone to speak on their behalf. Those respondents who had attended more than one session were asked about the final session only. Three of the seven attended without any kind of representation. In one case the respondent was accompanied by a welfare rights officer, one a trade union and in another case some other representative.

Those who had attended their session without representation were asked why they did not have a representative with them. Of the four who attended without a representative, two said that they did so because they did not think that they needed anyone to represent them and the other two gave other reasons. Of the four respondents who attended their mediation or conciliation without representation, only one said that they had felt at a disadvantage because they had not been represented at the session. The remainder said that they felt at *no* disadvantage without representation.

Assessment of mediation and conciliation

Most mediation or conciliation sessions were fairly brief. In one case the respondent said that the final session had lasted for less than 30 minutes and five respondents said that the session had lasted for between half an hour and two hours.

Most respondents felt that during the mediation/conciliation session they had had the opportunity to say all (3 respondents) or most (1 respondent) of what they wanted to say. One respondent reported that they had said "some" of what they wanted to say, and two respondents thought that they had said very little or none of what they wanted to say. One respondent thought that there were important facts about their problem that they felt did not get discussed at the session.

Respondents were divided on the question of how well the mediator/conciliator had understood their case. Three respondents said that the mediator had understood the case very well, two said that the mediator had understood the case well, one thought the mediator had not understood the case well and another thought that the mediator had not understood the case well at all. Of the seven respondents who attended mediation four thought that the mediator was entirely neutral, one thought that the mediator had favoured the respondent and two had thought that the mediator had favoured the other side party to the mediation.

Of the seven respondents who attended mediation/conciliation sessions, two said that they would definitely go to mediation/conciliation again if in the were ever in a similar position , two said that they would probably do so again, one thought that they would *probably not* repeat the experience and one respondent said that they would *definitely not* do it again if in the same position.

Of those who attended mediation/conciliation sessions, five reported that an agreement had been reached at the end of the final session and of these, three thought that the agreement reached was fair and one thought that the agreement reached had *not* been fair (one respondent did not answer the question).

Although the number of cases in which mediation or conciliation was attempted was very small indeed, the broadly positive assessments of the experience made by the few respondents who experienced this form of alternative dispute resolution process are consistent with the England and Wales findings and other recent research on experiences of mediation[1].

[1] Cf Genn 1998, op cit; and Mulcahy et al, *Mediating Medical Negligence Claims— An Option for the Future?* HMSO, 1999; Gwynn Davis et al, Evaluating Publicly Funded Meditation Services, Legal Services Commission, 2000; see also Mackay and Brown, *Community Mediation in Scotland,* CRU 1999 and J Lewis, *The Role of Mediation in Family Disputes,* CRU 1999.

COURT AND TRIBUNAL HEARINGS

Among respondents to the main questionnaire about 9% reported that there had been a court, tribunal or arbitration hearing in connection with their dispute. Of those who said that there had been no hearing about 3% said that papers had been sent to a court or tribunal for a decision without a hearing.

Among those who stated that there had been a court or tribunal hearing about their dispute, nearly three-quarters (74%) said that they had started the action and about one-quarter (26%) said that the action had been started against them. This breakdown is rather different from that in England and Wales where the proportions were divided about half and half.

It was reported in Chapter 5 that among those whose case went to a court or tribunal hearing, about 44% were dealt with by the Sheriff Court ordinary procedure, about 19% went to the Sheriff Court small claims procedure, about one quarter went to a tribunal, some four per-cent went to the Sheriff Court summary procedure, and about three percent went to the Court of Session, although the identification of courts may be somewhat unreliable. A further five respondents said that their case had come before an Ombudsman.

About one-third of those respondents who reported that there had been a court or tribunal hearing in connection with their problem said that they attended the final hearing of the matter (34%).

Advice and representation

Most of those who actually attended court or tribunal hearings had received advice about resolving their dispute (92%) and of those who were advised, a little over half (57%) had received legal advice from a solicitor about the problem.

Of those attending hearings in a court or tribunal, about a quarter (23%) said that they attended without anyone accompanying them, about 66% were accompanied by a solicitor; and one percent said that an advice worker accompanied them[2].

Although it would be illuminating fully to analyse representation according to the type of court or tribunal attended, the number attending most types of courts was so small that the analysis is limited.

[2] The numbers add up to more than 100% because respondents mentioned all of those who accompanied them.

Those who attended hearings without representation were asked why they had attended unrepresented. The most common reason given was that the respondent did not think that they needed anyone to represent them. The next most common reason given was that the respondent could not afford to have a representative. A few unrepresented respondents said that they had been advised to represent themselves at the hearing. In response to the question of whether they had felt at a disadvantage without an advocate at the hearing, most said that they felt at *no* disadvantage[3].

Assessments of representatives' performance at hearings were generally favourable. About half (52%) thought that they had been represented very well and a further one-quarter (25%) thought that they had been represented fairly well. However, about one quarter of respondents thought that they had not been well represented, all of whom were respondents who lost their case at their hearing.

In a little under a half of cases respondents said that they had won their case (46%). A little over one half (51%) said that they had lost the case, and the remainder (four percent) gave another response.

Assessment of court and tribunal hearings

In most cases the final hearing attended by respondents lasted for less than 30 minutes (49%), with a further one-third lasting for up to two hours. A small minority (10%) lasted for one day, but none lasted longer than one day.

Most respondents had little difficulty understanding what was going on at the hearing, although a minority (14%) said that they could not understand why particular questions were being asked; and a similar proportion said that they were not sure who were the various people at the hearing.

Levels of satisfaction with court and tribunal proceedings were not particularly high in relation to the ability to get points across during the hearing, and the levels of satisfaction were significantly lower than in England and Wales. Only about one-quarter of those attending hearings said that they had had the opportunity to say everything they had wanted to say during the hearing (as compared with nearly two thirds

---

[3] Similar reasons for lack of representation at court hearings have been found elsewhere. Cf, Genn and Genn, 1989, op. cit. However that study found that applicants at tribunal hearings often felt at a distinct disadvantage without representation.

in England and Wales). Over one-third reported that they had said none of what they wanted to say. About two thirds of those who had trouble getting points across during the hearing said that there had been important facts about their problem which they felt did not get discussed at the hearing.

On the question of the judge's or tribunal's understanding of their case, only about one quarter of those who attended hearings thought that the decision-maker had understood the case very well (27% as compared with 50% of those attending court and tribunal hearings in England and Wales), and another fifth thought the decision-maker had understood the case fairly well. The remaining respondents were divided between those who thought that the decision-maker had not understood the case very well (28%) or not at all well (23%).

Assessments of impartiality were also not particularly positive. Only one-fifth of respondents attending hearings felt that the judge/tribunal "favoured" neither side (as compared with 47% in England and Wales), while six percent thought the judge/tribunal favoured the respondent and nearly three quarters (73%) thought that the judge/ tribunal favoured the opposing side (as compared with 33% in England and Wales)[4].

These findings suggest a relatively high level of dissatisfaction with court and tribunal proceedings among those who attended hearings, and a significantly higher level of dissatisfaction than that found in England and Wales. The dissatisfaction may simply be a reflection of the fact that a relatively high proportion of respondents in Scotland reported having lost at their hearing and, as we saw in the last Chapter, there was a clear association between the outcome of cases and perceptions of fairness.

Despite the level of expressed dissatisfaction, however, a high proportion of respondents reported that they would be prepared to go to a court or tribunal again if faced with similarly circumstances. Most respondents who attended hearings said that they would definitely (62%) or probably (31%) go to court again if they found themselves in the same position again. No respondents said that they would definitely not go again although about nine percent said that they would probably not go to a court or tribunal again if in the same position[5].

---

[4] It is of course possible that some respondents interpreted this question to be asking whether the judge/tribunal thought that one side or the other had the stronger case rather than whether the judge/tribunal was in some way biased against or in favour of the respondent.

[5] Baldwin 1997, Lord Chancellor's Department, op cit., pp 24–25.

Answers to qualitative interviews provided some insights into respondents' experiences of attending a court or tribunal, particularly of the anxiety, the foreignness of the surroundings and the vocabulary of the law. For example:

"[The industrial tribunal] wasnae' as formalised as sitting in a court-room. But there was still all the 'Stand up for the tribunal person', the court officials and what-have-you. I did feel later 'Och, I said this, I could have said that . . . and it's because you feel under pressure and everything: you're nervous; you're under pressure; 'cos as soon as they call your name, your mouth goes dry, your throat tightens up and your heart's going -your adrenaline's pumping . . . Sometimes, I think if someone would just take you aside beforehand and say 'This is what's going to happen' . . . the actual process in the court. You know who's who and does what. I would like to have known who this guy was who was actually sitting there to make this decision. We had quite a while to wait, as well; there was a long time sitting in waiting rooms which didn't really help things, but at the same time you never had any idea about what was going to happen."

"I just sat and listened to him in [the industrial tribunal] and thought, 'You know, why try and trip people up in court?' and I thought, 'Well, I'm telling it as it is as I remember it; you know, why try to confuse me?' I thought there must be something better than this. But I think there's a big fear factor, fear of the process of law from normal, ordinary working people."

"I had to go to court once because I had not restrained my dog properly. It just went by in a haze. I was treated like a criminal. I put my hands in my pockets and she says to me 'Take your hands out of your pockets—you're in a court of law.' I was shocked by the whole thing, because I had never been in trouble in my life before. And I was admonished, but I don't even know what that means. I was really upset. I don't know if that was guilty or not guilty or whatever. But I was admonished."

Evidence from qualitative interviews about experiences of attending court as a party, witness or, indeed juror, provide graphic descriptions of how individuals felt on entering the alien world of the court: anxiety, difficulty of coping with vocabulary, misunderstandings of procedure. The significance of respondents' expectations and how those expectations are formed are discussed further below.

SECTION 2. EXPLORING ATTITUDES TO THE LEGAL SYSTEM

"I think the court system can be very intimidating. You know, the image that comes across on television or whatever,—whether corrupted as well. An awful lot of the Scots law situation I think is corrupted and contaminated by English law. Simply through the media. Most of the media is not based with a Scottish law filter. They see an English law filter, or an American legal framework, from television. And I think that does actually kind of distort people's impressions of Scots law actually."

In order to explore general attitudes to the legal system five statements were read out to all respondents to the main survey, whether or not they had taken any action to try and resolve their problem, and respondents were asked to say how much they agreed or disagreed with each statement. The statements were largely drawn from comments made by members of the public during focus group discussions at the developmental stage of the research. The introduction to the attitude statements deliberately set the context, which was worded as follows: *"I would now like to ask you a few general questions about your feelings about the justice system in Britain. I am going to read out a few statements—please tell me for each one how much you agree or disagree with it."* Three of the statements were posed in positive terms and two in negative terms and the statements were always read to respondents in the following order:

(a) "If I went to court with a problem, I am confident that I would get a fair hearing.

(b) "Most judges are out of touch with ordinary people's lives."

(c) "Lawyers' charges are reasonable for the work they do."

(d) "Courts are an important way for ordinary people to enforce their rights."

(e) "The legal system works better for rich people than for poor people."

These attitude statements about the justice system in Scotland produced, on the whole, rather negative responses. The responses to the survey questions were consistent with the views and attitudes that had been expressed by members of the public who joined focus group discussions during the developmental stage of the project. They are also consistent with the findings in England and Wales. Analysis of attitudes in relation to respondents' demographic characteristics and experience of the legal system displayed few *consistent* differences of view between groups, although there was some interesting variation in response to individual questions depending on social group and experience of involvement with the legal system . These are discussed in relation to each question.

The generally negative response to attitudes statements posed on the main survey questionnaire was also reflected in many of the qualitative interviews conducted after the main survey and during which respondents were asked completely open questions about their attitudes to the courts, the judiciary and the legal system as a whole. Some typical responses to this open questioning are presented in relation to each of the attitude statements in the main survey in order to flesh out some of the perceptions that the public in Scotland holds of the courts and the legal system more generally.

THE IMPORTANCE OF COURTS FOR ENFORCING RIGHTS

It seems clear that the idea of courts as a place in which ordinary citizens can enforce rights is important in the national consciousness. The symbolic value of the courts, irrespective of any immediate concerns of the public about access and cost, is demonstrated by the two-thirds of respondents who agreed or strongly agreed with the statement "*Courts are an important way for ordinary people to enforce their rights*" (Figure 7.1). The question, however, is estimating the extent to which the public subscribes to the ideal of the courts and commitment to the rule of law. To that extent the question is rather different from the others which are tapping experience, expectations and beliefs. The results were very similar to those obtained in England and Wales, although the proportion agreeing was somewhat lower than in England and Wales where almost three quarters of respondents agreed or strongly agreed with the statement.

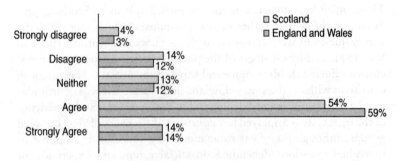

Figure 7.1 "Courts are an important way for ordinary people to enforce their rights" (Base = All respondents 472 weighted).

There were no significant differences in response to this question among respondents depending on demographic characteristics, education or income. However, the type of problem about which respondents were being interviewed and the outcome of their case did appear to be significantly associated with differing responses. Respondents who had experienced employment problems, neighbour problems and problems with landlords were significantly more likely than respondents interviewed about other types of problems to *disagree* with the statement that courts were important for enforcing rights (about one-quarter in each group disagreed or strongly disagreed with the statement). Respondents whose problem had been dealt with by a court or tribunal and those whose problem remained unresolved were also significantly more likely to *disagree* with the statement than those whose problem had been resolved by means of an agreement (28% and 25% respectively disagreeing with the statement). Indeed, those respondents who had been involved in any kind of legal proceedings while trying to resolve their problem were significantly more likely than those who had not been involved in legal proceedings to *strongly disagree* with the statement (13%).

Respondents' experience of using advisers to deal with their most recent problem did not appear to be related to their attitude to the importance of courts. Those respondents who took no action at all to deal with their problem were not *more* likely than those who took some action to *disagree* with the statement. Respondents who lost their case in a court or tribunal were predictably more likely to *disagree* with the statement than those who had won their case, suggesting that a negative experience of legal proceedings has an impact on expressed support for the legal system.

It seems then that although there is a high level of agreement with the idea of the significance of the courts as a place for enforcing individual rights, those expressing *least* confidence were respondents who had had recent experience of involvement with the legal system in the process of attempting to resolve their problems and disputes, and those who had failed to achieve any kind of resolution to their problem.

FAIRNESS OF THE COURTS

A second attitude statement aimed at tapping broad confidence in the legal system concerned perceptions of the fairness of courts (*"If I went*

to court with a problem I am confident that I would get a fair hearing").
Questions such as this have been used in numerous studies in the
United States to measure the degree of "diffuse support" for the courts.
Diffuse support recognises the legitimacy of an institution, even in the
face of decisions viewed as wrong or inimical to the individual's own
interests[6]. Diffuse support is regarded as more generalised and more
persistent than the kind of specific support measured by questions
aimed at evaluating the extent to which institutions have achieved specific objectives. It is therefore a reasonable indication of underlying
confidence in the courts.

The results of the analysis of questionnaire responses to the proposition that the respondent would receive a fair hearing in court,
shows that about three in five respondents agreed with the statement
(59%), although only one in twenty respondents was prepared to say
that they strongly agreed with the statement. What is also somewhat
disconcerting about the responses to this question in the context of
public confidence in the judicial system is that about fifteen percent of
respondents could not, or would not, commit themselves to a view on
the question of the fairness of proceedings. Although this is not necessarily a negative finding, it is clearly not a positive finding to a statement probing confidence in the court system. As Figure 7.2 shows,
these findings are, again, largely consistent with those obtained in
England and Wales.

There were no significant differences in the response to this attitude
question depending on gender, education, income, or problem type.
There were, however, some interesting differences in responses related
to age and experience of the legal system. Respondents under 25 and
those over 65 were the most likely to *agree* with the statement, and
those between the ages of 45 and 54 were the most likely to *disagree*
with the statement, with over one third in that age group (38%) disagreeing. Moreover, those respondents whose problem had led to some
involvement in legal proceedings and those whose problem led to a
court or tribunal decision, were significantly more likely than other
groups to *disagree* with the statement. Over one half of those whose
problem had been resolved on the basis of a court or tribunal decision
disagreed with the statement (52%), although there was no significant
difference depending on whether they had won or lost their case. This
finding reinforces the impression of respondents in Scotland emerging

[6] G Caldeira (1991) quoted in Olsun and Huth (1998) "Explaining Public Attitudes
Towards Local Courts", *The Justice System Journal*, vol 20/1 p 42.

from experiences of the legal system with rather negative attitudes. To this extent the results are somewhat different from those in England and Wales where it seemed that recent experience of using the legal system was *not* significantly associated with more negative attitudes towards that system.

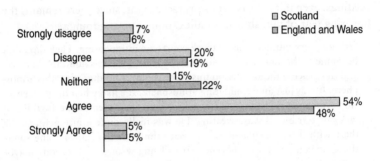

Figure 7:2 "If I went to court with a problem, I am confident that I would get a fair hearing". (Base = All respondents 472 weighted).

Perceptions of courts

"I feel that law courts ought to be reserved for murder, rape, pollution, huge fraud, seriously bad driving, those sort of things, where a criminal law has been broken, and it's got serious effects on society. When it's a one to one situation, like unfair dismissal, like divorce, it shouldn't be in a major court with major costs. Barristers, in my opinion, have no place in that."

In order to probe perceptions and experiences of courts more deeply, open questions were asked about views on courts during qualitative interviews. These questions produced interesting responses. Although questioning about courts in interviews was always related to the civil courts, the instinctive response of most respondents was to make reference to features of the criminal courts. Many people found it hard to understand questions like *"What are the courts for?"* since their only understanding of courts was in a criminal context. Members of the public tend not to hold a distinction in their minds between civil and criminal courts. The public image of "court" is a place where criminals go to be tried. Several respondents to qualitative interviews had experiences of being in court as jury members, witnesses and sometimes as defenders for minor offences. In these cases views of courts were often based on personal experience of the criminal courts, which tended to reinforce the images gleaned from the media and exaggerated the emphasis on criminal rather than civil trials in peoples' expectations of courts.

The immediate connection made between courts and crime may lead members of the public to be reluctant to become involved in legal proceedings, even if it is to assert or protect a right, since there remains the lingering fear of punishment or allegation of wrongdoing:

"It's just very intimidating—I think courts are intimidating. They shouldn't be. Some of the older courts—like Paisley Sheriff Court's quite an old place, and this place. I thought, 'God this place is old!' And there was this atmosphere. It was just an intimidating atmosphere. It's like when the policeman stops you and says hello, you feel guilty when you haven't done anything. It was just terrible—I was sweating! He was really quite a nice man, sitting there with these wee glasses on . . . But I think it's the fear of doing something wrong, you know: it's the fear of being wrong or somebody maybe tripping you up 'cos you see this guy trying to cross-examine you."

"I was called as a witness in a motor vehicle case where a driver drove into the back of me and the police eventually pursued and caught him and found he was over the limit, so I was called as a witness. Notwithstanding all I was doing was standing up and saying what happened to me, I found that pretty nerve racking. Amongst other things, you are dealing with the police, and every time you see a police car you wonder 'what have I done wrong lately?' Partly the fact that you're standing up in public and talking and most of us don't do that regularly. Partly the fact that the court maintains some sort of aura about it. It's the formality. The fact that there is a guy up there wearing a wig. For many people it's the possibility that they will come off worse."

"I've only actually been in a court once, as a witness to a cyclist being knocked over in London, and it's quite nerve-wracking, even being a witness . . . I think it was just the size of the courtroom, the seriousness of it, and the fact that it was a justice situation."

The fact that respondents automatically interpreted "courts" as being "criminal courts" meant that their expressed lack of confidence in courts was often a reflection of dissatisfaction with the state of the criminal law and decisionmaking in criminal cases. Although some respondents to qualitative interviews had had personal experience of courts, such experience was generally of the criminal courts. Thus in discussing attitudes to courts, respondents often commented about juries, about criminal defenders and most often about the problem of lack of consistency in judicial sentencing of criminals and the failure of the law to address certain forms of behaviour seen as anti-social and worthy of punishment.

> "I wouldn't have any great confidence in the right person winning a case . . . Daily you lift a newspaper, you listen to television programmes where judgments have been weird. You think, 'How could that have happened?' You know, they've lost a case either because of a technicality, or a judge allows somebody that's raped a four-year-old girl to get six years in jail. Even in the civil side of things, the more money you've got, the more chance you have of winning. But in the criminal side of things, I have no great faith. I would not have any confidence, if I was innocent of something and I went to court, that I wouldn't be found guilty."

> "Fear of law comes from probably lack of knowledge. And television; newspapers . . . You don't read an awful lot about wee Joe Bloggs winning cases and stuff like this. And sometimes you realise that the system seems unfair, the law itself— when you have these judgments in law. You've got rapists getting off and murderers getting off on a technicality. I don't understand that: I think that's crazy."

The experience of being called as a juror or as a witness did not necessarily alleviate negative perceptions of courts that had been gleaned from the media. Indeed, in some cases the experience actually increased the level of negativity felt, for example:

> "The first time I went to court I was fine about it. And then I got in there and found there was a jury there, it was an assault and I was just a witness, but I mean I'd done nothing wrong I'd just treated this man. But there was a jury so it was all very serious. I just didn't know how to handle it and how frankly to speak. You're just frightened of opening your mouth and saying what you think. I felt stupid." [Doctor giving evidence]

> "It's such an artificial damn thing. I've been on Jury duty many times and I'm not saying it's Kafkaesque, but it's so damned artificial. I've been in quite serious trials in the High Court where you have lawyers around in the well of the court. It's a big theatrical situation. I know the dignity of the law must be maintained, but I think it's a load of nonsense. Guys in their wigs and their gowns."

> "I think they're really just a waste. They're there for the lawyers. The only experience I base that on is, I've been called as a witness now twice and that has been a waste of my time and of all of the others. We go there; we sit; we don't know what's happening—the cases are cancelled; you know, 'Come back tomorrow, we'll phone you' and you've got to come back again. You wonder how do they get through the workload, if they're waiting till the morning of the trial to decide a case is cancelled."

Not all respondents, however, disapproved of the majesty and mystery of court proceedings. A few respondents in qualitative interviews referred to the importance of the experience of court being mysterious and authoritative and that the trappings contributed to that:

> "I work in a university with gowns and hoods all over the place. I also belong to the cathedral where we wear vestments. I'm not intimidated by costume or grand places. Although I suppose that the fear might be quite considerable for some people, but if you take away all the trappings, are they going to feel they've been to court? Because that's when you feel you've got justice. OK it's psychological rubbish, but you need not only to get justice, but to feel that other people can see that you got it. We don't like the churches where they've stripped away everything, because we think they've stripped away the majesty, or mystery, and you need to feel something greater than yourself."

> "Intimidation in terms of the power and majesty of a court can be very useful in ascertaining what the truth is. I think if you made it too relaxed, you might never find out what the truth was in certain circumstances. But on the other hand, I think that it probably also intimidates people from telling everything; they will only say the bare minimum, to get out of there as quickly as possible."

> "Courts are there for punishment of transgressors and they have to be there and they have to be imposing and justice has to be seen to be done."

> "You have American courts (I've seen them on Sky TV)—well it's not actually courts, people go and agree that they be bound by the decision and it is by a judge and it's small—a sort of small claims court. And I feel that that is probably inappropriate, because if you go to court, you should go to the court and do it properly."

As these quotes illustrate, there is a need to reach a balance between formality, authority, and user-friendliness for lay people. This is not an easy balance to draw and will need to vary between different types of court and tribunal. This issue is discussed further in Chapter 8.

A few respondents had views on how the courts might be changed to make them less intimidating and more attractive to those attempting to seek redress for civil problems through the legal system. The suggestions usually stressed a reduced level of formality, removal of wigs and gowns, and more modern and egalitarian settings in which the parties might feel more able to put their case without legal representation.

> "They should have a court system set up like they used to have a children's panel in Scotland—there were three or four and they talk to the person, listen to the case and actually speak to them. They're not caught up in this gowns

and traditional set-up, where you can be relaxed and speak. Because you're speaking to your peers, you're speaking to people who are community based."

"If you could go to a small claims court . . . I know you've got the small claims court, where you don't necessarily need a lawyer: you can go and put the case—I don't know if we have that in Scotland—I think you have them in England . . . that kind of scenario where you're going to put it in your own words—you don't need the legal jargon. I think that would be like—I think that's a brilliant system; I think that's really good—it's accessible, and if you lose, it isn't going to cost you heaven and earth. I know they've got them in England, but I don't know if they've got them in Scotland. Scotland's really different from everyone else . . . but something like that where people can go, put their case in their own words for someone to listen to them without all the legal jargon."

"It's the witness box, the whole set-up; the rows, the beautiful wooden pews, and the judge up on his plinth at the front there. If it was more like a business conference room so everybody's all on the one level, it would be less intimidating—because the witness is up there in front of everybody and everybody's eyes are upon them and they're standing; whereas if they were sitting down, everybody was on the same level—maybe the judge was at the head of the table and everybody else had a space round about—I'm sure it might be more attractive. The tradition goes back to past years when you used to think that your doctor was God, your lawyer was God, and the judge was higher. And I think the old-fashioned courtroom is all bound up in the same sort of thing—the aura from the courtroom."

"Courts are usually old buildings which are very open and they are probably intimidating. I've never been to a court, but they obviously have public galleries, the press galleries. If they were smaller, more intimate environments, people would possibly be more likely to go to them. Anything that makes it easier for people to feel more comfortable should be looked at and should be developed."

"I've been to a local under court, like a summary court and it was very informal and the accused people were there and it was not like sitting in your living room, it's not as informal as that, but that was the basic process."

DIFFERENTIAL RESOURCES AND THE LEGAL SYSTEM

The scepticism conveyed in the responses to the question about fairness of hearings may, in part, be a reflection of the very strong feelings aroused by a related attitude statement suggesting that the wealthy have an advantage in the legal system. About seven in ten respondents agreed or strongly agreed with the proposition that the legal system works better for the rich than the poor. Only fourteen percent of all respondents disagreed with the statement and only two percent strongly disagreed, although about 14% of respondents did not offer a view. Ironically, as we have seen in Chapter 3, it is the middle classes who both feel, and appear to be, disadvantaged in terms of access to legal advice in relation to both the wealthy and the poor.

There were, on the whole, rather few differences between groups of respondents associated with view of the legal system working best for those with resources. There was no difference among age groups or in relation to education. Men were somewhat more likely to agree strongly with the statement (44% as compared with 31% of women strongly agreeing) and those respondents who were interviewed about an accidental injury or a tribunal matter were significantly more likely to agree with the statement than those experiencing other problem types. Respondents most likely to disagree with the statement were those dealing with consumer disputes or divorce and separation problems. Unsurprisingly, income was significantly associated with responses to this question. Respondents on the highest incomes were most likely to disagree with the statement and those on *middle incomes* were the most likely to agree or strongly agree with the statement. This is consistent with the discussion in Chapter 3, which indicated concerns among respondents to the main survey about the problems of middle income groups in achieving access to justice.

Responses to this particular attitude question did not appear to vary significantly depending on involvement in legal proceedings for the most recent problem, or whether respondents had obtained advice about the most recent problem, nor on the outcome of the case.

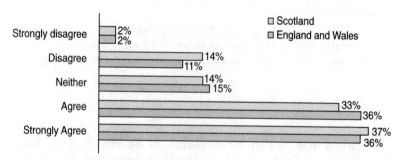

Figure 7.3 "The legal system works better for rich people than for poor people". (Base = All respondents 472 weighted).

Consistent with responses in England and Wales, interviews with respondents in Scotland revealed strong views about the extent to which resources were important to the ability to take advantage of the legal system and in the determination of outcome. There was a common perception that high quality legal expertise was expensive, but was also crucial to achieving a successful outcome. Thus, those who can afford to pay for good quality legal advice will inevitably have an advantage over those who cannot afford to pay for anything at all, and those who can afford to pay *more* will have a further advantage. For example:

"What good, what good was it? You go to the law and you think, 'That's okay if you've got money. If you've got money you can get good people . . . If you've got money and you can have the technique, the time and the effort.' I just feel, quite honestly, if we'd have had the money to pay for a lawyer then we'd have got a better service." (Redundancy case—represented in tribunal by free adviser)

"If you go to the civil court..if someone has good finances, they have more opportunity to employ a more competent or a more experienced lawyer or barrister and from that point of view you get what you pay for. Probably the cards are stacked against you to some extent. The system as it is set up is probably a fair system, but the results of the system with the opportunity if you've got more finances to employ better legal brains, it's probably weighted in favour of getting better justice for the rich than there is for the poor."

A second theme that emerged in qualitative interviews, relating to the impact of differential resources on the outcome of cases, was the problem of individuals battling against large corporations. Several respondents expressed a keen appreciation of the effect of power imbalances between opponents in the attempt to secure a satisfactory resolution of civil disputes and problems.

"You've got to look very carefully at the type of organisation you're taking on, because the larger the organisation the more likely they are to start delaying things and the legal costs are mounting. What for the ordinary person is a lot of money, it's just a drop in the ocean to the multi-national."

"You read in the papers that people can't afford to continue on something that's probably really right—it's a good cause but they can't afford to . . . It's a corporate thing. The corporate guys have got the money. The little individual guy—unless he's got the wherewithal, unless he gets legal aid—couldn't do it, whether it's right or wrong. As far as I'm concerned, you still have to have money, and the law will work better for money . . . There is a few cases when you'll read that someone has battled this big corporation and won, but how often does that happen?"

"I think it's not so much the wealthy, but the people with more power. If it's a large insurance company then I think the law would stick more with their side, partly because they've got the might to back it up. I mean they can afford all the best lawyers and such."

"It's probably intimidating for the ordinary person to take on a large corporation, because they feel that they have limited resources where the equivalent resources that a large corporation would have are almost infinite in comparison. And there might be a feeling of powerlessness, even though they might feel that they are right in terms of natural justice and in terms of what the law might eventually decide. But they may not have the resources to keep going, to get to that point of resolution."

A third common theme related to problems over the accessibility of legal aid and the plight of those on middle incomes. As reported in Chapter 3, concern was expressed that, unlike the rich and the poor, the middle income groups were effectively excluded from access to justice. For example:

"The courts are very important for the people who need them. It's important to know that it's there behind you, in case you have a problem, that there's some remedy, because I'm sure it would be soul-destroying if you felt there was something legally wrong in your life that you couldn't get sorted out. I'm sure costs it must put people off. I'm sure there's a lot of people out there with grievances that could be dealt with through the courts, whether it's against a big company or whether it's a divorce or family law or whatever. And it'll be the fees. It'll be the lack of support from the legal aid system. It's the in-between—it's the people that are not well enough off to pay it themselves, and the people who are not poor enough to actually get the legal aid. It's the ones actually in between. And that batch of people in between seems to be getting bigger, because the legal aid system seems to be getting tougher to get."

"Probably someone who's getting Legal Aid has got more access to the legal system than someone who's in the position where they've maybe got enough money, but they're running the risk of losing it all if they lose the case. The likes of ourselves where, OK we're not rich, but we do have a wee bit of savings, well personally I would think twice about taking the legal system unless I had a case that I knew was really watertight."

THE COST OF ADVICE FROM LAWYERS

"Very often with the law it's difficult to measure what you're actually getting for your money. Whereas if you build a house, or you buy a car, you can actually see it—it is tangible. With the law, you have loads of words, which no-one seems to really understand..The law's one of these thing where you don't really see value for money unless you've won. If you've lost it's just a load of words."

Concern about the extent to which the legal system requires resources is directly reflected in, or perhaps a reflection of, a widespread belief that the cost of legal advice is unaffordable for most ordinary people. About seven out of ten respondents disagreed or strongly disagreed with the suggestion that lawyers' charges are reasonable for the work that they do (70%) and as figure 7.4 indicates, the responses to this question in Scotland were almost identical to those given in England and Wales[7].

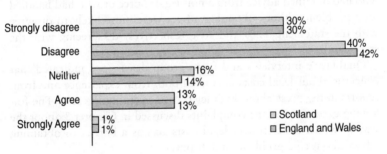

Figure 7.4 "Lawyers' charges are reasonable for the work they do" (Base = All respondents 472 weighted).

Despite the widespread disagreement with the statement there were one or two differences between groups in their response to the question. Although there was no significant difference in response related to different age groups, gender, education, problem type or outcome of problem, there were differences related to income and the type of advice obtained about the problem that respondents had been trying to resolve. The analysis of response in relation to income tends to support

[7] It is also broadly in line with the findings of The Law Society of Scotland's 1998 public opinion survey on solicitors.

the complaints made by middle-income groups. Respondents with household incomes of below £10,000 and those with incomes over £41,000 were the most likely to agree with the suggestion that lawyers' charges are reasonable for the work that they do. In both income groups about one in five respondents agreed with the statement, and this finding is consistent with responses in England and Wales.

There was little difference in response according to the type of problem that respondents had experienced although those who had been dealing with divorce and separation problems were among the most likely to agree (20% agreeing and 3% strongly agreeing) as were those who had problems with their landlord (23% agreeing and none strongly agreeing).

There were also some differences in views depending on whether or not respondents had obtained advice to deal with their most recent problem. Among those who had obtained legal advice, about 15% agreed or strongly agreed that lawyers' charges are reasonable for the work that they do and about six in ten (62%) disagreed. Respondents who had obtained advice from a non-legal source or who had handled with problem without obtaining advice were more likely to disagree with the statement (72% and 76% respectively disagreeing with the statement).

Qualitative interviews and focus group discussions indicated that concerns about legal costs emanated both from experience and from reports in the press about high legal costs accruing in cases. The following extracts echo the complaints discussed in Chapter 3 about the way in which concern over legal costs acts as a barrier to obtaining advice about civil problems and disputes:

"You hear reports in the news about these poor people that have got involved in court cases. Okay, they're phenomenal amounts of money you're talking about and big huge cases to be reported on the television, but seeing all their cases lost and they've got to pay thousands and thousands of pounds' worth of costs. So, it puts you off a little bit, even if it's a small thing you're thinking about—It is definitely the money you're thinking about."

"I think solicitors are fine to have around when you need them: obviously they're needed for the purchase of a house and if you were involved in a legal situation you would need someone to show you around the law or to defend your position. But my own personal opinion of solicitors is that they're just an overpaid profession. I don't know how they reach their scale of fees."

"Solicitors in my experience so far—they've usually accomplished just about what you asked them to, but at great expense. I do feel that the legal profession is charging everybody a lot of money for what they do, it has got the point where you think before you speak. Because if you talk to a solicitor for an hour, that's an hour's bill you've got, which is not a very good idea usually, they're not cheap."

THE JUDICIARY

A final attitude question posed to all respondents that provoked rather negative responses concerned the judiciary. Respondents were asked whether or not they agreed with the statement that most judges were out of touch with ordinary peoples' lives. The wording of the attitude statement was borrowed from expressions that occurred frequently during open-ended focus group discussions with members of the public during developmental work prior to the main survey. The strength and consistency of feeling expressed during group discussions were confirmed in the survey responses and then further elaborated during open questioning in qualitative interviews.

Among respondents to the main survey questionnaire, about seven in ten respondents (70%) agreed or strongly agreed with the statement, 17% disagreed or strongly disagreed with the statement, and a little over one in ten (13%) felt unable to agree or disagree with the statement. As Figure 7.5 demonstrates, the responses to this question were, again, virtually identical to those obtained in England and Wales.

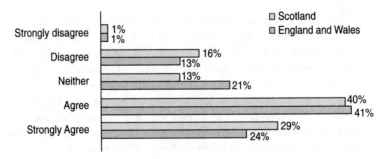

Figures 7.5 "Most judges are out of touch with ordinary people's lives" (Base = All respondents 472 weighted).

In common with the results in England and Wales, there were no significant differences in the response to this question in Scotland depending on age, gender or income. However, there were significant differences depending on, education, experience of the legal system, and problem type and in this respect the findings are different from those in England and Wales. As far as education is concerned, the Scottish data suggest that better educated respondents were more likely to *disagree* with the statement than less well-educated respondents. Almost one-quarter of those with degree-level qualifications *disagreed* with the statement, and almost one in five of those with Scottish Highers or equivalent *disagreed*. Those respondents whose problem had led to a court or tribunal decision were by far the most likely to strongly agree or agree with the statement. Some 41% of those whose case led to a court or tribunal decision *strongly agreed* with the statement and a further 46% of this group agreed with the statement. Where a respondent had lost their case in court or tribunal about 56% strongly agreed with the statement. Moreover, among those who obtained legal advice at some point about their problem, about 40% strongly agreed with the statement. These findings seem to suggest that although negative views about the judiciary are held across social boundaries, the level of negativity is *more pronounced* among those respondents with recent direct experience of involvement with the legal system. To this extent the findings are somewhat different from England and Wales where involvement with the legal system was not significantly associated with increased or decreased levels of negativity. They are, however, consistent with the pattern of findings on experiences and attitudes to the judicial system in Scotland, which indicates that *direct experience increases levels of negativity*.

The view that judges are out of touch, or at least the sentiment conveyed by the statement, was an issue about which respondents in qualitative interviews appeared to hold relatively strong views. In each qualitative interview respondents were asked completely open questions about their views of judges. The question generally stimulated negative responses relating to perceptions of remoteness based on social distance, inconsistency in sentencing, and examples of insensitive judicial comments reported in the media. There also appeared to be some disapproval of court robes and wigs which were seen as being anachronistic and which possibly contributed to the impression of judges being outdated.

It is notable that although only a minority of respondents had ever met or appeared before a judge, respondents were nonetheless generally opinionated and fluent on this subject. This is because judges, and caricatures of judges, through media communication, regularly enter the homes of the public, and because the behaviour of judges has a high public salience. The public has a view, because of the importance attached to the office of judge in the public imagination. The occasionally strong disapproval expressed attached to the imagined typical incumbent. It also reflects a degree of apprehension, which may be a necessary part of social order, but is not wholly functional in the context of a modern civil justice system.

The opinions expressed about the judiciary during qualitative interviews tended to cluster around several themes: remoteness, values, and dress. There were also quite thoughtful concerns about appointment, training and accountability. The extracts from interview transcripts speak for themselves.

Remoteness

The common allegation of remoteness was sometimes seen as a natural consequence of advanced age, but also a result of background and isolation from modern culture:

"My impression of the judge in these court cases, is somebody who sits there in wigs; terribly old—old dodderers.. They have no idea. Like, 'Who's B&Q?' They have no knowledge of the real world; they're locked in this legal little timewarp. As I say, blinkered, aye."

"I don't think it's a fair system. It's too black and white. I know the law doesn't probably allow for grey areas, but there are grey areas in life; and then it's down to a man's judgment. And he might be one of these older guys with the wigs and that doesn't know who the Spice Girls are and what have you; no knowledge of the world."

"They make statements and, y'know, you think 'Where is this guy? Does he live in the real world?' I mean, it's like trying to explain poverty to somebody that's never had to go without a meal. . . . How can [a judge] take their background into a situation if he's so far removed from the real world . . . what kind of judgment call can he make on this other person's background?"

"They don't seem to have much of a clue about life when you read about them in the papers. It's like they've not got a scooby about what ordinary people do or say or anything else. You know, they're lords and that's it. They've got their own standards and everything and some of them don't even think the way we think. Reading about them in the paper, they don't have a clue about ordinary life."

"I think the judges should be accountable. When you see some of the daft judgments handed down..the judge in one of the rape cases not so long ago, he said more or less that the girl had asked for it and things like that. Well I mean things like that just shouldn't be said. I think it demeans the whole justice system when you get people like that. It used to be that judges never spoke out of line at all. I'm talking about real accountability. They've also got their fears and they should be accountable that way."

As in England and Wales, respondents in Scotland tended to offer an image of judges as being male and elderly. The problem of advanced age was seen to lie less in the possibility of failing intellectual powers and more in an inability to empathise with the values of contemporary society and the problems of the daily lives of those whom they judge:

"I think they're old and they're not quite with it. We live in a different time now, say from my granny's time, where morals are different. I think most judges are probably over 60 years old. I think there are very intelligent thirty, forty year olds who could do a really good job and have a more balanced view on what today's life's about. I think most judges are pretty well-off. They earn a good living and therefore they don't really have a real understanding of poverty and how that can affect people day to day."

"I think they're a bit doddery when they're sitting there. I'm not saying they're not intelligent people; they're very intelligent people . . . I think there should be more women judges and all younger. Half of these judges should be retired. I don't mean any disrespect to them, but they've been through the system and I think it comes to a point where you can overstay your welcome.

Values

There was also some concern that the values and biases of a predominantly male and privileged professional group would heavily influence judicial decision-making. One or two respondents thought that the appointment of more women to the bench might act as some kind of corrective to this perceived tendency:

"From having viewed things in the sheriff courts here, I feel that the way a sheriff in a Scottish court treats people depends on their accent and how they're dressed and if you go in with a reasonable accent and wearing a suit and a tie, you will get a much, a much kinder hearing from the sheriff than you will if you go in jeans and a t-shirt and talk with a local accent. I think that's highly unfair, but it's just the way it goes."

"I think women have got more understanding, more of the heart that goes into us. I don't know whether it's the mothering instincts in them."

"We have got to have faith in the judiciary. . . . I have a reasonable amount of faith. But it starts to fray at the edges where you hear all the Old Boys' Network. I think it would be better if judges come from across the spectrum of backgrounds in the country. But when you find that an awful lot of them went to the right schools, the right universities, and it's part of the establishment, and isn't really representative of modern society. Women, for example.—Obviously grossly under-represented. I'd have a lot more faith if they were clearly more representative of society."

Interestingly, however, there was also some evidence in qualitative interviews of a different perception of Scotland by comparison with England and Wales. At least a couple of Scottish respondents thought that Scotland was less hierarchical than England and that the problems of rigid class distinctions were less acute north of the border:

"Scotland I think is a smaller country and I think it is less hierarchical [than England] because of its size, by the very definition. I think also because of the different legal system. I think there is a difference there; I think with the Scottish parliament as well: I think there's a sense of movement there, of something fresh, because it will have a lot of power to make laws which will affect people. So I think there is a sense that we are moving on here. Scotland has never had the same tradition of public schools quite the same way as England—you know, the Oxbridge kind of axis. It's never been quite the same in Scotland, never been as strong."

"I can't see any reason to say they're out of touch. I think that's one thing where Scotland probably does better than England. There's less likelihood here of people at the top of the system being an elitist group, who went to those kind of schools where they don't keep in touch . . . I think Eton and Harrow probably still produce elitist people who haven't the remotest idea how ordinary folk live, I don't think from what I've seen and heard that justice in Scotland has that problem."

Dress

Although respondents were not specifically asked questions about judicial dress, respondents often raised the subject when they were explaining their views of the judiciary. In general, there was little support expressed for wigs and gowns. Rather it was felt that they merely accentuated age, distance, and a degree of menace.

"I see these wigs and I think what is the point of wearing a wig? Is there a point? Keeping your head warm? Wigs and robes to me are really outdated. They're for ceremonial occasions. What's the point other than to intimidate people? And the presence—makes him feel better and makes the other people feel worse."

"Certainly in the Court of Session, they're antiquated: you have a judge sitting up in a red robe and a big fancy wig, which I think's a nonsense in present-day society. Okay, people say 'Oh, but it instils a sense of gravitas into the whole proceedings.' To my mind it just makes it more unapproachable . . . The common man in the street doesn't normally bump into Your Lordships—these people are called lords; they sit up in an elevated place with their robes and their wigs. It just appears to me that it kind of alienates the general public rather than thinking that they're getting a fair crack of the whip or gives them what I think is access to justice."

Appointments procedure and training

Additional concerns expressed by a few respondents related to the obscure processes by which members of the judiciary were appointed, perceived lack of training and lack of accountability[8]. In common with some respondents in England and Wales, some Scottish respondents felt that appointment to judicial office was based more on networks than merit. For example:

"Judges aren't appointed by passing an exam. Judges aren't appointed solely on merit. It's not what you know; it's who you know. I know it for sure. The sheriffs who are in the sheriff court are not appointed by any system of selection which has any relevance in a modern society: there is no exam that they've passed; there is no procedure which they go through. They are just selected because 'Oh he's been doing this for a number of years and he's quite a good guy.' I mean, the number of [poor] sheriffs there are in this

---

[8] These interviews were carried out two years before the announcement from the Scottish Executive in 2001 that it proposed to introduce a Judicial Appointments Board.

country is incredible . . . They need a far greater assessment of people's abilities. . . . It doesn't provide a sensible judiciary."

"I think people would feel more secure if they knew how they got their jobs; is there any kind of training that goes along with it at that level? They make final decisions; what they say goes and I think if people knew that there was training, for example, so that they weren't distanced away from people. If there was some kind of ongoing work in anti-discriminatory training; anti-racist training, that kind of thing. I think they can be [discriminatory]. You do get these big sensational cases where they've come out and they've made some very sexist comment or some decision they've made has been very very sexist. Also this whole thing about how black people are perceived when they go to court. I think they can often be treated a bit harsher. I wouldn't be able to tell you where they were, but I think there are statistics that kinda' back that up, the amount of black people that are actually in custodial sentences. If there was a way to actually get bad judges out, in the way you would in any profession—I don't think people have the confidence that that happens."

"I don't really [have confidence] but that's not through experience, it's just through television, news reports and stuff like that. You hear about them all being eighty-year-old and all that kind of thing, completely out of touch with society. I probably reckon that's true, but that's more to do with the system's fault, they don't produce young Sheriffs. It's all old barristers that get the jobs. I don't know whether that is a good or a bad thing, because it takes a lot of experience to be a Sheriff or a Judge as such. The rate the law changes at the moment, and it's changing quite rapidly I think, it's quite hard for them to keep up with it. I don't think they receive adequate training or anything like that. As far as I'm aware, once they've been made a Sheriff, or a Judge, then that's the end of their training, it's up to themselves to provide themselves with the right, correct information. Through the courts, which isn't right, because it can lead to a lot of mistakes. But, that's just opinions again, I don't know if that's facts, you know? Which is probably another big problem, I don't think there's enough facts given out to the general public on how the whole court system works."

Positive views of the judiciary

Not all views expressed about the judiciary were negative. A minority of respondents in the survey questionnaire and in qualitative interviews expressed some level of approval of the judiciary and an appreciation of the demands of the job. There was also the positive side to age, which some respondents felt would bring experience and even wisdom. For example:

"I shouldn't think they are [out of touch], I only know one Sheriff, who certainly is not out of touch, and I know his age is nearer seventy than sixty, but he's certainly not out of touch— far from it, and I don't see any reason to believe the rest are. I presume somebody has a look occasionally to see if anybody's verging on senility, other than that, if you've been involved in law and you've been living for fifty, sixty years, you ought to know more than other people, not less."

"I've met quite a few outwith the court and I would say that in general I think they basically just trying to do a job. I don't think that they're in any way consciously biased. Perhaps it's years of dealing with cases and cynicism on the part of some of the older ones that makes them perhaps appear biased. I don't really feel that they are [out of touch]. They are probably all middle-class so they may be out of touch with the pressures that are on unemployed people, the long-term unemployed and people like that; or people who are living in deprived areas."

"I think the majority's pretty fair. Again too removed, far too removed from society. I would think there might be some 'old fools' amongst them, but I think to have reached that level of probity and trust must make them, not better people, but far more impartial in judgement."

CONCLUSION

The survey data together with information from focus groups discussions and qualitative interviews offer some rather disconcerting evidence on experiences of, and attitudes to the legal system in Scotland. The experiences of Scottish respondents who had been involved in court and tribunal hearings seem to be somewhat less positive than those of respondents in England and Wales and this was reflected in broader attitudinal questions about courts and judges. However, those with experience of court hearings, even within a sample of members of the public selected because of their experience of justiciable problems, comprise a minority. Expectations of courts, judges, and lawyers are shaped more often by televised representations of courts and rather negative newspaper reporting. Most people's experience of courts is as a spectator—watching and reading about what goes on in high-profile and generally criminal cases. Respondents were well aware of the power of the media to shape attitudes and expectations and several had suggestions about the need for better education about the system of justice:

"Obviously television educates you quite a bit. The only source of education on the law that I would say was through watching things. I watch documentaries and real things like this. Education is about the only things you could do to make law [seem less inaccessible]."

"I think people have to be exposed to real courts more. I think there needs to be publicity to combat the television version of courts. With the exception of a programme which I thought was called Night Court which was a very informal sort of programme, most court scenes appear to be showing the talents of the actor playing the legal council—their rantings and ravings. If people think that a real court is half like that, they will do anything to avoid going near it, because this guy's going to brow beat them, they will be made to look a fool. They will give the wrong answer, they will drop themselves in the soup when they've done nothing wrong."

"You don't get taught how the court system works, you just have to pick it up through life, I presume. I definitely think it should be taught. I don't think there's ever going to be a person that doesn't have to go through the court at some point in their life, no matter how good a life they live. So I reckon it should probably be part of lifestyle studies in school and things like that, where they're given career advice. It would be quite helpful and it would make people more eager to go to court, rather than just writing off their problems."

"I think if there was more general education in terms of things like consumer rights, so that the general public behaved a bit more of the way Americans do—Americans tend to know what their rights are and will go and complain to shops and restaurants and hotels. I think you would then find, on the converse, the shops, restaurants and hotels would then start to behave better and would probably cut down the number of instances where people had to resort to the law. I think in this country we're just a wee bit reticent about complaining, and so we let them off with murder."

The responses to attitude questions about the legal system suggest that although the public in Scotland regard courts as important, there is some lack of confidence in the fairness of hearings, a belief that the courts serve the interests of the wealthy, and that the judiciary are remote and out of touch. There is also a strong view that lawyers' charges are unreasonably high. In all of these respects, the findings were indistinguishable from those in England and Wales. The findings are also broadly consistent with recent surveys of public perceptions of the courts in the United States. A recent review of the findings of 23 statewide surveys suggests that the public is poorly informed about the role of the courts and court procedures and unaware of court reforms that had been implemented[9]. The review of the surveys also concludes that the public "holds certain strong negative images of the state courts: that trial courts are difficult to access, slow to reach decisions, costly to use, difficult to understand . . .'[10]. Other negative perceptions of the courts include a perception of unfairness resulting from racial bias in the courts. However, the strongest and most widespread perception apparently relates to the belief that "the rich are far more likely than others to prevail in legal proceedings."[11]

The most recent study to be published in the United States on "Public Trust and Confidence in the Justice System" involved a survey of 1,826 Americans in early 1999. Respondents were asked to express their opinions regarding the "courts in their community".[12] The results of the study revealed a number of areas of public dissatisfaction with the courts. For example, over two-thirds of respondents did not agree that it was affordable to bring cases to court; 87% felt that having a lawyer contributed a lot to the cost of going to court; only 10% of respondents felt that courts in their communities handled cases in an excellent manner; and 70% of African-Americans felt that as a group they were treated somewhat worse or fare worse than other groups by courts. Some 44% of respondents felt that judges were out of touch with what was going on in their community.

The evidence of qualitative interviews in the present study revealed some ignorance about the legal system and a widespread inability to distinguish between criminal and civil courts. As a result of this confusion about the work of the courts attitudes towards the judicial system are strongly influenced by media stories about criminal cases and televised representations of criminal trials. The assumption that "court" means a criminal court contributes to a reluctance voluntarily to become involved in court proceedings. Respondents' views of the legal system often conveyed a sense of alienation from the institutions and processes of the law, despite the fact that the courts are regarded as important and that they would be used if something terrible occurred. There is a lack of sympathy with the jargon of the law, the mystifying procedures of the courts, and the closed world of the legal profession. Fears about the cost of embarking on legal proceedings and

[9] David B Rottman, *Public Trust and Confidence in the State Courts: A Primer*, National Center for State Courts, Working Paper, March 1999.
[10] Ibid p 4.
[11] Ibid p.5.
[12] *How the Public Views The State Courts: A 1999 National Survey*, National Center for State Courts, May 1999.

a belief that resources are crucially important to the outcome of litigation lead many people to feel that the courts are largely irrelevant to their lives and to the resolution of their problems. The view of judges as inconsistent, old and remote is simply a part of this picture.

These are important matters. The courts have an important role in maintaining social order, in providing for the peaceful resolution of disputes and in protecting citizens from arbitrary power. Public confidence in the judicial system is also fundamental to the legitimacy that enables the courts to rely on voluntary compliance with promulgated decisions[13].

[13] Recent research in England and Wales suggests that failing confidence in the criminal courts is leading to an increase in jury acquittal rates (see research in progress by Gary Slapper on juries reported *Sunday Times* 28 January 2001).

8

Paths to Justice Scotland:
Which Way Now?

In this chapter we highlight some of the key findings of the study and discuss some of the broader conclusions that might be drawn from those findings, identifying, where relevant, areas in need of further research. Finally, we explore some of the implications of the survey for policymakers, particularly in relation to community legal services in Scotland.

Ubiquitous problems

Justiciable problems that are more than trivial are a feature of life. Many involve substantial threats to the security and comfort of individuals. Others involve financial loss or the danger of loss. Still others involve merely muddle and inconvenience. The results of this survey revealed a relatively high incidence of justiciable problems within the population of Scotland. Over a five year period about 26% of the Scottish population experienced one or more problems or events for which a legal remedy is available, the most common being problems with landlords, faulty goods and services, money problems, and problems to do with home ownership. This pattern of problem incidence was very similar to that found in England and Wales although in England and Wales consumer problems and money problems headed the list. The chief difference between the two jurisdictions, however, was in the incidence levels. In Scotland respondents to the screening survey reported *fewer* experiences of each problem type during the survey reference period, and this important difference is discussed further below.

The survey also established that problems tend to come in clusters. Respondents who reported having experienced a justiciable problem in the previous five years often experienced a problem more than once *and* more than one type of problem. Pairs of problems that commonly tend to cluster together were: divorce and family matters; family matters and children; money problems and family matters; money problems and living in rented accommodation; employment problems and money problems.

Responding to problems

The most common strategy adopted by members of the public in Scotland when faced with a justiciable problem was to try and sort out the problem or to take some direct personal action that might lead to a resolution of the problem. Only a tiny minority of people faced with a justiciable problem took no steps to resolve the problem and when this occurred it was most often because of a belief that nothing could be done about the problem. Those who appeared simply to "lump" their problems were also unlikely to have obtained outside advice about any problem in the past, suggesting that amongst these individuals at least there may be a persistent tendency to "lump" problems that stems either from pragmatism or a sense of fatalism or powerlessness. This was to some extent borne out by qualitative interviews in which respondents referred to the cost and trouble that flow from involvement with legal action and the perception that little could be done to solve problems and disputes.

About one in three respondents adopted a self-help strategy. Self-helpers who attempted to resolve their problem without taking outside advice were often required to show determination and creativity in order to secure a satisfactory resolution. Many were defeated in their attempts and gave up without ever seeking any assistance in their efforts.

Nearly two in three respondents obtained advice about resolving their problem, using a very wide range of more or less appropriate advisers. The most commonly used advisers were solicitors in private practice and CABx. The propensity to obtain advice and the choice of advisers varied significantly depending on the type of problem being faced. Issues relating to divorce and family matters, accidental injury, ownership of residential property, and landlord and tenant disputes were the most likely to be taken to solicitors, while matters relating to benefits, money, and employment disputes were the least likely to be taken to solicitors. These findings to some extent differ from those in

England and Wales where respondents were more likely than those in Scotland to consult solicitors about problems relating to employment and ownership of residential property, and less likely to consult solicitors about landlord and tenant problems. An analysis of use of solicitors by income showed that those on the lowest incomes in Scotland were as likely to obtain advice from a solicitor at some point about their problem as those on the highest incomes. This suggests a U shaped curve in which middle income respondents used solicitors less than either those on lower incomes or those who were better off. This is different from the results in England and Wales and indicates that while legal aid in Scotland is helping those with lower incomes to seek legal help it is failing the middle income who were originally covered by the scheme.

Achieving a result

When members of the public handled the resolution of their problems alone they met with varying degrees of success. Over half of those members of the public interviewed in the survey who dealt with their problem without advice or assistance eventually abandoned the matter. This is a relatively high figure that demonstrates the difficulty of achieving a resolution for many types of problem and the need for advice and assistance in enforcing rights and defending claims. It also indicates that the impact of justiciable problems in a high proportion of cases is apparently simply absorbed by the public, although it takes a toll. Over three in five of those who had failed to resolve their problem after taking some action to reach a resolution reported that they had found the whole business stressful, and over one in four reported that their health had suffered.

The evidence of the study demonstrates clearly, however, that success in resolving problems using self-help strategies depends on the type of problem being dealt with. Self-helpers who took on the other side in consumer matters were more successful in achieving a resolution of the problem by comparison with, say, those who tried to deal with employment problems alone. Success in handling the problem alone depends on the type of problem, the capability of the person dealing with the problem and the intransigence of the opposition. Self-helpers faced with intransigence either gave up or sought help. This means that the problems taken to advisers are, by definition, the more serious and intractable.

The problems most frequently taken to advisers in Scotland were those concerning divorce and separation, accidental injury, disputes over residential property, and employment. Those least likely to find their way to advisers were consumer problems, tribunal issues, and money problems. The problems that were most often taken *directly* to solicitors or those that finally end up with solicitors advising in Scotland are divorce and separation problems, accidental injury, disputes over residential property and landlord and tenant disputes. This reflects the seriousness of these matters to individuals, the extent to which the legal system is perceived as being relevant to the resolution of the problem or to securing a remedy, and to some extent the availability of legal aid or other means of subsidising legal costs.

Some problems appear to have a generally low rate of resolution, for example employment problems, neighbour problems and problems with landlords, particularly where the respondent has a low level of educational attainment. Problems with higher rates of resolution were divorce and separation problems, consumer problems, accidental injury, and problems relating to ownership of property, particularly where the respondent had high levels of educational attainment.

What emerges clearly from the approach of the public in Scotland to the resolution of justiciable disputes is the very limited use made of formal legal proceedings. Almost nine in ten justiciable problems were dealt with either successfully or unsuccessfully apparently without any legal proceedings being commenced, without an ombudsman being contacted or any other ADR processes being used. This is despite the fact that almost two in three members of the public took some advice about trying to resolve their problem, and that of those, about half received advice from a solicitor at some point about their problem.

Making Choices

This simplified account of the outcome of justiciable problems obscures the complexity of the factors that influence choices about whether to take action, what kind of action to take, how much to persevere and when to give up. At each stage in the process that follows the recognition that something bad has happened or is about to happen, the decision about what to do will be determined by a vast range of factors: Do people have any inkling of what their rights and remedies might be? Do they have the knowledge or confidence to pursue those rights and remedies? Do they feel able to handle the matter alone? If not do they know where to go for help? If they know where to go for help can they access that help, when accessibility depends on the willingness or ability to pay (or be paid for), or on the willingness or ability to join long queues during normal working hours.

All of these matters have to be evaluated against the nature of the threat to be averted or the value to be gained, the uncertainty of the outcome in the light of the obduracy of the opponent, and within the context of beliefs about the expense and trauma involved in bringing the law to bear in the enforcement or defence of rights. The study revealed clearly the error in thinking about legal or other advice needs in relation to what certain kinds of "people" do, rather than focusing on what people do *in relation to particular problems*. The most self-reliant and confident people will, for certain kinds of problems almost automatically obtain legal advice, because the matter is important and because it is immediately characterised as a problem for which legal assistance is required.

The importance of problem-type as well as person-type in influencing the approach taken to the resolution of justiciable problems means that policy aimed at providing more effective access to successful dispute resolution must have regard not only to the *number* of justiciable problems confronted by the public, but to the *types* of problems experienced, and the ease or difficulty with which those problems can be resolved.

What do people want?

When faced with a justiciable event most people simply want to solve the problem or to obtain compensation for harm and loss. The impulse for punishment, revenge, apologies, or altruistic solutions is far less important than the desire to be rid of the problem, free of the threat, or compensated for the loss. In finding pathways to solutions, members of the public want routes that are quick, cheap, and relatively stress-free. That is true for all social groups. People want to get on with their lives as quickly as possible and few relish the thought of having to pay to obtain what they believe is their right or what is due to them. Individuals take action or defend their position largely (although not exclusively) because they believe that they have a moral claim to the outcome that they seek, however that belief has been formed and irrespective of the accuracy of the belief in strictly legal terms.

In seeking these solutions there is little evidence of any "rush" to law in Scotland. On the contrary, for most type of problems (excluding divorce and separation, accidental injury and tribunal matters) involvement in legal proceedings is a rare exception. However, the avoidance of legal proceedings requires some interpretation. Members of the public do not necessarily avoid law because they have an instinctive reluctance to press what they believe to be their legal rights. Most people *do* try to press their claims or defend their position, presumably by some reference to rights that have moral or legal force. Many express a strong sense of injustice and unfairness about the problem with which they have been faced. It is not the law that is remote from attempts to resolve justiciable problems, but rather it is formal legal proceedings that are largely remote from the resolution of many day to day justiciable problems. This remoteness derives from the real and imagined cost and discomfort of becoming involved in the procedures that currently exist for the resolution of civil disputes and claims. There is a widespread perception that legal proceedings involve uncertainty, expense and potential long-term disturbance and that only the most serious matters could justify enduring those conditions. Were there to be a revolution in public dispute resolution processes—and this means more than tinkering with procedures and small claims limits—public enthusiasm for mobilising the courts might increase. While it might not be regarded as a social good for the public to be engaged in perpetual litigation, the inability to secure redress for what are seen as morally justifiable claims and a sense of exclusion from the apparatus provided by the state for dispute resolution can lead to frustration, cynicism, apathy and lack of confidence in institutions.

BROAD COMPARISON WITH ENGLAND AND WALES

Landscape of justiciable disputes

An important finding to note is the significantly *lower* overall incidence rate of justiciable problems reported in Scotland as compared with England and Wales. While in Scotland about *one in four* respondents reported having experienced one or more justiciable problems during the survey reference period (26%), the figure in England and Wales was about *two in five* (40%). In Scotland respondents to the screening survey reported *fewer* experiences of each problem type, even in areas where the substantive law, the court procedures and the legal aid system were much the same in the two jurisdictions at the time of the surveys. In seeking to understand this difference, the discussion in Chapter 2 discounted the possibility that there is actually a lower incidence of justiciable problems in Scotland and instead suggested explanations for a substantial reporting difference to the screening survey between the population of England and Wales and that in Scotland. Such a reporting difference is likely to be the result of one or a combination of factors influencing the perceptions of respondents to the screening survey. For example, it is possible that a greater sense of fatalism or powerlessness among the Scottish population led to a systematic underreporting of problems. Underreporting might also have occurred because the Scottish population, with its strong socialist traditions, is more community-orientated than the English, and thus less likely to perceive disputes as being individual matters rather than collective problems. Finally, a less plausible explanation is that the population of Scotland is more hardy, self-reliant and self assured than that in England and Wales, and is thus less likely than the English to perceive problems and disputes as being "difficult to resolve". This is a subject that would clearly benefit from further, tightly focused research.

Response to problems

The response of members of the public in Scotland to justiciable problems was very similar to that in England and Wales. Overall about three percent of respondents did nothing ("the lumpers"), about one-third (32%) tried to resolve the problem without help ("the self-helpers") and about two thirds (65%) tried to resolve the problem with advice or help from an outside adviser ("the advised") (Figure 3.1). These figures are virtually identical with the results in England and Wales (5% lumpers; 35% self-helpers and 60% advised). Previous experience of advice-seeking in relation to justiciable problems was also similar in the two jurisdictions. A little over nine out of ten of Scottish respondents had received advice in the past from a wide range of advice sources, and about two out of three said that they had taken legal advice at least once in the past. These figures are almost identical with those reported in the England and Wales study.

Accounts of anticipated and real barriers to advice-seeking in Scotland were also consistent with those mentioned in England and

Wales. For example, fear of legal costs; inaccessibility of good quality advice about legal rights; previous negative experiences of legal advisers or legal processes; a sense of powerlessness about certain types of problem; and in some cases a sense of alienation from the legal system. Scottish respondents also made frequent references to legal aid "withering away" in Scotland. These perceptions are interesting in that they seem to reflect developments in England and Wales reported in the UK media, rather than any significant changes to legal aid in Scotland.

Use of advisers is again very similar in the two jurisdictions. Taking into account *all* of the sources of advice contacted by Scottish respondents while trying to resolve their justiciable problem, about one-quarter obtained advice from a solicitor *at some point* about trying to resolve their problem (representing almost one-half of all those who obtained any advice). This figure is virtually identical to that in England and Wales. About 14% of respondents in Scotland *at some point* contacted a CAB about trying to resolve the problem, representing about one in five of all those who sought advice (22%) about their problem and this is also very similar to the figure in England and Wales.

One difference between the two jurisdictions, however, was in the use of solicitors as *first* advisers by those on low incomes. Respondents in Scotland with incomes of below £10,000 were significantly *less* likely to seek *initial* advice from a solicitor than those in other income brackets. Similarly, they were significantly more likely to seek advice in the first instance from a CAB. These results are different from those in England and Wales where it was found that there was little variation between respondents in different income bands in their choice of first adviser. However, when we look at *all advice* obtained about trying to resolve the problem, and not just in relation to first advisers, the picture changes. In Scotland, respondents on the lowest incomes who sought advice about resolving their problem were as likely to obtain advice from a solicitor at some point as respondents on the highest incomes. This suggests that legal aid provision in Scotland makes it possible for individuals on the lowest incomes to have access to legal advice with at least the same frequency as those on higher incomes.

Outcomes

The analysis of the pattern of outcomes of justiciable problems and disputes in the two jurisdictions shows a remarkable consistency (see

Chapter 5, Figure 5.1). Indeed, in several cases the percentages are identical, for example in the proportion of cases successfully resolved by agreement without the use of advisers, the proportion abandoned by self-helpers and the proportion resolved by agreement following advice. The overall proportion involved in legal proceedings and the proportion decided on the basis of adjudication were also very similar in the two jurisdictions (although there was some variation depending on problem type[1]). Given the differences between the two jurisdictions in procedures and structures, this consistency of outcome is notable and raises interesting questions discussed further below.

One difference that emerged, however, was the somewhat greater concern expressed by respondents in Scotland about having to pay legal expenses as compared with England and Wales. This is interesting since the proportion of people offered legal aid in Scotland was significantly *higher* than the proportion offered legal aid in England and Wales.

Impact and perceptions of fairness

In reporting on negative and positive effects of sorting out problems, the pattern of effects in Scotland bears a striking resemblance to those found in England and Wales, which is notable bearing in mind the difference in culture, law and procedure. In so far as the Scottish results are distinctive in this area, there is a suggestion of slightly higher levels of experienced stress in Scotland, and an indication that in Scotland the perceived unpleasantness and uncertainty of legal proceedings swamp other more positive aspects of enforcing or defending rights.

Expectations of what could be achieved in trying to sort out justiciable problems were in general fairly similar in the two jurisdictions, although expressions of powerlessness and general pessimism were more common in Scotland than in England and Wales.

A conspicuous difference between the results of the two studies was in perceptions of the fairness of the decision or agreement that brought

---

[1] Involvement in legal proceedings in Scotland was most common in cases concerning divorce and separation, landlord and tenant problems, accidental injury, and ownership of residential property. Involvement in legal proceedings was least common in consumer disputes and neighbour disputes. Although this pattern is roughly consistent with that found in England and Wales, involvement in legal proceedings was higher in Scotland for landlord and tenant problems and lower than in England for divorce and separation problems, employment problems, and disputes over residential property.

the problem to an end. Among those respondents in Scotland whose dispute was resolved by an adjudicated decision only 48% said that the decision was fair, as compared with 71% in England and Wales. Another difference from England and Wales was the high proportion of respondents in Scotland who said that they had accepted an unfair agreement because of a general sense of powerlessness (23% as compared with 6% in England and Wales).

Although most Scottish respondents who had won their court or tribunal hearing thought that the decision was fair, as many as one in five (21%) were actually prepared to say that they thought the decision was unfair (as compared with 7% in England and Wales). This is an arguably perverse outcome but reinforces the impression that respondents who had been involved in legal proceedings in Scotland were left with a rather negative view of the legal system. Unsurprisingly in light of the previous finding, among those who lost at their hearing, the overwhelming majority of respondents in Scotland thought that the decision had been *unfair*. Only *one in ten* of losers were prepared to say that the decision was fair as compared with one in three losers in England and Wales. This indicates a substantially more negative view of court and tribunal hearings in Scotland.

Perceptions of the legal system

Among the minority of respondents whose problem had led to a court or tribunal hearing, levels of satisfaction with those proceedings were significantly *lower* than in England and Wales. Moreover, those respondents whose problem had led to some involvement in legal proceedings and those whose problem led to a court or tribunal decision, were significantly more likely than other groups to lack confidence in the fairness of the courts. Over one half of those whose problem had been resolved on the basis of a court or tribunal decision said that they would not be confident of a fair hearing if they had to go to court. To this extent the results are also somewhat different from those in England and Wales where it seemed that recent experience of using the legal system was *not* significantly associated with more negative attitudes towards that system.

However respondents in Scotland had very similar views to those south of the Border about the reasonableness of lawyers' charges and in Scotland broad perceptions of the judiciary were virtually identical to those in England and Wales. On the other hand, while in Scotland negative views about the judiciary are held across social boundaries, the level of negativity is *more pronounced* among those respondents with recent direct experience of involvement with the legal system. To this extent the findings are somewhat different from England and Wales where involvement with the legal system was not significantly associated with increased or decreased levels of negativity. They are, however, consistent with the pattern of findings on experiences and attitudes to the judicial system in Scotland, which indicates that *direct experience of the judicial system in Scotland tends to increase levels of negativity*.

DISCUSSION OF COMPARISON

Comparing legal systems

In many ways the *similarities* between the findings of the two studies are much greater and more interesting than the differences. Indeed, the frequency with which behaviour and outcomes are alike, when substantive law and procedures are significantly different presents us with something of a puzzle. Figure 5.1 (Chapter 5) encapsulates the puzzle. The figures for how people tackle justiciable events in the two jurisdictions, whether they seek advice, the type of advice they obtain, and whether the matter was successfully resolved or abandoned, are virtually identical. There were also virtually identically negative responses on questions about confidence in the legal system, courts, and the judiciary. How can this be, given the apparently significant differences in certain areas of law, and procedure and legal culture?

One possible explanation is that justiciable events are the stuff of everyday life and the problems of everyday life are pretty similar in Scotland and in England. For such problems any developed legal system will attempt to provide answers, and although the route to those solutions may vary from jurisdiction to jurisdiction, the outcome may look surprisingly alike, suggesting a functional similarity in legal systems that Scottish and English lawyers have rarely emphasised or acknowledged. Although the rules and procedures may appear distinctive to the lawyers, judges and academics who use and analyse them and to which they become attached (e.g. consideration, unjustified enrichment, pure economic loss, detailed pleadings, fast tracks, discovery rules) viewed pragmatically they lead to very similar outcomes.

A second and possibly related answer suggested by the two studies is that the satisfactory resolution of justiciable problems is ultimately likely to be influenced less by fine differences in technical rules and more by provision of clear guidance on the law, together with accessible, affordable court procedures that will encourage settlement or provide for relatively painless adjudication.

As our study shows, roughly one-third of justiciable problems were resolved with a bit of perseverance and a measure of goodwill on both sides. For such cases all that a legal system needs to do is to facilitate, or at least not get in the way. It can do this in two ways. Either by providing a fair, understandable, clear statement of norms[2] such that parties can predict easily how matters would be resolved if they went to court, or, alternatively, by providing a brooding omnipresence with the threat that the legal system will ultimately resolve disputes, usually in an arbitrary and painful way, if the dispute cannot be sorted out by the parties. On the second scenario, ironically, the more arbitrary, unpredictable and expensive the system is, the more it will force people to settle or abandon their dispute since the cost of going or being taken to court is too painful and expensive to be borne.

One-half of the justiciable problems about which respondents were interviewed led to no satisfactory resolution. What should the legal system offer this group? It should filter out cases without merit at an early stage to prevent individuals and the State from wasting resources, and assist the meritorious pursuer in overcoming the intransigence of the unreasonable defender, thus protecting the rights of the pursuer and enforcing the obligations of defenders. For this group the State needs to provide a State-sanctioned method of dispute resolution that is fair, comprehensible, predictable and affordable. However, the negativity expressed in both jurisdictions about the cost of seeking to resolve problems by resort to the legal system has two important effects: first, it discourages the use of the system to enforce rights or obligations among pursuers; and second, it encourages intransigence among defenders who recognise only too well the drawbacks of the system (the "OK, then sue me" syndrome). For this reason both jurisdictions have low rates of satisfactory resolution when all civil disputes and problems that arise are considered. The somewhat higher level of negativity expressed by the Scottish population about various aspects of the legal system, especially among previous users of that system, may account

---

[2] Marc Galanter, 'The Radiating Effects of Courts' in K Boyum and L Mather (Eds.), *Empirical Theories About Courts*, New York, Longman, 1983, pp 117–138.

for the lower proportion of Scottish disputants issuing legal proceedings as compared with England and Wales.

Negative perceptions of the legal system.

It would seem that much of the negativity expressed by respondents concerning the Scottish legal system stems from two sources. First, the media. Our study highlighted the fact that many respondents with negative impressions of their legal systems had never had first hand experience of the system. They had, however, repeatedly seen portrayals of courts, lawyers and judges on television or in the newspapers which might be misleading since they related to other jurisdictions, or more often, calculated to reduce confidence in the justice system because in this field "good news" stories are rarely of interest to the media.[3]

The second source, perhaps surprisingly, might have been the respondents' advisers, despite the fact that they may collectively take a pride in the distinctiveness of the Scottish legal system. It will be recalled that we found in chapter three that respondents who had taken advice expressed high satisfaction rates with their solicitors and other advisers. This accords with a string of studies in Scotland stretching back over fifteen years in which between 91% and 72% of respondents have been very or fairly satisfied with their solicitor.[4] Again, although there was a significant minority of respondents with a negative view of the Scottish justice system, the attitude questions in chapter seven suggested that about 60% of respondents retained a belief in the fairness of the Scottish system. However, more worryingly the survey found that, unlike England and Wales, those who had recent experience of the justice system were significantly more likely to have a negative view of the system than those who had never used it. How is this apparent paradox to be explained? Interestingly, the finding mirrors closely those of one of the earliest studies of Scottish perceptions of their legal

---

[3] The power of the media to influence public perceptions can be seen from the campaign by the Lord Chancellors Department focusing on "fat cat" lawyers and the English Law Society's counter campaign as to the effects of the legal aid cuts contained in the Access to Justice Bill 1999.

[4] Scottish Consumer Council (SCC) *Report of a Study of the Use of Solicitors* 1987; SCC, *Buying a House in Scotland*, 1988; A. Millar and S. Morris, *Legal Services in Scotland: Consumer Survey* CRU, 1992; SCC, *Civil Disputes in Scotland* 1997; System Three, *General Public Opinion Survey*, 1998; SCC, *Home Truths*, 2000. Perhaps inevitably satisfaction rates have begun to decline in recent years.

system, published 25 years ago.[5] In it Campbell found that only 66% of respondents believed that if they used the courts in Scotland justice would be achieved. Again the great majority of respondents who had used a solicitor were satisfied with his or her performance, but more negative about their legal system and other lawyers, than non-users of the system. Campbell's explanation of the paradox, derived from an American study[6] that had thrown up the same phenomenon, was that the problem lay with advisers' efforts to maintain control of the relationship with their clients. "To maintain the relationship the lawyer may . . . use 'institutional excuses'. The lawyer, to put it crudely, may blame the law, blame other lawyers, blame the judicial process: should things go wrong—or go too slowly—it is never the lawyer's fault but always that of other people. Clients thus emerge satisfied with their own lawyers but less than happy with the legal system as a whole."[7]

IMPLICATIONS FOR POLICY IN SCOTLAND

The study has demonstrated how common are non-trivial justiciable problems. It has also established that although in most cases action was taken to resolve the problem or to achieve a remedy, almost nine in ten problems did not involve any kind of formal court or tribunal proceeding, nor were they taken to ombudsmen, mediation or other alternative dispute resolution processes. In about half of all cases no resolution to the problem appears to have been achieved by means of agreement, judicial decision, or court order. These statistics suggest a large "dark figure" of hidden potential demand for the civil justice system. What are the likely implications of these and other key findings of the study for the operation of the civil justice system in Scotland and for the interests of the public in the context of the current reform agenda? The study has shown that strategies for dealing with justiciable problems are influenced principally by the nature of the problem, but also by a complicated mix of factors such as: the knowledge and capability of the individual; the capability of the individual or the resources available to them; and the accessibility of advice and assistance.

---

[5] C.M. Campbell, "Lawyers and their Public" 1976 *Juridical Review* 20.
[6] Missouri Bar Apprentice Hall Survey: A Motivational Study of Public Attitudes in Law Office Management, 1963.
[7] Campbell, *op.cit.* p.35. For a study of image management by US divorce attorneys which graphically illustrates Campbell's thesis in action, see, A. Sarat and W. Felstiner, "Lawyers and Legal Consciousness" 98 (1989) *Yale Law Journal* 1684.

Party capability

As far back as 1974 Marc Galanter[8] argued that "the fundamental problems of access to legality can best be visualised as problems of the capability of the parties. That is, that lack of capability poses the most fundamental, as well as the most neglected, barrier to access and that correspondingly, upgrading of party capacity holds the greatest promise for promoting access to legality. Party capability includes a range of personal capacities which can be summed up in the term "competence": ability to perceive grievance, information about availability of remedies, psychic readiness to utilise them, ability to manage claims competently, and to seek and utilise appropriate help." In Chapter Four we argued in a similar fashion that an individual's need for help (information, advice, letter writing, etc.) in tackling a justiciable problem would depend on their capability and resources, the importance of the problem to them and the intransigence of the opponent. Our research suggests that people's capacity to tackle such problems on their own varies considerably. Some individuals are predisposed to "lump" problems, some to seeking help.[9] Some have the knowledge and self-confidence to proceed on their own, perhaps with a minimum of information and knowledge.[10] Others are so traumatised by their problems that they simply cannot help themselves. Here the pragmatics of "lawcare" cut against the philosophy of some providers. The intellectual concern in the 1960s that professionals were part of the problem for those they were trying to help, because they encouraged dependency and robbed people of "their" problems,[11] has left a legacy. CABx in particular are committed to empowering their clients, to helping them to help themselves rather than doing things for them. This approach is designed to enhance party capability for those who survive the jammed phone lines and busy waiting rooms.[12]

---

[8] "Why the 'Haves' Come Out Ahead" 9 *Law and Society Rev*. 95.

[9] Our evidence (see Chapter 3) showed that lumpers and advice seekers tended to be consistently lumpers or advice seekers when faced with several justiciable problems over a period of time.

[10] However, as we have seen, even the most self-reliant and confident people will, for certain kinds of problems almost automatically obtain legal advice, because the matter is important and because it is immediately characterised as a problem for which legal assistance is required.

[11] Ivan Illich (et al) *Disabling Professions*, (London, Salem, 1977).

[12] S. Wexler, "Practising Law for Poor Persons" 79 (1970) Yale Law Journal 1049 at p.1055. "[I]t is better for poor people to acquire new skills than new dependencies".

However, we found some individuals were so paralysed by the problems confronting them that they wished to be saved, not helped. These individuals, often with low levels of capability in terms of education, income, confidence, verbal skill, literacy skill, and emotional fortitude are likely to need some help in resolving justiciable problems no matter what the importance of the problem and no matter how intransigent or accommodating the opposition. This need is, however, likely to be greatest where the problem is serious and the opponent is particularly intransigent[13].

If such people are to benefit from a Scottish community legal service, a "one size fits all" approach is unlikely to work. By recognising that the approach has to be tailored to the individual and her or his particular problem or cluster of problems, a community legal service programme will be able to adapt its response to the capacities of the clients. Surveys such as this and the Legal Services Research Centre's periodic needs survey for the Legal Services Commission offer guidance not only as to the incidence of justiciable problems, but of the likely demand for different types of information, advice and assistance, thus enabling informed resource allocation decisions to be made.

Community legal education and public portrayals of the justice system

As far as individual capability is concerned, it is likely that average levels of capability will rise rather than fall in the future. For example, an increasing proportion of the population is receiving higher education; greater emphasis is being placed in schools on improving standards of literacy and numeracy; computer literacy is taught at an early age. These developments should equip the public to make good use of information and advice about rights and obligations, about the legal system and about alternative dispute resolution processes, were that information to be made more readily available. At the moment there is

---

[13] There is evidence in some jurisdictions that as a result of the increasing complexity of modern society coupled with the movement to "care in the community" that advice agencies and community law centres are finding that a growing proportion of their caseload consists of the elderly or persons with mental health or intellectual impairment difficulties whose legal problems are invariably complex. Self-help is not an option for such clients. See J. Giddings and M. Robertson, " 'Informed litigants with nowhere to go', Unbundling Legal Aid Services in Australia". Unpublished paper at the International Legal Aid Group conference, Melbourne, June 2001.

no place in the national curriculum for information about the most basic rudiments of legal rights and obligations or the nature of the legal system. It is perhaps bizarre that although members of the public will have been taught to distinguish between, say different varieties of trees, they are unable as adults to distinguish between the criminal and civil courts. As the study has shown, "education" about rights and obligations and about the activity of courts is received through the haphazard and selective reports of journalists, whose primary interest is in selling newspapers, and via televised representations of legal proceedings in which the principal objective is entertainment. These "information" sources cannot satisfy the expressed need for greater understanding of rights, obligations and procedures for redress, nor is it desirable that they should be filling the knowledge gap. The evident influence of the media on the public imagination of the legal system is a direct result of the absence of any competing accurate and regular information flow.

There are challenges here for a Scottish community legal service, for the courts, for schools, and, indeed, for the judiciary in considering how a co-ordinated programme of public education could be mounted to provide a better understanding of matters that are fundamental to citizenship. The survey suggests that whatever may be the position amongst the Scottish judiciary and legal profession, many people in Scotland feel no pride or ownership in "their" justice system nor confidence in its ability to reach a fair result. It may never be easy to persuade the media to temper their staple diet of bad news stories concerning the justice system, but the case for far greater exposure of the Scottish courts on the television than the "one-off" series in the mid 1990s, seems unanswerable if we are to counter the levels of misinformation unwittingly conveyed in the media on a daily basis.

A clear message that emerges from the study is the profound need for knowledge and advice about obligations, rights, remedies, and procedures for resolving justiciable problems. This is a need that exists to varying degrees across all social, educational, and cultural boundaries and for all types of justiciable problem. It is a trite observation that citizenship requires knowledge, but the pervasive lack of the most rudimentary knowledge about legal rights and procedures for enforcing or defending rights can lead to an unnecessary level of helplessness even among the more competent and resourceful. Unfortunately there are few programmes of public education about rights, obligations and remedies that might equip the public to take steps to avoid disputes from arising or to deal confidently and appropriately with difficulties before they have escalated into something more intractable. At the moment the emphasis in advice provision tends to be geared towards disaster management, despite the fact that the provision of high quality advice at an early stage may be successful in preventing a potentially short-term problem from leading to a longer term chronic cluster of problems. As the experiences of respondents to the survey have graphically illustrated, accessing advice when a disaster is looming is as difficult as when the disaster has occurred. In some respects it may be more difficult since the most obvious sources of free advice such as CABx and generalist advice centres are reported by respondents to suffer from restricted opening hours requiring those in work to take time off in order to obtain advice. They also reportedly suffer from overcrowded offices, unanswered telephones and difficulties in arranging appointments.

Community legal education is also relevant to advice seeking behaviour. As we saw in Chapter Three, the Scottish patterns of advice seeking favoured by individuals with justiciable problems are largely comparable with the patterns in England Wales. While the use of solicitors as the first port of call in personal injury or divorce cases seems eminently sensible, the fact that they are more likely to be the first port of call than the CAB in consumer and neighbour cases, and never the first port of call in landlord and tenant cases seems to suggest a lack of accurate information in the public domain on the general expertise of solicitors and CAB respectively.[14] A directory of advisers and their expertise would seem to be a desirable feature for any Scottish community legal service, coupled with an education programme to enhance public awareness of the relative expertise and cost of different types of agency.

In the United States and a variety of Commonwealth jurisdictions, as well as England and Wales, technology is increasingly being used to tackle the information deficit. Free or low-cost telephone hotlines are being used to provide pre-recorded tapes on a wide range of legal fields or legal information and/or advice tailored to the individual circumstances of the client. Usually the service will include the facility for a referral to a relevant specialist if there is one in the local vicinity. Again in British Columbia, Victoria (Australia) and in England, websites have

---

[14] It also supports Lindley over Kempson in their debate as to the rationality of existing patterns of advice seeking by the public. See A. Lindley, "Access to Legal Advice" 7(4) 1997 *Consumer Policy Review* 139 and E. Kempson, *Legal Advice and Assistance* (London, 1989).

been established with information on a wide range of legal topics linked to a database of providers.[15] As yet, these have not become fully interactive, but the experience of the Technology Initiative Grants of the USA Legal Services Corporation suggests that this will not be long delayed. Thus since 2000 the Legal Aid Society of Orange County, California has been participating in a project entitled I-CAN (Interactive Community Assistance Network) designed to make "self-help" information available through a web site and through Internet interactive self-help kiosks. Clients accessing this multi-lingual system view video clips explaining the law, complete court forms on screen, and then electronically file them in a variety of proceedings, including domestic violence actions. I-CAN is tied into the legal system's provider community to expedite access and referral. This is an example of the Internet addressing the "latent legal market" described by Richard Susskind[16] and there can be little doubt that it has a key role to play in any Scottish community legal service. However, although in theory information technology offers possibilities for easy access to information, there is still a considerable way to go before the average adult member of the public will possess the skill to access such information.

Aside from levels of computer literacy there is also the matter of ordinary literacy to be addressed. According to a 1998 survey of 8,000 members of the public aged 16 to 60 for whom English was their first language, around sixteen percent of the adult population was judged to be functionally illiterate and in some areas of the country one in four adults were unable to read a parcel label. This casts severe doubts on the merits of pursuing an "information only" approach to helplines and websites without providing the wherewithal to obtain legal advice and assistance in appropriate cases. It follows that any Scottish community legal service will need to take account of the incidence of justiciable problems, the clustering of problems, and the seriousness and intractability of certain types of problem. All of these shape whether the need is for information alone or for advice and/or assistance and representation.

---

[15] For example, www.bcpl.gov.bc.ca/ell, www.legalonline.vic.gov.au, www.austlii.edu.au, www.justask.org.uk

[16] R.Susskind, *The Future of Law* (Oxford University Press, 1998).

Court procedures and access to justice

Our results indicate that a high proportion of problems remains unresolved and that the legal system in Scotland could be doing better in meeting the needs of citizens. At best barriers to access contribute to the sense of lack of ownership of the civil justice system expressed by the Scottish population in the survey. At worst a perception of unenforceable rights and sense of alienation from the system might encourage undesirable forms of self-help.

The response to these concerns south of the border has been the fundamental reforms of civil procedure devised by Lord Woolf and implemented in April 1999. In recognition of a "crisis" in access to civil justice, the reforms were designed to alter the landscape of civil litigation in the future. Lord Woolf's vision for the new culture and approach to civil litigation involved greater emphasis on settlement and court control of litigation. He introduced a single, simplified, plain English set of rules for the High Court and county courts operated by the judiciary in the light of an "overriding objective"—the exhortation to deal with cases "justly". This is achieved by ensuring that parties are on an equal footing; by saving expense; by dealing with cases in a proportionate manner with regard to the amount of money at stake, the importance and complexity of the issues in dispute, and the financial position of the parties. The overriding objective also requires that cases are dealt with expeditiously and fairly, and that court resources are allocated in an appropriate manner. The judiciary have acquired wide case-management powers, including the initial allocation of civil actions to one of a number of "tracks"[17], responsibility for ensuring that civil actions are dealt with proportionately, and the power to penalise parties and their solicitors for failure to deal expeditiously with cases.

Settlement is encouraged by the use of pre-action protocols, which provide a framework for parties to follow so that they may resolve or clarify the issues in a dispute prior to the issue of court proceedings. The centrality of out of court settlement in the new landscape has led

---

[17] The "small claims track" for cases with a value of up to £5,000 (excluding personal injury actions with a value over £1,000; and all housing actions which have been removed from the small claims jurisdiction); the "fast track" for cases with a value of between £5,000 and £15,000 (involving fixed trial dates, simplified procedures, limited trial length and capping of costs payable to counsel for appearing at a fast track trial); and the "multi-track" for cases over £15,000 or of particular complexity, where judges are required actively to manage the progress of the action.

to a growing interest in diverting cases away from the courts and toward private dispute resolution processes such as mediation, conciliation and arbitration (ADR). In order to ensure that parties and their legal representatives actively explore the possibility of achieving settlement by private ADR, the new rules of court give judges the power to direct parties to try to settle their differences by means of ADR and to stay court proceedings for this purpose[18].

The emphasis in the Woolf reforms on proportionality, speed, limited procedures and pressure toward early case-settlement was designed to drive down the cost of litigation to parties, to make court procedure more comprehensible and thus improve access to justice. Although the evidence of this survey reveals similar problems of access to civil justice in Scotland, comparable changes to civil justice procedures have only been introduced in a few discrete court procedures in Scotland. Whether such changes would be beneficial on a widespread basis, however, is worthy of debate and would need to be informed by assessments of the effectiveness of the reforms south of the border.

A recent and rather flimsy evaluation of the impact of the reforms produced by the Lord Chancellor's Department[19] has reported some interesting findings. First, that there has been a *drop* in the number of claims issued since the introduction of the reforms in April 1999, in particular in the types of claim where the new Civil Procedure Rules have been introduced. Second, that the pre-action protocols are thought to be promoting settlement prior to the issue of proceedings. Third, that although small claims are now taking *longer* to reach a hearing, other cases are reaching trial more quickly. Finally, although the report suggests that it is "too early to provide a definitive view on costs", mounting anecdotal evidence and complaints by the Master of the Rolls reported in the media suggest that costs have actually increased. The experiences of court users and potential users of the courts await further research[20]. Thus while it seems reasonable to assume that one effect of the reforms has been to encourage early settlement and a

---

[18] Where the court of its own initiative considers that a stay of proceedings while the parties try to settle their case by alternative dispute resolution would be appropriate, the court will direct that the proceedings be stayed for one month. Civil Procedure Rule 26.4(2)(b). This can be extended for such a period as the court considers appropriate, 26.4(3).

[19] *Emerging Findings: An early evaluation of the Civil Justice Reforms*, Lord Chancellor's Department, March 2001.

[20] Some evidence on this may emerge from research being conducted by the Legal Services Commission.

reduction in the issue of court proceedings, it is unclear to what extent the reforms have facilitated the resolution of justiciable problems that might previously have been left unresolved. Further research will also be needed to judge whether the reforms have had a broader impact on perceptions of the accessibility of the civil justice system.

Alternative Dispute Resolution

The results of the study have demonstrated very clearly how little impact the development of mediation, conciliation and other ADR techniques has had on the way that the public in Scotland seeks to resolve their justiciable problems, or on the suggested strategies offered by those providing advice. Quite simply current ADR activity in the context of civil, and indeed family disputes, appears to be having a very limited impact on the public. The probable reasons for this are lack of knowledge about ADR services among the general public and to some extent among advisers and the legal profession; suspicion about what is a relatively new development; and also principled objections to the compromise of legal rights and entitlements[21]. This is clearly an area where there is much work to be done, not least in educating the profession and the public.

Helping the middle income

Our survey showed that those on lowest and the highest income were more likely to use solicitors than those with middle incomes. It also showed that those with middle incomes were most likely to assert that lawyers overcharge their clients. This may partially be explained by the fact that it is this group that falls just outside the legal aid limits in terms of eligibility. One solution for the policymakers would be to extend the upper eligibility limit whilst also extending contributions on a sliding scale up to 100% of the cost of the case (including the administrative costs of processing the application). This would extend the real benefit of legal aid—the ability to have one's liability for expenses if one loses modified by the Court—to middle income groups. An alternative may be to develop the concept of "unbundling legal services"[22]

[21] See Genn, 1998 op. cit., Mulcahy 1999, Davies 1999, for a discussion of recent experiments in mediating civil and family disputes.

[22] F. Mosten, "The Unbundling of Legal Services: Increasing Access" in R. Smith (Ed) *Shaping the Future: New Directions in Legal Services* (Legal Action Group, 1995).

or "discrete task representation", as it is sometimes known. Under this approach the representation of a client is broken into a series of separate tasks, some of which are handled by the lawyer and others by the client or a paralegal. It allows people to use a limited amount of legal service provision where it is most needed. This solution, however, is likely to be most useful for educated, highly legally competent, middle income groups rather than for those with low levels of party capability.[23]

The merits of organisation

Galanter in his classic 1974 study of disputing, points not only to the advantages which organisational "repeat-players" of the legal system gain over individual "one shotters" but to the fact that "parties differ in their capacity to utilise legal services". However, subsequent research into party capability indicates that the relative advantages between and among litigants are more nuanced than the terms *one shotter* and *repeat player* suggest.[24] Nevertheless there are undoubtedly advantages to be gained from aggregating claims e.g. though the use of class actions or sharing or reducing risks through the use of collective initiatives or resources. The latter is perhaps another area suitable for colonisation by a Scottish community legal service. By acting as an information clearing house in relation to specialist legal help and assistance and introducing effective referral systems the community legal service reduces the costs associated with dispute resolution, for one shot litigants.

Views on the judiciary

The views expressed as to the Scottish judiciary must be a matter of concern, even if they are largely the result of the misleading media portrayals or "bad news" stories discussed earlier. To some extent the establishment of the Judicial Appointments Board may address this. However, if these perceptions are to be reversed not only will that Board have to reflect broadly the composition of Scottish society in its

[23] See Giddings and Robertson, *op.cit.*
[24] J. Grossman, H. Kritzer and S. Macaulay, "Do the 'Haves' Still Come Out Ahead?" 33 (1999) *Law and Society Review* 803 at p.810.

composition—as the Judicial Appointments Advisory Committee in Ontario does—it will also have to have "regard to how representative the Bench is of Scottish society and how to encourage applications from under-represented groups".[25] Further, it is likely that the distorting judicial images fostered by the media will only be effectively countered by greater exposure of actual Scottish courts and judges on television.

LOOKING FORWARD

The evidence of this study has shown that despite efforts by members of the public to resolve their justiciable problems by means of self-help strategies and even after having enlisted the help of advisers, a high proportion of problems are abandoned without any resolution. Greater understanding about the law and greater certainty about the enforcement of legal rights and obligations in the civil context might have an impact on the behaviour of those who evade their responsibilities and obligations when the opportunity exists and when the likelihood of sanction is remote.

The objectives of any Scottish community legal service are likely to include the provision of general information about the law and legal system and the availability of legal services, as well as providing advice and assistance in the resolution of disputes. This survey has shown that there is a great unmet demand for such information, advice and assistance and that this demand runs across a wide income spectrum. The way in which priorities for the provision of services under a Scottish community legal service are set will inevitably determine the types of existing need that will be met. In setting those priorities attention should be paid to the volume of problems experienced by the public, the way in which problems of particular kinds tend to cluster, the seriousness and intractability of certain types of problems and differential need for assistance rather than advice.

---

[25] Speech by the Justice Minister, Jim Wallace at Strathclyde University on 14th March 2001 announcing the establishment of the Judicial Appointments Board.

Appendix A

TECHNICAL REPORT

As explained in the introduction to the main report, the study comprised three distinct stages:

1. A face-to-face screening survey of the general population of adults (aged over 18), designed to estimate the prevalence of events for which a legal remedy exists ("justiciable problems") in the previous five years. This involved a random sample of 2,684 individuals ("the screening survey").
2. Follow-up face-to-face interviews with 472 individuals identified as having experienced a non-trivial justiciable problem ("the main survey").
3. In-depth qualitative interviews with 29 respondents who had experienced a justiciable problem ("the qualitative interviews").

SAMPLE DESIGN

The objective of the sample design was to achieve main interviews with 500 people who had experienced problems with a potential legal remedy. As it was not known what proportion of the population would be eligible for a main interview, as having experienced a problem with a potential legal remedy, it was necessary to draw the sample in two stages. The first stage was designed to allow the strike rate to be assessed so that an appropriate number of addresses could be issued at the second stage in order to achieve the target number of interviews.

The screening sample was drawn for the Postcode Address (Small Users) File (PAF). The population north of the Caledonian canal was excluded in order to avoid excessive fieldwork costs. Survey estimates for the Scottish population are therefore subject to a small bias due to the exclusion of this area which contains approximately 4% of the Scottish population. The sample was drawn in the following stages:

1. Postcode sectors with fewer than 550 delivery points were grouped together with an adjacent sector.
2. The list of sectors, including the grouped sectors, was stratified by region, population density and Census data for household tenure.
3. Sectors were selected systematically with probability proportional to the number of delivery points using a random start and fixed interval method.
4. A fixed number of delivery points were selected per selected sector.

THE ADVANCE LETTER

An advance letter was mailed to sampled households shortly before fieldwork was due to begin. Printed on SCPR letterhead and signed by a researcher, the letter introduced the subject matter of the study in general terms as "a study to investigate the extent to which people have problems in their daily lives which are difficult to sort out". The letter avoided mention of the legal system, the courts or access to justice and interviewers were briefed to avoid using these terms when introducing the survey. This approach was adopted in order to minimise the risk of respondents focusing on the sorts of problems which involve solicitors and courts to the exclusion of the wider types of problem of concern to the study. Another consideration was that mention of legal processes might discourage respondents who had not had contact with the legal system from co-operating with the study. A copy of the letter appears at Appendix C.

THE SCREENING SURVEY

A random sample of 2,684 individuals aged 18 or over were screened for whether or not they had experienced problems of various sorts over the past five or so years. The majority of these individuals were interviewed in person although in the case of partners a single interview was allowed to cover two individuals, with the respondent providing proxy information for their partner. In order to facilitate collection of screening details for a partner, the screening questionnaire separate columns for answers for respondents and partners to be recorded.

The screening questionnaire collected information about the following types of problems:

- Employment
- Owning residential property
- Renting out rooms or property
- Living in rented accommodation
- Faulty goods and services
- Money
- Divorce
- Family
- Children
- Accident or injury
- death of a child or partner as a result of an accident
- Discrimination in relation to sex/age/disability
- Unfair treatment by the police
- Immigration or nationality issues
- Receiving negligent or wrong medical or dental treatment

In addition to this range of justiciable "problems", respondents were also asked whether, apart from anything already reported, they had had legal action taken against them, had been threatened with legal action over a disagreement, or had started or had considered starting court proceedings for any reason.

For each type of problem respondents were presented with a show card listing common examples of these problems and asked the following questions:

- *"Since January 1992, have you (or your husband/wife/partner) had any problems or disputes that were difficult to solve to do with (PROBLEM TYPE)?"*.
- The number of such problems they had experienced in this period
- For up to three most recent problems of that type, whether they had done anything to resolve the problem.
- If they had done nothing to resolve the problem, the reason why not.
- The date when the problem or dispute began.

The following rules were adopted in classifying problems experienced by respondents:

- Where both the respondent and his/her partner were involved in a problem the problem was recorded for both individuals.
- Problems which started before January 1992 were included if they were on-going after that date.

- Problems which started before the respondent turned 18 years of age were excluded.
- Problems experienced by a respondents in their role as a business person were excluded.
- Situations in which the respondent was helping someone else out with their problem were not counted as a problem except where the respondent was acting on behalf of a child (under the age of 16).
- Criminal problems where a respondent had been legitimately questioned or arrested by the police were not counted. However, perceived unfair treatment by the police was counted as a type of discrimination problem.
- Problems which occurred abroad were excluded.

A copy of the screening questionnaire appears at Appendix C.

EVENT SELECTION FOR THE MAIN SURVEY

An event selection form was completed for each individual who had experienced an eligible problem and had either taken action over it or not taken action for a reason other than the triviality of the problem. 'Trivial' problems were defined as those where respondents stated that they felt the problem was not important or they had no dispute with anyone regarding it or they thought the other person in the dispute was right.

The event selection form was designed to identify a single problem to be asked about in the main interview and, in the case of shared problems, to identify the best person in the household to ask about this problem in the main interview. Where respondents had been involved in more than one problem within the reference period, the event selection form identified the *second most recent* problem as the one to be covered in the main interview.

A copy of the event selection form appears at Appendix C.

THE MAIN QUESTIONNAIRE

The main questionnaire focused on the single problem identified using the event selection form and covered the following issues in sequence:

1. The nature of the dispute.
2. Advice – sources of advice, the nature of advice received and the respondent's satisfaction with it.
3. Where no advice was sought, the reason why.
4. Objectives – the main reasons for taking action and the extent to which these were achieved.
5. Experiences of court and dispute resolution processes, including mediation, tribunals and dealings with ombudsmen.
6. Settlements reached, with or without help from advisers.
7. Amounts recovered.
8. Amounts paid out.
9. Dispute resolution: whether the dispute was ended by agreement or adjudication.
10. Costs – legal costs, financial support and other financial costs of the dispute.
11. General assessments of the experience of dealing with the problem: regrets, the impact of the problem and respondents' attitudes to the legal system.

A copy of the main interview questionnaire appears at Appendix C.

QUESTIONNAIRE DEVELOPMENT

The questionnaires and other fieldwork instruments were developed by the author and researchers at the *National Centre for Social Research*. The key elements of the design were discussed and agreed with members of the project Advisory Group convened by the Nuffield Foundation.

The questionnaire was based on the questionnaire used in the England and Wales survey which was carried out in 1998 following several stages of questionnaire development in the Spring and Summer of 1997, including focus group discussions with advice agencies, members of the public and solicitors and pilots of the questionnaire and other survey instruments. The questionnaire was adapted to reflect the different legal and institutional environment in Scotland. Focus group discussions were conducted in Edinburgh and a Scottish pilot survey was carried out.

FIELDWORK PROCEDURES AND RESPONSE RATES

Interviewers called at each issued address in order to check that it was a private address and to ascertain how many adults aged 18 or over lived there. Thirteen per cent of issued addresses were found to be ineligible because they were untraceable, were empty, demolished or not yet built, because they contained a business, institution or holiday home. (Table 1). At the remainder of addresses, which were private households, interviewers sought to establish how many adults aged 18 years or over lived there. This information was recorded for 77% of private households (Table 1).

Where the interviewers found more than one dwelling unit at the address they were required to list them all and then randomly select one dwelling unit to be contacted for the study, using instructions provided with the sample details.

Table 1 Incidence of private households and success rate for establishing the number of residents in them

	Number	%	%
Addresses issued for screening	2,550	100	
Of which:			
Contain no private households	341	13	
– not traced	17	1	
– empty, demolished, not yet built	160	6	
– business or institution only	137	5	
– other	27	1	
Contain private households	2,209	87	100
Of which:			
No information obtained about residents	504		23
– no contact made	183		8
– information refused on doorstep	290		13
– refusal to head office	31		1
Information obtained about residents	1,705		77

A total of 3,006 adults aged 18 or over were identified within the 1,705 addresses where information was obtained, an average of 1.8 adults per address. Screening interviews were completed with 2,684 of these adults, representing a response rate of 89% (Table 2).

Table 2 Success rate for screening individuals

	Number	%
Number of adults identified at addresses where information obtained	3,006	100
Of which:		
Number of adults not screened	322	11
Number of adults screened	2,684	89

A total of 612 respondents to the screening survey (23% of the sample) were classified as eligible for the main interview as having experienced one or more problems for which a legal remedy exists and having taken action or not taken action for a reason other than the triviality of the problem (Table 3). Where two or more adults in the same household had a shared problem only one was selected for the main interview, by a random method. Thus, of the 612 people who were eligible, 526 (86%) were issued for the main stage of fieldwork.

Table 3 Eligibility rate of screened adults

	Number	%	%
Number of adults screened	2,684	100	
Of which:			
Not eligible for main interview	2,072	77	
Eligible for main interview	612	23	100
Of which			
Not issued for main interview as shared problem covered by another interview in the household	86		14
Issued for main interview	526		86

At the main stage of fieldwork interviews were completed with 472 people, representing a response rate of 89% of the issued sample (Table 4).

Table 4 Response rate for main interview

	Number	%
Issued for main interview	526	100
No interview achieved	54	11
Interview completed	472	89

Taking the information in Tables 1 to 4 together a cumulative response rate can be calculated by multiplying together the proportion of private addresses at which information was obtained (77%), the proportion of identified adults who were screened (89%) and the proportion of selected adults for whom a main interview was completed (89%). This calculation produces a cumulative response rate of 61%.

FIELDWORK

The survey was carried out in Spring and Autumn of 1998 by interviewers of the *National Centre for Social Research*. Interviewers were personally briefed by project researchers in briefing conferences in regional centres. Fieldwork was managed by staff at the *National Centre's* offices in Brentwood and by a network of local field managers. Following the *National Centre's* usual quality control procedures a proportion of interviews were supervised during the survey or had their work back-checked by the office by re-contacting respondents.

DATA PROCESSING AND ANALYSIS

Interviews were edited and coded at the *National Centre's* data processing department in Brentwood. Data were entered by keying. Initial analysis and weighting was carried out at the *National Centre* using Quantum. Subsequent analyses were carried out by the author and the *National Centre* using SPSS analysis software.

WEIGHTING

The survey of problems for which a main interview was completed was designed to be representative of all problems experienced by adults in Scotland in the reference period of the past five years for which a legal remedy exists. The following strategy was applied:

SCREENING-SURVEY WEIGHT

Selection probability weight

If a sampled addresses contained more than one occupied dwelling units, then the interviewer had to select one (at random). Therefore, single address occupied units had higher chances of being selected than multiple address occupied units. To adjust for this, the multiple household indicator (MOI) was used when drawing the sample of addresses, so that an address with n occupied units appeared n-times in the sampling frame. This gave each occupied unit in the sample an equal chance of being selected. However, for the cases where the MOI used at the sampling stage was found to be incorrect when the fieldwork took place, an compensatory weight had to be applied. This is defined as:

Selection probability weight $= \dfrac{\text{no of occupied dwelling units in the sampled address}}{\text{MOI}}$

Non-response weight

In order to assess (and subsequently correct where possible) the extent of non-response bias, a comparison was made between the screen survey respondents and the total population in Scotland in terms of their age and sex profiles. The objective of this analysis was to estimate the probability of response in different subgroups and to adjust the weights accordingly.

The non-response weight is calculated as:

Non-response weight $= \dfrac{\text{total population \% within age/sex group}}{\text{total sample \% within age/sex group}}$

This weight adjusts for differential response rates by gender and age group.

The screening-survey weight is the product of the 'selection probability' weight and the 'non-response' weight, after trimming the few largest weights (above the 95%, and below the 5% percentiles) to avoid excess variance inflation due to weighting.

The table below shows the screen sample distribution by age and sex after weighting by the selection probability weight, the population distribution using mid-97 Scottish population estimates as well as the final weighted (by the screening weight) age/sex distribution[1].

%	Productives after selection probability weight	Mid-97 population estimates	Productives after final screening weight
Age			
18–24	9.1	11.5	11.0
25–34	18.2	20.4	18.4
35–44	19.0	18.7	19.1
45–54	16.4	16.5	16.8
55–64	14.4	13.2	13.6
65+	21.4	19.7	19.4
Missing	1.4		1.4
Gender			
Male	45.5	47.7	47.1
Female	53.4	52.3	51.8
Missing	1.1		1.1

SCALING THE WEIGHTS

The screening-survey weight was scaled by a constant factor, so that the weighted total sample size for the screening data is similar to the unweighted total (2,684).

---

[1] Where 'age' or 'sex' was missing, the non-response weight adjusted the distribution only for the non-missing variable.

MAIN-SURVEY WEIGHT

Number of problems weight

The survey was designed as a probability sample of 'problems' rather than of people. Ideally, those who had more than one problem during the reference period should have been included in the survey once for each problem. Alternatively, we might have included each person once but collected data about each problem. In practice, neither of these was possible; each respondent was selected just once and was asked only about their second more recent problem, if they had experienced more than one in the reference period. This produces a bias towards the problems of respondents who had fewer than the average number of problems over the reference period. To adjust for this tendency of problems experienced by respondents who had multiple problems to be under-represented in the unweighted sample a 'number of problems' weight was calculated equal to the number of eligible problems experienced over the reference period.

Shared problem weight

If a problem was shared by at least two persons in the same household, then only one person was asked to provide detailed information regarding the particular problem. This produces a bias towards problems that are not shared in the household. To adjust for this, a 'shared problem' weight was calculated. This was defined as follows:

- If a respondent belongs to a household where at least a member had a shared problem[2], then:
  shared problem weight = the number of non-main survey respondents in the household sharing the *same* problem as the respondent plus 1 (the respondent).
- For *all* other main-survey respondents, shared problem weight = 1.

The vast majority of the main sample respondents (85%) were assigned a 'shared problem' weight of 1 with 14% being assigned a weight of 2, four respondents were given a weight of 3 and only one a weight of 4.

The main-survey weight is the product of the 'screening weight', the 'number of problems' weight and the shared problem weight, after

[2] Coded as '54' in the Address Record File (ARF).

trimming the few largest weights (above the 95%, and below the 5% percentiles) to avoid excess variance inflation due to weighting.

Scaling the weights

The main-survey weight was scaled by a constant factor, so that the weighted total sample size for the main-survey data is similar to the unweighted total (472).

QUALITATIVE INTERVIEWS

The sample for the qualitative interviews was purposively selected in order to include a range of common problem types including personal injury problems, neighbour disputes, consumer disputes, employment disputes and family disputes. The sample was organised in five groups according to the what type of action the respondent took in response to the problem.

A Those who took no action to resolve problem
   (No to QA17 (a), and no to Q18(a), and no to QA32, and no to QA33).

B Those who took action to resolve problem and did so without using an adviser of any kind
   (No to QA17 (a) and Yes to QA32).

C Those who sought non-legal advice and dealt with the problem themselves
   (Yes to QA17 *but not* code 02, or 10, or 11, or 12, or 15).

D Those who sought legal advice and resolved problem without court hearin
   (Yes to QA17 code 02, or 10, or 11, or 12, or 15; AND No to QD1 (a); AND Yes to D14 (a)).

E Those who sought legal advice and resolved problems via court hearing
   (Yes to QA17 code 02, or 10, or 11, or 12, or 15 and Yes to QD1 (a)).

A total of 40 qualitative interviews were carried out by interviewers from the *National Centre's* qualitative research department in 1999. The interviewers were briefed and debriefed by the author and the author was responsible for the analysis of qualitative data. The topic guide for the qualitative interviews is reproduced in Table 5.

Table 5 Topic guide for qualitative follow-up interviews

1. Initial motivations for taking or not taking action
   - What effect was the problem having – impact on life/work/health?
   - Why did something have to be done?
   - Or why was nothing done despite effect of problem – was it lack of knowledge? Lack of money? Not wanting more trouble? Just too much bother? Too upset?
   - If no action taken, was there anything that could have been provided that would have assisted them to resolve the problem? Advice? Information? Support?

2. Reasoning leading to approach taken:
   - How did they formulate the problem?
   - What did they think could be done? Why did they think nothing could be done?
   - Feelings of blame, anger, injustice? Or not?

3. Objectives in taking action
   - What were they seeking?
   - What did they really want? [this needs careful probing]
   - Did anyone else have a part in framing those objectives or expectations?

4. Why did they seek advice or not seek advice:
   - What made them think advice was necessary?
   - What were they hoping for?
   - How did they come to go to that/those advisers?
   - What did they get from the adviser(s)?
   - Assessment of quality of adviser – knowledge, approach, how could they have been better?

5. Resolving the dispute:
   - What steps were taken with or without help to resolve the dispute?
   - How did it end (if at all)?
   - Why did it end in that way?
   - Responses to court based resolution processes
   - Responses to non-court based resolution processes

6. Assessments:
   Did they achieve their objectives? If not, why not?
   Was the outcome worth the effort expended?
   Whether took action or not: how would they act differently if they were faced with a similar situation in the future?
   How could the process have been made easier/better?
   How should a problem like theirs be dealt with in a well-ordered society?

   Positive aspects of dealing with the problem?
   Negative aspects of dealing with the problem?

Table 5 cont.

7. General attitudes to the civil justice system:
   • What are the courts for?
   • Should ordinary people be able to use the courts effectively?
   • What agencies, organisations, institutions should be made available to help people resolve problems such as theirs?

Appendix B

LOGISTIC REGRESSION ANALYSIS

The objective of the analysis was to identify and explain the factors and respondent characteristics that are important in influencing:

- whether the respondent sought advice for the problem
- whether the dispute was resolved
- whether the main objective was achieved
- perceived fairness of the outcome

The statistical method used was multiple logistic regression. Regression analysis is a versatile data analysis technique that can be used to study relations among variables. Logistic regression is a multi-variate statistical technique that is used to predict a binary dependent variable from a set of independent variables, i.e. the probability that an event will occur. There are many ways of identifying the significant independent variables, but the most well known way is by means of the 'forward stepwise selection'.

Using this method, initially the model contains only the constant and no independent variables. At each step, the value with the smallest significance level for the score statistic is entered into the model, provided that it is less than the chosen significance level (e.g. 0.05). All variables in the forward stepwise block that have been entered are then examined to see if they meet the removal criteria. If the significance level for the log likelihood of the model, or the significance level for Wald statistic for a variable exceeds the chosen cut-off point for removal (usually 0.1), the variables is removed from the model. If no variables meet removal criteria, the next eligible variable is entered into the model. The process continues until no variables meet the entry or removal criteria.

The analysis used the following 4 (binary) dependent variables (variable names are given in brackets using capital letters):

- whether any advice was sought about the problem (DEPEND1)
- whether the dispute was resolved i.e. agreement reached or court/tribunal/ombudsman's decision or order given (DEPEND2)

- whether the main objective was achieved (either completely or partly) (DEPEND3)
- whether the outcome achieved was fair (only for those who reached agreement or where there was a court/tribunal/ombudsman's decision or order) (DEPEND4)

The independent variables used in the analysis are:

- AGE2 – Age group
- DADTYP – Type of advice sought
- DADTYP1 – Type of advice and whether positive assistance given by CABx and other advisers
- DADSETT2 – Type of advice and problem resolved
- DAMOUNT3 – Type of remedy sought (revised to include two levels of lump sum)
- DINCOME2 – Income group
- DLAWATT – Attitude to law (whether confident of a fair hearing)
- DNEGEFF – Whether any negative effects while sorting out problem
- DPLAINT2 – Whether plaintiff or defendant
- DPROB – Problem type
- MJ3B2 – Employment status
- MJ3D2 – Social class
- MJ8B2 – Highest educational qualification
- SEX – Sex

Their use in the four models is summarised below:

	Depend1: whether any advice sought	Depend2: whether dispute resolved completely or partly	Depend3: whether main objective achieved	Depend4: whether outcome was fair
AGE2	X	X	X	X
DADTYP			X	
DADTYP1		X		
DADSETT2				X
DAMOUNT3	X	X	X	X
DINCOME2	X	X	X	X

	Depend1: whether any advice sought	Depend2: whether dispute resolved completely or partly	Depend3: whether main objective achieved	Depend4: whether outcome was fair
DLAWATT	X			X
DNEGEFF			X	X
DPLAINT2	X	X	X	X
DPROB	X	X	X	X
MJ3B2	X	X	X	X
MJ3D2	X		X	X
MJ8B2	X	X	X	
SEX	X	X	X	X

The following tables provide the regression coefficients (log odds), odds ratios and p-values for the logistic regression models discussed in the report. The models were fitted using SPSS (Statistical Package for the Social Sciences). The tables present the variables that are significant after a forward conditional stepwise logistic regression model for identifying the factors associated with advice seeking, settling disputes and fairness of outcome. Unless stated, all coefficients are compared with the theoretical average, i.e. there is no reference category. Tables are presented for only three of the four analyses described above as no factors were found to be significant for the third dependent variable of whether the main objective was achieved.

Table B1 Obtaining advice

Variable	Coef.	Odds ratio (log odds)	p-value
Income {DINCOME2}			0.029
Under £8,000	−0.15	0.86	0.508
£8,000–£14,999	0.47	1.60	0.049
£15,000–£28,999	−0.33	0.72	0.110
£29,000 and over	−0.50	0.61	0.022
Missing	0.50	1.65	0.113
Problem type [DPROB]			0.000
Employment	0.51	1.67	0.201
Neighbour problems	0.37	1.44	0.260

Table B1 cont.

Variable	Coef.	Odds ratio (log odds)	p-value
Divorce/separation	1.38	3.99	0.006
Accident or injury	0.89	2.43	0.067
Money (excluding benefits)	−0.98	0.38	0.000
Landlord and tenant	−0.20	0.82	0.519
Consumer problems	−1.21	0.30	0.000
Owning property	0.88	2.40	0.086
DSS/Education	−1.30	0.27	0.002
Other problem types	−0.34	0.71	0.250
Employment status [MJ3B2]			0.000
Self-employed	0.60	1.81	0.084
Managers	1.05	2.85	0.005
Foremen	−0.29	0.75	0.399
Other and NA	−0.38	0.68	0.038
Missing	−0.97	0.38	0.000
Constant	**1.29**		**0.000**

Table B2 Problem resolution (agreement/ court/ tribunal/ ombudsman decision)

Variable	Coef.	Odds ratio (log odds)	p-value
Remedy sought [DAMOUNT3]			0.003
Smaller lump sum: £500 or less	0.35	1.42	0.280
Larger lump sum: £501 or more	0.51	1.67	0.193
Money amount: regular payments	−0.21	0.81	0.422
No money amount	−0.66	0.52	0.000
Not applicable/not answered	0.00	1.00	0.993
Constant	**0.01**		**0.966**

Table B3 Perceived fairness of outcome

Variable	Coef.	Odds ratio (log odds)	p-value
Remedy sought [DAMOUNT3]			0.014
Smaller lump sum: £500 or less	0.16	1.17	0.837
Larger lump sum: £501 or more	−2.04	0.13	0.004
Money amount: regular payments	0.01	1.01	0.987
No money amount	1.13	3.10	0.014
Not applicable/not answered	0.75	2.11	0.090
Problem type [DPROB]			0.058
Employment	−1.48	0.23	0.562
Neighbour problems	7.12	1232.28	0.746
Divorce/separation	−1.57	0.21	0.529
Accident or injury	0.99	2.69	0.721
Money (excluding benefits)	−0.92	0.40	0.711
Landlord and tenant	−2.41	0.09	0.335
Consumer problems	0.42	1.52	0.868
Owning property	−1.29	0.27	0.611
DSS/Education	−0.56	0.57	0.827
Other problem types	−0.29	0.75	0.910
Negative effects [DNEGEFF]			0.008
Yes	−0.69	0.50	0.008
No/not answered	0.69	2.00	0.008
Attitude to courts [DLAWATT]			0.011
Positive (confident)	0.60	1.83	0.213
Neither positive nor negative/can't say	0.13	1.14	0.808
Negative (not confident)	−1.10	0.33	0.037
Not answered	0.36	1.44	0.752
Constant	**1.51**		0.542

CHAID ANALYSIS

Logistic regression analysis identified a number of factors that appeared to discriminate between people in terms of the various outcome measures. It was not, however, clear how these factors interact in order to produce a number of different and defined population subgroups with a specific size. To address this an analysis has been undertaken using the CHAID (CHi-squared Automatic Interaction Detector) module within SPSS, in order to divide the population into groups who differ in terms of advice seeking and settling disputes.

CHAID is a multivariate statistical technique, which operates broadly as follows: first, a dependent variable that divides the population into two or more groups is defined (for example, those who seek advice and those who do not). Second, a set of independent variables (possible discriminators) is identified for inclusion in the analysis. Third, the CHAID algorithm searches these independent variables and selects the variable that discriminates best in terms of the dependent variable (for example, having or not having had advice) and divides the population into groups based on this variable. Fourth, within each of these groups, CHAID searches through the remaining variables for the next best discriminator and further sub-divides the population within the group into sub-groups based on this variable. Finally, this sub-division process stops when no further split can be found that satisfies the chi-squared criterion for statistical significance.

The following tables provide the obtaining advice and resolving disputes rates for the population subgroups identified by CHAID and discussed in the report. The tables are presented in ascending order of the percentage obtaining advice and resolving the dispute respectively.

Table B4 Obtaining advice

GROUP	% of total	% seeking advice
Consumer problems, money problems (excluding benefits) and DSS/Education problems	38.8%	47%
Landlord and tenant problems, neighbour problems and miscellaneous other problems; women.	18.0%	60%
Landlord and tenant problems, neighbour problems and miscellaneous other problems; men.	14.8%	76%
Divorce or separation, employment problems, accident or injury problems and problems to do with owning property	28.4%	85%
Total	100.0%	

Table B5 Resolving problems

GROUP	% of total	% resolving
Problems to do with employment, neighbours, accident/injury, landlord and tenant, owning property or DSS/education *where* **no** money amount was sought in the dispute and the respondent's highest qualification was **not** an A level or degree.	11.2%	6%
Problems to do with employment, money, landlord and tenant or DSS/education or other miscellaneous problems *where* **no** money amount was sought in the dispute and the respondent's highest qualification was an A level or degree.	15.3%	23%
Divorce/separation, money problems, consumer problems or miscellaneous other problems *where* **no** money amount was sought in the dispute and the respondent's highest qualification was **not** an A level or degree.	10.8%	43%
Respondents who sought a money amount in their dispute (or did **not** specify what remedy they sought) and obtained legal advice or no advice at all.	32.2%	45%
Divorce/separation, consumer problems or problems to do with neighbours, accident or injury or owning property *where* **no** money amount was sought in the dispute and the respondent's highest qualification was an A level or degree.	18.4%	57%
Respondents who sought a money amount in their dispute (or did not specify what remedy they sought) and only obtained non-legal advice.	11.9%	69%
Total	100.0%	

Appendix A

35 NORTHAMPTON SQUARE
LONDON EC1V 0AX

SCPR
SOCIAL & COMMUNITY PLANNING RESEARCH

TELEPHONE 0171-250 1866
FAX 0171-250 1524

June - August 1998

Dear Sir or Madam,

I am writing to ask for your help with a study to investigate the extent to which people have problems in their daily lives which are difficult to sort out. We are interested in experiences in many aspects of life - working life, family life, money matters, renting or owning property and many more. This is the first national study of its kind which will seek to explore how people deal with their problems - some may seek advice or help from other people or organisations, some may try to sort out the problem on their own, others may do nothing. This study will enable us to identify successful and unsuccessful ways of dealing with problems, and we hope will lead to improvements in the advice and help available to people.

The study is being carried out by researchers at Strathclyde University, University College London and Social and Community Planning Research (an independent non-profit making research institute). The research is funded by the Nuffield Foundation.

So that we can get the national picture, we have selected addresses at random from a list kept by the Post Office of all addresses in Scotland, England and Wales. An SCPR interviewer will be calling at your address in the near future to ask your household to help with the study. The interviewer will carry an identification card with a photograph.

Even if you think you have not had any problems in the last few years we would still like to speak to you - without your help we will not be able to estimate the numbers of people in the population who have not experienced problems in recent years. The usefulness of the survey depends very much on the cooperation of all those selected and I do hope you will agree to take part.

The information you provide will be treated in the strictest confidence and the report of the study will be produced in such a way that no individuals will be identifiable.

If you have any queries about the survey, please contact Jean Vallance - the SCPR Area Manager - on 0141 762 2852.

Many thanks in anticipation of your help.

Yours sincerely,

Emily Charkin
Researcher

Appendix B

Head Office: 35 NORTHAMPTON SQUARE
LONDON EC1V 0AX
Tel: 0171 250 1866 Fax 0171 250 1524

SCPR
SOCIAL & COMMUNITY PLANNING RESEARCH

Field and DP Office: 100 KINGS ROAD
BRENTWOOD, ESSEX CM14 4LX
Tel: 01277 200 600 Fax: 01277 214 117

P1667
(Scotland)

SCREENING QUESTIONNAIRE   **1997**

SERIAL NO : ☐☐☐☐☐   PERSON NO. (Respondent): ☐☐

Card 2
201-05
206-07

DATE: ☐☐☐☐☐☐

Cd:208-9
210-15

START TIME: ☐☐☐☐
(24 hour clock) :

PERSON NO. (Partner): ☐☐
(if 'Yes' at Q1a below)

216-19
220-21
(Batch:
1358-82)

1a Can I just check, do you have a (husband/wife) or partner
living in this household?

Yes	1	**ASK b)**
No	2	**GO TO d)**

222

IF SPOUSE / PARTNER IN HOUSEHOLD
b **REFER TO ARF, AND TRANSFER PERSON NUMBER OF PARTNER AT TOP OF PAGE**

c **READ OUT:**
I would like to ask you about different sorts of problems you or your
(husband / wife / partner) might have had.

Please only include problems you have had <u>yourselves</u>, not situations
where you helped somebody else with *their* problem.

We are interested in those problems you or your (husband / wife / partner)
have experienced as <u>individuals</u>, not those experienced by your employer
or any business you might run.

We are also only interested in problems you or your (husband / wife / partner) had
since the age of 18.

ASK Q2 - Q17 FOR RESPONDENT <u>AND</u> PARTNER   **GO TO Q2**

IF <u>NO</u> SPOUSE / PARTNER IN HOUSEHOLD
d **READ OUT:**
I would like to ask you about different sorts of problems you might have had.

Please only include problems you have had <u>yourself</u>, not situations where
you helped somebody else with *their* problem.

We are interested in those problems you have experienced as an <u>individual</u>,
not those experienced by your employer or any business you might run.

We are also only interested in problems you had since the age of 18.

ASK Q2 - Q17 FOR RESPONDENT <u>ONLY</u>

2

SHOW SCREEN CARD A

2a Since January 1992, have you (or your husband/wife/partner) had any problems or disputes that were difficult to solve to do with employment?
CODE ALL THAT APPLY

Card 2

> INCLUDE ALL PROBLEMS
> SINCE JAN '92 EVEN IF
> **STARTED** BEFORE THEN.

> EXCLUDE PROBLEMS
> BEFORE AGE OF 18.
> INCLUDE IF BECAME 18
> DURING DISPUTE.

	Respondent	Partner	
... losing a job *(eg unfair dismissal, dispute about redundancy package)*	1	1	223-29
... getting pay or a pension	2	2	
... other rights at work *(eg maternity leave, sickness pay, holiday entitlement, working hours)*	3	3	
... changes to your terms and conditions of employment	4 b)	4 b)	
... unsatisfactory or dangerous working conditions	5	5	
... harassment at work	6	6	
... unfair disciplinary procedures	7	7	
NO, NONE OF ABOVE	0 → Q3	0 → Q3	

IF PROBLEM
SHOW SCREEN CARD A

b How many problems of this sort have you (has your husband / wife / partner) had since January 1992?

ENTER NUMBER: ☐☐   ☐☐   230-31

c COMPLETE GRID ON NEXT PAGE FOR RESPONDENT (AND PARTNER) FOR UP TO 3 PROBLEMS SINCE JANUARY 1992, STARTING WITH THE MOST RECENT.

WORK <u>DOWN</u> THE GRID FOR EACH PROBLEM

IF FOUR OR MORE PROBLEMS, TAKE THE THREE MOST RECENT.

3

	Respondent			Partner			
SHOW SCREEN CARD X (coloured) 2d Thinking of the (most recent / 2nd most recent / 3rd most recent) problem, did you (your husband/wife/partner) do any of the things on this card to try to resolve it? **CODE ALL THAT APPLY IN APPROP. COLUMN**	Most recent	2nd most recent	3rd most recent	Most recent	2nd most recent	3rd most recent	Cd 2
Talked/wrote to other side about problem	1*	1*	1*	1*	1*	1*	1st 32-38
Sought advice about trying to solve problem	2*	2*	2*	2*	2*	2*	2nd 39-45
Threatened other side with legal action	3*	3*	3*	3*	3*	3*	3rd 46-52
Went to court, tribunal or arbitration / Started a court or tribunal case or an arbitration	4*→g	4*→g	4*→g	4*→g	4*→g	4*→g	
Went to mediation or conciliation	5*	5*	5*	5*	5*	5*	
Took the problem to an ombudsman	6*	6*	6*	6*	6*	6*	
Took other action to try to solve problem	7*	7*	7*	7*	7*	7*	
(DID NOTHING)	8→e	8→e	8→e	8→e	8→e	8→e	
IF DID NOTHING **SHOW SCREEN CARD Y (coloured)** e Why did you (your husband/wife/partner) do nothing? **CODE ALL THAT APPLY**							
Other side was already taking action	0*	0*	0*	0*	0*	0*	1st 53-61
Thought it would cost too much	1*	1*	1*	1*	1*	1*	2nd 62-70
Thought it would take too much time	2*	2*	2*	2*	2*	2*	3rd 71-79
Did not think anything could be done	3*	3*	3*	3*	3*	3*	
Did not think it was very important	4	4	4	4	4	4	
No dispute with anybody / Thought the other person/side was right	5	5	5	5	5	5	
Was scared to do anything	6*	6*	6*	6*	6*	6*	
Thought it would damage relationship with other side	7*	7*	7*	7*	7*	7*	
Other reason (**SPECIFY**)	8*	8*	8*	8*	8*	8*	
f **INTERVIEWER CHECK e**							
At least one starred code ringed at e)	1→g	1→g	1→g	1→g	1→g	1→g	80
No starred codes ringed	2→next or Q3	2→next or Q3	2→next or Q3	2→next or Q3	2→next or Q3	2→next or Q3	Cd 3
g **IF AT LEAST ONE STARRED CODE** When did this problem or dispute begin? **ENTER DATE DISPUTE BEGAN.**							1st 10-13
MONTH	☐	☐	☐	☐	☐	☐	2nd 14-17
IF DON'T KNOW MONTH, ENTER 98 YEAR	☐	☐	☐	☐	☐	☐	3rd 18-21

4

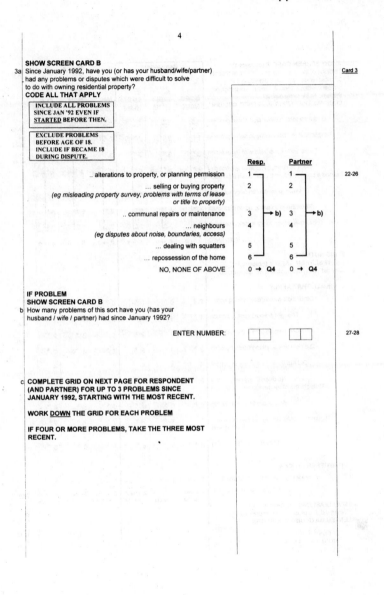

SHOW SCREEN CARD B
3a Since January 1992, have you (or has your husband/wife/partner) had any problems or disputes which were difficult to solve to do with owning residential property?
CODE ALL THAT APPLY

> INCLUDE ALL PROBLEMS SINCE JAN '92 EVEN IF STARTED BEFORE THEN.

> EXCLUDE PROBLEMS BEFORE AGE OF 18. INCLUDE IF BECAME 18 DURING DISPUTE.

Card 3

	Resp.	Partner	
.. alterations to property, or planning permission	1	1	22-26
... selling or buying property (eg misleading property survey, problems with terms of lease or title to property)	2	2	
.. communal repairs or maintenance	3 →b)	3 →b)	
... neighbours (eg disputes about noise, boundaries, access)	4	4	
... dealing with squatters	5	5	
... repossession of the home	6	6	
NO, NONE OF ABOVE	0 → Q4	0 → Q4	

IF PROBLEM
SHOW SCREEN CARD B
b How many problems of this sort have you (has your husband / wife / partner) had since January 1992?

ENTER NUMBER: ☐☐ ☐☐   27-28

c COMPLETE GRID ON NEXT PAGE FOR RESPONDENT (AND PARTNER) FOR UP TO 3 PROBLEMS SINCE JANUARY 1992, STARTING WITH THE MOST RECENT.

WORK <u>DOWN</u> THE GRID FOR EACH PROBLEM

IF FOUR OR MORE PROBLEMS, TAKE THE THREE MOST RECENT.

5

SHOW SCREEN CARD X (coloured)

3d Thinking of the (most recent / 2nd most recent / 3rd most recent) problem, did you (your husband/wife/partner) do any of the things on this card to try to resolve it?
CODE ALL THAT APPLY IN APPROP. COLUMN

	Respondent			Partner			Cd 3
	Most recent	2nd most recent	3rd most recent	Most recent	2nd most recent	3rd most recent	
Talked/wrote to other side about problem	1*	1*	1*	1*	1*	1*	1st 29-35
Sought advice about trying to solve problem	2*	2*	2*	2*	2*	2*	2nd 36-42
Threatened other side with legal action	3*	3*	3*	3*	3*	3*	3rd 43-49
Went to court, tribunal or arbitration / Started a court or tribunal case or an arbitration	4*→g	4*→g	4*→g	4*→g	4*→g	4*→g	
Went to mediation or conciliation	5*	5*	5*	5*	5*	5*	
Took the problem to an ombudsman	6*	6*	6*	6*	6*	6*	
Took other action to try to solve problem	7*	7*	7*	7*	7*	7*	
(DID NOTHING)	8→e	8→e	8→e	8→e	8→e	8→e	

IF DID NOTHING
SHOW SCREEN CARD Y (coloured)

e Why did you (your husband/wife/partner) do nothing?
CODE ALL THAT APPLY

Other side was already taking action	0*	0*	0*	0*	0*	0*	1st 50-58
Thought it would cost too much	1*	1*	1*	1*	1*	1*	2nd 59-67
Thought it would take too much time	2*	2*	2*	2*	2*	2*	3rd 68-76
Did not think anything could be done	3*	3*	3*	3*	3*	3*	
Did not think it was very important	4	4	4	4	4	4	
No dispute with anybody / Thought the other person/side was right	5	5	5	5	5	5	
Was scared to do anything	6*	6*	6*	6*	6*	6*	
Thought it would damage relationship with other side	7*	7*	7*	7*	7*	7*	
Other reason (**SPECIFY**)	8*	8*	8*	8*	8*	8*	

f **INTERVIEWER CHECK e**

At least one starred code ringed at e)	1→g	1→g	1→g	1→g	1→g	1→g	77
No starred codes ringed	2→next or Q4	2→next or Q4	2→next or Q4	2→next or Q4	2→next or Q4	2→next or Q4	Cd 4

g **IF AT LEAST ONE STARRED CODE**
When did this problem or dispute begin?
ENTER DATE DISPUTE BEGAN.

| IF DON'T KNOW MONTH, ENTER 98 | MONTH | | | | | | 1st 10-13 2nd 14-17 |
| | YEAR | | | | | | 3rd 18-21 |

6

SHOW SCREEN CARD C

4a Since January 1992, have you (or your husband/wife/partner
had any problems or disputes that were difficult to solve
to do with renting out rooms or property to a lodger or tenant?
INCLUDE PROBLEMS/DISPUTES RELATED TO CROFTING
CODE ALL THAT APPLY

Card 4

> EXCLUDE PROBLEMS/DISPUTES TO DO
> WITH RESPONDENT'S BUSINESS

> INCLUDE ALL PROBLEMS
> SINCE JAN '92 EVEN IF
> STARTED BEFORE THEN.

> EXCLUDE PROBLEMS
> BEFORE AGE OF 18.
> INCLUDE IF BECAME 18
> DURING DISPUTE.

	Resp.	Partner	
... repeated non-payment of rent (rent arrears)	1	1	22-29
... repairs, return of deposits or early abandonment of tenancy	2	2	
...agreeing on council tax or housing benefit payments or other terms of the lease, missive or tenancy agreement	3	3	
... evicting a lodger or tenant	4 → b)	4 → b)	
... tenant sub-letting the property	5	5	
... problems with managing agents, factors or letting agents	6	6	
... complying with safety regulations	7	7	
... anti-social tenants	8	8	
NO, NONE OF ABOVE	0 → **Q5**	0 → **Q5**	

IF PROBLEM
SHOW SCREEN CARD C

b How many problems of this sort have you (has your
husband / wife / partner) had since January 1992?

ENTER NUMBER: ☐☐   ☐☐   30-31

c **COMPLETE GRID ON NEXT PAGE FOR RESPONDENT**
(AND PARTNER) FOR UP TO 3 PROBLEMS SINCE
JANUARY 1992, STARTING WITH THE MOST RECENT.

WORK DOWN THE GRID FOR EACH PROBLEM

IF FOUR OR MORE PROBLEMS, TAKE THE THREE MOST
RECENT.

7

4d SHOW SCREEN CARD X (coloured)
Thinking of the (most recent / 2ⁿᵈ most recent / 3ʳᵈ most recent) problem, did you (your husband/wife/partner) do any of the things on this card to try to resolve it?
CODE ALL THAT APPLY IN APPROP. COLUMN

	Respondent			Partner			
	Most recent	2ⁿᵈ most recent	3ʳᵈ most recent	Most recent	2ⁿᵈ most recent	3ʳᵈ most recent	
Talked/wrote to other side about problem	1*	1*	1*	1*	1*	1*	1ˢᵗ 32-38
Sought advice about trying to solve problem	2*	2*	2*	2*	2*	2*	2ⁿᵈ 39-45
Threatened other side with legal action	3*	3*	3*	3*	3*	3*	3ʳᵈ 46-52
Went to court, tribunal or arbitration / Started a court or tribunal case or an arbitration	4*→g	4*→g	4*→g	4*→g	4*→g	4*→g	
Went to mediation or conciliation	5*	5*	5*	5*	5*	5*	
Took the problem to an ombudsman	6*	6*	6*	6*	6*	6*	
Took other action to try to solve problem	7*	7*	7*	7*	7*	7*	
(DID NOTHING)	8→e	8→e	8→e	8→e	8→e	8→e	

IF DID NOTHING
SHOW SCREEN CARD Y (coloured)
e Why did you (your husband/wife/partner) do nothing?
CODE ALL THAT APPLY

Other side was already taking action	0*	0*	0*	0*	0*	0*	1ˢᵗ 53-61
Thought it would cost too much	1*	1*	1*	1*	1*	1*	2ⁿᵈ 62-70
Thought it would take too much time	2*	2*	2*	2*	2*	2*	3ʳᵈ 71-79
Did not think anything could be done	3*	3*	3*	3*	3*	3*	
Did not think it was very important	4	4	4	4	4	4	
No dispute with anybody / Thought the other person/side was right	5	5	5	5	5	5	
Was scared to do anything	6*	6*	6*	6*	6*	6*	
Thought it would damage relationship with other side	7*	7*	7*	7*	7*	7*	
Other reason (SPECIFY)	8*	8*	8*	8*	8*	8*	

f INTERVIEWER CHECK e

At least one starred code ringed at e)	1→g	1→g	1→g	1→g	1→g	1→g	80
No starred codes ringed	2→next or Q5	2→next or Q5	2→next or Q5	2→next or Q5	2→next or Q5	2→next or Q5	Cd 5

g IF AT LEAST ONE STARRED CODE
When did this problem or dispute begin?
ENTER DATE DISPUTE BEGAN.

IF DON'T KNOW MONTH, ENTER 98 MONTH	☐☐	☐☐	☐☐	☐☐	☐☐	☐☐	1ˢᵗ 10-13 2ⁿᵈ 14-17
YEAR	☐☐	☐☐	☐☐	☐☐	☐☐	☐☐	3ʳᵈ 18-21

8

SHOW SCREEN CARD D

5a Since January 1992, have you (or your husband/wife/ partner) had any problems or disputes that were difficult to solve ... to do with living in rented accommodation?
INCLUDE PROBLEMS/DISPUTES RELATED TO CROFTING
CODE ALL THAT APPLY

INCLUDE ALL PROBLEMS
SINCE JAN '92 EVEN IF
STARTED BEFORE THEN.

EXCLUDE PROBLEMS
BEFORE AGE OF 18.
INCLUDE IF BECAME 18
DURING DISPUTE.

	Resp.	Partner	
... poor or unsafe living conditions	01	01	22-41
... getting a deposit back from the landlord or council	02	02	
... renting out rooms to lodgers or sub-letting	03	03	
... getting other people in the accommodation to pay their share of the bills	04	04	
... getting the landlord or council to do repairs *(eg dampness)*	05 →b)	05 →b)	
... agreeing on rent, council tax or housing benefit payments or other terms of the lease, missive or tenancy agreement	06	06	
...getting the landlord to provide a written lease, missive or tenancy agreement	07	07	
... neighbours *(eg disputes about noise, boundaries, access etc)*	08	08	
... harassment by the landlord	09	09	
... being evicted, or threatened with eviction	10	10	
NO, NONE OF ABOVE	00 → Q6	00 → Q6	

Card 5

IF PROBLEM
SHOW SCREEN CARD D
b How many problems of this sort have you (has your husband / wife / partner) had since January 1992?

ENTER NUMBER:

42-43

c **COMPLETE GRID ON NEXT PAGE FOR RESPONDENT (AND PARTNER) FOR UP TO 3 PROBLEMS SINCE JANUARY 1992, STARTING WITH THE MOST RECENT.**

WORK DOWN THE GRID FOR EACH PROBLEM

IF FOUR OR MORE PROBLEMS, TAKE THE THREE MOST RECENT.

9

SHOW SCREEN CARD X (coloured)

5d Thinking of the (most recent / 2nd most recent / 3rd most recent) problem, did you (your husband/wife/partner) do any of the things on this card to try to resolve it?
CODE ALL THAT APPLY IN APPROP. COLUMN

	Respondent			Partner			
	Most recent	2nd most recent	3rd most recent	Most recent	2nd most recent	3rd most recent	
Talked/wrote to other side about problem	1*	1*	1*	1*	1*	1*	1st 44-50
Sought advice about trying to solve problem	2*	2*	2*	2*	2*	2*	2nd 51-57
Threatened other side with legal action	3*	3*	3*	3*	3*	3*	3rd 58-64
Went to court, tribunal or arbitration / Started a court or tribunal case or an arbitration	4*→g	4*→g	4*→g	4*→g	4*→g	4*→g	
Went to mediation or conciliation	5*	5*	5*	5*	5*	5*	
Took the problem to an ombudsman	6*	6*	6*	6*	6*	6*	
Took other action to try to solve problem	7*	7*	7*	7*	7*	7*	
(DID NOTHING)	8→e	8→e	8→e	8→e	8→e	8→e	

IF DID NOTHING
SHOW SCREEN CARD Y (coloured)

e Why did you (your husband/wife/partner) do nothing?
CODE ALL THAT APPLY

Other side was already taking action	0*	0*	0*	0*	0*	0*	1st 10-18
Thought it would cost too much	1*	1*	1*	1*	1*	1*	2nd 19-27
Thought it would take too much time	2*	2*	2*	2*	2*	2*	3rd 28-36
Did not think anything could be done	3*	3*	3*	3*	3*	3*	
Did not think it was very important	4	4	4	4	4	4	
No dispute with anybody / Thought the other person/side was right	5	5	5	5	5	5	
Was scared to do anything	6*	6*	6*	6*	6*	6*	
Thought it would damage relationship with other side	7*	7*	7*	7*	7*	7*	
Other reason (SPECIFY)	8*	8*	8*	8*	8*	8*	

f **INTERVIEWER CHECK e**

At least one starred code ringed at e)	1→g	1→g	1→g	1→g	1→g	1→g	(73)
No starred codes ringed	2→next or Q6	2→next or Q6	2→next or Q6	2→next or Q6	2→next or Q6	2→next or Q6	

g **IF AT LEAST ONE STARRED CODE**
When did this problem or dispute begin?
ENTER DATE DISPUTE BEGAN.

MONTH

IF DON'T KNOW MONTH, ENTER 98

YEAR

1st 37-40
2nd 41-44
3rd 45-48

10

SHOW SCREEN CARD E

6a Since January 1992, have you (or your husband/wife/partner) had any problems or disputes that were difficult to solve to do with receiving faulty goods or services - some examples are shown on this card?

		Resp.		Partner
INCLUDE ALL PROBLEMS SINCE JAN '92 EVEN IF STARTED BEFORE THEN.	Yes	1 → b)	1 → b)	49
EXCLUDE PROBLEMS BEFORE AGE OF 18. INCLUDE IF BECAME 18 DURING DISPUTE.	No	2 → Q7	2 → Q7	

IF PROBLEM
SHOW SCREEN CARD E

b How many problems of this sort have you (has your husband / wife / partner) had since January 1992?

ENTER NUMBER: ☐☐ ☐☐   50-51

c COMPLETE GRID ON NEXT PAGE FOR RESPONDENT (AND PARTNER) FOR UP TO 3 PROBLEMS SINCE JANUARY 1992, STARTING WITH THE MOST RECENT.

WORK **DOWN** THE GRID FOR EACH PROBLEM

IF FOUR OR MORE PROBLEMS, TAKE THE THREE MOST RECENT.

11

SHOW SCREEN CARD X (coloured)

6d Thinking of the (most recent / 2nd most recent / 3rd most recent) problem, did you (your husband/wife/partner) do any of the things on this card to try to resolve it?
CODE ALL THAT APPLY IN APPROP. COLUMN

	Respondent			Partner			
	Most recent	2nd most recent	3rd most recent	Most recent	2nd most recent	3rd most recent	Cd 6
Talked/wrote to other side about problem	1*	1*	1*	1*	1*	1*	1st 52-58
Sought advice about trying to solve problem	2*	2*	2*	2*	2*	2*	2nd 59-65
Threatened other side with legal action	3*	3*	3*	3*	3*	3*	3rd 66-72
Went to court, tribunal or arbitration / Started a court or tribunal case or an arbitration	4*→g	4*→g	4*→g	4*→g	4*→g	4*→g	
Went to mediation or conciliation	5*	5*	5*	5*	5*	5*	
Took the problem to an ombudsman	6*	6*	6*	6*	6*	6*	
Took other action to try to solve problem	7*	7*	7*	7*	7*	7*	
(DID NOTHING)	8→e	8→e	8→e	8→e	8→e	8→e	

IF DID NOTHING
SHOW SCREEN CARD Y (coloured)

e Why did you (your husband/wife/partner) do nothing?
CODE ALL THAT APPLY

							Cd 7
Other side was already taking action	0*	0*	0*	0*	0*	0*	1st 10-18
Thought it would cost too much	1*	1*	1*	1*	1*	1*	2nd 19-27
Thought it would take too much time	2*	2*	2*	2*	2*	2*	3rd 28-36
Did not think anything could be done	3*	3*	3*	3*	3*	3*	
Did not think it was very important	4	4	4	4	4	4	
No dispute with anybody / Thought the other person/side was right	5	5	5	5	5	5	
Was scared to do anything	6*	6*	6*	6*	6*	6*	
Thought it would damage relationship with other side	7*	7*	7*	7*	7*	7*	
Other reason (SPECIFY)	8*	8*	8*	8*	8*	8*	

f INTERVIEWER CHECK e

At least one starred code ringed at e)	1→g	1→g	1→g	1→g	1→g	1→g	(76)
No starred codes ringed	2→next or Q7	2→next or Q7	2→next or Q7	2→next or Q7	2→next or Q7	2→next or Q7	

g IF AT LEAST ONE STARRED CODE
When did this problem or dispute begin?
ENTER DATE DISPUTE BEGAN.

IF DON'T KNOW MONTH, ENTER 98

MONTH □□ □□ □□   □□ □□ □□

YEAR □□ □□ □□   □□ □□ □□

1st 37-40
2nd 41-44
3rd 45-48

12

SHOW SCREEN CARD F
7a Since January 1992, have you (or your husband/wife/
partner) had any problems or disputes that were difficult
to solve ... to do with money?
CODE ALL THAT APPLY

> **EXCLUDE PROBLEMS/DISPUTES TO DO
> WITH RESPONDENT'S BUSINESS OR
> EMPLOYER**

> **INCLUDE ALL PROBLEMS
> SINCE JAN '92 EVEN IF
> STARTED BEFORE THEN.**

> **EXCLUDE PROBLEMS
> BEFORE AGE OF 18.
> INCLUDE IF BECAME 18
> DURING DISPUTE.**

	Resp.	Partner	
... getting someone to pay money that they owe	01	01	49-66
... insurance companies unfairly rejecting claims	02	02	
... incorrect or disputed bills	03	03	
... incorrect or unfair tax demands (including Council Tax)	04	04	
... the DSS not giving benefits, pensions, grants or loans that you (or your husband/wife/partner) are legally entitled to	05 → b)	05 → b)	
... being given incorrect information or advice about insurance, pensions or other financial products	06	06	
... mismanagement of a pension fund to which you (or your husband/wife/partner) contribute	07	07	
... unfair refusal of credit as a result of incorrect information about you (or your husband/wife/partner)	08	08	
... unreasonable harassment from creditors	09	09	
NO, NONE OF ABOVE	00 → Q8	00 → Q8	

IF PROBLEM
SHOW SCREEN CARD F
b How many problems of this sort have you (has your
husband / wife / partner) had since January 1992?

ENTER NUMBER: ☐☐   ☐☐   67-68

c **COMPLETE GRID ON NEXT PAGE FOR RESPONDENT
(AND PARTNER) FOR UP TO 3 PROBLEMS SINCE
JANUARY 1992, STARTING WITH THE MOST RECENT.**

WORK DOWN THE GRID FOR EACH PROBLEM

**IF FOUR OR MORE PROBLEMS, TAKE THE THREE MOST
RECENT.**

13

	Respondent			Partner			Cd 7
SHOW SCREEN CARD X (coloured) 7d Thinking of the (most recent / 2nd most recent / 3rd most recent) problem, did you (your husband/wife/partner) do any of the things on this card to try to resolve it? **CODE ALL THAT APPLY IN APPROP. COLUMN**	Most recent	2nd most recent	3rd most recent	Most recent	2nd most recent	3rd most recent	
Talked/wrote to other side about problem	1 *	1 *	1 *	1 *	1 *	1 *	1st 69-75
Sought advice about trying to solve problem	2 *	2 *	2 *	2 *	2 *	2 *	Cd 8 10-16
Threatened other side with legal action	3 *	3 *	3 *	3 *	3 *	3 *	3rd 17-23
Went to court, tribunal or arbitration / Started a court or tribunal case or an arbitration	4 * →g	4 * →g	4 * →g	4 * →g	4 * →g	4 * →g	
Went to mediation or conciliation	5	5	5	5	5	5	
Took the problem to an ombudsman	6 *	6 *	6 *	6 *	6 *	6 *	
Took other action to try to solve problem	7 *	7 *	7 *	7 *	7 *	7 *	
(DID NOTHING)	8 → e	8 → e	8 → e	8 → e	8 → e	8 → e	
IF DID NOTHING **SHOW SCREEN CARD Y (coloured)** e Why did you (your husband/wife/partner) do nothing? **CODE ALL THAT APPLY**							
Other side was already taking action	0 *	0 *	0 *	0 *	0 *	0 *	1st 24-32
Thought it would cost too much	1 *	1 *	1 *	1 *	1 *	1 *	2nd 33-41
Thought it would take too much time	2 *	2 *	2 *	2 *	2 *	2 *	3rd 42-50
Did not think anything could be done	3 *	3 *	3 *	3 *	3 *	3 *	
Did not think it was very important	4	4	4	4	4	4	
No dispute with anybody / Thought the other person/side was right	5	5	5	5	5	5	
Was scared to do anything	6 *	6 *	6 *	6 *	6 *	6 *	
Thought it would damage relationship with other side	7 *	7 *	7 *	7 *	7 *	7 *	
Other reason (**SPECIFY**)	8 *	8 *	8 *	8 *	8 *	8 *	
f INTERVIEWER CHECK e							
At least one starred code ringed at e)	1 → g	1 → g	1 → g	1 → g	1 → g	1 → g	(77)
No starred codes ringed	2→next or Q8	2→next or Q8	2→next or Q8	2→next or Q8	2→next or Q8	2→next or Q8	
g IF AT LEAST ONE STARRED CODE When did this problem or dispute begin? **ENTER DATE DISPUTE BEGAN.** MONTH	☐☐	☐☐	☐☐	☐☐	☐☐	☐☐	1st 51-54 2nd 55-59 3rd 60-63
IF DON'T KNOW MONTH, ENTER 98 YEAR	☐☐	☐☐	☐☐	☐☐	☐☐	☐☐	

14

8a Can I just check, have you (or has your husband/wife partner) been involved in divorce proceedings, even if no divorce was obtained, since January 1992? **INCLUDE PROCEEDINGS AGAINST CURRENT OR PREVIOUS SPOUSE**

INCLUDE EVEN IF PROCEEDINGS **STARTED** BEFORE JAN'92.	EXCLUDE PROCEEDINGS BEFORE AGE OF 18. INCLUDE IF BECAME 18 DURING PROCEEDINGS.

	Resp.	**Partner**	
Yes	1 * → b)	1 * → b)	64
No	2 → **Q9**	2 → **Q9**	

IF YES
b When did these divorce proceedings begin?
ENTER DATE DIVORCE PROCEEDINGS STARTED.

IF DON'T KNOW MONTH, ENTER 98

65-68

Month

Year

SHOW SCREEN CARD G
9a Since January 1992, have you (or your husband/wife/partner) had any experience of any of the things on this card to do with relationships and other family matters?
CODE ALL THAT APPLY

INCLUDE ALL PROBLEMS SINCE JAN '92 EVEN IF **STARTED** BEFORE THEN.	EXCLUDE PROBLEMS BEFORE AGE OF 18. INCLUDE IF BECAME 18 DURING DISPUTE.

	Resp.	Partner	
...division of money, pensions or property in connection with divorce or separation	1	1	69-74
... getting or paying maintenance or child support payments	2	2	
... fostering or adopting children or becoming a legal guardian	3 → b)	3 → b)	
... violent or abusive relationships with a partner, ex-partner or other family member	4	4	
... problems after the death of a family member or partner *(eg disputed wills, division of property, funeral arrangements, succession of tenancy)*	5	5	
NO, NONE OF ABOVE	0 → **Q10**	0 → **Q10**	

IF PROBLEM
SHOW SCREEN CARD G
b How many experiences of this sort have you (has your husband / wife / partner) had since January 1992?

ENTER NUMBER:

75-76

c COMPLETE GRID ON NEXT PAGE FOR RESPONDENT (AND PARTNER) FOR UP TO 3 PROBLEMS SINCE JANUARY 1992, STARTING WITH THE MOST RECENT.

WORK **DOWN** THE GRID FOR EACH PROBLEM

IF FOUR OR MORE PROBLEMS, TAKE THE THREE MOST RECENT.

15

SHOW SCREEN CARD X (coloured)

9d Thinking of the (most recent / 2nd most recent / 3rd most recent) problem, did you (your husband/wife/partner) do any of the things on this card to try to resolve it?
CODE ALL THAT APPLY IN APPROP. COLUMN

Cd 9

	Respondent			Partner		
	Most recent	2nd most recent	3rd most recent	Most recent	2nd most recent	3rd most recent	
Talked/wrote to other side about problem	1 *	1 *	1 *	1 *	1 *	1 *	1st 10-16
Sought advice about trying to solve problem	2 *	2 *	2 *	2 *	2 *	2 *	2nd 17-23
Threatened other side with legal action	3 *	3 *	3 *	3 *	3 *	3 *	3rd 24-30
Went to court, tribunal or arbitration / Started a court or tribunal case or an arbitration	4 *→g	4 *→g	4 *→g	4 *→g	4 *→g	4 *→g	
Went to mediation or conciliation	5 *	5 *	5 *	5 *	5 *	5 *	
Took the problem to an ombudsman	6 *	6 *	6 *	6 *	6 *	6 *	
Took other action to try to solve problem	7 *	7 *	7 *	7 *	7 *	7 *	
(DID NOTHING)	8 → e	8 → e	8 → e	8 → e	8 → e	8 → e	

IF DID NOTHING
SHOW SCREEN CARD Y (coloured)
e Why did you (your husband/wife/partner) do nothing?
CODE ALL THAT APPLY

Other side was already taking action	0 *	0 *	0 *	0 *	0 *	0 *	1st 31-39
Thought it would cost too much	1 *	1 *	1 *	1 *	1 *	1 *	2nd 40-48
Thought it would take too much time	2 *	2 *	2 *	2 *	2 *	2 *	3rd 49-57
Did not think anything could be done	3 *	3 *	3 *	3 *	3 *	3 *	
Did not think it was very important	4	4	4	4	4	4	
No dispute with anybody / Thought the other person/side was right	5	5	5	5	5	5	
Was scared to do anything	6 *	6 *	6 *	6 *	6 *	6 *	
Thought it would damage relationship with other side	7 *	7 *	7 *	7 *	7 *	7 *	
Other reason (SPECIFY)	8 *	8 *	8 *	8 *	8 *	8 *	

f **INTERVIEWER CHECK e**

At least one starred code ringed at e)	1 → g	1 → g	1 → g	1 → g	1 → g	1 → g	(78)
No starred codes ringed	2→next or Q10	2→next or Q10	2→next or Q10	2→next or Q10	2→next or Q10	2→next or Q10	

g **IF AT LEAST ONE STARRED CODE**
When did this problem or dispute begin?
ENTER DATE DISPUTE BEGAN.

IF DON'T KNOW MONTH, ENTER 98	MONTH	☐☐	☐☐	☐☐	☐☐	☐☐	☐☐	1st 58-61 2nd 62-65 3rd 66-69
	YEAR	☐☐	☐☐	☐☐	☐☐	☐☐	☐☐	

16

10a Can I just check, do you (or your husband/wife/partner)
have any children aged 23 or younger?

	Resp.	Partner	
Yes, children aged 23 or younger	1 → b)	1 → b)	70
No	2 → Q11	2 → Q11	
Can't say	8 → Q11	8 → Q11	

IF HAS CHILDREN AGED 23 OR YOUNGER
SHOW SCREEN CARD H
b Since January 1992, have you (or your husband/wife/
partner) had any problems or disputes that were difficult
to solve ... to do with children who were under 18 at
the time?
CODE ALL THAT APPLY

> INCLUDE ALL PROBLEMS
> SINCE JAN '92 EVEN IF
> STARTED BEFORE THEN.

	Resp.	Partner	
... residence and contact (custody and access) arrangements for children	1	1	71-75
...children being on the At Risk Register/Child Protection register	2	2	
... involvement with the Children's Panel about a child thought to be at risk/children being taken into care	3 → c)	3 → c)	
... abduction (or threatened abduction) of the children	4	4	
...children going to the school you (or your husband/wife/ partner) want, or receiving the type of education they need (eg special needs)	5	5	
... children being unfairly excluded or suspended from school	6	6	

> EXCLUDE CHILDREN'S PANEL
> INVOLVEMENT ABOUT CHILD
> OFFENDING

	Resp.	Partner	
NO, NONE OF ABOVE	0 → Q11	0 → Q11	

IF PROBLEM
SHOW SCREEN CARD H
c How many problems of this sort have you (has your
husband / wife / partner) had since January 1992?

ENTER NUMBER: ☐☐ ☐☐   76-77

d **COMPLETE GRID ON NEXT PAGE FOR RESPONDENT**
(AND PARTNER) FOR UP TO 3 PROBLEMS SINCE
JANUARY 1992, STARTING WITH THE MOST RECENT.

WORK DOWN THE GRID FOR EACH PROBLEM

IF FOUR OR MORE PROBLEMS, TAKE THE THREE MOST
RECENT.

17

SHOW SCREEN CARD X (coloured)	Respondent			Partner			Cd 10
10e Thinking of the (most recent / 2nd most recent / 3rd most recent) problem, did you (your husband/wife/partner) do any of the things on this card to try to resolve it? CODE ALL THAT APPLY IN APPROP. COLUMN	Most recent	2nd most recent	3rd most recent	Most recent	2nd most recent	3rd most recent	
Talked/wrote to other side about problem	1*	1*	1*	1*	1*	1*	1st 10-16
Sought advice about trying to solve problem	2*	2*	2*	2*	2*	2*	2nd 17-23
Threatened other side with legal action	3*	3*	3*	3*	3*	3*	3rd 24-30
Went to court, tribunal or arbitration / Started a court or tribunal case or an arbitration	4*→h	4*→h	4*→h	4*→h	4*→h	4*→h	
Went to mediation or conciliation	5*	5*	5*	5.*	5*	5*	
Took the problem to an ombudsman	6*	6*	6*	6*	6*	6*	
Took other action to try to solve problem	7*	7*	7*	7*	7*	7*	
(DID NOTHING)	8→f	8→f	8→f	8→f	8→f	8→f	

IF DID NOTHING
SHOW SCREEN CARD Y (coloured)
f Why did you (your husband/wife/partner) do nothing?
CODE ALL THAT APPLY

Other side was already taking action	0*	0*	0*	0*	0*	0*	1st 31-39
Thought it would cost too much	1*	1*	1*	1*	1*	1*	2nd 40-48
Thought it would take too much time	2*	2*	2*	2*	2*	2*	3rd 49-57
Did not think anything could be done	3*	3*	3*	3*	3*	3*	
Did not think it was very important	4	4	4	4	4	4	
No dispute with anybody / Thought the other person/side was right	5	5	5	5	5	5	
Was scared to do anything	6*	6*	6*	6*	6*	6*	
Thought it would damage relationship with other side	7*	7*	7*	7*	7*	7*	
Other reason (SPECIFY)	8*	8*	8*	8*	8*	8*	

g **INTERVIEWER CHECK f**

At least one starred code ringed at f)	1→h	1→h	1→h	1→h	1→h	1→h	(80)
No starred codes ringed	2→next or Q11	2→next or Q11	2→next or Q11	2→next or Q11	2→next or Q11	2→next or Q11	

h **IF AT LEAST ONE STARRED CODE**
When did this problem or dispute begin?
ENTER DATE DISPUTE BEGAN.

MONTH ☐☐ ☐☐ ☐☐ ☐☐ ☐☐ ☐☐

| IF DON'T KNOW |
| MONTH, ENTER 98 |

YEAR ☐☐ ☐☐ ☐☐ ☐☐ ☐☐ ☐☐

1st 58-61
2nd 62-65
3rd 66-69

18

SHOW SCREEN CARD I

11a Since January 1992, have you (or your husband/wife/partner)
suffered any injury or health problem because of an accident or
because of poor working conditions?
Some examples are shown on this card.
IF YES: Did you (he/she) have to see a doctor or dentist or go to a
hospital as a result of this?

> INCLUDE ALL PROBLEMS
> SINCE JAN '92 EVEN IF
> STARTED BEFORE THEN.

> EXCLUDE PROBLEMS
> BEFORE AGE OF 18.
> INCLUDE IF BECAME 18
> DURING DISPUTE.

<u>Card 10</u>

	Resp.	Partner	
Yes - suffered injury or health problem; went to doctor/dentist/hospital	1 → b)	1 → b)	70
Yes - suffered injury or health problem; did <u>not</u> go to doctor/hospital	2 → Q12	2 → Q12	
No	3 → Q12	3 → Q12	

IF CODE 1 AT a)
SHOW SCREEN CARD I

b How many problems of this sort have you (has your
husband / wife / partner) had since January 1992
- please only include those where you had to see
a doctor or dentist or go to hospital?

ENTER NUMBER:

71-72

c COMPLETE GRID ON NEXT PAGE FOR RESPONDENT
(AND PARTNER) FOR UP TO 3 PROBLEMS SINCE
JANUARY 1992, STARTING WITH THE MOST RECENT.

WORK <u>DOWN</u> THE GRID FOR EACH PROBLEM

IF FOUR OR MORE PROBLEMS, TAKE THE THREE MOST
RECENT.

19

SHOW SCREEN CARD X (coloured)
11d Thinking of the (most recent / 2nd most recent / 3rd most recent) problem, did you (your husband/wife/partner) do any of the things on this card to try to resolve it?
CODE ALL THAT APPLY IN APPROP. COLUMN

	Respondent			Partner			
	Most recent	2nd most recent	3rd most recent	Most recent	2nd most recent	3rd most recent	Cd 10
Talked/wrote to other side about problem	1*	1*	1*	1*	1*	1*	1st 73-79 Cd 11
Sought advice about trying to solve problem	2*	2*	2*	2*	2*	2*	2nd 10-16
Threatened other side with legal action	3*	3*	3*	3*	3*	3*	3rd 17-23
Went to court, tribunal or arbitration / Started a court or tribunal case or an arbitration	4*→g	4*→g	4*→g	4*→g	4*→g	4*→g	
Went to mediation or conciliation	5*	5*	5*	5*	5*	5*	
Took the problem to an ombudsman	6*	6*	6*	6*	6*	6*	
Took other action to try to solve problem	7*	7*	7*	7*	7*	7*	
(DID NOTHING)	8→e	8→e	8→e	8→e	8→e	8→e	

IF DID NOTHING
SHOW SCREEN CARD Y (coloured)
e Why did you (your husband/wife/partner) do nothing?
CODE ALL THAT APPLY

	Most recent	2nd most recent	3rd most recent	Most recent	2nd most recent	3rd most recent	
Other side was already taking action	0*	0*	0*	0*	0*	0*	1st 24-32
Thought it would cost too much	1*	1*	1*	1*	1*	1*	2nd 33-41
Thought it would take too much time	2*	2*	2*	2*	2*	2*	3rd 42-50
Did not think anything could be done	3*	3*	3*	3*	3*	3*	
Did not think it was very important	4	4	4	4	4	4	
No dispute with anybody / Thought the other person/side was right	5	5	5	5	5	5	
Was scared to do anything	6*	6*	6*	6*	6*	6*	
Thought it would damage relationship with other side	7*	7*	7*	7*	7*	7*	
Other reason (SPECIFY)	8*	8*	8*	8*	8*	8*	

f **INTERVIEWER CHECK e**

	Most recent	2nd most recent	3rd most recent	Most recent	2nd most recent	3rd most recent	
At least one starred code ringed at e)	1→g	1→g	1→g	1→g	1→g	1→g	(77)
No starred codes ringed	2→next or Q12	2→next or Q12	2→next or Q12	2→next or Q12	2→next or Q12	2→next or Q12	

g **IF AT LEAST ONE STARRED CODE**
When did this problem or dispute begin?
ENTER DATE DISPUTE BEGAN.

MONTH	☐☐	☐☐	☐☐	☐☐	☐☐	☐☐	1st 51-54 2nd 55-58 3rd 59-62
IF DON'T KNOW MONTH, ENTER 98 YEAR	☐☐	☐☐	☐☐	☐☐	☐☐	☐☐	

20

12a Can I just check, since January 1992, has a child or partner of yours
    .(or a child or ex-partner of your husband/wife/partner)
    died as a result of an accident?

Card 33

> INCLUDE DEATHS BEFORE 1992, IF
> RESP. / PARTNER TOOK OR
> THOUGHT ABOUT TAKING SOME
> ACTION SINCE 1992.

> EXCLUDE DEATHS IF RESPONDENT
> OR CURRENT PARTNER UNDER AGE
> OF 18 AT THE TIME.
> INCLUDE IF BECAME 18 DURING
> ANY FOLLOWING ACTION

		Resp.	**Partner**	
Yes		1 → **b)**	1 → **b)**	10
No		2 → **Q13**	2 → **Q13**	

IF CODE 1 AT a)
b Can I just check has this happened once, or more than once?
   IF MORE THAN ONCE, ESTABLISH NUMBER OF
   FATAL ACCIDENTS

                    ENTER NUMBER OF FATAL ACCIDENTS: ☐☐   ☐☐   11-12

c COMPLETE GRID ON NEXT PAGE FOR RESPONDENT
   (AND PARTNER) FOR UP TO 3 ACCIDENTS SINCE
   JANUARY 1992, STARTING WITH THE MOST RECENT.

   WORK <u>DOWN</u> THE GRID FOR EACH ACCIDENT

   IF FOUR OR MORE ACCIDENTS, TAKE THE THREE MOST
   RECENT.

21

SHOW SCREEN CARD X (coloured)

12d Thinking of the (most recent / 2nd most recent / 3rd most recent) accident, did you (your husband/wife/partner) do any of the things on this card to try to find out how it happened? CODE ALL THAT APPLY IN APPROP. COLUMN

Cd 33

	Respondent			Partner			
	Most recent	2nd most recent	3rd most recent	Most recent	2nd most recent	3rd most recent	
Talked/wrote to other side about problem	1*	1*	1*	1*	1*	1*	1st 13-19
Sought advice about trying to solve problem	2*	2*	2*	2*	2*	2*	2nd 20-26
Threatened other side with legal action	3*	3*	3*	3*	3*	3*	3rd 27-33
Went to court, tribunal or arbitration / Started a court or tribunal case or an arbitration	4*→g	4*→g	4*→g	4*→g	4*→g	4*→g	
Went to mediation or conciliation	5*	5*	5*	5*	5*	5*	
Took the problem to an ombudsman	6*	6*	6*	6*	6*	6*	
Took other action to try to solve problem	7*	7*	7*	7*	7*	7*	
(DID NOTHING)	8 → e	8 → e	8 → e	8 → e	8 → e	8 → e	

IF DID NOTHING
SHOW SCREEN CARD Y (coloured)

e Why did you (your husband/wife/partner) do nothing?
CODE ALL THAT APPLY

	Most recent	2nd most recent	3rd most recent	Most recent	2nd most recent	3rd most recent	
Other side was already taking action	0*	0*	0*	0*	0*	0*	1st 34-42
Thought it would cost too much	1*	1*	1*	1*	1*	1*	2nd 43-51
Thought it would take too much time	2*	2*	2*	2*	2*	2*	3rd 52-60
Did not think anything could be done	3*	3*	3*	3*	3*	3*	
Did not think it was very important	4	4	4	4	4	4	
No dispute with anybody / Thought the other person/side was right	5	5	5	5	5	5	
Was scared to do anything	6*	6*	6*	6*	6*	6*	
Thought it would damage relationship with other side	7*	7*	7*	7*	7*	7*	
Other reason (SPECIFY)	8*	8*	8*	8*	8*	8*	

f **INTERVIEWER CHECK e**

	Most recent	2nd most recent	3rd most recent	Most recent	2nd most recent	3rd most recent	
At least one starred code ringed at e)	1 → g	1 → g	1 → g	1 → g	1 → g	1 → g	61
No starred codes ringed	2→next or Q13	2→next or Q13	2→next or Q13	2→next or Q13	2→next or Q13	2→next or Q13	

g **IF AT LEAST ONE STARRED CODE**
When did this accident happen?
ENTER DATE ACCIDENT OCCURRED.

MONTH

| IF DON'T KNOW MONTH, ENTER 98 |

YEAR

1st 62-65
2nd 66-69
3rd 70-73

22

SHOW SCREEN CARD J
13a Since January 1992, have you (or your husband/wife/partner)
had any problems or disputes that were difficult to solve ... to
do with any of these issues?
CODE ALL THAT APPLY

Card 11

| EXCLUDE CASES OF POLICE |
| NOT DOING JOB PROPERLY |

| INCLUDE ALL PROBLEMS |
| SINCE JAN '92 EVEN IF |
| STARTED BEFORE THEN. |

| EXCLUDE PROBLEMS |
| BEFORE AGE OF 18. |
| INCLUDE IF BECAME 18 |
| DURING DISPUTE. |

	Resp.	Partner	
... being discriminated against because of race, sex or disability	1	1	63-67
... unfair treatment by the police *(eg assault by the police, or being unreasonably arrested)*	2	2	b)
... immigration or nationality issues	3	3	
... being given medical or dental treatment that was negligent or wrong	4	4	
... defamation *(your reputation or good name being publicly questioned)*	5	5	
NO, NONE OF THESE	0 → Q14	0 → Q14	

IF PROBLEM
SHOW SCREEN CARD J
b How many problems of this sort have you (has your
husband / wife / partner) had since January 1992?

ENTER NUMBER: ☐☐   ☐☐   68-69

c **COMPLETE GRID ON NEXT PAGE FOR RESPONDENT
(AND PARTNER) FOR UP TO 3 PROBLEMS SINCE
JANUARY 1992, STARTING WITH THE MOST RECENT.**

WORK DOWN THE GRID FOR EACH PROBLEM

**IF FOUR OR MORE PROBLEMS, TAKE THE THREE MOST
RECENT.**

23

SHOW SCREEN CARD X (coloured)

13d   Thinking of the (most recent / 2nd most recent / 3rd most recent) problem, did you (your husband/wife/partner) do any of the things on this card to try to resolve it?
CODE ALL THAT APPLY IN APPROP. COLUMN

	Respondent			Partner			
	Most recent	2nd most recent	3rd most recent	Most recent	2nd most recent	3rd most recent	Cd 11
Talked/wrote to other side about problem	1*	1*	1*	1*	1*	1*	1st 70-76 Col 12
Sought advice about trying to solve problem	2*	2*	2*	2*	2*	2*	2nd 10-16
Threatened other side with legal action	3*	3*	3*	3*	3*	3*	3rd 17-23
Went to court, tribunal or arbitration / Started a court or tribunal case or an arbitration	4*→g	4*→g	4*→g	4*→g	4*→g	4*→g	
Went to mediation or conciliation	5*	5*	5*	5*	5*	5*	
Took the problem to an ombudsman	6*	6*	6*	6*	6*	6*	
Took other action to try to solve problem	7*	7*	7*	7*	7*	7*	
(DID NOTHING)	8 → e	8 → e	8 → e	8 → e	8 → e	8 → e	

IF DID NOTHING
SHOW SCREEN CARD Y (coloured)

e   Why did you (your husband/wife/partner) do nothing?
CODE ALL THAT APPLY

Other side was already taking action	0*	0*	0*	0*	0*	0*	1st 24-32
Thought it would cost too much	1*	1*	1*	1*	1*	1*	2nd 33-41
Thought it would take too much time	2*	2*	2*	2*	2*	2*	3rd 42-50
Did not think anything could be done	3*	3*	3*	3*	3*	3*	
Did not think it was very important	4	4	4	4	4	4	
No dispute with anybody / Thought the other person/side was right	5	5	5	5	5	5	
Was scared to do anything	6*	6*	6*	6*	6*	6*	
Thought it would damage relationship with other side	7*	7*	7*	7*	7*	7*	
Other reason (SPECIFY)	8*	8*	8*	8*	8*	8*	

f   **INTERVIEWER CHECK e**

At least one starred code ringed at e)	1 → g	1 → g	1 → g	1 → g	1 → g	1 → g	(78)
No starred codes ringed	2→next or Q14	2→next or Q14	2→next or Q14	2→next or Q14	2→next or Q14	2→next or Q14	

g   **IF AT LEAST ONE STARRED CODE**
When did this problem or dispute begin?
ENTER DATE DISPUTE BEGAN.

MONTH ☐☐   ☐☐   ☐☐   ☐☐   ☐☐   ☐☐

IF DON'T KNOW MONTH, ENTER 98

YEAR ☐☐   ☐☐   ☐☐   ☐☐   ☐☐   ☐☐

1st 51-54
2nd 55-58
3rd 59-62

24

14a Apart from anything you have already told me about in this
interview - since January 1992, has any legal action been taken against you
(or your husband/wife/partner), for example have you been sent a
solicitor's letter or had court proceedings started against you?

Card 12

EXCLUDE ACTION BY POLICE
ABOUT ALLEGED CRIME

		Resp.	Partner	
INCLUDE ALL ACTION SINCE JAN '92 EVEN IF STARTED BEFORE THEN.	Yes	1* → b)	1* → b)	63
	No	2 → **Q15**	2 → **Q15**	

EXCLUDE ACTION
BEFORE AGE OF 18.
INCLUDE IF BECAME 18
DURING DISPUTE.

INCLUDE SUMMARY
WARRANT PROCEDURE FOR
RECOVERY OF DEBTS

IF YES
b How many legal actions have been taken against you (your
husband/wife/partner) since January 1992?
**EXCLUDE CASES COVERED EARLIER
IN INTERVIEW**

EXCLUDE CRIMINAL
PROSECUTIONS

WRITE IN NUMBER:

64-65

c FOR EACH LEGAL ACTION, STARTING
WITH THE MOST RECENT:
When did the dispute which led to this legal
action begin?

IF 4 OR MORE LEGAL
ACTIONS, ASK ABOUT 3
MOST RECENT

IF DON'T KNOW
MONTH, ENTER 98

	Respondent			Partner		
	Most recent	2nd most recent	3rd most recent	Most recent	2nd most recent	3rd most recent
MONTH						
YEAR						

1st
66-69
2nd
70-73
3rd
74-77

25

ALL

15a Apart from this, since January 1992 have you (has
your husband/wife/partner) been <u>threatened</u> with
legal action by anyone?

Card 13

		Resp.	Partner	
INCLUDE SHERIFF OFFICERS DEBT RECOVERY	Yes	1 → b)	1 → b)	10
	No	2 → Q16	2 → Q16	

INCLUDE SHERIFF
OFFICERS DEBT
RECOVERY

EXCLUDE CRIMINAL
PROSECUTIONS

INCLUDE ALL SUCH
PROBLEMS SINCE JAN '92
EVEN IF STARTED
BEFORE THEN.

EXCLUDE PROBLEMS
BEFORE AGE OF 18.
INCLUDE IF BECAME 18
DURING DISPUTE.

IF YES

b Did you (your husband/wife/partner) disagree with what
the other party was demanding (on any of these occasions)?

	Resp.	Partner	
Yes, disagreed	1 * → c)	1 * → c)	11
No	2 → Q16	2 → Q16	

IF DISAGREED

c Now I would like you to think of the occasions on which
you were (your husband/wife/partner was) threatened with
legal action and did not agree with what was being demanded.
On how many occasions has this happened since January 1992?
**EXCLUDE ACTUAL LEGAL ACTIONS AND
THREATENED CRIMINAL PROSECUTIONS**

WRITE IN NUMBER: ☐☐   ☐☐   12-13

d **FOR EACH THREATENED LEGAL ACTION,
STARTING WITH THE MOST RECENT:**
When did the dispute that led to this threat
being made begin?

		Respondent			Partner		
		Most recent	2nd most recent	3rd most recent	Most recent	2nd most recent	3rd most recent
IF 4 OR MORE THREATS, ASK ABOUT 3 MOST RECENT							
IF DON'T KNOW MONTH, ENTER 98	MONTH	☐☐	☐☐	☐☐	☐☐	☐☐	☐☐
	YEAR	☐☐	☐☐	☐☐	☐☐	☐☐	☐☐

1st
14-17
2nd
18-21
3rd
22-25

26

ALL

16a **SHOW SCREEN CARD K**
(Apart from anything you have already told me about in this interview), have you (has your husband/wife/partner) had any other problems since January 1992 for which you have done or thought about doing any of the things on this card?

Card 13

> **INCLUDE ALL SUCH PROBLEMS SINCE JAN '92 EVEN IF STARTED BEFORE THEN.**

> **EXCLUDE PROBLEMS BEFORE AGE OF 18. INCLUDE IF BECAME 18 DURING DISPUTE.**

	Resp.	Partner	
Yes	1 * → b)	1 * → b)	26
No	2 → Q17	2 → Q17	

IF YES

b On how many occasions have you (has your husband/wife/partner) done this?
EXCLUDE CASES COVERED EARLIER IN INTERVIEW.

WRITE IN NUMBER: ☐☐   ☐☐   27-28

c **FOR EACH PROBLEM/DISPUTE FOR WHICH RESPONDENT STARTED OR CONSIDERED STARTING COURT PROCEEDINGS, STARTING WITH THE MOST RECENT:**
When did the dispute that led to you (thinking about) starting court proceedings begin?

> **IF 4 OR MORE SUCH PROBLEMS OR DISPUTES, ASK ABOUT 3 MOST RECENT**

> **IF DON'T KNOW MONTH, ENTER 98**

	Respondent			Partner		
	Most recent	2nd most recent	3rd most recent	Most recent	2nd most recent	3rd most recent
MONTH	☐☐	☐☐	☐☐	☐☐	☐☐	☐☐
YEAR	☐☐	☐☐	☐☐	☐☐	☐☐	☐☐

1st 29-32
2nd
33-36
3rd
37-40

17a Can I check, how old were you (was your husband/wife/partner) on your (his/her) last birthday?

	Resp.	Partner	
ENTER AGE:	☐☐	☐☐	41-42

b **CODE SEX:**

Male	1	1	43
Female	2	2	

18a **INTERVIEWER CHECK Q2-16 RESPONDENT COLUMN**

27

Are any starred (*) codes ringed in respondent column?
(All starred codes are shaded in grey)

Yes	1	GO TO b)
No	2	GO TO c)

IF YES
b| Respondent is eligible for main interview.

BEFORE PROCEEDING WITH AN EVENT SELECTION FORM WITH THE
RESPONDENT, PLEASE CHECK THAT (S)HE WAS 18 OR OVER AT THE
OF THE PROBLEM(S) CODED.

> INCLUDE IF BECAME 18
> DURING DISPUTE

IF (S)HE WAS UNDER 18 AT THE TIME OF A PROBLEM, IT SHOULD NOT
HAVE BEEN CODED - GO BACK AND AMEND APPROPRIATE QUESTION
AND SUBSEQUENT ROUTING. YOU MAY ALSO NEED TO AMEND THE
CODE GIVEN AT A18a).

> NOW GO TO Q19

IF NO STARRED CODES IN RESPONDENT COLUMN
c| My office may want to check on my work - would you be happy
for someone to contact you about this interview?

Yes	1	ASK d)	(55)
No	2	GO TO f)	

IF YES
d| Could I have your telephone number in case someone from
my office wants to talk with you?

Telephone number given	1	GO TO e)	(56)
Refused / No telephone	2	GO TO f)	

IF NUMBER GIVEN
e| WRITE IN TELEPHONE NUMBER ON FRONT PAGE OF ARF

IF NO STARRED CODES IN RESPONDENT COLUMN
f| Sometime in the future we may want to come back and interview you
again. Would you be willing for us to do this?

Yes / Maybe	1	(57)
No	2	

19a| **INTERVIEWER CHECK Q1a, page 1**

Spouse / partner in household (code 1 at Q1a)	1	GO TO b)
No spouse / partner in household (code 2)	2	END. GO TO Q20.

45

IF SPOUSE / PARTNER IN HOUSEHOLD
b| **INTERVIEWER CHECK Q2-16 PARTNER COLUMN**
Are any starred (*) codes ringed?
(All starred codes are shaded in grey)

Yes	1	GO TO c)
No	2	END. GO TO Q20.

46

28

IF YES

c. Partner is eligible for main interview.

Card 13

BEFORE PROCEEDING WITH AN EVENT SELECTION FORM WITH THE PARTNER, PLEASE CHECK THAT (S)HE WAS 18 OR OVER AT THE OF THE PROBLEM(S) CODED.

> INCLUDE IF BECAME 18 DURING DISPUTE

IF (S)HE WAS UNDER 18 AT THE TIME OF A PROBLEM, IT SHOULD NOT HAVE BEEN CODED - GO BACK AND AMEND APPROPRIATE QUESTION AND SUBSEQUENT ROUTING. YOU MAY ALSO NEED TO AMEND THE CODE GIVEN AT A19a).

Q20. **INTERVIEWER TO COMPLETE:**

TIME NOW: 47-50
(24 hour clock)

INTERVIEWER NAME: _____

INTERVIEWER NUMBER: 51-54

29

INTERVIEWER:
IF RESPONDENT REPORTS A PROBLEM, AND YOU ARE NOT SURE WHETHER IT
IS WITHIN SCOPE FOR THE SURVEY, PLEASE TAKE THE DETAILS DOWN HERE,
AND CONTACT THE OFFICE BEFORE PROCEEDING WITH A MAIN INTERVIEW.

Appendix C

Head Office: 35 NORTHAMPTON SQUARE
LONDON EC1V 0AX
Tel: 0171 250 1866 Fax 0171 250 1524

SCPR

Field and DP Office: 100 KINGS ROAD
BRENTWOOD, ESSEX CM14 4LX
Tel: 01277 200 600 Fax: 01277 214 117

P1667   **1997**

Event Selection Form
N.B. One form per eligible person
(i.e. one each for respondent **and** partner where both eligible, even if regarding the same problem/dispute)

Card 14
01-05
06-07
Cd:08-09
10-15
16-19

SERIAL NO : [ ][ ][ ][ ][ ]   PERSON NO: [ ][ ]

DATE: [ ][ ][ ][ ][ ]   START TIME: [ ][ ][ ][ ] (24 hour clock)

1. **CHECK SCREENING QUESTIONNAIRE CAREFULLY AND TRANSFER DATES OF ALL PROBLEMS FROM APPROPRIATE COLUMN TO THE CALENDAR BELOW, ALONG WITH THE APPROPRIATE SCREENING QUESTION NUMBER(S).** *(Posn. of dates marked with symbol ■ in left-hand column)*

1986		1987		1988		1989		1990		1991	
Month	Question Number	Month	Question Number	Month	Question Number	Month	Question Number	Month	Question Number	Month	Question Number
Jan		Jan		Jan		Jan		Jan		Jan	
Feb		Feb		Feb		Feb		Feb		Feb	
March		March		March		March		March		March	
April		April		April		April		April		April	
May		May		May		May		May		May	
June		June		June		June		June		June	
July		July		July		July		July		July	
August		August		August		August		August		August	
Sept		Sept		Sept		Sept		Sept		Sept	
Oct		Oct		Oct		Oct		Oct		Oct	
Nov		Nov		Nov		Nov		Nov		Nov	
Dec		Dec		Dec		Dec		Dec		Dec	

1992		1993		1994		1995		1996		1997	
Month	Question Number	Month	Question Number	Month	Question Number	Month	Question Number	Month	Question Number	Month	Question Number
Jan		Jan		Jan		Jan		Jan		Jan	
Feb		Feb		Feb		Feb		Feb		Feb	
March		March		March		March		March		March	
April		April		April		April		April		April	
May		May		May		May		May		May	
June		June		June		June		June		June	
July		July		July		July		July		July	
August		August		August		August		August		August	
Sept		Sept		Sept		Sept		Sept		Sept	
Oct		Oct		Oct		Oct		Oct		Oct	
Nov		Nov		Nov		Nov		Nov		Nov	
Dec		Dec		Dec		Dec		Dec		Dec	

2

2a) **INTERVIEWER CHECK CALENDAR AND RECORD:**

			Cd 14
One problem/dispute only	1	**GO TO b)**	20
More than one problem/dispute	2	**GO TO c)**	

IF ONE PROBLEM/DISPUTE ONLY
b) FROM THE CALENDAR, ENTER THE SCREEN QUESTION NUMBER AND
VERY BRIEFLY DESCRIBE THE PROBLEM FOR FUTURE IDENTIFICATION
(eg "neighbour dispute" / "faulty washing machine").

Screen question number   Type of problem   21-22

Q [ ][ ]   _____

_____

REMAINING QUESTIONS RELATE TO THIS PROBLEM

GO TO d)

IF MORE THAN ONE PROBLEM/DISPUTE
c) FROM THE CALENDAR, ESTABLISH THE <u>SECOND MOST RECENT</u>
PROBLEM/DISPUTE.

ENTER BELOW THE SCREEN QUESTION NUMBER AND VERY BRIEFLY
DESCRIBE THE PROBLEM FOR FUTURE IDENTIFICATION
(eg "neighbour dispute" / "faulty washing machine").

Screen question number   Type of problem   23-24

Q [ ][ ]   _____

_____

REMAINING QUESTIONS RELATE TO THIS PROBLEM

ALL
d) **INTERVIEWER CODE:**

Event Selection Form already completed with another household member concerning this selected problem/dispute	1	**END.**	25
Others	2	**ASK e)**	

IF CODE 2 AT d)
e) Including yourself, how many people aged 18 or over were involved
on <u>your side</u> of the problem or dispute?

CODE: One (respondent only)

IF VERY LARGE NUMBER OF PEOPLE INVOLVED, ASK FOR ESTIMATED NUMBER	
INCLUDE IF BECAME 18 DURING DISPUTE	

01	**CONDUCT MAIN INTERVIEW WITH RESPONDENT.**	26-27

OR ENTER NUMBER OF PEOPLE
INVOLVED (<u>INCLUDING</u> RESPONDENT): [ ][ ]   **ASK Q3**

3

IF MORE THAN ONE PERSON INVOLVED

Q3a) Were any of these other people on your side members of
your <u>current</u> household?

Yes	1	ASK b)	28
No	2	CONDUCT MAIN INTERVIEW WITH RESPONDENT.	

IF YES

b) Are you the best person in the household to answer
questions about this problem or dispute?

Yes	1	CONDUCT MAIN INTERVIEW WITH RESPONDENT.	29
No	2	ASK c)	

IF NO

c) ESTABLISH WHICH OTHER HOUSEHOLD MEMBER IS
BEST PERSON TO INTERVIEW ABOUT THE PROBLEM.

ENTER HIS/HER NAME: _____

AND PERSON NUMBER: ☐☐   30-31
(FROM ARF GRID ON PAGES 5-8)

d) INTERVIEWER CODE:

Person named at c) has been interviewed or is due to be interviewed about <u>another</u> problem/dispute	1	GO TO e)	32
Others	2	CONDUCT MAIN INTERVIEW WITH PERSON NAMED AT c)	

IF CODE 1 AT d)

e) EXPLAIN THAT OTHER PERSON IS ALREADY BEING INTERVIEWED
ABOUT ANOTHER PROBLEM.
ATTEMPT MAIN INTERVIEW WITH RESPONDENT ABOUT PROBLEM
DESCRIBED AT Q2 OF THIS EVENT SELECTION FORM.

a) TIME NOW: ☐☐☐☐   33-36
(24 hour clock)

b) INTERVIEWER NAME: _____

c) INTERVIEWER NUMBER : ☐☐☐☐☐☐   37-40

Batch:
41-45

Appendix D

Head Office: 35 NORTHAMPTON SQUARE
LONDON EC1V 0AX
Tel: 0171 250 1866 Fax 0171 250 1524

SOCIAL & COMMUNITY
SCPR
PLANNING RESEARCH

Field and DP Office: 100 KINGS ROAD
BRENTWOOD, ESSEX CM14 4LX
Tel: 01277 200 600 Fax: 01277 214 117

P1667
Scotland

MAIN QUESTIONNAIRE

1997

Card 15

SERIAL NUMBER:		**PERSON NUMBER:**	01-05
RECORD TIME NOW:			06-07
			Cd:08-09
			10-13

A1. CHECK EVENT SELECTION FORM (Q2b/Q2c):

Screen question number Q2 (employment)	01	**GO TO A2, page 2**	14-15
Screen question number Q3 (owning residential property)	02	**GO TO A3, page 2**
Screen question number Q4 (renting out rooms or property)	03	**GO TO A4, page 2**
Screen question number Q5 (living in rented accommodation)	04	**GO TO A5, page 2**
Screen question number Q6 (faulty goods or services)	05	**GO TO A6, page 3**
Screen question number Q7 (money)	06	**GO TO A7, page 3**
Screen question number Q8 (divorce proceedings)	07	**GO TO A8, page 3**
Screen question number Q9 (family matters)	08	**GO TO A9, page 3**
Screen question number Q10 (children)	09	**GO TO A10, page 4**
Screen question number Q11 (accident or injury)	10	**GO TO A11, page 4**
Screen question number Q12 (fatal accident of child or partner)	11	**GO TO A11, page 4**
Screen question number Q13 (discrimination / police / immigration / medical treatment)	12	**GO TO A12, page 4**
Screen question number Q14 (legal action taken against respondent)	13	
Screen question number Q15 (threatened with legal action)	14	**GO TO A13, page 4**
Screen question number Q16 (started / thought about starting case in court / tribunal / arbitration / going to mediation / ombudsman)	15	

(Batch
3279-83

2

IF SCREEN Q2 (*employment*)
A2. (Can I just check), who (were / are) you in dispute or disagreement with - was it your employer, a work colleague or some other person or organisation?
CODE ALL THAT APPLY

Employer	1	1516-18
Work colleague(s)	2	**GO TO A14, page 5**
Other person / organisation	3	

(SPECIFY) _____

IF SCREEN Q3 (*owning residential property*)
A3. **SHOW CARD A.**
(Can I just check), who (were / are) you in dispute or disagreement with?
CODE ALL THAT APPLY

Feuholder / Superior / Owner	01	1519-28
Neighbour	02	
Bank / Building society / Mortgage company	03	**GO TO A14, page 5**
Insurance company	04	
Estate agent	05	
Surveyor	06	
Council / Local Authority	07	
Squatters	08	
Other person / organisation	09	

(SPECIFY) _____

IF SCREEN Q4 (*renting out rooms or property*)
A4. **SHOW CARD B.**
(Can I just check), who (were / are) you in dispute or disagreement with?
CODE ALL THAT APPLY

Tenant / Lodger	1	1529-32
Managing agent / Factor / Letting agent	2	**GO TO A14, page 5**
Council / Local Authority	3	
Other person / organisation	4	

(SPECIFY) _____

IF SCREEN Q5 (*living in rented accommodation*)
A5. **SHOW CARD C.**
(Can I just check), who (were / are) you in dispute or disagreement with?
CODE ALL THAT APPLY

Landlord / Council / Housing association	1	1533-37
Neighbour(s)	2	
Co-tenant(s) / Flat mate(s)	3	**GO TO A14, page 5**
Lodger / Sub-tenant	4	
Other person / organisation	5	

(SPECIFY) _____

3

IF SCREEN Q6 (*faulty goods / services*)
A6. SHOW CARD D.
(Can I just check), who (were / are) you in dispute or disagreement with?
CODE ALL THAT APPLY

Shop / Mail order company / Travel agent	1	1538-41
Tradesman (eg plumber, electrician, double glazing installation, car mechanic)	2	
Professional (eg lawyer, accountant, surveyor)	3	**GO TO A14, page 5**
Other person / organisation	4	
(SPECIFY) _____		

IF SCREEN Q7 (*money*)
A7. SHOW CARD E.
(Can I just check), who (were / are) you in dispute or disagreement with?
CODE ALL THAT APPLY

Bank / building society / mortgage company / credit card company	01	1542-51
Utility company (eg gas, electricity, water)	02	
Insurance company	03	
Pension company	04	**GO TO A14, page 5**
Inland Revenue	05	
Other business	06	
Employer	07	
Council / Local authority	08	
DSS	09	
Accountant / financial adviser	10	
(Ex) husband / wife / partner	11	
Other family member	12	
Other person / organisation	13	
(SPECIFY) _____		

IF SCREEN Q8 (*divorce proceedings*)
A8. IN SUBSEQUENT QUESTIONS,
"...OTHER SIDE..." = (EX) HUSBAND / WIFE

GO TO A14, page 5

IF SCREEN Q9 (*family matters*)
A9. SHOW CARD F.
(Can I just check), who (were / are) you in dispute or disagreement with?
CODE ALL THAT APPLY

(Ex) Husband / wife / partner	1	1552-
Other family member	2	
Local authority / Social Work Department	3	
Fostering or adoption agency	4	**GO TO A14, page 5**
Child Support Agency (CSA)	5	
Other person / organisation	6	
(SPECIFY) _____		

4

A10.
IF SCREEN Q10 (*children*)
SHOW CARD G.
(Can I just check), who (were / are) you in dispute or disagreement with?
CODE ALL THAT APPLY

(Ex) Husband / wife / partner	1	1558-62
Other family member	2	
Local authority / Social Work Department	3	**GO TO A14, page 5**
School / Teacher / Local Education Authority (LEA)	4	
Other person / organisation	5	
(SPECIFY) _____		

A11.
IF SCREEN Q11 (*accident / injury / fatal accident of child or partner*)
SHOW CARD H.
(Can I just check), who (were / are) you in dispute or disagreement with?
CODE ALL THAT APPLY

Employer	1	1563-67
Council / Local authority	2	
Shop	3	
Restaurant / café / bar	4	**GO TO A14, page 5**
Driver of car, van, bicycle, motorcycle or other vehicle	5	
Other person / organisation	6	
(SPECIFY) _____		

A12.
IF SCREEN Q12 (*discrimination etc*)
SHOW CARD I.
(Can I just check), who (were / are) you in dispute or disagreement with?
CODE ALL THAT APPLY

Police	1	1568-71
Immigration authorities	2	
Hospital / Doctor / dentist / other medical practitioner	3	**GO TO A14, page 5**
Other person / organisation	4	
(SPECIFY) _____		

A13.
IF SCREEN Q13-15 (*legal action taken/threatened/started*)
(Can I just check), who (were / are) you in dispute or disagreement with?
WRITE IN:

_____

1572-7

5

1610-29

ALL

A14. PLEASE ESTABLISH AN APPROPRIATE WORD OR PHRASE TO DESCRIBE THE PERSON / ORGANISATION THAT RESPONDENT WAS IN DISPUTE OR DISAGREEMENT WITH.

THROUGHOUT THE QUESTIONNAIRE, WHERE QUESTIONS REFER TO "...OTHER SIDE...". YOU SHOULD INSERT THE APPROPRIATE WORD OR PHRASE

A15a) Can you tell me in more detail exactly what the problem or dispute (was / is) about?

IF NECESSARY:

PROBE: What (was / is) the key thing that you and ... OTHER SIDE ... (were / are) in dispute about?

PROBE FOR THE KEY ARGUMENTS OF <u>BOTH SIDES</u>

GUIDANCE ABOUT LEVEL OF DETAIL REQUIRED:

e.g. IF DISPUTE ABOUT LOSS OF JOB
Threatened or actual loss of job (dismissal / early retirement / redundancy)?
Disputed grounds for loss of job or dispute about package on leaving (eg pension, redundancy package) or something else?

IF NEIGHBOUR DISPUTE:
Dispute about boundaries, noise levels, communal maintenance or other problem?
Respondent complaining about other side, or other side complaining about respondent?

IF DISPUTE WITH LANDLORD ABOUT EVICTION:
Actual or threatened eviction? On what grounds? Did respondent dispute these grounds?

IF DISPUTE ABOUT CHILD SUPPORT PAYMENTS:
Payments by respondent or other party?
If previous agreement not being met - in what way? Why?

IF DISPUTE ABOUT FAULTY SERVICE:
In what way was the service faulty?
Was respondent withholding payment, or was the other side refusing to complete job, or what?

b) PLEASE ESTABLISH AN APPROPRIATE WORD OR PHRASE TO DESCRIBE THE PROBLEM / DISPUTE / SITUATION.

THROUGHOUT THE QUESTIONNAIRE, WHERE QUESTIONS REFER TO "...PROBLEM ..." YOU SHOULD EITHER INSERT THE APPROPRIATE WORD OR PHRASE OR REFER TO "THIS PROBLEM/ DISPUTE".

c) INTERVIEWER: SUBSEQUENT QUESTIONS OFFER DIFFERENT TENSES. USE AS APPROPRIATE FOR EACH RESPONDENT.

6

ALL
A16a) **SHOW CARD J**
Before I ask you some more detailed questions about ...PROBLEM,
can you look at this card and tell me whether you have *ever* contacted
any of the people or organisations on this card <u>about any matter</u>?

	Yes	1	**ASK b)**
	No	2	**GO TO A17**

1630

IF YES
b) **SHOW CARD J**
Which ones?
CODE ALL THAT APPLY

1631-74

Citizens Advice Bureaux (CAB)	01
Law Centre	02
Welfare Rights Officer (WRO)	03
Consumer advice centre /Trading Standards Officer	04
Other advice agency / worker	05
Employer	06
Trade Union or Staff Association	07
Professional body *(eg BMA, Law Society)*	08
Trade association *(eg ABTA, Which, AA)*	09
Solicitor	10
Advocate	11
Claims agency *(eg Direct Legal / Quantum)*	12
Court staff	13
Ombudsman	14
Other legal consultant *(eg employment law / immigration law consultant)*	15
Member of Parliament (MP) or Local councillor	16
Local council department/Local authority	17
Housing association	18
Social worker / Social Work Department	19
Police	20
Religious organisation *(eg church, mosque, synagogue)*	21
Insurance company	22

7

A17a) **SHOW ADVISER CARD**
Now please think about ...PROBLEM. (Did you have / Have you had) any contact at any stage
with any of the people or organisations on this card about ... PROBLEM...?
(IF NECESSARY: - please do not include contact with ...OTHER SIDE)
MAKE SURE RESPONDENT READS FULL LIST.

	Yes, contact with adviser(s)	1	ASK b)	
IF YES	No	2	GO TO A18	1710

b) **SHOW ADVISER CARD**
Who did you contact first about ... PROBLEM?
RING ONE CODE IN 1ST COLUMN BELOW

	1st	2nd	3rd	4th	5th	$6^{th}/7^{th}$ etc	
Citizens Advice Bureaux (CAB)	01	01	01	01	01	01	1st
Law Centre	02	02	02	02	02	02	1711-2
Welfare Rights Officer (WRO)	03	03	03	03	03	03	2nd
Consumer advice centre / Trading Standards Officer	04	04	04	04	04	04	1713-4
Other advice agency / worker	05	05	05	05	05	05	3rd
Employer	06	06	06	06	06	06	1715-6
Trade Union or Staff Association	07	07	07	07	07	07	4th
Professional body *(eg BMA, Law Society)*	08	08	08	08	08	08	1717-8
Trade associations *(eg ABTA, Which, AA)*	09	09	09	09	09	09	5th
Solicitor	10	10	10	10	10	10	1719-20
Advocate	11	11	11	11	11	11	6th
Claims agency *(eg Direct Legal / Quantum)*	12	12	12	12	12	12	1721-30
Court staff	13	13	13	13	13	13	
Ombudsman	14	14	14	14	14	14	
Other legal consultant *(eg employment law / immigration law consultant)*	15	15	15	15	15	15	
Member of Parliament (MP) or Local councillor	16	16	16	16	16	16	
Local council department/Local authority	17	17	17	17	17	17	
Housing association	18	18	18	18	18	18	
Social Worker / Social Work Department	19	19	19	19	19	19	
Police	20	20	20	20	20	20	
Religious organisation *(eg church, mosque, synagogue)*	21	21	21	21	21	21	
Insurance Company	22	22	22	22	22	22	
Other person / organisation	23	23	23	23	23	23	
(SPECIFY) _____							
No further advice sought	00	00	00	00	00	00	

c) Who did you contact next?
RING ONE CODE IN 2ND COLUMN ABOVE

d) Who did you contact next?
RING ONE CODE IN 3RD COLUMN ABOVE

e) Who did you contact next?
RING ONE CODE IN 4TH COLUMN ABOVE

f) Who did you contact next?
RING CODE IN 5TH COLUMN ABOVE

g) Who did you contact next?
RING CODE IN 6TH COLUMN ABOVE
IF CONTACTED MORE THAN 6 SOURCES, CODE ALL THAT APPLY IN '6ᵗʰ/7ᵗʰ' COLUMN ABOVE.

> **ONLY INCLUDE** PARTNER / FRIENDS / RELATIVES IF THEY ARE ONE OF THE TYPES OF ADVISERS ON THE CARD.
>
> IF CONTACTED MORE THAN ONE OF THE SAME TYPE OF ADVISER, EG MORE THAN ONE SOLICITOR CONSULTED, RING CODE FOR SOLICITOR IN AS MANY COLUMNS AS IS APPROPRIATE.

8

ALL

A18a) SHOW ADVISER CARD
(Did / Have) you (try / tried) UNsuccessfully to contact any of the (other) people or organisations on this card for help or advice about...PROBLEM?

Yes	1	ASK b)
No	2	GO TO c)

1731

IF YES
b) SHOW ADVISER CARD
Who?
CODE ALL THAT APPLY

Citizens Advice Bureaux (CAB)	01
Law Centre	02
Welfare Rights Officer (WRO)	03
Consumer advice centre /Trading Standards Officer	04
Other advice agency / worker	05
Employer	06
Trade Union or Staff Association	07
Professional body *(eg BMA, Law Society)*	08
Trade association *(eg ABTA, Which, AA)*	09
Solicitor	10
Advocate	11
Claims agency *(eg Direct Legal / Quantum)*	12
Court staff	13
Ombudsman	14
Other legal consultant *(eg employment law / immigration law consultant)*	15
Member of Parliament (MP) or Local councillor	16
Local council department/Local authority	17
Housing association	18
Social worker / Social Work Department	19
Police	20
Religious organisation *(eg church, mosque, synagogue)*	21
Insurance company	22
Other person / organisation (SPECIFY)	23

1732-41

c) SHOW ADVISER CARD
(Did /Have) you consider(ed) contacting any of the (other) people or organisations on this card for help or advice about...PROBLEM?

Yes	1	ASK d)
No	2	GO TO A19

1742

9

IF YES
d) SHOW ADVISER CARD
Who?
CODE ALL THAT APPLY

Citizens Advice Bureaux (CAB)	01	1743-56
Law Centre	02	
Welfare Rights Officer (WRO)	03	
Consumer advice centre /Trading Standards Officer	04	
Other advice agency / worker	05	
Employer	06	
Trade Union or Staff Association	07	
Professional body *(eg BMA, Law Society)*	08	
Trade association *(eg ABTA, Which, AA)*	09	'
Solicitor	10	
Advocate	11	
Claims agency *(eg Direct Legal / Quantum)*	12	
Court staff	13	
Ombudsman	14	
Other legal consultant *(eg employment law / immigration law consultant)*	15	
Member of Parliament (MP) or Local councillor	16	
Local council department/Local authority	17	
Housing association	18	
Social worker / Social Work Department	19	
Police	20	
Religious organisation *(eg church, mosque, synagogue)*	21	
Insurance company	22	
Other person / organisation (SPECIFY)	23	

e) Why did you decide not to contact .. ADVISERS MENTIONED AT d)?
PROBE FULLY. RECORD VERBATIM.

OR CODE: (Intend to / May) contact in future   01

1757-66

A19a) INTERVIEWER CHECK A17a), page 7

Contact with adviser(s) about problem (code 1 at A17a)	1	**GO TO b)**	1767
No contact with adviser (code 2 at A17a)	2	**GO TO A31, page 16**	

10

IF ADVISER CONTACTED
b) **INTERVIEWER CHECK page 7 - A17b) GRID, COLUMN 1 FOR 1ˢᵀ ADVISER CONTACTED**

c) Before you consulted .. 1ˢᵀ ADVISER ,.., had there been any contact between you and ...OTHER SIDE... to try to sort out ...PROBLEM?

Yes	1	**GO TO f)**	1768
No	2	**ASK d)**	

IF NO
d) Before you consulted ...1ˢᵀ ADVISER..., had you <u>tried</u> to contact ...OTHER SIDE... to sort out ...PROBLEM?

Yes	1	1769
No	2	

e) And before you consulted ...1ˢᵀ ADVISER..., had ...OTHER SIDE... tried to contact you to sort out ...PROBLEM?

Yes	1		1770
No	2	**GO TO A20**	
(Can't say)	8		

IF CONTACT BETWEEN TWO PARTIES
f) Did you manage to come to any sort of agreement with .. OTHER SIDE... before you consulted .. 1ˢᵀ ADVISER?

Yes	1	**ASK g)**	1771
No	2	**GO TO A20**	
(Can't say)	8		

IF YES
g) What sort of agreement?
PROBE FULLY. RECORD VERBATIM.

1772-81

A20a) What made you think of contacting ....1ˢᵗ ADVISER...?   1810-1?
CODE ALL THAT APPLY

It was advised or suggested by a partner / friend / relative / work colleague	1
Saw (or heard) advertisement for ...ADVISER	2
Previous experience of similar situation	3
Other (*specify*)	4

_____

_____

(Can't say)	8

11

b) When did you contact ...1ˢᵀ ADVISER?
ENTER MONTH AND YEAR.
. **ESTIMATE ACCEPTABLE.**

MONTH: ☐☐

YEAR: ☐☐

1814-17

c) About how long after .. PROBLEM.. started was this?

CODE ONE ONLY

As soon as problem started	01
1- 2 weeks	02
3 - 4 weeks	03
5 - 6 weeks	04
2 months	05
3 months	06
4 months	07
5 months	08
6 months	09
More than 6 months	10
(Can't say)	98

1818-19

d) **INTERVIEWER CHECK GRID AT A17b), page 7**

One adviser contacted	1	**GO TO e)**
Two or three advisers contacted	2	**GO TO f)**
Four or more advisers contacted	3	**GO TO g)**

1820

IF ONE ADVISER CONTACTED
e) NOW PLEASE COMPLETE GRID ON NEXT PAGE FOR THE ADVISER CONTACTED
(RECORDED AT A17b)

<u>WORK DOWN</u> THE FIRST COLUMN UNTIL YOU REACH THE BOTTOM OF PAGE 15.

IF TWO OR THREE ADVISERS CONTACTED
f) NOW PLEASE COMPLETE GRID ON NEXT PAGE FOR EACH ADVISER CONTACTED,
STARTING IN FIRST COLUMN WITH THE FIRST ADVISER CONTACTED (RECORDED AT A17b)

<u>WORK DOWN</u> THE 1ˢᵀ COLUMN UNTIL YOU REACH THE BOTTOM OF PAGE 15, THEN RETURN
TO PAGE 12 AND COMPLETE THE 2ᴺᴰ COLUMN FOR THE 2ᴺᴰ ADVISER CONTACTED.

IF FOUR OR MORE ADVISERS CONTACTED
g) NOW PLEASE COMPLETE GRID ON NEXT PAGE FOR THE **FIRST TWO** ADVISERS CONTACTED,
STARTING IN FIRST COLUMN WITH THE FIRST ADVISER CONTACTED (RECORDED AT A17b)

OUT OF THE REMAINING 3ᴿᴰ / 4ᵀᴴ, 5ᵀᴴ etc ADVISERS RECORDED AT 17b),
ESTABLISH **WHICH ADVISER DID THE MOST FOR THE RESPONDENT.**
THEN COMPLETE THE THIRD COLUMN FOR THIS ADVISER.

<u>WORK DOWN</u> EACH COLUMN UNTIL YOU REACH THE BOTTOM OF PAGE 15, THEN RETURN TO
PAGE 12 AND COMPLETE FURTHER COLUMNS AS APPROPRIATE FOR SUBSEQUENT ADVISERS.

12

		1st ADVISER	2nd ADVISER	3rd ADVISER
A21	**INTERVIEWER CHECK A17b)** WRITE IN TYPE OF 1st ADVISER IN COLUMN 1, TYPE OF 2nd ADVISER IN COLUMN 2 ETC *(eg CAB, Solicitor)*	1821-2	1926-7	2026-7
A22	(Sometimes people seek advice from friends or relatives who work in particular jobs such as advice agencies or the legal profession). Can I just check, was ...ADVISER... that you contacted a friend or relative of yours?	1823	1928	2028
	Yes	1	1	1
	No	2	2	2
A23	**SHOW CARD K** When you contacted .. ADVISER ... about .. PROBLEM, what sort of advice or help were you looking for? **CODE ALL THAT APPLY**	1824-30	1929-35	2029-35
	Advice about my legal rights	1	1	1
	Advice about procedures *(eg how to deal with summons, court procedures)*	2	2	2
	Advice about ways to solve the problem	3 → A24	3 → A24	3 → A24
	Advice about financial position	4	4	4
	Someone to represent me in court / tribunal	5	5	5
	Other advice or help (SPECIFY IN ROW BELOW)	6 ↓ ROW 1	6 ↓ ROW 2	6 ↓ ROW 3

ROW 1 (1st ADVISER)	1831-40
	GO TO A24

ROW 2 (2nd ADVISER)	1936-45
	GO TO A24

ROW 3 (3rd ADVISER)	2036-45
	GO TO A24

		1st ADVISER	2nd ADVISER	3rd ADVISER
A24	Did .. ADVISER.. think that there was something that could be done about .. PROBLEM... - either by you, or with the help of someone else?	1841	1946	2046
	Yes	1	1	1
	No	2	2	2
A25.	**SHOW CARD L** Did ...ADVISER... give you advice about any of the things on this card at any time? **CODE ALL THAT APPLY**	1842-44	1947-49	2047-49
	Your legal rights	1	1	1
	Procedures / what to do next *(eg how to deal with summons, court procedures)*	2	2	2
	The financial position	3	3	3
	None of these types of advice	4	4	4

13

		1st ADVISER	2nd ADVISER	3rd ADVISER
A26a)	**SHOW CARD M** Did ...ADVISER... suggest that you do any of the things on this card? **CODE ALL THAT APPLY**	1845-49	1950-54	2050-54
	Contact other side to try to resolve the problem	1	1	1
	Seek advice or help from another person / organisation	2	2	2
	Threaten other side with legal action	3 → b	3 → b	3 → b
	Go to court, tribunal or arbitration / start a court, tribunal or arb. case against other side	4	4	4
	Go to mediation / conciliation	5	5	5
	Take the problem to an ombudsman	6	6	6
	None of these	0 → A27	0 → A27	0 → A27
b)	**INTERVIEWER CHECK a)**	1850	1955	2055
	Advised to seek advice from other person/organisation (code 2 at a)	1 → c	1 → c	1 → c
	Others	2 → A27	2 → A27	2 → A27
c)	**IF ADVISED TO SEEK ADVICE FROM OTHER** Who did (s)he suggest that you contact for advice or help? **CODE ALL THAT APPLY**	1851-60	1956-65	2056-65
	Citizens Advice Bureaux (CAB) 01	01	01	01
	Law Centre 02	02	02	02
	Welfare Rights Officer (WRO) 03	03	03	03
	Consumer advice centre / Trading Standards Officer 04	04	04	04
	Other advice agency / worker 05	05	05	05
	Employer 06	06	06	06
	Trade Union or Staff Association 07	07	07	07
	Professional body 08	08	08	08
	Trade associations 09	09	09	09
	Solicitor 10	10	10	10
	Advocate 11	11	11	11
	Claims agency 12	12	12	12
	Court staff 13	13	13	13
	Ombudsman 14	14	14	14
	Other legal consultant 15	15	15	15
	Member of Parliament (MP) or Local councillor 16	16	16	16
	Local council department/Local authority 17	17	17	17
	Housing association 18	18	18	18
	Social Worker / Social Work Department 19	19	19	19
	Police 20	20	20	20
	Religious organisation 21	21	21	21
	Insurance Company 22	22	22	22
	Other person / organisation 23 (SPECIFY)	23	23	23
	(Can't say) 98	98	98	98

14

A27	**SHOW CARD N** Did ...ADVISER... give you any of the types of help on this card? **CODE ALL THAT APPLY**	1ˢᵗ ADVISER 1861-66	2ⁿᵈ ADVISER 1966-71	3ʳᵈ ADVISER 2066-71
	None of these types of help	0	0	0
	Contacted other side on my behalf	1	1	1
	Negotiated with other side on my behalf	2	2	2
	Contacted another person/organisation on my behalf	3	3	3
	Helped me to contact another person/organisation (e.g. by making an appointment, giving me a list of people to approach)	→ A28	→ A28	→ A28
	Accompanied me to court/ tribunal/ arbitration/ mediation	5	5	5
	Spoke on my behalf in court/ tribunal/ arbitration/ mediation	6	6	6
	Gave me other advice or help (specify in row below)	7 ↓ ROW 1	7 ↓ ROW 2	7 ↓ ROW 3

ROW 1 (1ˢᵗ ADVISER)   1867-76

GO TO A28

ROW 2 (2nd ADVISER)   1972-81

GO TO A28

ROW 3 (3ʳᵈ ADVISER)   2072-81

GO TO A28

A28a)	Did you actually meet .. ADVISER . face-to-face?		1910	2010	2110
	Yes	1 → b	1 → b	1 → b
	No	2 → c	2 → c	2 → c
b)	**IF MET ADVISER FACE-TO-FACE** How far did you have to travel to see ...ADVISER? **IF ADVISER = EMPLOYER** **CODE "NO TRAVEL"**	1911	2011	2111
	(No travel / Adviser travelled to respondent)	0	0	0
	Less than 5 miles	1	1	1
	5 - 14 miles	2	2	2
	15 - 29 miles	3	3	3
	30 - 49 miles	4	4	4
	50 miles or more	5	5	5
	(Can't say)	8	8	8

15

		1st ADVISER	2nd ADVISER	3rd ADVISER
A28c)	About how many times did you speak to .. ADVISER.., either in person or on the phone?	1912	2012	2112
	Never	1	1	1
	Once or twice	2	2	2
	3 - 5 times	3	3	3
	6 - 10 times	4	4	4
	11 - 15 times	5	5	5
	16 - 20 times	6	6	6
	More than 20 times	7	7	7
	(Can't say)	8	8	8
A29	Overall, how helpful did you find the advice or help you received from .. ADVISER...READ OUT...	1913	2013	2113
	..very helpful,	1	1	1
	fairly helpful,	2	2	2
	not very helpful	3	3	3
	or not at all helpful?	4	4	4
	(Can't say)	8	8	8
A30a)	Would you recommend other people in your situation to consult ...TYPE OF ADVISER ..? PROBE: Definitely or probably (not)?	1914	2014	2114
	Yes - definitely	1→ c	1→ c	1→ c
	Yes - probably	2→ c	2→ c	2→ c
	Probably not	3→ b	3→ b	3→ b
	Definitely not	4→ b	4→ b	4→ b
	(Can't say)	8→ c	8→ c	8→ c
b)	**IF WOULD NOT RECOMMEND** Why is that?	RECORD IN ROW I BELOW	RECORD IN ROW II BELOW	RECORD IN ROW III BELOW
	ROW 1 (1st ADVISER)			1915-24
				GO TO c
	ROW 2 (2nd ADVISER)			2015-24
				GO TO c
	ROW 3 (3rd ADVISER)			2115-24
				GO TO c
c)	**INTERVIEWER CHECK A17b, page 7**	1925	2025	2125
	Further adviser coded at A17b)	1→A21, next col. page 12	1→A21, next col. page 12	1→A21, next col. page 12
	No further adviser coded	2→ B1, page 22	2→ B1, page 22	2→ B1, page 22

16

IF NO ADVISER CONTACTED

A31. Can I just check, as far as you know (did / does) ...OTHER SIDE... have a solicitor or other adviser to help them deal with .. PROBLEM?

2126-35

IF YES: Who?

CODE ALL THAT APPLY

Citizens Advice Bureaux (CAB)	01
Law Centre	02
Welfare Rights Officer (WRO)	03
Consumer advice centre /Trading Standards Officer	04
Other advice agency / worker	05
Employer	06
Trade Union or Staff Association	07
Professional body *(eg BMA, Law Society)*	08
Trade association *(eg ABTA, Which, AA)*	09
Solicitor	10
Advocate	11
Claims agency *(eg Direct Legal / Quantum)*	12
Court staff	13
Ombudsman	14
Other legal consultant *(eg employment law / immigration law consultant)*	15
Member of Parliament (MP) or Local councillor	16
Local council department/Local authority	17
Housing association	18
Social worker / Social Work Department	19
Police	20
Religious organisation *(eg church, mosque, synagogue)*	21
Insurance company	22
Other person / organisation (SPECIFY)	23

_____

No advice or help	00
Can't say	98

A32a) (Was there / Has there been) any contact between you and ...OTHER SIDE... to try to sort out ...PROBLEM?

Yes, contact with other side	1	**GO TO A33**
No	2	**ASK b)**
(No other side in this problem/dispute)	3	**GO TO A33**

2136

IF NO

b) (Did you <u>try</u> / Have you <u>tried</u>) to contact ...OTHER SIDE... to sort out ...PROBLEM?

Yes, tried to contact other side	1
No	2

2137

17

c) (Did / Has) ...OTHER SIDE... (try / tried) to contact you   2138
to sort out ...PROBLEM?

Yes	1
No	2
(Can't say)	8

IF NO ADVISER CONTACTED
A33 (Apart from this), (did you do / have you done) anything else   2139-48
about ... PROBLEM ?
CODE ALL THAT APPLY

Threatened other side with legal action	01
Went to court, tribunal or arbitration / started court, tribunal or arbitration case against other side	02
Went to mediation or conciliation	03
Took the problem to an ombudsman	04
Sought advice or help from other person / organisation (*specify*)	05
Paid other side some money	06
Other action (*specify*)	07
No - done nothing	00
(Can't say)	98

A34a) **INTERVIEWER CHECK A32a)**

Yes, contact with other side	1	**GO TO B1, page 22**	2149
No	2	**GO TO b)**	
(No other side in this problem/dispute)	3	**GO TO c)**	

IF NO CONTACT
b) **INTERVIEWER CHECK A32b)**

Respondent tried to contact other side	1	**GO TO B1, page 22**	2150
No attempted contact	2	**GO TO c)**	

IF NO ATTEMPTED CONTACT / NO OTHER SIDE
c) **INTERVIEWER CHECK A33**

Respondent did something else (code 01-06)	1	**GO TO B1, page 22**	2151
Others (code 00 or 98)	2	**ASK A35**	

18

IF NO ACTION TAKEN
A35a) Do you intend to do anything about .. PROBLEM ?
. **IF YES:** Definitely or probably?
IF NO: Probably not or definitely not?

Yes, definitely	1	
Yes, probably	2	**GO TO A36**
Maybe	3	
Probably not	4	**ASK b)**
Definitely not	5	

2152

IF DOES NOT INTEND TO DO ANYTHING
b) Why don't you intend to do anything about ... PROBLEM?
PROBE FULLY. RECORD VERBATIM.

2153-62

GO TO A41, page 21

IF (MAYBE) INTENDS TO DO SOMETHING
A36. What do you intend to do?
CODE ALL THAT APPLY

2163-72

Contact the other side	01
Threaten other side with legal action	02
Go to court, tribunal or arbitration / start court, tribunal or arbitration case against other side	03
Go to mediation or conciliation	04
Take the problem to an ombudsman	05
Seek advice or help from other person / organisation (*specify*)	06
Pay other side some money	07
Other (planned) action (*specify*)	08
(Can't say)	98

19

A37a) I would now like to ask you about what you want to achieve by
doing something about ...PROBLEM.
What is the <u>main</u> thing you want to achieve in trying to sort
out ...PROBLEM?
PROBE FULLY. RECORD VERBATIM.

2210-19

b) What other things (if any) do you want to achieve?
PROBE FULLY., RECORD VERBATIM.

2220-29

OR CODE: No other things   00

A38a) All in all, how likely do you think it is that you will achieve
what you want ...**READ OUT**...

2230

...very likely,	1	**GO TO A39**
fairly likely,	2	
not very likely,	3	**ASK b)**
or not at all likely?	4	
(Can't say)	8	**GO TO A39**

IF NOT LIKELY
b) Why do you say that?
PROBE FULLY. RECORD VERBATIM.

2231-40

IF INTENDS TO DO SOMETHING ABOUT PROBLEM
A39a) **INTERVIEWER CHECK ANSWERS GIVEN AT A37a) AND b),
AND CODE:**

Respondent wanted to get **money** from other side	1	**GO TO d)**
Respondent wanted other side to **reduce** amount of money he/she/they were asking for *(eg bill / child support etc)*	2	**GO TO c)**
Others	3	**GO TO b)**

2241

IF OTHERS
b) Can I just check, are you trying to get ...OTHER SIDE... to pay you
some money?

2242

Yes	1	**GO TO d)**
No	2	**GO TO A41, page 21**

20

IF WANTED REDUCTION IN BILL / EXPECTED PAYMENTS etc
c) I would now like to ask you some questions about when you
decided that you wanted ...OTHER SIDE... to reduce the amount
of money (he/she/they) was/were asking you for.

Can I just check, were you trying to get a reduction in a *bill* that you
were being asked to pay, or a reduction in *regular payments* that
you were being asked to make?

2243

Bill	1	GO TO A40
Reduced payments	2	GO TO A41
Both	3	GO TO A40
Can't say	8	GO TO A41

IF WANTS OTHER SIDE TO PAY MONEY
d) Can I just check, are you trying to get a lump sum of money
or regular payments from ...OTHER SIDE...?

2244

Lump sum of money from other side	1	ASK A40
Regular payments from other side (eg maintenance, benefits etc).	2	GO TO A41
Both	3	ASK A40
Can't say	8	

IF WANTS LUMP SUM / REDUCED BILL / CAN'T SAY
A40a) How much money are you trying to get ...OTHER SIDE... to
(pay / reduce the bill or payment by)?
PROMPT WITH CODES IF NECESSARY
ESTIMATE ACCEPTABLE

INCLUDE MONEY OWED AND
COMPENSATION

2245-46

£50 or less	01	
£51 - £100	02	
£101 - £200	03	
£201 - £500	04	
£501 - £750	05	
£751 - £1,000	06	
£1,001 - £1,500	07	
£1,501 - £3,000	08	ASK b)
£3,001 - £5,000	09	
£5,001 - £10,000	10	
£10,001 - £15,000	11	
£15,001 - £25,000	12	
£25,001 - £50,000	13	
£50,001 - £75,000	14	
£75,001 - £100,000	15	
More than £100,000	16	
(Can't say)	98	GO TO A41

21

IF VALUE GIVEN AT a)
b) Where did you get the idea from that you could expect to get
this amount of money?   2247-55
CODE ALL THAT APPLY

Suggested or advised by *friend / relative / work colleague*	01
Suggested or advised by *other person / organisation* (*specify*)	02
Reports in the *media* about these kinds of cases	03
Previous experience of similar kind of situation	04
Other (*specify fully*)	05
(Can't say)	98

IF NO ACTION (YET) TAKEN
A41. Can I just check, (has / did) ...OTHER SIDE...threaten(ed) you
with legal action at any stage, or taken you to court to sort out ...PROBLEM?   2256

Yes	1	**GO TO C1, page 26**
No	2	**GO TO H4, page 62**

22

SECTION B: OBJECTIVES

IF ANY ACTION TAKEN

B1a) Thinking back to when you first decided to do something about
...PROBLEM..., what was the <u>main</u> thing you wanted to achieve?
RECORD VERBATIM IN COLUMN 1 OF TABLE AGAINST "MAIN AIM"

b) (Did / Have) you achieve(d) this aim?
IF YES: Completely or partly?
RING CODE IN COLUMN 2

c) At that stage, were there any <u>other</u> things you hoped to achieve?
RECORD VERBATIM AGAINST "2ⁿᵈ AIM", "3ʳᵈ AIM" etc
IF NO OTHER THINGS, CODE 00 AGAINST "2ⁿᵈ AIM" BELOW

FOR EACH AIM RECORDED, ASK:

d) (Did / Have) you achieve(d) this aim?
IF YES: Completely or partly?
RING CODE IN COLUMN 2

Column 1	Column 2	
Things respondent hoped to achieve	Whether achieved or not	
Main aim: 2257-63	Achieved completely 1	2264
	Achieved partly 2	
	Not achieved 3	
	Too early to say 4	
2ⁿᵈ aim: 2265-71	Achieved completely 1	2272
	Achieved partly 2	
	Not achieved 3	
OR CODE: (No other aims) 00	Too early to say 4	
3ʳᵈ aim: 2273-79	Achieved completely 1	2280
	Achieved partly 2	
	Not achieved 3	
OR CODE: (No other aims) 00	Too early to say 4	
4ᵗʰ aim: 2310-16	Achieved completely 1	2317
	Achieved partly 2	
	Not achieved 3	
OR CODE: (No other aims) 00	Too early to say 4	

B2a) You've now told me about what you wanted to achieve *initially*.
During the course of trying to sort out ...PROBLEM..., (have / did)
you change(d) your mind at any time about what you want(ed) to
achieve?

Yes	1	**ASK b)**
No	2	**GO TO B3**
Can't say	8	

23

IF YES

b) What other things did you decide that you wanted to achieve?
RECORD EACH NEW AIM IN COLUMN 1 OF TABLE AGAINST "NEW AIM 1", "NEW AIM 2" etc

OR CODE: No other things | 00 GO TO B3 | (2319-20)

c) **FOR EACH 'NEW' AIM RECORDED, ASK:**
(Did / Have) you achieve(d) this aim? **IF YES:** Completely or partly?
RING CODE IN COLUMN 2

Column 1		Column 2	
Other things respondent hoped to achieve		Whether achieved or not	
New aim 1:	2319-25	Achieved completely 1	2326
		Achieved partly 2	
		Not achieved 3	
		Too early to say 4	
New aim 2:	2327-33	Achieved completely 1	2334
		Achieved partly 2	
		Not achieved 3	
OR CODE: (No other aims) 00		Too early to say 4	
New aim 3:	2335-41	Achieved completely 1	2342
		Achieved partly 2	
		Not achieved 3	
OR CODE: (No other aims) 00		Too early to say 4	
New aim 4:	2343-49	Achieved completely 1	2350
		Achieved partly 2	
		Not achieved 3	
OR CODE: (No other aims) 00		Too early to say 4	

B3a) All in all, when you first decided to do something about ...PROBLEM...,
how likely did you think it was that you would achieve what you
wanted ...**READ OUT**...

...very likely,	1	**GO TO B4**	2351
fairly likely,	2		
not very likely,	3		
or not at all likely?	4	**ASK b)**	
(can't say)	8		

IF NOT LIKELY

b) Why did you think that?
PROBE FULLY. RECORD VERBATIM. 2352-61

24

B4a) INTERVIEWER CHECK ANSWERS GIVEN IN
GRIDS AT B1 AND B2

Respondent wanted to get **money** from other side	1	GO TO d)	2362
Respondent wanted other side to **reduce** amount of money he/she/they was/were asking for *(eg bill, child support etc)*	2	GO TO c)	
Others	3	GO TO b)	

IF OTHERS
b) Can I just check, were you trying to get ...OTHER SIDE... to pay you some money?

Yes	1	GO TO d)	2363
No	2	GO TO C1, page 26	

IF WANTED REDUCTION IN BILL / EXPECTED PAYMENTS etc
c) I would now like to ask you some questions about when you decided that you wanted ...OTHER SIDE... to reduce the amount of money (he/she/they) was asking you for.
Can I just check, were you trying to get a reduction in a *bill* that you were being asked to pay, or a reduction in *regular payments* that you were being asked to make?

2364

Bill	1	GO TO B5
Reduced payments	2	GO TO C1, page 26
Both	3	GO TO B5
Can't say	8	GO TO C1, page 26

IF WANTED TO GET MONEY
d) I would now like to ask you some questions about when you decided that you wanted some money from ...OTHER SIDE.
Can I just check, at that stage were you trying to get a lump sum of money or regular payments from ...OTHER SIDE...?

Lump sum of money from other side	1	ASK B5	2365
Regular payments from other side (eg maintenance, benefits etc).	2	GO TO C1, page 26	
Both	3	ASK B5	
(Can't say)	8		

25

IF WANTED LUMP SUM / CAN'T SAY / REDUCED BILL
B5a) How much money were you trying to get ...OTHER SIDE... to
(pay / reduce the bill or payment by)?
PROMPT WITH CODES IF NECESSARY
ESTIMATE ACCEPTABLE

INCLUDE MONEY OWED AND COMPENSATION		

IF AMOUNT OF MONEY SOUGHT CHANGED OVER TIME, ASK ABOUT LATEST AMOUNT		

£50 or less	01	2366-67
£51 - £100	02	
£101 - £200	03	
£201 - £500	04	
£501 - £750	05	
£751 - £1,000	06	
£1,001 - £1,500	07	
£1,501 - £3,000	08 **ASK b)**	
£3,001 - £5,000	09	
£5,001 - £10,000	10	
£10,001 - £15,000	11	
£15,001 - £25,000	12	
£25,001 - £50,000	13	
£50,001 - £75,000	14	
£75,001 - £100,000	15	
More than £100,000	16	
(Can't say)	98 **GO TO C1, page 26**	

IF VALUE GIVEN AT a)
b) Where did you get the idea from that you could expect to get
this amount of money?
CODE ALL THAT APPLY

Suggested or advised by *friend / relative / work colleague*	01	2368-77
Suggested or advised by *other person / organisation* (specify)	02	
Reports in the *media* about these kinds of cases	03	
Previous experience of similar kind of situation	04	
Other (specify fully)	05	
(Can't say)	98	

26

SECTION C: MEDIATION

C1a) **SHOW CARD O**
On this card are some examples of organisations that offer mediation
or conciliation to people to help resolve disputes.
Did <u>you</u> attend any mediation or conciliation sessions with any of
these types of organisations to try to resolve ... PROBLEM ... ?

Yes - help received	1	**ASK b)**	2410
No	2		
(Mediation / conciliation session planned for future)	3	**GO TO D1, page 31**	
(Can't say)	8		

IF YES
b) **SHOW CARD O**
What was the name of the organisation?
CODE ONE ONLY

Advisory, Conciliation and Arbitration Service (ACAS)	01	2411-12
Comprehensive Accredited Lawyer Mediators (CALM)	02	
Centre for Dispute Resolution (CEDR)	03	
Mediation Bureau	04	
Academy of Experts	05	
Chartered Institute of Arbitrators	06	
Family Mediation Scotland (FMS)	07	
ACCORD	08	
SFLA	09	
Other mediation/conciliation organisation (SPECIFY)	10	
_____		
(Can't say)	98	

c) How many (mediation / conciliation) sessions were there?   2413

One	1
Two	2
Three	3
Four or more	4

d) (I would now like to ask you a few questions about the <u>final</u>
(mediation / conciliation) session).

What was the date of the (final) mediation / conciliation session?   2414-1

WRITE IN MONTH AND YEAR: ☐☐ **19** ☐☐
ESTIMATE ACCEPTABLE.

27

C2a) **SHOW CARD P**
At the (final) mediation / conciliation session, were you accompanied by
any of the people on this card?

Advocate	1		2418-22
Solicitor	2		
Law Centre adviser	3		
Advice worker (CAB / WRO)	4		
Trade Union or Staff association representative	5	**ASK b)**	
Partner / friend / relative	6		
Other (SPECIFY)	7		
Not accompanied	0	**GO TO C4**	

IF ACCOMPANIED
b) **SHOW CARD P**
Was there anyone at the mediation / conciliation session(s) to speak
on your behalf?
IF YES: Who spoke on your behalf?

Advocate	1		2423-2?
Solicitor	2		
Law Centre adviser	3		
Advice worker (CAB / WRO)	4	**ASK C3**	
Trade Union or Staff Association representative	5		
Partner / friend / relative	6		
Other (SPECIFY)	7		
No-one to speak on respondent's behalf	0	**GO TO C4**	
(Can't say)	8		

IF REPRESENTED AT MEDIATION SESSION
C3a) How well do you feel that your (advocate / solicitor / adviser)
represented you at the (mediation / conciliation) session
... READ OUT ...

...very well,	1	242
fairly well,	2	
not very well,	3	
or not at all well?	4	
(Can't say)	8	

c) Do you think you would have been better off without
a (advocate / solicitor / adviser) to represent you?

Yes	1		24?
No	2	**GO TO C5**	
Maybe	3		
(Can't say)	8		

28

IF NO-ONE TO SPEAK ON RESP'S BEHALF

C4a) Why did you not have anyone representing you at the
(mediation / conciliation) session?
CODE ALL THAT APPLY
PROBE: Any other reason?

Could not afford it	1
Was advised that I should represent myself	2
Didn't think I needed anyone to represent me	3
Other (*specify fully*)	4

2430-34

_____

_____

(Can't say)	8

b) Did you feel that you were at a disadvantage because you
did not have anybody to speak on your behalf?

Yes	1
No	2
(Can't say)	8

2435

IF MEDIATION/CONCILIATION

C5a) **SHOW CARD P**
Did ...OTHER SIDE... have anyone to speak on (his / her / their)
behalf at the (mediation / conciliation) session?
IF YES: Who spoke on ...OTHER SIDE's... behalf?
CODE ALL THAT APPLY

Advocate	1	
Solicitor	2	
Law Centre adviser	3	
Advice worker (CAB / WRO)	4	**ASK b)**
Trade Union or Staff Association representative	5	
Partner / friend / relative	6	
Other (SPECIFY)	7	

2436-40

_____

No-one to speak on other side's behalf	0	**GO TO C6**
(Can't say)	8	

b) How well do you feel that ...OTHER SIDE...'s (advocate / solicitor / adviser)
represented (him / her / them) ... READ OUT ...

...very well,	1
fairly well,	2
not very well,	3
or not at all well?	4
(Can't say)	8

244

29

C6a) How long did the (mediation / conciliation)
session last?
CODE ONE ONLY

Less than 30 minutes	01
30 minutes, under 2 hours	02
2 hours, under 4 hours	03
4 hours, under a day	04
Whole day	05
Two days	06
Three days or more	07
Can't say	98

2442-3

b) **SHOW CARD Q**
Did you feel that you had an opportunity to say what you wanted
to say during the (mediation / conciliation) session - please choose
your answer from this card?

2444

I had an opportunity to say ... everything I wanted to say	1	GO TO C7
...most of what I wanted to say	2	
...some of what I wanted to say	3	
...very little of what I wanted to say	4	ASK c)
... none of what I wanted to say	5	
(Can't say)	8	

IF DID NOT SAY EVERYTHING (S)HE WANTED
c) Were there any important facts about ... PROBLEM... which
you feel did not get discussed at the (mediation / conciliation) session?

Yes	1
No	2
(Can't say)	8

2445

C7a) How well do you think that the (mediator / conciliator)
understood your case ... READ OUT ....

...very well,	1
fairly well,	2
not very well,	3
or not at all well?	4
(Can't say)	8

2446

b) Did you feel that the (mediator / conciliator) tended to favour
one of the parties?

Yes - favoured respondent	1
Yes - favoured other party	2
No	3
Can't say	8

2447

30

c) If you were in the same position again, would you be prepared
to go to (mediation / conciliation) again?
IF YES: Probably or definitely?
IF NO: Probably not or definitely not?

Yes, probably	1	2448
Yes, definitely	2	
Probably not	3	
Definitely not	4	
Maybe	5	
(Can't say)	8	

C8a) Can I just check, did you come to an agreement at the end of the
(mediation / conciliation) session?

Yes, agreement reached	1	**ASK b)**	2449
No	2	**GO TO D1, page 31**	

IF AGREEMENT REACHED
b) Do you think the agreement reached was fair?

Yes	1	**GO TO D1, page 31**	2450
No	2	**ASK c)**	
(Can't say)	8	**GO TO D1, page 31**	

IF NO
c) Why do you say that?
PROBE FULLY. RECORD VERBATIM.   2451-60

31

SECTION D: COURT / TRIBUNAL / ARBITRATION / OMBUDSMAN

D1a) (Was there / Has there been) a court, tribunal or arbitration hearing about
... PROBLEM... - even if you didn't attend it?

IF NO COURT HEARING YET, CODE "NO"	EXCLUDE ANY ASSOCIATED CRIMINAL PROCEEDINGS STARTED BY THE POLICE.

Yes - court / tribunal / arbitration hearing	1	**GO TO D3**		2461
No	2	**ASK b)**		

IF NO
b) Sometimes papers are sent to a court, tribunal or arbitration and
a decision is made without a hearing. Can I just check, (have / were)
papers about ...PROBLEM... (been) sent to a court, tribunal or arbitration
for such a decision?

Yes, papers sent to court/ tribunal/ arbitration for decision without a hearing	1	**GO TO D2**	2462
No	2	**ASK c)**	

IF NO
c) Has ...PROBLEM...come before an Ombudsman?

Yes - came before ombudsman	1	**GO TO D10, page 36**	2463
No	2	**GO TO D12, page 37**	

IF PAPERS SENT TO COURT etc FOR DECISION WITHOUT HEARING
D2a) **SHOW CARD R**
What kind of court or tribunal was it?
CODE ONE ONLY

Sheriff court / small claims procedure	01	2464-65
Sheriff court / summary cause	02	
Sheriff court / ordinary	03	
Court of Session	04	
Industrial Tribunal	05	
Social Security Appeal Tribunal (SSAT)	06	
Other tribunal (SPECIFY)	07	
_____		
Other court (SPECIFY)	08	
_____		
Other arbitration (SPECIFY)	09	
_____		
Can't say	98	

b) Can I check, did you start the action or was the action
started against you?
CODE ONE ONLY

Respondent started action	1	2466
Action started against respondent	2	**GO TO D10, page 36**
(Can't say)	8	

32

IF HEARING IN COURT / TRIBUNAL / ARBITRATION
D3a) **SHOW CARD R**
What kind of court or tribunal was it?
CODE ONE ONLY

Sheriff court / small claims procedure	01	2467-68
Sheriff court / summary cause	02	
Sheriff court / ordinary	03	
Court of Session	04	
Industrial Tribunal	05	
Social Security Appeal Tribunal (SSAT)	06	
Other tribunal (SPECIFY)	07	
Other court (SPECIFY)	08	
Other arbitration (SPECIFY)	09	
Can't say	98	

b) Can I check, did you start the action or was the action
started against you?
CODE ONE ONLY

Respondent started action	1	2469
Action started against respondent	2	
(Can't say)	8	

c) How many hearings or arbitrations have there been - please
include all hearings, whether or not you attended them?

One	1	2470
Two	2	
Three	3	
Four or more	4	
(Can't say)	8	

d) (I would like to ask you a few questions about the <u>final</u>
hearing or arbitration).
What was the date of (your / that) hearing or arbitration?
WRITE IN MONTH AND YEAR
ESTIMATE ACCEPTABLE.

☐☐ **19** ☐☐   2471-74

IF PROCEEDINGS ON-GOING, GIVE DATE OF MOST RECENT HEARING / ARBITRATION	OR CODE: (Can't say) 9998

D4a) Did you attend the (hearing / arbitration) yourself?

Yes, attended hearing / arbitration	1	**ASK b)**	2475
No	2	**GO TO c)**	

33

IF YES

b) **SHOW CARD P**

Were you accompanied by any of the people on this card?

CODE ALL THAT APPLY

Advocate	1	2510-14
Solicitor	2	
Law Centre adviser	3	
Advice worker (CAB / WRO)	4	**ASK c)**
Trade Union or Staff Association representative	5	
Partner / friend / relative	6	
Other (SPECIFY)	7	

Not accompanied	0	**GO TO D6**
(Can't say)	8	

IF ACCOMPANIED / DID NOT ATTEND HEARING

c) **SHOW CARD P**

Was there anyone at the (hearing / arbitration) to speak on your behalf
- please do not include witnesses who gave evidence for you?

IF YES: Who spoke on your behalf?

CODE ALL THAT APPLY

Advocate	1	2515-19
Solicitor	2	
Law Centre adviser	3	
Advice worker (CAB / WRO)	4	**ASK D5**
Trade Union or Staff Association representative	5	
Partner / friend / relative	6	
Other (SPECIFY)	7	

No-one to speak on respondent's behalf	0	**GO TO D6**
(Can't say)	8	

IF REPRESENTED AT HEARING / ARBITRATION

D5a) How well do you feel that your (advocate / solicitor / adviser)
represented you at the (hearing / arbitration) ... READ OUT ...

...very well,	1	2520
fairly well,	2	
not very well,	3	
or not at all well?	4	
(Can't say)	8	

b) Do you think you would have been better off without
a (advocate / solicitor / adviser) to represent you?

Yes	1	2521
No	2	**GO TO D7**
Maybe	3	
(Can't say)	8	

34

IF NO-ONE TO SPEAK ON RESP'S BEHALF
D6a) Why did you not have anyone representing you at the
(hearing / arbitration)?
CODE ALL THAT APPLY
PROBE: Any other reason?   2522-26

Could not afford it	1
Was advised that I should represent myself	2
Didn't think I needed anyone to represent me	3
Other (*specify fully*)	4

_____

_____

_____

(Can't say)	8

b) Did you feel that you were at a disadvantage because you
did not have anybody to speak on your behalf?   2527

Yes	1
No	2
(Can't say)	8

IF HEARING / ARBITRATION
D7a) **SHOW CARD P**
Did ...OTHER SIDE... have anyone to speak on (his / her / their)
behalf at the (hearing / arbitration) - please do not include witnesses
who gave evidence for (him/her/them)?
IF YES: Who spoke on (his / her / their) behalf?
CODE ALL THAT APPLY

Advocate	1	2528-32
Solicitor	2	
Law Centre adviser	3	
Advice worker (CAB / WRO)	4	**ASK b)**
Trade Union or Staff Association representative	5	
Partner / friend / relative	6	
Other (SPECIFY)	7	
No-one to speak on respondent's behalf	0	**GO TO D8**
(Can't say)	8	

c) How well do you feel that ...OTHER SIDE...'s (advocate / solicitor / adviser)
represented (him / her / them) at the (hearing / arbitration)... READ OUT ...
CODE ONE ONLY

...very well,	1	2533
fairly well,	2	
not very well,	3	
or not at all well?	4	
(Can't say)	8	

35

D8a) How long did the (hearing / arbitration) last?
PROMPT IF NECESSARY
CODE ONE ONLY

Less than 30 minutes	1
30 minutes - 2 hours	2
2 - 4 hours	3
Whole day	5
Two days	6
Three days or more	7
Can't say	8

2534

b) **INTERVIEWER CHECK D4a), page 32**

2535

Respondent attended hearing / arbitration	1	**ASK c)**
Others	2	**GO TO D10, page 36**

IF ATTENDED HEARING / ARBITRATION
c) Did you have any difficulties understanding what was going
on at the (hearing / arbitration) - for example....
... READ OUT AND CODE YES OR NO FOR EACH....

	Yes	No	(Can't say)	
..the (court / tribunal / arbitration) procedures?	1	2	8	2536
... why particular questions were being asked?	1	2	8	2537
... who the various people at the (hearing / arbitration) were?	1	2	8	2538

d) **SHOW CARD Q**
Did you feel that you had an opportunity to say what you wanted
to say at the (hearing / arbitration) - please choose your answer
from this card?

2539

At the hearing, I had an opportunity to say ... everything I wanted to say	1	**GO TO D9**
...most of what I wanted to say	2	
...some of what I wanted to say	3	
...very little of what I wanted to say	4	**ASK e)**
... none of what I wanted to say	5	
(Can't say)	8	

IF DID NOT SAY EVERYTHING (S)HE WANTED
e) Were there any important facts about ... PROBLEM... which
you feel did not get discussed at the (hearing / arbitration)?

2540

Yes	1
No	2
(Can't say)	8

D9a) How well do you think that the (sheriff / judge / tribunal / arbitrator)
understood your case ... READ OUT ....

2541

...very well,	1
fairly well,	2
not very well,	3
or not at all well?	4
(Can't say)	8

36

b) Did you feel that the (sheriff / judge / tribunal / arbitrator) favoured
one of the parties?

Yes - favoured respondent	1	2542
Yes - favoured other party	2	
No	3	
Can't say	8	

c) If you were in the same position again, would you be prepared
to go to (court / tribunal / arbitration) again?
IF YES: Probably or definitely?
IF NO: Probably not or definitely not?

Yes, probably	1	2543
Yes, definitely	2	
Probably not	3	
Definitely not	4	
Maybe	5	
(Can't say)	8	

IF PROBLEM PUT BEFORE COURT / TRIBUNAL / ARBITRATION / OMBUDSMAN
D10a) Can I just check, was a decision given by the
(sheriff / judge / tribunal / arbitrator / ombudsman)?
CODE 'YES' IF CASE 'THROWN OUT OF COURT'
CODE 'NO' IF SETTLED OUT OF COURT

Yes, decision given	1	**ASK b)**	2544
No	2	**GO TO D12, page 37**	
(Case ongoing / Still awaiting decision)	3	**GO TO F1, page 50**	

IF DECISION GIVEN
b) Did you win or lose the case?

Respondent won	1	2545
Respondent lost	2	
Other (*specify*) _____	3	
(Can't say)	8	

c) Do you think the (sheriff's / judge's / tribunal's / arbitrator's / ombudsman's)
decision was fair?

Yes	1	**GO TO e)**	2546
No	2	**ASK d)**	
(Can't say)	8	**GO TO e)**	

IF NO
d) Why do you say that?   2547-56
PROBE FULLY. RECORD VERBATIM.

e) **INTERVIEWER CHECK D4a), page 32**

Respondent attended hearing / arbitration	1	**GO TO g)**	2557
Others	2	**GO TO f)**	

37

IF OTHERS
.f) **INTERVIEWER CHECK D1c, page 31**

Case came before Ombudsman	1	**ASK g)**	2558
Others	2	**GO TO D11**	

IF ATTENDED HEARING / CASE CAME BEFORE OMBUDSMAN
g) How clearly did the (sheriff / judge / tribunal / arbitrator / ombudsman)
explain the reasons for (the / his / her) decision - READ OUT...

...very clearly,	1	2559
fairly clearly,	2	
not very clearly,	3	
or not at all clearly?	4	
(Can't say)	8	

D11. What would you say was the main reason that you did not come
to an agreement or settlement with ...OTHER SIDE...before
(the hearing / the arbitration / sending the case to the Ombudsman)?
PROBE FULLY. RECORD VERBATIM.

2560-69

GO TO E1, page 41

**IF PROBLEM NOT COME BEFORE COURT / TRIBUNAL /
ARBITRATION / OMBUDSMAN (YET)**
D12a) Can I just check, was a court, tribunal or arbitration case ever started -
for a court case, this would mean that a writ or summons was issued?

Yes, court / tribunal / arbitration case started	1	**ASK b)**	2570
No	2	**GO TO D14**	
Can't say	8		

IF YES
b) **SHOW CARD R**
What kind of court or tribunal was it?
CODE ONE ONLY

Sheriff court / small claims procedure	01	2571-72
Sheriff court / summary cause	02	
Sheriff court / ordinary	03	
Court of Session	04	
Industrial Tribunal	05	
Social Security Appeal Tribunal (SSAT)	06	
Other tribunal (SPECIFY)	07	
_____		
Other court (SPECIFY)	08	
_____		
Other arbitration (SPECIFY)	09	
_____		
Can't say	98	

38

c) Can I check, did you start the action or was the action started against you?
CODE ONE ONLY

Respondent started action	1
Action started against respondent	2
(Can't say)	8

2573

D13. Can I just check, was a date ever set for ... PROBLEM ... to come before a court, tribunal or arbitrator?

Yes, date set for hearing	1
No	2
(Can't say)	8

2574

IF NO DECISION GIVEN / NOT (YET) COME BEFORE COURT/TRIBUNAL/ARBITRATION
D14a) (Can I just check) did you at any stage reach an agreement or settlement with ...OTHER SIDE...to end the dispute?

Yes, agreement / settlement reached	1	**ASK b)**
No	2	**GO TO F1, page 50**
(Problem resolved itself without agreement)	3	

2575

IF AGREEMENT / SETTLEMENT REACHED
b) **SHOW ADVISER CARD**
Did you reach this agreement with the help of any of the people on this card? **IF YES:** Who?
CODE ALL THAT APPLY

Citizens Advice Bureaux (CAB)	01
Law Centre	02
Welfare Rights Officer (WRO)	03
Consumer advice centre /Trading Standards Officer	04
Other advice agency / worker	05
Employer	06
Trade Union or Staff Association	07
Professional body (eg BMA, Law Society)	08
Trade association (eg ABTA, Which, AA)	09
Solicitor	10
Advocate	11
Claims agency (eg Direct Legal / Quantum)	12
Court staff	13
Ombudsman	14
Other legal consultant (eg employment law / immigration law consultant)	15
Member of Parliament (MP) or Local councillor	16
Local council department/Local authority	17
Housing association	18
Social worker / Social Work Department	19
Police	20
Religious organisation (eg church, mosque, synagogue)	21
Insurance company	22
Other person / organisation (SPECIFY)	23

2610-19

No help from anyone on this card	00

39

c) **SHOW ADVISER CARD**

Did ...OTHER SIDE... have a solicitor or other adviser to help with coming to this agreement? **IF YES:** Who?

CODE ALL THAT APPLY

Citizens Advice Bureaux (CAB)	01
Law Centre	02
Welfare Rights Officer (WRO)	03
Consumer advice centre /Trading Standards Officer	04
Other advice agency / worker	05
Employer	06
Trade Union or Staff Association	07
Professional body (eg BMA, Law Society)	08
Trade association (eg ABTA, Which, AA)	09
Solicitor	10
Advocate	11
Claims agency (eg Direct Legal / Quantum)	12
Court staff	13
Ombudsman	14
Other legal consultant (eg employment law / immigration law consultant)	15
Member of Parliament (MP) or Local councillor	16
Local council department/Local authority	17
Housing association	18
Social worker / Social Work Department	19
Police	20
Religious organisation (eg church, mosque, synagogue)	21
Insurance company	22
Other person / organisation (SPECIFY)	23
_____	
No advice or help	00
(Can't say)	98

2620-29

d) Who made the first move to settle the dispute - was it you, (your solicitor/adviser) or ...OTHER SIDE?

CODE ONE ONLY

Respondent	1
Respondent's solicitor / adviser	2
Other side	3
Other side's solicitor / adviser	4
Both sides	5
Other (SPECIFY) _____	6
(Can't say)	8

2630

e) When was this agreement reached?

WRITE IN MONTH AND YEAR
ESTIMATE ACCEPTABLE.

☐☐ 19 ☐☐

2631-34

OR CODE: (Can't say) 9998

40

D15a) **INTERVIEWER CHECK D13, page 38**

Date set for hearing	1	**ASK b)**
Others	2	**GO TO D16**

2635

IF PROCEEDINGS STARTED AND DATE SET FOR HEARING
b) How soon before the hearing date did you come to the
agreement / settlement?
CODE ONE ONLY

Day of hearing	1
Less than one week	2
One week, less than one month	3
One month, less than 3 months	4
3 months, less than 6 months	5
6 months or more	6
(Can't say)	8

2636

c) Why was it settled at that stage, rather than at a (court / tribunal / arbitration) hearing?
PROBE FULLY. RECORD VERBATIM.

2637-46

GO TO E1, page 41

IF CODE 2 AT D15a)
D16a) **INTERVIEWER CHECK D1a), D1b) AND D1c) - page 31**

Problem came before court / tribunal / arbitration / ombudsman	1	**ASK b)**
(i.e. code 1 at D1a, D1b or D1c)		
Others	2	**GO TO E1, page 41**

2647

IF COURT / TRIBUNAL / ARBITRATION / OMBUDSMAN
b) Why was the case settled at that stage, rather than waiting for a
decision from the (court / tribunal / arbitration / ombudsman)?
PROBE FULLY. RECORD VERBATIM.

2648-57

41

SECTION E: IF AGREEMENT REACHED / DECISION GIVEN

E1a) I would now like to ask you about what was agreed or decided.
If there has been more than one agreement, settlement or decision
about ...PROBLEM, I would like to ask you in detail about the most recent one.

Can I first check, has there been more than one agreement or decision
reached about ...PROBLEM?
IF YES: How many?

No, one only	1
Yes, more than one agreement - two	2
- three	3
- four or more	4

2658

b) **SHOW CARD S**
Can I just check, during the course of trying to sort out
...PROBLEM..., have any of the circumstances on this card
applied to you?

> - LEGAL ADVICE OR REPRESENTATION FROM A
>   SOLICITOR, ADVOCATE OR OTHER LEGAL CONSULTANT
> - PROBLEM CAME BEFORE COURT / TRIBUNAL /
>   ARBITRATION
> - COURT / TRIBUNAL / ARBITRATION CASE STARTED
> - PROBLEM WENT TO MEDIATION OR CONCILIATION
> - PROBLEM WENT TO OMBUDSMAN

Yes, card applied	1	**ASK c)**
No	2	**GO TO d)**

2659

IF YES
c) **SHOW CARD S**
The circumstances on the card almost always lead to legal costs.
Sometimes, it is agreed that the other side will pay your legal costs
- these costs might not necessarily be paid directly to you; they may
be paid directly to your solicitor or other legal adviser.

> LEGAL COSTS MAY BE
> REFERRED TO AS LEGAL
> EXPENSES

Can I just check, (in the most recent agreement or decision) was
it decided that ...OTHER SIDE... should pay any of <u>your</u> legal costs?

Yes	1
No	2
(No legal costs or expenses)	3
(Can't say)	8

2660

d) (Apart from legal costs) was it decided that ...OTHER SIDE...
should pay you any money for anything else?

> **REDUCTION IN BILL = YES**

Yes	1	**ASK e)**
No	2	**GO TO f)**

2661

42

IF YES
e) **SHOW CARD T**
- Did this money include compensation for anything - that is money to
make up for any pain, distress or inconvenience you have suffered,
or any money that you have lost?
IF YES: What was this compensation for?
CODE ALL THAT APPLY

Yes, compensation to make up for :	
- pain	01
- distress	02
- inconvenience	03
- money lost	04
- extra expenses incurred as a result of the problem	05
Impaired ability to do things (eg loss of mobility, loss of sight, etc)	06
Damage to property	07
- something else (SPECIFY)	08

2662-67

No compensation   09

(Can't say)   98

f) **INTERVIEWER CHECK E1c) AND E1d), page 41**

Other side to pay money *(code 1 at E1c) and/or code 1 at E1d)*	1	**ASK g)**
Others	2	**GO TO E4**

2668

IF OTHER SIDE TO PAY MONEY TO RESPONDENT
g) (Including any compensation and legal costs), how much
money was it decided that ...OTHER SIDE... should pay?
WRITE IN AMOUNT OF MONEY AS APPROPRIATE BELOW:
EITHER AS A TOTAL AMOUNT *(Option 1)* **OR AS REGULAR PAYMENTS** *(Option 2)*

IF 2+ SOURCES OF PAYMENT ENTER <u>TOTAL</u>

IF A BILL WAS REDUCED, ENTER AMOUNT REDUCED BY

2669-74

Option 1: **TOTAL AMOUNT OF MONEY:**   Total: £ ☐☐☐☐☐☐

OR

Option 2: **REGULAR PAYMENTS:**   Regular payments: £ ☐☐☐☐

2675-78

RING APPROPRIATE CODE TO INDICATE
HOW OFTEN PAYMENTS TO BE MADE:

Weekly	1
Fortnightly	2
Monthly	3
Quarterly	4
Six monthly	5
Yearly	6
Other (SPECIFY)	7
(Can't say)	8)

2679

43

E2a) Was this more, less or about the same amount of money
as you had hoped for?
IF MORE: Much more or a bit more than you hoped for?
IF LESS: Much less or a bit less than you hoped for?   2710

Much more than hoped for	1	GO TO E3
A bit more than hoped for	2	
A bit less than hoped for	3	ASK b)
Much less than hoped for	4	
About the same	5	GO TO E3
(Can't say)	8	

IF LESS
b) **INTERVIEWER CHECK D10a), page 36**

Decision given by sheriff /judge /tribunal /arbitrator /ombudsman	1	GO TO E3
Others (including D10a not asked)	2	ASK c)

2711

IF NO DECISION GIVEN
c) Why did you accept this amount of money, rather than trying to
get more?
PROBE FULLY.   RECORD VERBATIM.   2712-21

IF OTHER SIDE TO PAY MONEY
E3a) Since the (agreement was reached / decision was given), have you
had any difficulties actually obtaining this money from ...OTHER SIDE...?   2722

Yes	1	ASK b)
No	2	GO TO E8, page 47

IF YES
b) Since the (agreement was reached / decision was given),
(have you done / did you do) anything to try to get ...OTHER SIDE... to
pay the money?
CODE ALL THAT APPLY

Yes - wrote to the other side	1	2723-27
- spoke to (or tried to speak to) the other side	2	
- threatened other side with legal action	3	
- started court or tribunal proceedings against other side	4	
- other (*specify*)	5	GO TO E8, page 47
No - did not do anything	0	

44

IF NO ARRANGEMENT FOR OTHER SIDE TO PAY MONEY

E4a) **SHOW CARD S**
Please look at this card again about the sorts of things which lead to legal costs.
Can I just check, (in the most recent agreement or decision) was it decided that you should pay any of ...OTHER SIDE's... legal costs?

> LEGAL COSTS MAY BE
> REFERRED TO AS LEGAL
> EXPENSES

> - LEGAL ADVICE OR REPRESENTATION FROM A
>   SOLICITOR, ADVOCATE OR OTHER LEGAL CONSULTANT
> - PROBLEM CAME BEFORE COURT / TRIBUNAL /
>   ARBITRATION
> - COURT / TRIBUNAL / ARBITRATION CASE STARTED
> - PROBLEM WENT TO MEDIATION OR CONCILIATION
> - PROBLEM WENT TO OMBUDSMAN

Yes	1	ASK b)	2728
No	2		
(No legal costs)	3	GO TO c)	
(Can't say)	8		

IF YES

b) How much was it agreed that you should pay to cover these legal costs?

2729-34

WRITE IN:

Other side's legal costs: £ ☐☐☐☐☐

OR CODE: (Can't say)   999998

c) And (apart from legal costs) was it decided that you should pay ...OTHER SIDE... any money for anything else?

Yes	1	ASK d)	2735
No	2	GO TO e)	

IF YES

d) **SHOW CARD T**
Did this money include compensation for anything - that is money to make up for any pain, distress or inconvenience that ...OTHER SIDE... suffered, or any money that (he / she / they) lost?
IF YES: What was this compensation for?
CODE ALL THAT APPLY

Yes, compensation to make up for :		
- pain	01	2736-41
- distress	02	
- inconvenience	03	
- money lost	04	
- extra expenses incurred as a result of the problem	05	
Impaired ability to do things (eg loss of mobility, loss of sight, etc)	06	
Damage to property	07	
- something else (SPECIFY)	08	
_____		
No compensation	09	
(Can't say)	98	

e) **INTERVIEWER CHECK E4a) AND c)**

Respondent to pay money	1	ASK E5	2742
(code 1 at E4a) and/or code 1 at E4c)			
Others	2	GO TO E8, page 47	

45

IF RESPONDENT TO PAY MONEY TO OTHER SIDE
E5a) (Apart from ...OTHER SIDE's... legal costs), how much money was it
decided that you should pay ...OTHER SIDE?
INCLUDE COMPENSATION
WRITE IN AMOUNT OF MONEY AS APPROPRIATE BELOW:
EITHER AS A TOTAL AMOUNT *(Option 1)* **OR AS REGULAR PAYMENTS** *(Option 2)*

2743-48

Option 1: **TOTAL AMOUNT OF MONEY:**   Total: £ ☐☐☐☐☐☐

OR

2749-52

Option 2: **REGULAR PAYMENTS:**   Regular payments: £ ☐☐☐☐

RING APPROPRIATE CODE TO INDICATE
HOW OFTEN PAYMENTS TO BE MADE:

Weekly	1
Fortnightly	2
Monthly	3
Quarterly	4
Six monthly	5
Yearly	6
Other (SPECIFY)	
_____	7
(Can't say)	8

2753

b) Was this more, less or about the same amount as ...OTHER SIDE...
had originally asked for?

More than other side had asked for	1
Less than asked for	2
About the same	3
(Can't say)	8

2754

E6a) Was it more, less or about the same amount of money
as you had expected to pay?
IF MORE: Much more or a bit more than you expected?
IF LESS: Much less or a bit less than you expected?

2755

Much more than expected	1	**ASK b)**
A bit more than expected	2	
A bit less than expected	3	
Much less than expected	4	
About the same	5	**GO TO E7**
(Can't say)	8	

IF MORE THAN EXPECTED
b) **INTERVIEWER CHECK D10a), page 36**

Decision given by sheriff /judge /tribunal /arbitrator /ombudsman	1	**GO TO E7**
Others	2	**ASK c)**
(including D10a not asked)		

2756

46

IF NO DECISION GIVEN
c) Why did you agree to pay this amount of money, rather than
negotiating a lower figure?
PROBE FULLY. RECORD VERBATIM.

2757-66

E7a) Since the (agreement was reached / decision was given), have you
paid any of the money?

Yes	1	**GO TO E8**	2767
No	2	**ASK b)**	

IF NOT ANY OF THE MONEY
b) How likely do you think it is that you will pay the
money ... READ OUT ....

... very likely,   1   2768
fairly likely,   2
not very likely,   3
or not at all likely?   4

(Can't say)   8

c) Since the (agreement was reached / decision was given),
has ...OTHER SIDE... done anything to try to get you to pay
the money?
CODE ALL THAT APPLY

Yes - wrote to me   1   2769-73

- spoke to (or tried to speak to) me   2

- threatened me with legal action   3

- started court or tribunal proceedings against me   4
  (*i.e. sent me a writ or summons*)

- other (*specify*)   5

_____

_____

No - has not done anything   0

(Can't say)   8

d) Why have you not (yet) paid the money?
PROBE FULLY. RECORD VERBATIM.

2810-19

47

IF AGREEMENT MADE / DECISION GIVEN

E8a) (Apart from the money payment), were any other arrangements agreed or decided, for example that you or ...OTHER SIDE... would do something, or stop doing something?

Yes	1	**ASK b)**	2820
No	2	**GO TO E11**	

IF YES

b) What was agreed / decided?
PROBE FULLY. RECORD VERBATIM.   2821-30

c) **INTERVIEWER CODE FROM ANSWER GIVEN AT b)**

Certain action / behaviour required of respondent only	1	**ASK E9**	2831
Action / behaviour required of other side only	2	**GO TO E10**	
Action / behaviour required of both sides	3	**ASK E9**	

IF ACTION REQUIRED OF RESPONDENT

E9a) Have you kept to (your part of) these agreed arrangements?

Yes	1	**GO TO c)**	2832
No	2	**ASK b)**	

IF NO

b) Why is that?
PROBE FULLY. RECORD VERBATIM.

2833-42

c) **INTERVIEWER CHECK E8c)**   2843

Certain action / behaviour required of respondent only	1	**GO TO E11**	
Action / behaviour required of both sides	3	**ASK E10**	

IF ACTION REQUIRED OF OTHER SIDE

E10a) Has ...OTHER SIDE... kept to (his / her / their) part of these agreed arrangements?   2844

Yes	1	**GO TO E11**	
No	2	**ASK b)**	

48

IF NO

b) Have you done anything to try and make ...OTHER SIDE... keep
to the agreed arrangements?
CODE ALL THAT APPLY

Yes - wrote to the other side	1	2845-49
- spoke to (or tried to speak to) the other side	2	
- threatened other side with legal action	3	**GO TO E11**
- started court or tribunal proceedings against other side	4	
- other (*specify*)	5	

No - did not do anything	0	**ASK c)**

IF DONE NOTHING TO ENFORCE AGREEMENT

c) Why is that?
PROBE FULLY. RECORD VERBATIM.   2850-59

IF AGREEMENT REACHED / DECISION GIVEN

E11a) Before this (agreement was reached / decision was given), had you rejected   2860
any offers... from ...OTHER SIDE... - by this I mean formal offers from
(him/her/them) to pay you money or to do something else to resolve the
dispute?

Yes	1
No	2

b) And before this (agreement was reached / decision was given), did you make
any offers that were rejected by...OTHER SIDE...?
IF NECESSARY: By this I mean formal offers to pay ...OTHER SIDE...
money or to do something else to resolve the dispute?

Yes	1	2861
No	2	

IF AGREEMENT REACHED / DECISION GIVEN

E12a) **INTERVIEWER CHECK D10a), page 36**

Decision given by sheriff /judge /tribunal /arbitrator /ombudsman	1	**GO TO E13**	2862
Others	2	**ASK b)**	

IF OTHERS

b) Taking everything into consideration, do you think that the
agreement was fair?

Yes	1	**GO TO E13**	2863
No	2	**ASK c)**	

49

IF NO
c) In what ways do you think it was unfair?
PROBE FULLY. RECORD VERBATIM.

2864-73

d) Why did you agree to settle the case if you did not
think that it was fair?
PROBE FULLY. RECORD VERBATIM.

2910-19

IF AGREEMENT / DECISION
E13a) Did the (agreement / decision) actually end the dispute between
you and ...OTHER SIDE...?
IF YES: Completely or only partly?

2920

Yes, completely	1	**GO TO G1, page 53**
Yes, partly	2	**ASK b)**
No	3	

IF PARTLY / NO
b) Is the problem still on-going?

2921

Yes, problem still on-going	1	**GO TO F4, page 51**
No, problem resolved	2	**ASK c)**

IF PROBLEM RESOLVED
c) How did the problem resolve itself?
PROBE FULLY. RECORD VERBATIM.

2922-31

GO TO G1, page 53

50

SECTION F: IF NO AGREEMENT REACHED / NO DECISION GIVEN

F1a) Can I just check, is the problem still on-going?

Yes, problem still on-going	1	GO TO F2
No, problem resolved	2	ASK b)

2932

IF PROBLEM RESOLVED
b) How did the problem resolve itself?
PROBE FULLY. RECORD VERBATIM.

2933-42

IF NO AGREEMENT / DECISION
F2a) SHOW ADVISER CARD
(Did / Does)...OTHER SIDE... have a solicitor or other adviser at any stage
to help sort out .. PROBLEM?
IF YES: Who?
CODE ALL THAT APPLY

Citizens Advice Bureaux (CAB)	01
Law Centre	02
Welfare Rights Officer (WRO)	03
Consumer advice centre /Trading Standards Officer	04
Other advice agency / worker	05
Employer	06
Trade Union or Staff Association	07
Professional body (eg BMA, Law Society)	08
Trade association (eg ABTA, Which, AA)	09
Solicitor	10
Advocate	11
Claims agency (eg Direct Legal / Quantum)	12
Court staff	13
Ombudsman	14
Other legal consultant (eg employment law / immigration law consultant)	15
Member of Parliament (MP) or Local councillor	16
Local council department/Local authority	17
Housing association	18
Social worker / Social Work Department	19
Police	20
Religious organisation (eg church, mosque, synagogue)	21
Insurance company	22
Other person / organisation (SPECIFY)	23

2943-52

No advice or help	00
(Can't say)	98

51

b) (Before the problem was resolved,) did you at any stage reject any offers from ...OTHER SIDE... - by this I mean formal offers from (him/her/them) to pay you money or to do something else to resolve the dispute?

Yes	1	2953
No	2	

c) And did you make any offers to ...OTHER SIDE... that were rejected?
IF NECESSARY: By this I mean formal offers to pay ...OTHER SIDE.... money or to do something else to resolve the dispute?

Yes	1	2954
No	2	

F3. INTERVIEWER CHECK F4a)

Problem still on-going	1	ASK F4	2955
Problem resolved	2	GO TO F6	

IF PROBLEM STILL ON-GOING
F4a) Apart from what you have already told me about, are you doing anything else to sort out this problem?

Yes	1	GO TO c)	2956
No	2	ASK b)	

IF NO
b) Do you intend to do anything about .. PROBLEM ?
IF YES: Definitely or probably?
IF NO: Probably not or definitely not?

Yes, definitely	1		2957
Yes, probably	2	ASK c)	
Maybe	3		
Probably not	6		
Definitely not	4	GO TO F5	
Maybe	5		
(Can't say)	8		

IF DOING / LIKELY TO DO SOMETHING
c) What are you doing or planning to do?
CODE ALL THAT APPLY

Contact the other side	01	2958-67
Threaten other side with legal action	02	
Go to court, tribunal or arbitration / start court, tribunal or arbitration case against other side	03	
Go to mediation or conciliation	04	
Take the problem to an ombudsman	05	
Seek advice or help from other person / organisation (specify)	06	
Pay other side some money	07	
Other (planned) action (specify)	08	
(Can't say)	98	

52

d) Do you think that you will be able to sort out ... PROBLEM?
   IF YES: Definitely or probably?
   IF NO: Probably not or definitely not?

2968

Yes - definitely	1	
Yes - probably	2	
Probably not	3	**GO TO G1, page 53**
Definitely not	4	
(Can't say)	8	

IF NOT PLANNING TO DO ANYTHING ABOUT PROBLEM
F5 Why don't you intend to do anything about ... PROBLEM?
   PROBE FULLY.   RECORD VERBATIM.

2969-78

**IF NOT PLANNING TO DO ANYTHING /
PROBLEM RESOLVED ITSELF WITHOUT AGREEMENT**
F6 What would you say was the main reason that you (did / have)
   not manage(d) to come to an agreement or settlement with
   ..OTHER SIDE?
   PROBE FULLY.   RECORD VERBATIM.

3010-19

53

SECTION G: COSTS

ALL
G1a) **INTERVIEWER CHECK E1b), page 41**

			3020
Yes, card applied *(i.e. legal costs probably incurred)*	1	**GO TO c)**	
No	2	**ASK b)**	

IF NO
b) **SHOW CARD S**
Can I just check, during the course of trying to sort out
…PROBLEM…, (did / have) any of the circumstances on this card
(apply / applied) to you?

- LEGAL ADVICE OR REPRESENTATION FROM A
  SOLICITOR, ADVOCATE OR OTHER LEGAL CONSULTANT
- PROBLEM CAME BEFORE COURT / TRIBUNAL /
  ARBITRATION
- COURT / TRIBUNAL / ARBITRATION CASE STARTED
- PROBLEM WENT TO MEDIATION OR CONCILIATION
- PROBLEM WENT TO OMBUDSMAN
	LEGAL COSTS MAY BE
	REFERRED TO AS LEGAL
	EXPENSES,

			3021
Yes, card applied *(i.e. legal costs probably incurred)*	1	**ASK c)**	
No	2	**GO TO G9**	

IF CARD APPLIED
c) Can I just check, during the course of trying to sort out …PROBLEM…,
(were you / have you been) offered any financial support from any of
the following sources…
…**READ OUT AND CODE YES OR NO FOR EACH**…

	Yes	No	Can't say	
…Legal Aid?	1	2	8	3022
…Legal Expenses Insurance?	1	2	8	3023
…Trade Union or Staff Association?	1	2	8	3024
Employer?	1	2	8	3025

d) **INTERVIEWER CHECK c)**

			3026
Respondent offered at least one type of support (at least one code 1 at c)	1	**ASK G2**	
Others	2	**GO TO G6**	

IF OFFERED FINANCIAL SUPPORT
G2a) **INTERVIEWER CHECK G1c)**

			3027
Respondent offered Legal Aid	1	**ASK b)**	
Others	2	**GO TO G3**	

IF OFFERED LEGAL AID
b) You said you were offered Legal Aid. Did you accept it?

			3028
Yes	1	**GO TO d)**	
No	2	**ASK c)**	

54

IF NO
c) Why was that?
PROBE FULLY. RECORD VERBATIM.

3029-38

GO TO G3

IF LEGAL AID ACCEPTED
d) Was this Legal Aid backing withdrawn at at any stage?

Yes	1	
No	2	
(Can't say)	8	

3039

G3a) **INTERVIEWER CHECK G1c), page 53**

Respondent offered Legal Expenses Insurance	1	ASK b)
Others	2	GO TO G4

3040

b) You said that you were offered Legal Expenses Insurance. Was this Legal Expenses Insurance backing withdrawn at at any stage?

Yes	1	
No	2	
(Can't say)	8	

3041

c) **SHOW CARD S**
(This card shows examples of the sorts of things which lead to legal costs).
(Did / Has) Legal Expenses Insurance actually (pay / paid) any money to cover your legal costs?

3042

> - LEGAL ADVICE OR REPRESENTATION FROM A SOLICITOR, ADVOCATE OR OTHER LEGAL CONSULTANT
> - PROBLEM CAME BEFORE COURT / TRIBUNAL / ARBITRATION
> - COURT / TRIBUNAL / ARBITRATION CASE STARTED
> - PROBLEM WENT TO MEDIATION OR CONCILIATION
> - PROBLEM WENT TO OMBUDSMAN

LEGAL COSTS MAY BE REFERRED TO AS LEGAL EXPENSES

Yes	1	ASK d)
No	2	
Not yet but expected to	3	GO TO G4
(Can't say)	8	

IF YES
d) How much did the Legal Expenses Insurance pay to cover these legal costs?
ESTIMATE ACCEPTABLE

£ [ ][ ][ ][ ][ ][ ]   3043-48

(Can't say)   999998

55

G4a) INTERVIEWER CHECK G1c), page 53

Respondent offered financial support from Trade Union/ Staff Assocn.	1	**ASK b)**	3049
Others	2	**GO TO G5**	

IF OFFERED TRADE UNION SUPPORT
b) You said you were offered financial support from your
Trade Union or Staff Association. Did they withdraw their backing at
at any stage?

Yes	1	3050
No	2	
(Can't say)	8	

G5a) INTERVIEWER CHECK G1c), page 53

Respondent offered financial support from employer	1	**ASK b)**	3051
Others	2	**GO TO G6**	

IF OFFERED EMPLOYER SUPPORT
b) You said that you were offered financial support by your
employer. Did your employer withdraw this backing at
any stage?

Yes	1	3052
No	2	
(Can't say)	8	

c) **SHOW CARD S**
(This card shows examples of the sorts of things which
lead to legal costs).
(Did / Has) your employer actually (pay / paid) any money to
cover your legal costs?

- LEGAL ADVICE OR REPRESENTATION FROM A
  SOLICITOR, ADVOCATE OR OTHER LEGAL CONSULTANT
- PROBLEM CAME BEFORE COURT / TRIBUNAL /
  ARBITRATION
- COURT / TRIBUNAL / ARBITRATION CASE STARTED
- PROBLEM WENT TO MEDIATION OR CONCILIATION
- PROBLEM WENT TO OMBUDSMAN
	**LEGAL COSTS MAY BE
	REFERRED TO AS LEGAL
	EXPENSES**

Yes	1	**ASK d)**	3053
No	2		
Not yet but expected to	3	**GO TO G6**	
(Can't say)	8		

IF YES
d) How much did your employer pay to cover these
legal costs?
ESTIMATE ACCEPTABLE

£ ☐☐☐☐☐☐   3054-59

(Can't say)   999998

56

G6a) SHOW CARD S
(This card shows examples of the sorts of things which lead to legal costs).
Can I just check, did any person or organisation offer to cover your legal
costs on a "no win, no fee" basis?
IF NECESSARY:
- by this, I mean did they offer to cover your legal costs if you
lost the case? This arrangement is sometimes referred to as
speculative fees.

> - **LEGAL ADVICE OR REPRESENTATION FROM A
>   SOLICITOR, ADVOCATE OR OTHER LEGAL CONSULTANT**
> - **PROBLEM CAME BEFORE COURT / TRIBUNAL /
>   ARBITRATION**
> - **COURT / TRIBUNAL / ARBITRATION CASE STARTED**
> - **PROBLEM WENT TO MEDIATION OR CONCILIATION**
> - **PROBLEM WENT TO OMBUDSMAN**

> LEGAL COSTS MAY BE
> REFERRED TO AS LEGAL
> EXPENSES

Yes, offered on a "no win, no fee" basis	1	ASK b)	3060
No	2	GO TO G7	
(Can't say)	8		

IF YES
b) Who was this?
CODE ALL THAT APPLY

Solicitor	1	3061-65
Advocate	2	
Claims agency (eg Direct Legal / Quantum)	3	
Other legal consultant (eg employment law / immigration law consultant)	4	
Partner / friend / relative	5	
Other (SPECIFY)	6	

_____

c) Did you have a written agreement about this "no win, no fee"
arrangement?

Yes	1	3066
No	2	
(Can't say)	8	

d) Was this "no win, no fee" offer withdrawn at any stage?

Yes	1	3067
No	2	
(Can't say)	8	

G7a) SHOW CARD S
(Apart from this) can I just check, (were you / have you been) offered any financial
support by any other person or organisation - this may have been an offer to pay some
of your legal costs, or to provide legal advice or services free of charge?

> - **LEGAL ADVICE OR REPRESENTATION FROM A
>   SOLICITOR, ADVOCATE OR OTHER LEGAL CONSULTANT**
> - **PROBLEM CAME BEFORE COURT / TRIBUNAL /
>   ARBITRATION**
> - **COURT / TRIBUNAL / ARBITRATION CASE STARTED**
> - **PROBLEM WENT TO MEDIATION OR CONCILIATION**
> - **PROBLEM WENT TO OMBUDSMAN**

> LEGAL COSTS MAY BE
> REFERRED TO AS LEGAL
> EXPENSES

Yes	1	ASK b)	3068
No	2	GO TO G8	

57

IF YES
b) Who offered you this support?
CODE ALL THAT APPLY

Solicitor	1
Advocate	2
Claims agency (eg Direct Legal / Quantum)	3
Other legal consultant (eg employment law / immigration law consultant)	4
Partner / friend / relative	5
Other (SPECIFY)	6

3069-74

_____

c) Was this offer of financial support withdrawn at any stage?

Yes	1
No	2
(Can't say)	8

3110

d) And did (this person or organisation / any of these people or organisations) actually pay any money to cover your legal costs?

Yes	1	**ASK e)**
No	2	
Not yet, but expected to	3	**GO TO G8**
(Can't say)	8	

3111

IF YES
e) How much did (he/she/they) pay to cover these legal costs?
ESTIMATE ACCEPTABLE

£ ▢▢▢▢▢▢

3112-17

(Can't say)   999998

G8a) **SHOW CARD S**
And did **you** personally have to pay any of your legal costs?

- **LEGAL ADVICE OR REPRESENTATION FROM A SOLICITOR, ADVOCATE OR OTHER LEGAL CONSULTANT** - **PROBLEM CAME BEFORE COURT / TRIBUNAL / ARBITRATION** - **COURT / TRIBUNAL / ARBITRATION CASE STARTED** - **PROBLEM WENT TO MEDIATION OR CONCILIATION** - **PROBLEM WENT TO OMBUDSMAN** -INCLUDE STATUTORY CLAWBACK	Yes	1	**ASK b)**
	No	2	
	Not yet, but expect to	3	**GO TO G9**
	(Can't say)	8	

3118

LEGAL COSTS MAY BE REFERRED TO AS LEGAL EXPENSES

IF YES
b) How much did you pay?
ESTIMATE ACCEPTABLE

3119-24

£ ▢▢▢▢▢▢

(Can't say)   999998

58

c) How much had you expected to pay?
ESTIMATE ACCEPTABLE

£ ☐☐☐☐☐☐   3125-30

ASK d)

OR CODE: (Nothing)   000000

(Can't say)   999998   **GO TO G9**

IF EXPECTED AMOUNT GIVEN
d) Where did you get the idea from that you might have to pay (that amount / nothing)?
CODE ALL THAT APPLY

Suggested or advised by *friend / relative / work colleague*   01   3131-40

Suggested or advised by *other person / organisation* (specify)   02

_____

Previous experience of similar kind of situation   03

Other (*specify fully*)   04

_____

_____

(Can't say)   98

G9a) As far as you know, during the course of trying to sort out ...PROBLEM...,
(was ....OTHER SIDE... / has ....OTHER SIDE... been) offered any financial
support from any of the following sources...
...**READ OUT AND CODE YES OR NO FOR EACH...**

	Yes	No	Can't say	
...Legal Aid?	1	2	8	3141
...Legal Expenses Insurance?	1	2	8	3142
...Trade Union?	1	2	8	3143
Employer?	1	2	8	3144

b) And as far as you know, did any person or organisation offer to cover
...OTHER SIDE's.... legal costs on a "no win, no fee" basis?
IF NECESSARY:
- by this, I mean did they offer to cover (his/her/their) legal costs if
(he/she/they) lost the case?

Yes, offered on a "no win, no fee" basis   1   3145

No   2

(Can't say)   8

59

G10. (Were you / Have you been) worried at any stage about having to pay any
legal costs - either your own costs or ...OTHER SIDE's...costs?
IF YES: Your costs or ...OTHER SIDE's?
CODE ONE ONLY

Yes - worried about paying own legal costs	1	3146
Yes - worried about paying other side's legal costs	2	
Yes - worried about both	3	
No	4	
(Can't say)	8	

ALL
G11a) **SHOW CARD U**
(Were there / Have there been) any (other) financial costs
related to sorting out ....PROBLEM - some examples are
shown on this card?
IF YES: What were these costs for?
CODE ALL THAT APPLY

Loss of earnings	1		3147-51
Cost of travelling	2		
(eg to visit lawyers / advice agencies / court etc)		**ASK b)**	
Cost of telephone calls	3		
Other costs *(specify)*	4		
_____			
No other financial costs (yet)	0	**GO TO c)**	
(Can't say)	8		

IF COSTS INCURRED
b) **SHOW CARD V**
About how much in total were these costs?
ESTIMATE ACCEPTABLE

£10 or less	01	
£11 - £50	02	3152-53
£51 - £100	03	
£101 - £200	04	
£201 - £500	05	
£501 - £750	06	
£751 - £1,000	07	
£1,001 - £1,500	08	
£1,501 - £3,000	09	
£3,001 - £5,000	10	
£5,001 - £10,000	11	
More than £10,000	12	
(Can't say)	98	

ALL
c) (Did you have / Have you had) to take any time off work, or use
any of your annual leave to sort out ...PROBLEM?

Yes	1	3154
No / Not yet	2	

60

SECTION H: OVERALL ASSESSMENT AND ATTITUDES

IF ACTION TAKEN

H1a) Thinking back to when you first decided to do something about ...PROBLEM..., how long had you thought that it would take to solve the problem?

CODE ONE ONLY

PROBE FOR ESTIMATE

Less than a week	01	3155-56
1 week less than 2 weeks	02	
2 weeks, less than a month	03	
1 - 2 months	04	
3 - 4 months	05	
5 - 6 months	06	
7 - 9 months	07	
10 - 12 months	08	
More than a year	09	
(Can't say)	98	

b) **INTERVIEWER CHECK E13b) page 49 OR F1a) page 50**

Yes, problem still on-going	1	**GO TO H2**	3157
No, problem resolved	2	**ASK c)**

IF PROBLEM RESOLVED

c) Did (Has) solving this problem take(n) a shorter time than you expected, about as long as you expected, or a longer time than you expected?

IF SHORTER: Much shorter or a bit shorter?
IF LONGER: Much longer, or a bit longer?

Much shorter than expected	1	3158
A bit shorter than expected	2	
About as long as you expected	3	
A bit longer than expected	4	
Much longer than expected	5	
(Can't say)	8	

IF ACTION TAKEN

H2a) Looking back over the experience of trying to sort out.. PROBLEM (so far), is there anything about the way in which you handled the situation that you regret?

Yes	1	**ASK b)**	3159
No	2	**GO TO H3**

IF YES

b) What is that?
PROBE FULLY. RECORD VERBATIM.

3160-69

61

IF ACTION TAKEN

H3a) Can I just check, (were you / have you been) in paid work at any time
during the course of sorting out .. PROBLEM?

Yes	1	**ASK b)**
No	2	**GO TO c)**

3170

IF YES

b) **SHOW CARD W**

As a result of trying to sort out this problem, (did / have)
you experience(d) any of the things on this card?

CODE ALL THAT APPLY

Had to take time off work due to stress	1
Chances of promotion were badly affected	2
Relationships with colleagues suffered	3
Had to move to another job	4
Other effect on working life (SPECIFY)	5
None of these effects	0

3171-75

c) **SHOW CARD X**

As a result of trying to sort out this problem, (did / have)
you experience(d) any of the things or feelings on <u>this</u> card?

CODE ALL THAT APPLY

The experience has made me feel that I have some control over my situation	01
I have found the experience of trying to sort out ...PROBLEM ...stressful	02
I have had difficulty sleeping	03
My health has suffered	04
I am glad to (be enforcing / have enforced) my rights	05
My relationships with family and friends have suffered	06
I am glad to (be clearing / have cleared) my name	07
I have had to move to another house / flat	08
I have had to move to another area	09
Other effect on life (SPECIFY)	10
None of these effects	00

3210-29

62

H4a) I would now like to ask you a few general questions about your
feelings about the justice system in Britain.

SHOW CARD Y
I am going to read out a few statements - please tell me for each
one how much you agree or disagree with it.
READ OUT EACH STATEMENT BELOW AND RING ONE CODE FOR EACH

		Strongly Agree	Agree	Neither agree nor disagree	Disagree	Strongly Disagree	(Can't say)	
a)	If I went to court with a problem, I am confident that I would get a fair hearing	1	2	3	4	5	8	3230
b)	Most judges are out of touch with ordinary people's lives	1	2	3	4	5	8	3231
c)	Lawyers' charges are reasonable for the work they do	1	2	3	4	5	8	3232
d)	Courts are an important way for ordinary people to enforce their rights	1	2	3	4	5	8	3233
e)	The legal system works better for rich people than for poor people	1	2	3	4	5	8	3234

63

SECTION J: CLASSIFICATION

ALL

J1a) And now a few questions about yourself to help us to analyse
the findings of the survey.
ASK OR CODE:
Firstly, your legal marital status - can I just check,
are you .. READ OUT ...

... married and living with your (husband/wife),	1	GO TO J2

3235

married and separated from your (husband / wife),	2	
... widowed,	3	ASK b)
.. divorced,	4	
...or single and never married?	5	

IF SEPARATED / WIDOWED / DIVORCED / SINGLE

b) Can I just check, are you living with someone as a couple ?

Yes	1
No	2

3236

J2a) **SHOW CARD Z**
Which of the phrases on this card best describes what you were doing last
week, that is the seven days ending last Sunday?
CODE ONE ONLY

In paid work as employee / self-employed - <u>full-time</u> (30 or more hours per week) - *or temporarily away from full-time job*	01	

3237-38

In paid work as employee / self-employed - <u>part-time</u> (less than 30 hours per week) - *or temporarily away from part-time job*	02	GO TO J3

In full-time education - *or on vacation from full-time education*	03	ASK b)
In part-time education - *or on vacation from part-time education*	04	
On government training scheme	05	
Waiting to take up paid work	06	
Unemployed	07	
Long-term sick or disabled	08	
Wholly retired from work	09	
Looking after the home / family	10	
Doing something else (SPECIFY) _____	11	

64

IF NOT IN PAID WORK LAST WEEK
b) Can I just check, apart from government schemes, have you been in
paid work at any time in the last ten years - please do NOT include
part-time or vacation work you may have done while you were a
full-time student?

Yes - in paid work in the last 10 years	1	**ASK J3**
No - not in paid work in the last 10 years	2	**GO TO J6**

3239

IF IN PAID WORK IN LAST 10 YEARS
J3a) Now I'd like to ask you about your current (most recent) job.
What is (was) the name or title of the job?
IF 2+ JOBS AT ONCE, TAKE MAIN JOB
(IF QUERIED, MOST REMUNERATIVE)

b) What kind of work do (did) you do most of the time?
PROBE FULLY.

SOC ☐☐☐   3240-42

ES ☐☐   3243-44

c) What materials or machinery do (did) you use?
PROBE FULLY.

SEG ☐☐   3245-46

SC ☐   3247

d) What skills or qualifications are (were) needed for the job?
PROBE FULLY.

J4a) Are (were) you ... READ OUT....

.. an employee	1	**ASK b)**
or self-employed?	2	**GO TO J5**

3248

IF EMPLOYEE
b) Do (did) you supervise, or are (were) you responsible
for other people's work?

Yes	1	**ASK c)**
No	2	**GO TO d)**

3249

65

. IF YES
c) How many people?

1 - 4	1	3250
5 - 24	2	
25 - 99	3	
100 - 499	4	
500 or more	5	
(Can't say)	8	

d) Including yourself, about how many people are (were) employed at the place where you work(ed)?

1 - 4	1	3251
5 - 24	2	
25 - 99	3 GO TO J6	
100 - 499	4	
500 or more	5	
(Can't say)	8	

IF SELF-EMPLOYED
J5a) Do (Did) you have any employees?

Yes	1 ASK b)	3252
No	2 GO TO J6	

IF YES
b) How many?

1 - 4	1	3253
5 - 24	2	
25 - 99	3	
100 - 499	4	
500 or more	5	
(Can't say)	8	

J6 SHOW CARD AA
Which of the letters on this card best represents the total income of your household at the moment - please think about your household income from all sources, before tax and other deductions?
ESTIMATE ACCEPTABLE

B	06	3254-55
C	13	
D	11	
F	09	
G	14	
H	12	
J	10	
K	04	
L	05	
M	08	
N	16	
O	03	
P	15	
Q	01	
T	02	
Z	07	
(Can't say)	98	
(Refused)	97	

66

J7 Are you a member of a Trade Union, Staff Association or
Professional association?

	Yes	1
	No	2

3256

J8a) Now a couple of questions about your education.
At what age did you finish your continuous full-time education?
IGNORE GAPS OF ONE YEAR OR LESS

WRITE IN AGE: ☐☐

3257-58

OR CODE: (Never went to school) 96
(Still in full-time education) 97

b) **SHOW CARD BB**
Please look at this card and tell me whether you have any of the qualifications listed.
Please start at the top of the list and tell me the first one you come to that you have obtained.
CODE FIRST TO APPLY

No qualifications	00

3259-60

Degree / Higher degree (or degree level qualification)
Teaching qualification
HNC/HND
SCOTBEC / TEC or SCOTVEC Higher, BEC/TEC Higher or BTEC Higher
City and Guilds Full Technological Certificate
Nursing qualification (SRN, SCM, RGN, RM RHV, Midwife)
GSVQ / GNVQ - Levels 4 & 5
SVQ / NVQ - Levels 4 & 5

01

SCE Higher / SLC Higher / SUPE Higher / "A" levels / "AS" levels /
Scottish certificate of 6th year studies
ONC/OND
SCOTBEC / TEC or SCOTVEC not Higher
BEC / TEC / BTEC not Higher
Higher School Certificate
City and Guilds Advanced / Final
GSVQ/GNVQ - Level 3 / Advanced / Intermediate
SVQ/NVQ - Levels 2 & 3

02

SCE Ordinary (Bands A-C)
Standard Grade (Levels 1-3)
SLC Lower or Ordinary
SUPE Lower or Ordinary
"O" level passes (Grades A-C if after 1975)
GCSE (Grades A-C)
CSE (Grade 1)
School Certificate or Matric
City and Guilds Craft / Ordinary level
GSVQ / GNVQ - Levels 1 & 2 / Foundation
SVQ / NVQ - Level 1

03

SCE Ordinary (Bands D & E)
Standard grade (Level 4,5)
CSE Grades 2-5
GCE "O" level Grades D & E (if after 1975)
GCSE (Grades D, E, F, G)
Clerical or commercial qualifications
Apprenticeship
City and Guilds Foundation

04

CSE Ungraded   05

Other qualifications (specify) _____   06

_____

(Can't say)   98

67

J9a) **SHOW CARD CC**
In which of these ways do you occupy this accommodation?

Own it outright	1	3261
Buying it with the help of mortgage or loan	2	**GO TO J10**
Pay part rent and part mortgage (shared ownership)	3	
Rent it	4	**ASK b)**
Live here rent-free (including rent-free in relative's / friend's property; excluding squatting)	5	
(Squatting)	6	**GO TO J10**

IF RENT / RENT-FREE
b) Do you rent from the council, a housing association, from an employer or from a private individual?

Council / Local Authority / New Town Devt / Scottish Homes	1	3262
Housing associations / Charitable or co-operative trusts	2	
Employer	3	
Privately	4	
(Bed and breakfast)	5	
Other (SPECIFY) _____	6	

J10a) **SHOW CARD DD**
Finally, to which of these groups do you consider you belong?
CODE ONE ONLY

White	01	3263-64
Black - Caribbean	02	
Black - African	03	
Black - neither Caribbean nor African	04	
Indian	05	
Pakistani	06	
Bangladeshi	07	
Chinese	08	
None of these	09	
Can't say	98	
Refused	97	

b) Thank you very much for your help.
My office may want to check on my work - would you be happy for someone to contact you about this interview?

Yes	1	**ASK c)**	(3276)
No	2	**GO TO e)**	

IF YES
c) Could I have your telephone number in case someone from my office wants to talk with you?

Telephone number given	1	**GO TO d)**	(3277)
Refused / No telephone	2	**GO TO e)**	

68

. **IF NUMBER GIVEN**
d) WRITE IN TELEPHONE NUMBER ON FRONT PAGE OF ARF

ALL
e) Sometime in the future we may want to come back and interview you
again. Would you be willing for us to do this?   (3278)

                                            Yes / Maybe   1
                                                     No   2

J11 **RECORD TIME NOW:**   [ ][ ][ ][ ]   3265-68
     (24 hour clock)

J12 **RECORD INTERVIEW LENGTH:** [ ][ ][ ]   3269-71
     (minutes)

J13 **INTERVIEWER NAME:** _____

J14 **INTERVIEWER NUMBER:** [ ][ ][ ][ ][ ][ ]   3272-75